BAUDELAIRE
As a Literary Critic

❧ BAUDELAIRE ❧
AS A LITERARY CRITIC

SELECTED ESSAYS
INTRODUCED AND TRANSLATED BY

LOIS BOE HYSLOP
AND
FRANCIS E. HYSLOP, JR.

1964
THE PENNSYLVANIA STATE UNIVERSITY PRESS
UNIVERSITY PARK, PENNSYLVANIA

Library of Congress Catalog Card Number: 64-15067

Copyright © 1964 by The Pennsylvania State University
All Rights Reserved
Printed in the United States of America by Vail-Ballou Press, Inc.

Typography and binding design by Marilyn Shobaken

TO
DEAN FREDERICK R. MATSON
For His Unfailing Encouragement

❧ FOREWORD

Interest in Baudelaire's critical writing has increased greatly during the past twenty years; it has even been suggested that his critical work is as remarkable as his poetry. Editions of his essays have multiplied in France, and recently Jonathan Mayne has made the greater part of Baudelaire's art criticism available in English. It has seemed to us useful to do the same for what Baudelaire called his *Literary Notices.*

Since Baudelaire viewed his criticism as a unified whole, it has been necessary to include significant excerpts from the art criticism in order to follow the evolution of his aesthetic ideas and the development of his critical thought. It would have been possible to put all the criticism in one volume, but since Mayne has already translated most of the essays on art in his book, *The Mirror of Art,* it seemed reasonable to confine ourselves primarily to the *Literary Notices,* which Baudelaire himself had planned to publish in a separate volume. Furthermore, lengthy discussions of artists and pictures might have been distracting to readers chiefly concerned with literature.

Baudelaire not only showed extraordinary discernment in his judgment of contemporaries such as Hugo, Poe, Leconte de Lisle, Balzac, Flaubert and others, but he also made valuable and provocative comments about obscure writers and forgotten books. Moreover, from his analysis of the literature of his time he developed a body of important general aesthetic ideas which have proved fruitful in the study and even in the creation of modern art and literature.

We have included virtually all of Baudelaire's literary articles. A few essays of minor importance and several miscellaneous pieces have been put in an appendix. Some fragmentary notes about Ponsard, Laclos, and Villemain have been omitted entirely. The preface to "Mesmeric Revelation" and the notes for a projected study of Realism have been included in the main body of the text in order to preserve the continuity of Baudelaire's critical thought.

The essays have been arranged in chronological order and are prefaced by explanatory notes. In general, we have left titles in French, except for those of the articles that we have translated. The few quotations from Latin and from French poetry have been left untranslated.

We should like to acknowledge our indebtedness to Jacques Crépet's superlative edition of Baudelaire's work, which is the basis of every scholarly work about the poet and critic. In a personal way we are grateful to Professor William T. Bandy for his suggestions, information, and continued interest.

We wish also to express our appreciation for grants-in-aid received from the Central Fund for Research of The Pennsylvania State University.

The Bald Eagle Press of State College, Pennsylvania, has graciously granted us permission to use the preface to "Mesmeric Revelation" and the two important essays on Poe that appeared in 1856 and 1857, which were originally translated for *Baudelaire on Poe*, copyright 1952.

The Oxford University Press has kindly granted us permission to use the translation of a long letter from Baudelaire to Richard Wagner, which appeared in our earlier book, *Baudelaire: A Self-Portrait*, and also for the use of short excerpts from other letters contained in the same volume, copyright 1957.

Lois Boe Hyslop

Francis E. Hyslop, jr.

University Park,
Pennsylvania

January 9, 1964

❦ CONTENTS

CONTENTS

❦ INTRODUCTION

"It is impossible for a poet not to contain within himself a critic. Therefore the reader will not be surprised that I consider the poet as the best of all critics." [1] Readers of Baudelaire's essays seem to agree so far as Baudelaire himself is concerned. Today the author of *Les Fleurs du Mal* is generally recognized as one of the most lucid critics of the nineteenth century and has been called the father of modern art criticism and the first aesthetician of his age. In spite of inevitable errors of judgment, no other critic so surely recognized the great among his contemporaries. And what is even more important, no other critic has succeeded so well not only in reflecting and analyzing works of art but also in generalizing from them, in seeking and discovering the principles that underlie artistic expression, in formulating what might be called a philosophy of criticism.

In his own day Baudelaire's extraordinary talent for criticism was largely overlooked by the general public. During the long months in Brussels while he waited in despair for the publisher's contract that never came, he would look in the shop windows at the trivial books on display and wonder if he would ever succeed in having anything of his own printed again.

It was only after his death that he attained full recognition. With the passing years his reputation has come to equal and even surpass that of Sainte-Beuve and Gautier who were recognized as giants by their age. Today Baudelaire's superiority to Sainte-Beuve in his judgment of nineteenth century writers goes unchallenged. Obtuseness and timidity, combined with a certain amount of malice, too often mar Sainte-Beuve's evaluation of his contemporaries. Unlike Baudelaire, he was more at ease in his appraisal of the past and, unlike him, he relied almost entirely upon a biographical and historical method which led him to explain the work almost wholly in terms of the man and the period.

Théophile Gautier, well known for his critical introduction to the posthumous edition of *Les Fleurs du Mal,* was far more prolific than Baudelaire and far more widely read. But his poetic and descriptive criticism lacks the penetration that distinguishes the work of his friend and admirer. In contrast to Baudelaire, Gautier seems undiscriminating and overly indulgent.

The reputations of other eminent critics of the period, such as Edmond Scherer, Barbey d'Aurevilly, Jules Janin, Armand de Pontmartin and Abel Villemain, have faded with the years. To-day Pontmartin is known chiefly as a clever journalist; Janin and Villemain are almost completely forgotten except by specialists, while Barbey and Scherer with their strong moral prejudices have lost much of their former importance. Ironically, Scherer and Pontmartin are often mainly remembered today for their intemperate attacks on *Les Fleurs du Mal.*

Baudelaire alone among his contemporaries has survived changes of taste and has remained as notable a critic of art as of literature. It has often been said, in fact, that Baudelaire's art criticism is more interesting and more significant than his literary criticism. To arbitrarily divide the criticism into two categories, however, is to deny its fundamental unity which stems logically and inevitably from his belief in the unity of all the arts. Artistic expression of any kind is for Baudelaire the work of a creative imagination by means of which the artist is enabled to discover spiritual reality through physical appearances and sensations. Hence, one art can not be divorced from another. The *Salon of 1859,* to mention only one example, is as necessary to a full understanding of Baudelaire's conception of literature as it is to his conception of the plastic arts. In fact, the definition and glorification of the imagination that appears in this essay is only a further development of an idea which Baudelaire had already explored in his third essay on Poe. Had he not given it such eloquent expression in 1859, undoubtedly he would have done so elsewhere—perhaps in his essay on Victor Hugo—for his conception of the imagination was one that was essential to all his critical thought.

2

From the very beginning of his career it is apparent that Baudelaire believed in the interrelation of all the arts. In his first important critical work, the *Salon of 1845*, his observations are as applicable to literature as to painting. His emphasis on originality, his condemnation of imitation and of the substitution of technical skill for personal vision are echoed in a charming, though rather slight review of *Norman Stories* (1845) and frequently recur in later essays, whether on literature or the plastic arts. Only a year later, in the *Salon of 1846*, Baudelaire lays the foundation for a criticism that will prove valid for all the arts and encourages the artists of his day to emulate the novelist Balzac in his brilliant exploitation of modern beauty and the heroism of modern life.

It is, then, because he views all artists as alike in purpose and because he sees all the arts as closely related that Baudelaire's criticism should be read as a whole, and that it is unfair to say that he excels in one category or the other. That the poet was well aware of this relationship is revealed in a letter he wrote from Belgium when he was hoping to find a publisher for his critical work: "Although these articles, unknown for the most part, have appeared at long intervals, they are bound together by a single and systematic thought." [2] It might almost be said that, like *Les Fleurs du Mal*, the critical essays possess their own secret architecture.

In his literary criticism, as well as in his art criticism, Baudelaire deliberately chose to write about his contemporaries. It was, of course, inevitable that he should have omitted a few well-known authors whose works were deserving of recognition. Tantalizing references to writers such as Balzac and Chateaubriand, for example, make the reader wish that he had expanded his comments into full-length articles such as those on Hugo or Flaubert.

It was just as inevitable that Baudelaire should have discussed a few minor figures who are now forgotten. The fact that he was commissioned by Eugène Crépet to write on ten of his contemporaries partly explains the choice of certain names which otherwise might have been omitted. Baudelaire himself, however, could well have justified their inclusion by reminding us, as he did in his article on Constantin Guys, that "everything is not in Raphael, everything is not in Racine; that there is much that is good, sound and delightful in the *poetae minores*."

Moreover, it is important to remember that it is not so much the artist as what is said about the artist that is of interest in Baudelaire's critical essays. In almost every article, regardless of the subject, the reader finds penetrating observations and challenging ideas that excite his thought and stimulate his imagination.

In a letter written to Ancelle from Belgium in 1866 Baudelaire listed the writers whom he excluded from the "modern rabble": Chateaubriand, Balzac, Stendhal, Mérimée, de Vigny, Flaubert, Banville, Gautier, and Leconte de Lisle.[3] Of these he failed to write formal studies on Chateaubriand, Balzac, Stendhal, Mérimée, and de Vigny, although occasional references to them are sometimes almost as revealing as an extended essay.

For Balzac in particular Baudelaire felt the greatest admiration.[4] It is true that in one of his first articles, "How a Genius Pays his Debts," he is plainly satirizing his more successful contemporary, but even here the satire is directed not at the novelist's accomplishments but rather at his questionable method of using ghost writers in an effort to increase his earnings.

From 1846 on, Baudelaire expresses only the highest praise for the author of *La Comédie Humaine*. Although he is conscious of Balzac's lapses of style, he is willing to overlook his verbosity and his clumsy phraseology in his admiration for the creative genius that is everywhere apparent. In one of the most perceptive pages to be found in his criticism, Baudelaire analyzes the source of this genius and, like Philarète Chasles before him, attributes much of Balzac's greatness to his extraordinary visionary powers.[5] This view of Balzac as a visionary rather than a realist has been adopted by most modern critics and has inspired a recent critic, Albert Béguin, to write a volume of criticism entitled *Balzac Visionnaire*.

4

From the frequent references to Chateaubriand in his essays, letters, and *Journaux Intimes*, it is clear that Baudelaire considered the author of *Le Génie du Christianisme* a master of French language and style worthy of being ranked with La Bruyère and Buffon. It was Chateaubriand who, according to Baudelaire, had created the "great school of melancholy"; his principal contribution had been "to sing the sad glory of melancholy and ennui." Baudelaire must have found in *René* the same artistic morbidity that he admired in Poe; he may also have recognized some of the same neurasthenic qualities that he observed in himself.

For many years Baudelaire had contemplated writing an article on dandyism which was to center about Chateaubriand as the "father" of the movement, but in spite of his "incorrigible liking" for that "old dandy," he failed, for one reason or another, to carry out his intention.

It is unfortunate that Baudelaire did not devote a critical study to the work of Alfred de Vigny whom he deeply admired and respected both as a man and as a poet. The two writers had much in common, as Henri Peyre has so well observed, from their ideas on progress and on modern society to their deification of the imagination.[6] Yet Baudelaire seldom mentions the elder poet either in his critical essays or in his correspondence. Only one statement can be found that justifies the inclusion of de Vigny's name among those which he had listed for Ancelle: "Victor Hugo, Sainte-Beuve, Alfred de Vigny rejuvenated, or better still renewed, French poetry, dead since the time of Corneille." [7]

It is interesting to discover that de Vigny was one of the few major poets of the period who recognized the greatness of *Les Fleurs du Mal*, which he once called *Les Fleurs du Bien*. Ill and dying of cancer, he received Baudelaire with the utmost courtesy at the time of the latter's candidacy for the French Academy and later wrote him a charming letter expressing admiration for his poetry, "as yet too little appreciated and too superficially judged." [8]

5

Baudelaire's failure to write about Stendhal and Mérimée is equally disappointing. Although he mentions an occasional service that Mérimée had performed on his behalf, he says nothing whatever about his work. His personal admiration for Mérimée, however, is expressed in a flattering comparison to Delacroix and in terms which describe Baudelaire as much as they do his subject: "He had the same slightly affected coolness, the same icy cloak concealing a shy sensibility and an ardent passion for the good and the beautiful; under the same hypocritical egoism, he had the same devotion to secret friends and to cherished ideas." [9]

Mérimée, on his side, was considerably less charitable toward the poet and critic whom he once called a "poor, inexperienced boy weary of life because he has been deceived by a grisette." He showed even less understanding of Baudelaire's genius when he dismissed *Les Fleurs du Mal* as "mediocre and completely innocuous, showing only an occasional spark of poetry." [10]

As for Stendhal, Baudelaire says nothing at all of his novels, either in his criticism or elsewhere. He was, however, impressed by the critical views of his predecessor, whether on art, love, or America, and there is no doubt that he borrowed heavily from him in formulating some of his own aesthetic ideas. Margaret Gilman in *Baudelaire the Critic* has succeeded admirably in showing the full extent of Stendhal's influence on the development of Baudelaire's critical thought. [11]

To those who are acquainted with Baudelaire's correspondence it comes as no surprise that in his letter to Ancelle he omitted the names of Lamartine and Alfred de Musset. As a schoolboy Baudelaire had eagerly read both poets and had been especially influenced by the rich harmonies and gentle melancholy of Lamartine's verse. His first poem, "Incompatibilité," written at the age of seventeen, has indeed a distinctly Lamartinian ring.

But Baudelaire's enthusiasm was short-lived. In his first essay on Poe (1852) he complains that in spite of the "astonishing merits" which make them "the idols of weak and sentimental souls," Lamartine and Musset "lack will power and are not sufficiently masters of themselves." Some years later, in a letter (February 18, 1860) to the scholar, critic, and journalist, Armand Fraisse, he frankly expresses his contempt for the sentimental and undisciplined art of the author of *Les Nuits*: "Except at the age of one's first communion, in other words at the age when everything having to do with prostitutes and silken ladders produces a religious effect, I have never been able to endure that *paragon of lady-killers*, his spoiled child's impudence, invoking heaven and hell about hotel room adventures, his muddy torrent of mistakes in grammar and prosody, and finally his utter incapacity to understand the work through which a reverie becomes a work of art. Someday you will find that you are enthusiastic only about perfection and you will scorn all those effusions of ignorance. I ask your pardon for speaking so sharply about certain things; incoherence, banality and carelessness have always caused me an irritation that is perhaps too acute." [12]

Baudelaire's irritation is even more apparent in his judgment of George Sand whose moral ideas he despised as much as her "famous *flowing style*, so dear to the bourgeoisie." Veiled references to the "republican poetess" and to the "priestess of love" are to be found in his article on Marceline Desbordes-Valmore. But it is in his *Journaux Intimes*, a collection of miscellaneous notes begun about 1855 and continued until the time of his last illness, that he gives free vent to his distaste. Exasperated by her moral, social, and political ideas, so opposed to his own belief in original sin and to his aristocratic conception of literature, he becomes frankly contemptuous in the notations which serve as his indictment: "She is stupid, she is dull, she is garrulous. Her ideas on morals show the profundity of judgment and the delicacy of feeling of a concierge or a kept woman." Or again, "she claims that a true Christian does not believe in Hell . . . she has good reasons to wish to abolish Hell." So violent is Baudelaire's reaction to this "Prudhomme

7

of immorality" that even if he had chosen to write an article on Sand, it might well have been refused publication, as happened in the case of his essay on Hégésippe Moreau commissioned by Eugène Crépet.

Baudelaire is far more kindly toward Dumas *père*, though understandably his name does not appear among those which he had listed for Ancelle. Writing to Sainte-Beuve as late as March 30, 1865, he readily admits the fascination he felt on reading the swashbuckling novels and dramas written with such unflagging gusto: "Alexandre Dumas has just left us. That good man came to show himself off with his usual ingenuousness. Even while forming a line to shake his hand, the Belgians made fun of him. That is disgraceful. A man may be respected for his *vitality*. The vitality of a Negro, to be sure. But I think that many others who like me are fond of the serious have been carried away by *La Dame de Montsoreau* and by *Balsamo*." [13]

The possibly inadvertent omission of Hugo's name among those mentioned to Ancelle is much more startling and requires more explanation, especially since Baudelaire had written an article on Hugo and a review of *Les Misérables* several years earlier. Baudelaire's attitude toward Victor Hugo had always been somewhat ambivalent. In the *Salons of 1845* and *1846* he had disparaged the poet for his artificiality and for his pedantic use of symmetry and antithesis, faults that are more damning in Hugo's earlier works where they are less often redeemed by some of his more solid virtues. Even in the earlier work of Hugo, however, Baudelaire notes the "nobility" and the "majesty" which mark the poetry of his great contemporary and praises his admirable and curious dexterity in handling his tools.

In 1859 Baudelaire seems to have undergone a change of heart. In his article on Gautier as well as in the *Salon of 1859* he expresses the highest regard for Hugo's work. It is true that his flattering remarks may have been prompted by the hope of obtaining a letter-preface from Hugo for his article on Gautier which he was planning to re-publish in the form of a brochure. But in all fairness it must be added that the publication of *Les*

Contemplations (1856) and of *La Légende des Siècles* (1859–1883) had done much to change his opinion. There can be no doubt of his sincerity when he wrote to his mother in July, 1857, at the time of the publication of *Les Fleurs du Mal*: "I know that the book with its faults and merits will take its place in the memory of the literary public beside the best poems of V. Hugo, of Th. Gautier and even of Byron." [14] Baudelaire's use of the word "best" does much to explain his seemingly contradictory views about Hugo. There was much in Hugo that displeased and annoyed him. There was also much that he deeply admired and that he recognized in his more dispassionate moments as being truly great. To express the hope that his poetry would take its place beside the "best poems" of Hugo, Gautier, and Byron was indirectly the highest compliment he could pay his contemporaries.

The sincerity of his admiration for what was best in Hugo is confirmed by another letter to his mother written in 1859: "I am very surprised by what you say about *La Légende des Siècles*. It may be that you are wearied by lines that are often choppy and broken, sometimes epic, sometimes lyric. But Hugo has never been so picturesque or so astonishing as at the beginning of *Rathbert* (Le Concile d'Ancône), *Zim-Zizimi*, *Le Mariage de Roland*, *La Rose de l'Infante*; they reveal dazzling powers which he alone possesses." [15]

Unfortunately Hugo's political and social ideas, like those of George Sand, exasperated and infuriated his critic. Repelled by the exiled poet's conception of himself as "saviour of the human race," by his democratic and utilitarian ideas, by his belief in progress, Baudelaire reverted to his former disparaging attitude both in his *Journaux Intimes* and in his correspondence. Poverty and ill-health only served to increase the resentment and hostility that he felt in the face of Hugo's great fame and fortune. In spite of the breach between the two writers, however, it must be admitted that in his article of 1862 Baudelaire was extraordinarily successful in perceiving and defining the real greatness of Victor Hugo.

Almost as surprising as the omission of Hugo's name was his failure to mention Sainte-Beuve. Of all his predecessors perhaps none had influenced Baudelaire more than the famous critic.[16] The intimate, psychological tone of his early novel *Volupté* and of his *Poésies de Joseph Delorme* was greatly admired by him and is clearly reflected in *Les Fleurs du Mal*. In an early, somewhat mediocre poem which he sent to the elder writer, Baudelaire acknowledged his debt in the most flattering terms, and as late as 1862 he still called himself "the incorrigible lover of *Rayons Jaunes* and of *Volupté*."

The relationship between the two men was always most cordial, and Baudelaire remained genuinely fond of "l'oncle Beuve" in spite of the critic's failure, either through timidity or through lack of understanding, to come to the defense of his disciple.

* * *

The distinguished critic and scholar, Henri Peyre, has pointed out that "no other poet, not even Goethe or Coleridge, has been as great in the realm of criticism as Baudelaire, while still remaining a poet. No one has combined to the same degree intelligence and sensibility, analysis and synthesis, the exploration of the often troubled abysses of his own inner world and the ability to penetrate the universe of other creators." [17] A careful reading of Baudelaire's criticism unquestionably justifies such extravagant praise and leads one to inquire by what means he succeeded so well in reflecting and distilling beauty, whether in literature, in the plastic arts, or in music. What system or method did he follow? What did he believe to be the nature and function of criticism?

Baudelaire himself raised the question as early as 1846. "What is the use of criticism?" he asks in the opening chapter of the *Salon of 1846*. In the provocative pages that follow he brilliantly sums up his creed and expresses certain ideas that will become the core of his critical thought: "I sincerely believe that the best criticism is that which is amusing and poetic; not a cold, mathematical criticism which, under the pretext of explaining everything, shows neither hate nor love, and deliberately divests itself of every vestige of temperament. . . ."

It is clear from the outset that, for Baudelaire, criticism is intensely personal. The critic's task is not to remain impassive before a work of art but to reveal, freely and deliberately, all the pleasure or displeasure he may feel. Moreover, criticism is like art itself in that the relation of the critic to a work of art is much the same as the relation of the artist to nature: "since a beautiful picture is nature reflected by an artist, the best criticism will be the reflection of that picture by an intelligent and sensitive mind." In both cases the subjective element is unavoidable. The critic must subject himself to the vision of the artist, he must feel the experience that the artist has sought to express, yet at the same time he must "reflect" that experience through his own temperament. In his essay on Wagner this subjective element is especially apparent. Never has Baudelaire succeeded more brilliantly in translating an artistic experience while relying on his own personal response. In the opening paragraph he warns the reader that he intends to speak in his own name, for the use of "I, rightly considered impertinent in many cases, implies nevertheless a great modesty; it confines the writer within the strictest limits of sincerity. By reducing his task, it makes it easier." [18]

If criticism is the translation of an artistic experience, then the best criticism of a picture may be a sonnet or an elegy, Baudelaire reminds us half in jest. Readers of *Les Fleurs du Mal* will be inclined to agree. In poems such as "Les Phares" and "Don Juan aux Enfers" he has succeeded admirably in showing all the magnificent resources of his critical and poetic genius.

But such criticism, Baudelaire warns us, is destined for anthologies of poetry. "Criticism properly speaking" is justified only if it is "biased, impassioned, partisan, that is to say written from an exclusive point of view, but from a point of view that opens up the widest horizons." A surprising and somewhat paradoxical statement at first glance, but one that is completely in accord with his own practice. Believing as he did that beauty was the sole purpose of art, Baudelaire was always ready to defend it, especially when it went unrecognized or was misunderstood, as in the cases of Delacroix, Flaubert, and Wagner. At the same time he stood equally ready to heap scorn and condemnation on everything that tended to degrade or debase it, whether the materialistic and utilitarian conceptions of the School of Good Sense or the "incoherence, banality, and carelessness" of Hégésippe Moreau and Alfred de Musset.

This broad point of view, so essential in criticism, he goes on to explain, depends in turn on the critic's ability to recognize the "individualism" or the "temperament" of the artist in question. "An artist must possess something essentially *sui generis* by virtue of which he is *he* and not another," Baudelaire was to write many years later in his essay on Wagner.[19] This being the case, the critic must be conscious of all that which constitutes originality: "the mind of the critic, like that of the poet, must be open to beauty of every kind." [20] He must be able to discover the vision, the dream, the inner world of the artist; above all, he must perceive the particular beauty which distinguishes that artist from all others.

Baudelaire's reliance on a personal response to works of art is made more abundantly clear in his article on the Exposition Universelle of 1855 in which he frankly abandons all fixed criteria and preconceived systems:

More than once I have tried, like all my friends, to confine myself within a system in order to preach freely. But a system is a kind of damnation which forces us into a perpetual recantation; it is always necessary to invent another, and the exertion required is a cruel punishment. And my system was always beautiful, vast, spacious, convenient, neat, and above all complete. At least, it seemed so to me. And always a spontaneous, unexpected product of universal vitality would come along and give the lie to my childish, antiquated knowledge, that pitiable daughter of Utopia. No matter how much I changed or broadened the criterion, it always fell short of expressing universal man and never caught up with the multiform and multicolored beauty that moves in the infinite spirals of life. Constantly condemned to the humiliation of a new conversion, I made an important decision. To escape the horror of these philosophical apostasies, I proudly resigned myself to modesty: I was content to feel; I sought refuge in an impeccable naïveté. I humbly beg pardon of academic minds of all types who occupy the various workshops of our artistic factory. It is there that my philosophic conscience has found repose; and I can affirm, at least in so far as a man can answer for his virtues, that my mind now enjoys a greater impartiality.[21]

Yet whether or not he fully realized it, Baudelaire was indeed following a method—one, in fact, that he had partially described in 1846 and that he restated in 1855: "I was content to feel." To sense the artist's experience and to re-create it for the reader was, however, only one step in the very subjective method he had evolved. At the same time he was endeavoring more to understand the "mysterious intentions and the method" that lay behind the work. In his remarkable essay on Wagner (1861) he tells how he sought "to penetrate more deeply into the understanding of these singular works, . . . to discover the why and the wherefore, and to transform pleasure into knowledge." [22] Consciously or unconsciously, Baudelaire was articulating what he himself had been doing for some time and what might be called the key to his critical approach. In spite of himself, he had found a "system," one that allowed him the utmost freedom and that revealed to the fullest extent both his superb poetic imagination and his keen analytical mind. The question, "What is the use of criticism?" asked by him in 1846 was not fully answered until 1861. Only then does it become clear that, for Baudelaire, criticism was not merely the re-creation of the beauty contained in a work of art but also the search, through analysis and generalization, of the laws that govern artistic phenomena.

Although his "system" was valid for all the arts, Baudelaire tends to use it less in his literary criticism than elsewhere. Here more often than not, he neglects the re-creation of the experience and moves directly to extract the essence of what he had read. Criticism becomes less a translation than a meditation. Often it contains biography, personal or historical considerations, and digressions that are more or less related to the subject. But almost always he shows a rare ability to enter into the work of the writer, to single out its strength and its weaknesses, to assimilate it until it becomes his own. In the essay on Pierre Dupont he says: "To perform the work well, you *must get right inside* the protagonist, you must become so thoroughly imbued with the emotions that he expresses and feel them so perfectly that the work seems to be your very own." [23] It was this ability to enter into the "arcana of the work" that made it possible for Baudelaire to recognize and define the genius of such writers as Flaubert, Hugo, and Leconte de Lisle.

* * *

Art, like life itself, has for Baudelaire only one goal, one justification. Just as dandyism is a means of cultivating beauty in "natural" and hence imperfect man, so art is a means by which the banalities and ugliness of nature can be transformed into beauty. Except for a brief period when he was attracted to a more utilitarian conception of art, Baudelaire continues to view the pursuit of beauty as the primary goal of all artistic expression: "[The arts] always represent the expression of the beautiful through the feelings, the passions, and the dreams of each man. . . ." [24]

It is at once apparent that the poet and critic considers beauty as something variable rather than absolute and that he believes its character is determined to a large extent by the temperament or the sensibility of the artist. To clarify his position even further he adds: "All forms of beauty, like all possible phenomena, contain something absolute and something particular. Absolute and eternal beauty does not exist or rather it is only an abstraction skimmed off the surface of a variety of beauties. The characteristic element of each form of beauty comes from the passions; and since we have our particular passions, we have our own beauty." [25]

Baudelaire's statement does much to explain his scorn for the Neo-Classicism of the Pagan School which he expressed so frankly in his essay of 1852. By attempting to reproduce the eternal element that is found in the past and by neglecting the circumstantial element belonging to the present, the writers of the Pagan School had forfeited all claim to originality. Baudelaire may still have been thinking of them when many years later he wrote in his essay on Constantin Guys: "Woe unto him who seeks in antiquity anything other than pure art, logic, and general method! By plunging too deeply into the past, he loses sight of the present; he renounces the values and privileges provided by circumstances; for almost all our originality comes from the stamp that *time* imprints upon our feelings." [26]

At one moment in his career, Baudelaire, under the influence of Poe, rejected the part played by the passions in the creation of beauty. In his essay of 1857 he agreed with Poe that "passion is *natural*, too natural not to introduce an offensive, discordant tone into the domain of pure beauty, too familiar and too violent not to scandalize the pure Desires, the gracious Melancholies and the noble Despairs which inhabit the supernatural regions of poetry." [27]

But his rejection was only temporary, and in later essays he returns to his fundamental belief in the role played by the passions. He attributes the genius of Wagner and Delacroix in large part to the power of the passions which moved and inspired them. It was the passions that enabled Wagner to express both the carnal and mystical aspects of man: "through this passion he adds something superhuman to everything; through this passion he understands and makes everything understood." Similarly, Delacroix possessed "an immense passion, reinforced by a formidable will . . . the two signs that mark the most unmistakable geniuses." [28]

It might be said in passing that Baudelaire's own poetry

sprang largely from his passions. The most casual reading reveals how they color his thought, suggest his themes, and tie his poetry to life itself. Poe, on the other hand, by excluding the passions (except what might be called a passion for death and decay) is too often lacking in humanity. The women he sings are not flesh and blood creatures like those of the French poet, but rather "creatures of marble in a world of frozen music." [29] Pale, bloodless phantoms, they seem to dwell only in the world of the dead.

Baudelaire's belief in the variable element of beauty is closely related to his idea of modernity: "Modernity is the transitory, the fugitive, the contingent, the half of art of which the other half is the eternal and the immutable." It is to be found everywhere, not least of all "in the spectacle of fashionable life and of thousands of stray souls—criminals and kept women— who drift about in the underground of a great city." [30]

In this emphasis on urban modernity Baudelaire was incorporating into his aesthetics ideas which were an important part of his own literary practice. His study of Samuel Cramer, the modern dandy of *La Fanfarlo*, the "Tableaux Parisiens" of *Les Fleurs du Mal*, and the *Petits Poèmes en Prose*, all show the inspiration of modern urban life.

Because Baudelaire puts extraordinary stress on the epic possibilities of contemporary life, heroism becomes one of the key words in his essays. As early as 1845 he encouraged true painters to "seize the epic character of contemporary life and make us see and understand, through color or design, how great and poetic we are in our cravats and our patent leather boots." In 1846 he again urges the artist to seek the beauty and heroism of modern life, "for just as all centuries and all peoples have had their forms of beauty, so inevitably we have ours. That is in the natural order of things." [31]

Fully as important as the heroic aspect of modernity is the mysterious beauty to be found everywhere in the teeming life of the city: "Parisian life is rich in poetic and marvelous subjects. The marvelous envelops and permeates us like the atmosphere itself, but we do not see it." [32] Fortunately, Daumier, Guys, Meryon, and Balzac had not failed to see it. In fact, it was because Balzac had so well portrayed this "poetic and marvelous" element of modern life that Baudelaire ends the *Salon of 1846* with a magnificent apostrophe to the creator of Rastignac, Vautrin, and Birotteau. Nor had Baudelaire himself failed to observe it. His ability to detect its presence in the life around him explains why, unlike the average Realist, he could say to the city of Paris in his unfinished epilogue to *Les Fleurs du Mal:* "You have given me your mud and I have turned it into gold." [33]

According to Baudelaire, all beauty necessarily contains an element of strangeness. Like Poe, who had cited Bacon's famous dictum, "There is no exquisite beauty without some strangeness in its proportions," he believes that the bizarre is "the indispensable condiment of all beauty." In his article on the Exposition Universelle he develops the idea a little further:

> *The beautiful is always strange.* I do not mean that it is deliberately, coldly strange, for in that case it would be a monster that has jumped the rails of life. I mean that it always contains a little strangeness, an artless, unpremeditated, unconscious strangeness, and that it is this strangeness that gives Beauty its specific character. It is its official stamp, its characteristic. Reverse the proposition and try to imagine a *commonplace beauty!* [34]

It is important to note that theoretically Baudelaire's emphasis on the strange has nothing to do with its shock value. On the contrary, like modernity, the bizarre is a necessary ingredient of the variable or transitory element of beauty. In fact, it seems to be almost the equivalent of this variable element, since, as Baudelaire goes on to point out, it is determined by "climate, milieu, race, religion, custom, and the artist's temperament."

Baudelaire associates beauty not only with the strange, but with melancholy and horror as well: "It is one of the astounding prerogatives of Art that the horrible, artistically expressed, becomes beauty; and that *sorrow,* when given rhythm and cadence, fills the mind with a serene *joy*." [35] The reader is at once reminded of "Hymne à la Beauté" where horror and murder are included among Beauty's jewels:

Tu marches sur des morts, Beauté, dont tu te moques;
De tes bijoux l'Horreur n'est pas le moins charmant,
Et le Meurtre, parmi tes plus chères breloques
Sur ton ventre orgueilleux danse amoureusement.

One has but to think of such poems as "Une Charogne" and "Une Martyre" to see how the poet himself has given artistic expression to horror, or of the magnificent sonnet "Recueillement," with its evocation of the slow, heavy coming of the night, to see how skillfully he has succeeded in giving sorrow a rhythm and cadence which, while producing a feeling of deep sadness, seem to "fill the mind with a serene joy."

Although Baudelaire's essays are filled with references to beauty, he expresses his own conception most completely in a long passage of the *Journaux Intimes*:

I have found a definition of Beauty—of *my* Beauty. It is something ardent and sad, something slightly vague, that allows for conjecture. I am going to apply my idea, if I may, to a concrete object, an object which happens to be the most interesting to society, the face of a woman. An attractive and beautiful face, a woman's face I mean, is one that makes us dream—though in a confused way—of both pleasure and sadness; that conveys an idea of melancholy, of lassitude, even of satiety—or a contrary idea such as ardor or a desire to live, joined with a recurring bitterness, such as might be caused by privation or despair. Mystery, regret are also characteristics of Beauty.

A handsome male face has no need to convey to a man—to a woman perhaps it may be different—that suggestion of sensual pleasure which in a woman's face, because it is usually more melancholy, is all the more provocative. But this face will also have something ardent and sad—spiritual needs, ambitions darkly suppressed—the suggestion of a seething, unused power—at times the suggestion of a revengeful indifference, (for the ideal type of the Dandy must not be excluded in this matter). Sometimes too—and this is one of the most interesting characteristics of beauty—it will convey mystery; and finally (so as to admit courageously how modern I feel in the matter of aesthetics) it will convey *unhappiness*. I do not claim that Joy cannot be associated with Beauty, but I do say that Joy is one of its most commonplace ornaments;—whereas Melancholy is, so to speak, her illustrious companion—so much so that I can scarcely imagine (could my mind be a bewitched mirror?) a type of Beauty in which there was no *Unhappiness*. Sustained— others might say obsessed—by these ideas, it is understandable that it would be difficult for me not to conclude that the most perfect type of masculine Beauty is *Satan*—as Milton conceived him.[36]

In this extended definition of beauty—*his beauty*—Baudelaire makes only a passing reference to its spiritual aspects. Elsewhere however, particularly in the Poe essay of 1857, he agrees with the American poet that "the principle of poetry is precisely and simply human aspiration toward a superior beauty," and he comes to view both poetry and music as a means of attaining the infinite, of glimpsing "the splendors beyond the tomb."

Not only in this spiritual view of beauty but also in his entire conception Baudelaire was obviously influenced by Poe, even to the extent of frankly paraphrasing many of his statements. Recent investigations, however, have shown that Poe's influence, both on Baudelaire's poetry and theory, was less important than was once believed. The discoveries of the distinguished Baudelaire scholar, W. T. Bandy, have proved that Baudelaire did not begin a systematic study of Poe until about 1852.[37] The *Salon of 1846*, on the other hand, clearly shows that by that date the French critic had already formulated most of his basic ideas about the nature of beauty. Thus it becomes apparent that Poe's influence lay mainly in strengthening and confirming ideas that Baudelaire had already conceived.

In his spiritual conception of beauty Baudelaire may also have been inspired, as Marcel Ruff suggests, by the German philosopher Schelling whose works had been translated into

French between 1842 and 1847. Baudelaire may have become interested in Schelling through his study of Thomas De Quincey who, he tells us, had read Kant, Fichte, and Schelling. In any case, Baudelaire's use of the phrase "the infinite in the finite" to characterize the beauty of Delacroix's painting seems to echo the words of Schelling: "Beauty is the manifestation of the divine in the terrestrial, of the infinite in the finite." [38]

*　　*　　*

Believing as he did that beauty was the principal goal of art, Baudelaire was naturally concerned with the means by which it might be attained. Although he had praised Chennevières in 1845 for his "sincere love of nature," his quotation from Heinrich Heine in the *Salon of 1846* shows that he soon came to distrust the direct imitation of nature: "In matters of art, I am a supernaturalist. I believe that the artist cannot find all his models in nature, but that the most remarkable are revealed to him in his soul, like the innate symbolism of innate ideas, and at the same instant."

Realism, "that silly cult of nature, untouched by the imagination," became more and more abhorrent to him, whether it was the realism of Courbet in painting, that of Feydeau and Champfleury in literature, or the photographic realism that resulted from the invention of the camera.

Nevertheless, for a short period of time (ca. 1844–1850), he had shown considerable interest in the Realist movement. He had shared in the democratic hopes of the period and he had been attracted by the ideas promulgated by such friends as Champfleury, Courbet, and Proudhon.[39] But his infatuation proved to be short-lived. A few years later he broke with "that rabble of vulgar artists and writers whose myopic intelligence takes refuge behind the vague and obscure term known as realism." Like Flaubert, he objected to having the term realism applied to his own art. To him it was "a repulsive insult flung in the face of every analyst, a vague and elastic word which for the ordinary man signifies not a new method of creation, but a minute description of trivial details." [40] A definition of poetry, contained among the notes for an article (1855) which was evidently intended as an indictment of Realism, shows how far he had moved away from the thinking of his former friends and associates: "Poetry is what is most real, what is completely true only in *another world*. This world [is] a hieroglyphic dictionary." [41]

From this time on Baudelaire became more and more convinced of the aesthetic danger resulting from a direct and servile imitation of nature. In the *Salon of 1859* he sounds a warning to both artists and writers:

> In recent years we have heard it said in a thousand different ways: "copy nature; copy only nature. There is no greater delight, no finer triumph than an excellent copy of nature." And this doctrine, so inimical to art, was alleged to apply not only to painting, but to all the arts, even to the novel, even to poetry. To these doctrinaires, so satisfied with nature, an imaginative man would certainly have had the right to answer: "I find it useless and tiresome to portray things as they are, because nothing that exists satisfies me. Nature is ugly, and I prefer the monsters of my imagination to the triteness of actuality.[42]

Even though he protested against a realistic presentation of nature, Baudelaire was not unaware of its "immortal freshness" or of the "magnificent décors . . . that nature constructs in her hours of genius." In a prose poem, "Le *Confiteor* de l'Artiste" (1862), he describes the artist's struggle with nature in his attempt to turn direct experience into artistic beauty. At first the writer experiences a great delight in gazing at the immensity of the sky and the sea. But soon he exclaims despairingly:

> The depth of the sky dismays me; its limpidity irritates me. The insensibility of the sea, the immutability of the spectacle revolt me . . . Is it necessary to suffer eternally, or to flee eternally from beauty? Nature, merciless enchantress, always victorious rival, leave me! Cease tempting my desires and my pride! The study of beauty

is a duel in which the artist cries out with fright before being vanquished.

It is curious to find that Baudelaire's aesthetic objection to the direct imitation of nature is related to his belief in original sin and to his consciousness of the existence of evil in the universe. In his eyes, nature "can counsel only crime. . . . it has created parricide and cannibalism, and a thousand other abominations." In contrast to the naturalistic conceptions of the eighteenth century with its denial of original sin, Baudelaire insists that "there is nothing that is not horrible in all the actions and desires of the purely natural man." [43]

A letter to the poet Fernand Desnoyers reiterates his belief that the spiritual essence of man is far more important than anything to be found in nature and at the same time expresses a distaste for undisciplined nature:

> But you know perfectly well that I can't become sentimental about vegetation and that my soul rebels against that strange new religion which to my mind will always have something shocking about it for every *spiritual* person. I shall never believe that the *souls of the gods live in plants, and* even if they did, I shouldn't be much concerned and I should consider my own soul of much greater value than that of sanctified vegetables. I have always thought, even, that there was something irritating and impudent about *Nature* in its fresh and rampant state.[44]

During the last years of his life Baudelaire seemed even more convinced that true reality was not to be found in the world around us. "Common sense tells us," he wrote in 1860 (*Les Paradis Artificiels*), "that the things of this world exist only incompletely and that true reality is to be found only in dreams." We are reminded of his comment many years earlier (*Salon of 1846*) that the most remarkable models exist not in nature, but in the artist's soul, and of his statement in 1855 that this world is only a "hieroglyphic dictionary" which allows the artist to discover true reality.

The interpretation of the "hieroglyphic dictionary" becomes then the major problem of the artist, whatever his medium. Many artists, including Baudelaire himself, had attempted to intensify their sense perceptions by artificial means such as drugs or alcohol. Baudelaire had even attempted to justify Poe's drunkenness as a means of recapturing the marvelous or frightening visions experienced in previous states of exaltation.

But Baudelaire early recognized the perils of this "dangerous road" which Poe, among others, had taken: "[Black] magic deceives them and produces for them a false light and a false happiness, whereas we, who are poets and philosophers, have regenerated our souls by continuous work and contemplation; by the assiduous exercise of will and by a fixed nobility of purpose, we have created for ourselves a truly beautiful garden." [45]

In a letter to Armand Fraisse, who had written a favorable review of *Les Paradis Artificiels*, Baudelaire renews his warning: "I have a horror of all stimulants because of the manner in which they amplify time and magnify everything. A continued spiritual orgy makes it not only impossible to be a businessman, but even a man of letters." [46]

It is imagination, "the queen of faculties," which alone, according to Baudelaire, can aid the poet to conquer nature and to discover true reality. It is imagination that enables him to interpret the hieroglyphic dictionary and thus to penetrate the mysteries of life, for imagination "casts a magical and supernatural light over the natural obscurity of things. . . . Imagination is the queen of truth, and the *possible* is one of the provinces of truth. It has a definite relationship with the infinite." [47]

Baudelaire does not, however, reject nature completely. For him it is a sort of springboard, a means of moving from reality to the artist's vision of reality: "External nature . . . is only an incoherent agglomeration of materials which the artist is invited to gather together and put in order, an *incitamentum*, an awakener of dormant faculties." Artists who have no imagination copy the dictionary; those "who obey imagination seek in the dictionary the elements which fit into their conception; then by arranging them artistically they give them an entirely new character." [48]

In its search for beauty, for the inner meaning of the exterior world, imagination is aided by reverie, contemplation, and dream. Reverie and contemplation are key words that recur again and again in Baudelaire's writings, whether in his poetry, his essays, or his *Journaux Intimes*. "The faculty of reverie," he writes in *Les Paradis Artificiels*, "is a divine and mysterious faculty; for it is in dreams that man communicates with the shadowy world which surrounds him. But in order to develop freely, this faculty has need of solitude; the more man concentrates, the more he tends to dream amply and profoundly." [49] An artist like Delacroix for whom imagination was the most important faculty and who, through reverie and concentration, could illuminate things with his mind was thus able to translate "the invisible, the impalpable, the dream."

Memory is still another means which aids the imagination to pursue its vision of beauty and to interpret the mysteries of the universe. As early as 1846 he had stressed its importance to the artist seeking to avoid a photographic realism: "memory is the chief criterion of art; art is a mnemotechny of the beautiful: now exact imitation spoils memory." [50] Years later in "The Painter of Modern Life" he again emphasizes the role played by memory and views it as a sort of catalytic agent which, by distinguishing between trivial detail and essential facts, helps the imagination to discern true reality.

But even more significant is Baudelaire's conception of memory as a means of stimulating the imagination to recall the *distant past*. Sense impressions, such as perfumes and sounds, may be used as a means of deliberate recall and help the poet to re-create or to recover the past. In his second essay on Poe, Baudelaire refers in Proustian language to the chain of impressions that follows some "exterior stimulus . . . such as the sound of a bell, a musical note, or a forgotten perfume." In *Les Paradis Artificiels* he reaffirms this idea: "And in such solemn circumstances, perhaps in death, and generally in the intense excitement created by opium, all the vast and complicated palimpsest of memory unfolds at once with all its superimposed layers of dead feelings, mysteriously embalmed in what we call oblivion." [51]

In his own poetry this "exterior stimulus" often serves as inspiration and becomes a means of restoring the past. So the perfume of Jeanne's hair is a:

> Charme profond, magique, dont nous grise
> Dans le présent le passé restauré! [52]

Through its magic charm the poet is enabled to rediscover the past, to see once again the white-capped waves of tropical seas, the dazzling fire of monotonous suns, and the ports filled with sails and masts that echo to the song of the sailors.

Proust, who was a great admirer of Baudelaire, was fascinated by the relationship of his own conception of memory to that of the poet: "In the case of Baudelaire, these even more numerous reminiscences are evidently less fortuitous and consequently, in my opinion, less decisive. It is the poet himself who, with more deliberation . . . voluntarily seeks in the scent of a woman's hair or breast the stimulating analogies that will evoke for him 'the azure of the immense, encircling sky' and 'a port filled with masts and flames.' " [53]

The word "voluntarily" is what differentiates Proust's idea of memory from that of Baudelaire. For Proust, memory must be involuntary if it is to be creative. For Baudelaire, imagination alone is creative, and memory is but its servant. As early as 1846 he had agreed with Hoffmann that "true memory, considered from a philosophical point of view, consists only in a very lively, easily aroused imagination, ready thereby to evoke in support of every sensation scenes from the past, while endowing them, as if by magic, with the life and character proper to each of them." [54]

Since memory has the power to revive childhood impressions with all their original freshness and vividness of detail and color, it becomes one of the chief instruments of genius. In *Les Paradis Artificiels*, Baudelaire goes so far as to maintain that these youthful impressions actually contain "the germ of the artist's strange reveries or, better still, of his genius." In *The Painter of Modern Life* he returns to this idea with a characteristically modern definition of genius: "Genius is only *childhood recovered* at will, childhood now endowed, in order to express itself, with virile organs and with an analytical mind that enables it to order and arrange all the materials accumulated involuntarily." [55]

Thus for Baudelaire a work of art—whether a picture, a poem, or a novel—continues to be in 1863 what it had been in 1846: "nature reflected by an artist." It is the artist's vision of beauty, inspired by contemplation and memory, and transformed by imagination into a work of art.

Perhaps the most important function of the Baudelairean imagination is its ability to perceive correspondences. In a letter to Toussenel in 1856 Baudelaire calls *"imagination . . .* the most *scientific* of the faculties because it alone understands *universal analogy* or what a mystic religion calls correspondence." A year later in his essay on Poe he reaffirms this belief: "Imagination is an almost divine faculty which perceives immediately and without philosophical methods the inner and secret relations of things, the correspondences, and the analogies." [56]

In both his essays and his famous sonnet it is apparent that correspondences may be either synaesthetic or transcendental, horizontal or vertical. In neither case, however, does he pretend that his conception is new or original. The often quoted line, "Perfumes, colors, and sounds respond to one another" is only the echo of ideas that had concerned many minds in both the eighteenth and nineteenth centuries, from Schelling and Madame de Staël to Sainte-Beuve, Balzac, Nerval, and Hoffmann, among others. Synaesthetic correspondences and analogies are for Baudelaire entirely normal and even inescapable: "What would be really surprising would be that sound *could not* suggest color, that colors *could not* convey a melody, and that sound and color were unsuited to translating ideas, things always having been expressed by a reciprocal analogy since the day when God created the world as a complex and indivisible whole." [57]

More important than the synaesthetic correspondences, at least so far as the critical essays are concerned, are the transcendental correspondences, those that exist between the visible and the invisible worlds. Influenced mainly by Swedenborg and Fourier, Baudelaire accepts a doctrine that is both pagan and Christian and that goes back almost to the beginning of time. Like others before him, he sees nature as a "forest of symbols," and "the earth and its spectacles as a revelation, as something in correspondence with Heaven." "Everything is hieroglyphic," he tells us in his essay on Hugo, and so the poet becomes a "translator, a decipherer." The universe is a vast storehouse of images and signs which must be digested and transformed. Aided by the imagination, the poet is enabled to find, even in the most natural and trivial spectacle, "chance objects that become speaking symbols."

From a study of the essays the reader might tend to assume that Baudelaire's own poetry continues what Lloyd James Austin calls the traditional "symbolique," that is to say a fixed system of symbols. In his excellent study of Baudelaire's poetry, Austin has pointed out that the symbolism of *Les Fleurs du Mal* is not so much a part of the traditional "symbolique" as it is a personal symbolism.[58] The symbols that the poet and critic finds in nature are less often concerned with transcendental reality than they are with his own personal mood or state of mind. Contrary to what the essays may sometimes suggest, the poet's imagination seldom takes us out of this world. Rather, it establishes a relation between exterior nature and the inner world of the poet, through the use of symbols which give concrete form to inner experience or idea. Thus the doctrine of universal analogies professed by Baudelaire becomes a sort of "aesthetician's myth," as Vivier has so aptly described it.

In her article, "From Imagination to Immediacy in French

Poetry" Margaret Gilman has shown how Baudelaire's views on imagination made him unique among French poets.[59] Whereas imagination played a primary role in both English and German Romanticism, its role in French Romanticism was largely secondary, in spite of the importance given it by a poet such as Alfred de Vigny.

It has often been thought that Baudelaire's conception of the imagination owes a great deal to Edgar Allan Poe, whose fame he did so much to assure among European readers. Once again the discoveries of W. T. Bandy tend to disprove or at least to minimize the claim.[60] It is true that Baudelaire might not have affirmed the importance of the imagination with such ardor, had he not found the confirmation of this idea in Poe. But it is well to recall that even in 1846 Baudelaire had indirectly exalted the imagination by giving the artist's temperament a pre-eminent role and by insisting that "the first task of the artist is to substitute man for nature and to protest against nature." [61]

The question is also sometimes asked if Baudelaire was influenced by Coleridge, since there is a rather close relationship between the ideas of the two writers. There is no evidence, however, that Baudelaire had ever read Coleridge, and it is generally conceded that he knew his ideas only indirectly, both through the works of Poe, who was strongly influenced by his English confrere, and through Mrs. Crowe whom he cites in the *Salon of 1859*.[62]

It seems quite evident, on the other hand, that it was Delacroix who did most to shape Baudelaire's conception of the imagination. Baudelaire had sought out the artist in 1845 and was enormously impressed by his theories and his work. On several occasions Baudelaire refers to Delacroix's observation that nature is only a dictionary, and in 1859 he associates this idea with his theory of the imagination. After the death of Delacroix in 1863, Baudelaire wrote a glowing article in which he paid final tribute to the artist "in [whose] eyes imagination was the most precious gift and the most important faculty." [63]

*   *   *

Important as imagination was to Baudelaire, it was not sufficient unless accompanied by a technical skill that made it possible for the artist to fully realize his conception. For him, as for Delacroix, imagination "remained impotent and sterile, if it did not have at its command a rapid skill which could follow the great, despotic faculty in all its impatient whims." [64] Imagination and inspiration had to be subjected to discipline. On this matter Baudelaire never changed his mind. In 1846 he had warned that the artist's naïveté and temperament should be "aided by all the means which technique provides." In the *Salon of 1859* he is even more explicit: "The more imagination one has, the more necessary it is to possess a technique which will accompany it on its adventures and overcome the difficulties it eagerly seeks out." [65]

One has only to think of his scorn for Musset, for George Sand, and for Moreau to recall the extent to which negligence and lack of discipline excited his anger. On the other hand, if he admired Gautier excessively, it was because the latter possessed a faultless style, because he was in complete command of his tools. "To handle a language skillfully is to practice a kind of suggestive magic," he once said in discussing Gautier.[66] This suggestive magic he found not only in Gautier, but also in Leconte de Lisle, Banville, Flaubert, and frequently in Hugo.

To attain the perfection and evocative magic of his own verse, Baudelaire followed the advice he gave others and reworked his poems with painstaking care. He was not a facile creator of images and rhymes, and his style was often the result of "severe labor pains," as he wrote to Godefroy in connection with his preface to the second volume of his Poe translations. In a letter to his mother he explains with what difficulty he succeeded in achieving the effect that he sought: "I don't know how many times you have spoken to me about *my facility* . . . Facility in conception or facility in expression? I have never had either one or the other, and it must be quite obvious that the little I have done is the result of very painful effort." [67]

It was this desire for perfection of form that explains his sympathy for art for art's sake, so alien in some respects to his nature. And it was his own mastery of poetic expression that explains much of the greatness of *Les Fleurs du Mal*. The anguish and despair, the sensual joys and spiritual needs that he voiced in his poetry would have moved us far less, had the expression been either weak or banal. Baudelaire himself never forgot that "idea and form are two beings in one" and that to neglect form is "to destroy poetry." [68]

* * *

It is unfortunate that Baudelaire failed to write an article on his conception of the nature and function of poetry. In a draft of a preface to *Les Fleurs du Mal*, he tells how he had intended to answer the question, "What is Poetry?" Discouraged by the hopelessness of the task, however, he abandoned the idea: "I was stopped by the appalling futility of explaining anything to anybody." [69] In spite of his failure to write a formal article on the subject, he made a number of provocative statements that throw an interesting light on poetry in general and on his own poetry in particular.

In the letter which Baudelaire wrote to Armand Fraisse criticizing the poetry of Musset, he inadvertently defines an aspect of poetry which is one of those most characteristic of *Les Fleurs du Mal*. Musset, he wrote, had never been able "to understand the work through which a reverie becomes a work of art." [70] His use of the word "reverie" seems to indicate his belief that poetry is above all the poet's vision of reality, that it is the poet's own inner world exteriorized and given perfection of form by a technique perfectly adapted to the subject.

In his notes on Realism Baudelaire gives, as we have seen, greater stress to the spiritual aspect of poetry: "Poetry is what is most real, what is completely true only in *another world*. This world [is] a hieroglyphic dictionary." Two years later in his 1857 essay on Poe he reaffirms the spiritual and transcendental nature of poetry, its ability to reveal the beauty and mystery of the invisible world:

It is at the same time by poetry and *through* poetry, by and *through* music that the soul glimpses the splendors beyond the tomb, and when an exquisite poem brings us to the verge of tears, those tears are not the proof of excessive pleasure; they are rather evidence of an aroused melancholy, of a condition of nerves, of a nature which has been exiled amid the imperfect and which would like to take possession immediately, on this very earth, of a revealed paradise.[71]

Less spiritual, but more characteristic of his own verse is the subtle observation that he makes in his essay on Banville: "Every lyric poet by virtue of his nature inevitably effects a return to the lost Eden." [72] Like Banville, Baudelaire himself often effects this return to a lost Eden, whether the Eden of his childhood, of tropical seas and skies, or of happiness that he had once known with his dark-skinned mistress. It is in these poems that, through his use of memory and imagination, he has succeeded in recapturing an idealized past and in restoring it to the present.

But the definition which best explains Baudelaire's conception of poetry and of art in general is found in the opening lines of "Philosophic Art." "What is the modern conception of pure art? It is to create a suggestive magic containing both the object and the subject, the world outside the artist and the artist himself." [73] This superb formula not only characterizes much of Baudelaire's own evocative verse, but also became the basis of the poetic theory of the Symbolists.

*   *   *

The question of the relation of art and morality was one that preoccupied Baudelaire throughout most of his career. Much has been written about the contradictory nature of his views. Poems such as "J'Aime le Souvenir" or "La Muse Malade," built on amoral pagan themes and written early in his career, indicate that for a time he shared the Neo-Classical views of such friends and associates as Banville and Ménard. It was not long, however, before he was to renounce the ideas of the Classical Revival completely.

In 1848 Baudelaire was carried away by enthusiasm for the Revolution, and for a short time his ideas of art were influenced by the democratic and social ideals of the period. His association with Proudhon, his intimate friendship with Pierre Dupont, his early memories of industrial strife and of the misery of the working class in Lyons, all contributed to the utilitarian conception of art that he upheld for a few short years. Not long afterward (1851), he praised the rather mediocre verse of Pierre Dupont who, like him, believed that "art should be inseparable from morality and utility," and he denounced the "puerile Utopia of the school of *art for art's sake.*" In another article written at about the same time he condemned the "Pagan School" for its rejection of reason and passion, and concluded that literature must "walk hand in hand with science and philosophy." [74]

Baudelaire soon realized, however, that he had gone to extremes and that the relationship of morality to art was not as direct and explicit as he had thought. In "The Respectable Drama and Novel" he expresses the view that was to become the basis of his thought from that time on. Art is useful, he maintains, "because it is art"; pernicious art, he adds, is that which distorts the conditions of life.[75]

There is no doubt that Baudelaire's discovery of Poe and de Maistre did much to encourage his return to a more aristocratic conception of art.[76] But though he highly approves Poe's attack on utility, "the great heresy of modern times," he is quick to add: "I do not mean that poetry does not ennoble manners—let there be no mistake about it—and that its final result is not to raise man above the level of vulgar interests; that would obviously be an absurdity. I say that, if the poet has pursued a moral aim, he has diminished his poetic force; and it is not rash to wager that his work will be bad." [77]

Whereas Poe considers that art and morality must be completely divorced from each other, Baudelaire acknowledges that
a certain morality is implicit in all great art. For the author of
Les Fleurs du Mal the moral intention of the artist must never
be explicit; art must never become the handmaiden of morality.
As he reminds the reader in his review of *Madame Bovary*,
"the logic of the work satisfies all the claims of morality, and
it is for the reader to draw his conclusions from the conclusion." [78] So he admires Hugo when he is an unintentional
moralist, but despises the explicit moralizing that he finds in
Les Misérables and other works.

Nowhere is Baudelaire's conception of the relation of art
to morality made more clear than in his letter to Swinburne
written a few years before his death: "I am not so much a
moralist as you obligingly pretend to believe. I simply believe
(as you do, no doubt) that every poem, every work of art that
is *well done,* naturally and necessarily suggests a *moral.* It is up
to the reader. I even have a very decided hatred for any exclusively moral *intention* in a poem." [79] It seems reasonable, therefore, to suppose that Baudelaire was not really serious when, in
his notes on *Les Liaisons Dangereuses,* he observed that "all
books are immoral." [80]

*　　*　　*

It is generally acknowledged that the aesthetic ideas expressed by Baudelaire in his remarkable essays on art, literature,
and music are not entirely new or original. His debts to Diderot,
Delacroix, Poe, and others are many, yet from the old he has
always succeeded in forging something new. Like his own fic-
tional character, Samuel Cramer, "he was at the same time all
the artists he had studied and all the books he had read, and
yet, in spite of this talent for mimicry, he remained profoundly
original." [81]

Not only are the essays fascinating studies of aesthetic
problems, which challenge the reader and provoke him to serious
thought, but also they constitute a remarkably sound basis for

the critical judgment of the artists he chose to discuss. There are times when his criticism is uneven and contradictory, when ill-health, poverty and frustration caused him to lash out in a nervous rage and to exaggerate the expression of his disapproval. At moments like these, irritated by unsympathetic personalities and exasperated by ideas that appeared naïve or sentimental, he would condemn a Moreau or a Musset to limbo and relegate the great Victor Hugo to the ranks of the lesser great.

As a matter of principle, moreover, Baudelaire constantly asserted the right to contradict himself. And in the case of Victor Hugo and the disciples of Art for Art's Sake at least, it is important to note that the contradictory elements of his criticism are as much the result of the growth and development of his aesthetic ideas as they are of personal caprice. Judged as a whole, the critical works of Baudelaire give ample evidence of coherence, of the "single and systematic thought," which he claimed for it in Brussels.

Above all it may be said that Baudelaire adhered to his own ideal of criticism. His is certainly not "a cold, mathematical criticism which, under the pretext of explaining everything, shows neither hate nor love, and deliberately divests itself of every vestige of temperament." On the contrary, it is indeed "biased, impassioned, partisan . . . and written from a point of view that opens up the widest horizons." The reader may agree or disagree, but he will seldom fail to admire and will certainly never find himself bored.

L. B. H.
F. E. H., Jr.

THE SALON OF 1846

PREFACE

The *Salon of 1845*, which was Charles Baudelaire's first important publication, is of interest today not so much for its judgment of individual pictures and artists as for its ringing affirmation that artistic novelty and heroic effect may be found —and should be sought—in modern life:

No one heeds tomorrow's wind; and yet the heroism of *modern life* surrounds us and crowds in upon us. We are too stifled by our true feelings not to be aware of them. There is no lack either of subjects or of colors with which to make epics. The *painter*, the real painter, will be he who can seize the epic character of contemporary life and make us see and understand, through color or design, how great and poetic we are in our cravats and our patent leather boots. Let us hope that next year the true seekers will give us the extraordinary pleasure of celebrating the advent of the *new!*

It is significant that Baudelaire's concern for modernity dates back to the very beginning of his career. He himself found some of his finest poetic inspiration in modern urban life and, in his essays, he urges both artists and writers to do likewise. His final and perhaps most important article, *The Painter of Modern Life,* was to be a sort of glorification of the artistic nd literary potentialities of contemporary life.

Baudelaire himself was so dissatisfied with the *Salon of 1845* that he is said to have destroyed all the copies that remained unsold. Champfleury, while explaining that the critic's action was prompted by his distress at its lack of personality, suggests somewhat maliciously that he may also have been conscious of the similarity of his ideas to those of Heine and Stendhal.[1] He adds: "The Utopia of this strange artist was to show himself to the public in all his vigor and in complete mastery of all his powers, and one must admire him for the respect that he had for his work." [2]

The *Salon of 1846* breaks away from the conventional pattern that the critic had followed in 1845 and reveals a Baudelaire who had suddenly found himself, who was indeed "in complete mastery of all his powers." In this brilliant essay he subordinates the criticism of individual artists and works to a thoughtful discussion of general aesthetic ideas which are as pertinent to literature as they are to the plastic arts. Baudelaire's personal contacts with Delacroix whom he had met in 1845 may have helped to crystallize many of these ideas and to encourage his break with traditionalism.

Almost all the important conceptions which came to make up Baudelaire's aesthetics appear in the essay in more or less embryonic form—modernity, which he had already praised in 1845, correspondences, imagination, supernaturalism. Here likewise we find a striking definition and analysis of Romanticism which, though it owes much to Stendhal, is given new life and meaning by Baudelaire.

Baudelaire was more aware of the historic chain of events than is often realized and, early in 1846 before composing his *Salon*, had somewhat cryptically called attention to the "filiation" between Neo-Classic and Romantic art and literature.[3] He himself was a Romanticist of the second generation, and the qualities that he emphasizes—"intimacy, spirituality, color, aspiration toward the infinite"—apply to his own work and also explain to a great extent his admiration for the poetry of Sainte-Beuve by whom he had been strongly influenced while still a boy in school.

Although Baudelaire continued to admire much about Romanticism, he never failed to condemn the excesses and the lack of restraint and discipline found among "the adepts of the false Romantic School." He himself differed from his predecessors in being sharply self-critical. A notation in his *Journaux Intimes*, "I reason too much," suggests that at times he believed himself overly rational. The reader may not concur, but he will undoubtedly agree that Baudelaire's critical intelligence was of fundamental importance in everything that he wrote.

It is worth noting that, as early as 1846, Baudelaire shows a marked preference for suggestion rather than detailed description, for imagination rather than realistic observation. It is mainly for these reasons that he views Eugène Delacroix rather than Victor Hugo as the real head of the Romantic School. Hugo in whose work "there is nothing to guess" . . . who "doesn't omit a blade of grass or a reflection from the streetlight" has become a "painter in poetry," while Delacroix who opens up "deep avenues to the most adventurous imagination . . . is often unconsciously a poet in painting."

WHAT IS THE USE OF CRITICISM?

What is the use?—A huge and terrible question mark that seizes criticism by the collar from the very first page in the first chapter.

The artist reproaches criticism first of all for not being able to teach anything either to the bourgeois—who want neither to paint nor to write verses—or even to art, from whose womb criticism has come.

And yet how many artists nowadays owe their paltry renown to criticism alone! Perhaps that is the real fault of criticism.

You have seen a Gavarni depicting a painter bent over his canvas; behind him is a thin, grave, staid gentleman in a white tie, holding his latest article in his hand.[4] "If art is noble, criticism is holy."—"Who says that?"—"Criticism!" If the artist plays the leading role so easily, it is because the critic is obviously like so many others of his kind.

As to the technical means and methods drawn from the works themselves, I know full well that the criticism of today has other pretentions; for that reason it will always recommend drawing to colorists and color to draughtsmen. It has such rational and sublime taste! The public and the artist have nothing to learn here. These things are learned in the studio, and the public is concerned only with the result.

I sincerely believe that the best criticism is that which is amusing and poetic; not a cold, mathematical criticism which, under the pretext of explaining everything, shows neither hate nor love, and deliberately divests itself of every kind of temperament, but—since a beautiful picture is nature reflected by an artist—the best criticism will be the reflection of that picture by an intelligent and sensitive mind. Thus the best criticism of a picture may well be a sonnet or an elegy.

But this kind of criticism is destined for anthologies and for readers of poetry. As for criticism properly speaking, I hope that philosophers will understand what I am going to say: to be just, that is to be justifiable, criticism should be biased, impassioned, partisan, that is to say written from an exclusive point of view, but from a point of view that opens up the widest horizons.

To extol line to the detriment of color, or color at the expense of line, is doubtless a point of view; but it is neither very broad nor very just, and it shows a great ignorance of individual cases.

You do not know to what degree nature has mingled the taste for line and the taste for color in each mind, nor by what mysterious means she effects the fusion that results in a picture.

Thus a broader point of view will be individualism properly understood; one that will require of the artist naïveté and the sincere expression of his temperament, aided by all the means which his technique provides.* He who lacks temperament is

* In connection with individualism properly understood, see the article on William Haussoullier in the *Salon of 1845*.[5] In spite of all the criticism directed at me in this matter, my opinion remains unchanged; but it is necessary to understand the article.

not worthy of painting pictures, and—since we are tired of imitators and especially of eclectics—such a person ought rather to assist a painter with temperament. That is what I shall prove in one of my last chapters.

Armed with a sure criterion, a criterion drawn from nature, the critic should henceforth perform his duty with impassioned enthusiasm; for being a critic does not keep him from being a man, and passion unites similar temperaments and exalts reason to new heights.

Somewhere Stendhal has said: "Painting is nothing more than a construction in ethics!" If the word ethics is interpreted more or less freely, the same may be said of all the arts. Since they always represent the expression of the beautiful through the feelings, the passions and the dreams of each man—that is to say, variety in unity or the various aspects of the absolute—criticism invariably borders on metaphysics.

Since each century and each people has given expression to its own beauty and its own ethics—and if by Romanticism we mean the most recent and the most modern expression of beauty—in the eyes of the reasonable and impassioned critic, the great artist will be the one who will add the greatest amount of Romanticism to the requirement of naïveté which has been mentioned above.

WHAT IS ROMANTICISM?

Few people today will care to give this word a real and concrete meaning; yet will they dare maintain that a whole generation would be willing to battle for several years over a flag that is not a symbol? If we were to recall recent disturbances, it would become obvious that if few Romanticists remain, it is because few of them found Romanticism; yet all sought it sincerely and honestly.

Some were concerned only with the choice of subjects; they lacked the temperament to deal with their subjects. Others, still believing in a Catholic society, sought to reflect Catholicism in their works. To call oneself a Romanticist and to study the past systematically is to contradict oneself. Some have blasphemed the Greeks and Romans in the name of Romanticism; but you can make Romanticists of the Greeks and Romans only if you are one yourself. Truth in art and local color have led many others astray. Realism had existed for a long time before that great battle, and besides, to compose a tragedy or a picture for M. Raoul Rochette is to run the risk of being contradicted by anyone who happens to be more learned than M. Raoul Rochette.[6]

Romanticism lies neither in choice of subject nor in exact truth, but in the manner of feeling.

They looked for it outside themselves, but it was only to be found within.

For me, Romanticism is the most recent, the most contemporary expression of the beautiful.

There are as many kinds of beauty as there are habitual ways of seeking happiness.

This is clearly explained by the philosophy of progress. Thus, just as there have been as many ideals as there have been ways in which people understand morality, love, religion, etc., so Romanticism will not consist in perfect execution, but in a conception analogous to the morality of the period.

It is because some have associated it with technical perfection that we have had the rococo of Romanticism, unquestionably the most intolerable of all its forms.

Thus, above all, it is necessary to know those aspects of nature and those situations of man which were disdained or unknown to the artists of the past.

To speak of Romanticism is to speak of modern art—that is, of intimacy, spirituality, color, aspiration toward the infinite, expressed by all the means available to the arts.

Hence it follows that there is an obvious contradiction between Romanticism and the works of its principal adherents. . . .

I do not know if any analogist has firmly established a complete scale of colors and feelings, but I do remember a passage in Hoffmann which expresses my idea perfectly and which will please all those who sincerely love nature: "It is not only in dreams or in the drifting thoughts that precede sleep, but also in the period when I am still awake and listening to music that I find an analogy and a close relation between colors, sounds, and perfumes. It seems to me that all these things have been brought into existence by the same ray of light and that they must unite in a marvelous harmony. The scent of brown and red marigolds always produces a magical effect on my being. It makes me fall into deep reverie and then I hear as if from a distance the solemn, deep tones of the oboe. . . ." [7]

EUGÈNE DELACROIX

. . . During the unhappy period of revolution which I mentioned a moment ago and whose many mistakes I have recorded, Eugène Delacroix was often compared to Victor Hugo. People had their romantic poet, they had to have a corresponding painter. This absolute insistence on finding counterparts and equivalents in the different arts often leads to strange blunders, and in this case offers further proof of a lack of comprehension. The comparison must surely have seemed painful to Eugène Delacroix, perhaps to both; for if my definition of Romanticism (intimacy, spirituality, etc.) places Delacroix at the head of this movement, it naturally excludes M. Victor Hugo. The comparison has remained in the banal realm of accepted ideas, and these two prejudices still survive in superficial minds. We must put an end to this sophomoric nonsense once and for all. I beg all those who have felt the need to create a certain aesthetic of their own and to deduce the causes from the results to carefully compare the productions of these two artists.

M. Victor Hugo, whose nobility and majesty I certainly do not wish to belittle, is a craftsman much more adroit than inventive, a workman far more correct than creative. Delacroix is sometimes clumsy, but yet essentially creative. M. Victor Hugo reveals a system of uniform alignments and contrasts in all his pictures, both lyric and dramatic. With him eccentricity itself assumes symmetrical forms. He abundantly possesses and coldly employs all the modulations of rhyme, all the resources of antithesis, all the tricks of apposition. He is a decadent or transitional composer who uses his tools with a truly admirable and extraordinary dexterity. M. Hugo was by nature an academician before he was born and, if we were still living in the days of fabulous marvels, I should be inclined to believe that, whenever he passed before their dour sanctuary, the green lions of the Institute would murmur to him in prophetic tones: "You will belong to the Academy!"

For Delacroix, justice is slower. His works, on the contrary, are poems, great poems naïvely conceived and executed with the insolence customary to genius.* In the works of the former, there is nothing to guess; for he takes so much pleasure in showing his skill that he doesn't omit a blade of grass or a reflection from the streetlight. The latter in his works opens up deep avenues to the most adventurous imagination. The first possesses a certain serenity, let us say rather a certain disinterested egoism which envelops all his poetry with an indefinable coldness and placidity—qualities which the stubborn and splenetic passion of the second, in conflict with the patience necessary to his craft, does not always permit him to retain. The one begins with detail, the other with an intimate understanding of his subject, with the result that one goes only skin deep, while the other tears out the entrails. Too materialistic, too concerned with the exterior aspects of nature, M. Victor Hugo has become a painter in poetry; Delacroix, always respectful of his ideal, is often unconsciously a poet in painting. . . .

* By the naïveté of genius must be understood a knowledge of technique combined with *gnothi seauton,* but a humble knowledge that leaves the leading role to temperament.

ON THE HEROISM OF MODERN LIFE

... Before trying to discover the epic side of modern life and to prove through examples that our age is no less fertile in sublime themes than the past, it may be said that, just as all centuries and all peoples have had their forms of beauty, so inevitably we have ours. That is in the natural order of things.

All forms of beauty, like all possible phenomena, contain something eternal and something transitory—something absolute and something particular. Absolute and eternal beauty does not exist, or rather it is only an abstraction skimmed off the surface of a variety of beauties. The characteristic element of each form of beauty comes from the passions and, since we have our particular passions, we have our own beauty.

Except for Hercules on Mount Oeta, Cato of Utica, and Cleopatra, whose suicides are not *modern* suicides, what suicides do you see in the pictures of the old masters? (The first killed himself because his burning garments became intolerable; the second because there was nothing more he could do for liberty; and the voluptuous queen because she had lost both her throne and her lover. But none of them destroyed himself in order to change skins with a view to metempsychosis.) Among pagan lives, devoted to the senses, you will not find a suicide like that of Jean Jacques [Rousseau], or even like the strange and marvelous suicide of Raphaël de Valentin.[8]

As for the dress, the outer garb of the modern hero—although the time is past when would-be painters dressed like the Grand Panjandrum and smoked pipes as long as shotguns—yet the studios and society are still full of people who would like to poeticize Antony with a Greek cloak or a parti-colored garment.[9]

And yet, has not this much maligned garb its own native beauty and charm? Is it not the necessary garb of our suffering age which wears the symbol of perpetual mourning even on its thin black shoulders? Notice how the black suit and the frock coat possess not only their political beauty, which is the expression of universal equality, but also their poetic beauty, which is the expression of the public soul—an endless procession of hired mourners, political mourners, amorous mourners, bourgeois mourners. We are all of us celebrating some funeral.

A uniform livery of mourning bears witness to equality; and as for the eccentrics who used to attract attention with their bold, violent colors, today they are satisfied with nuances in cut and design rather than nuances in color. Do not those puckered creases, playing like serpents around the mortified flesh, have their own mysterious grace? . . .

To return to our principle and essential problem, that of knowing whether we possess a specific beauty inherent in our new passions, I notice that most artists who have dealt with modern themes have restricted themselves to public and official subjects, to our victories and our political heroism. And even so, they do it grudgingly and because they are commissioned and paid by the government. However, there are subjects to be found in private life that are far more heroic.

The spectacle of fashionable life and of thousands of stray souls—criminals and kept women—who drift about in the underground of a great city, the *Gazette des Tribunaux* and the *Moniteur* all prove to us that we need only open our eyes to become aware of our heroism.

Should a minister, harassed by the impertinent curiosity of the opposition, express once and for all—with that haughty, sovereign eloquence peculiar to him—his contempt and disgust for all ignorant, annoying opposition, that very evening you will be sure to overhear everywhere on the Boulevard des Italiens these words: "Were you in the Chamber today? Did you see the minister? Good Heavens, how handsome he was! I have never seen anything so fine!"

Evidently there are such things as modern beauty and heroism!

A little farther on you may hear: "K.— or F.— has been commissioned to do a medal on that subject; but he won't be able to do it; he can't understand that kind of thing!"

Evidently there are artists more or less qualified to understand modern beauty.

Or else: "That magnificent scoundrel! Not even Byron's pirates are so grand and so scornful. Could you believe that he pushed aside the Abbé Montès and rushed straight to the guillotine, shouting: 'Don't destroy my courage!' "

This remark alludes to the bravado of a criminal about to die, a great Protestant, vigorous and poised, whose fierce courage was undaunted by the sight of the instrument of death! [10]

All these words falling from your lips are proof that you believe in a new and special beauty which is neither that of Achilles nor of Agamemnon.

Parisian life is rich in poetic and marvelous subjects. The marvelous envelops and permeates us, like the atmosphere itself; but we do not see it.

The *nude*—so dear to artists and so necessary to success—is as frequent and as important today as it was in the past:—in bed, in the bath, in the anatomical theater. The resources and the themes of painting are equally abundant and varied; but there is a new element—modern beauty.

For the heroes of the Iliad cannot compare with you, O Vautrin, O Rastignac, O Birotteau,—nor with you, O Fontanarès, who dared not publicly recount your sorrows wearing the funereal and rumpled frock coat of today; nor with you, O Honoré de Balzac, you the most heroic, the most amazing, the most romantic and the most poetic of all the characters that you have drawn from your fertile bosom! [11]

PREFACE TO MESMERIC REVELATION

Baudelaire first became acquainted with Poe in 1847 when he read in a socialist newspaper, *La Démocratie Pacifique*, several stories translated by Isabelle Meunier, the English-born wife of the socialist publisher, Victor Meunier. His enthusiasm was at once aroused and the following year (1848) he himself published a translation of Poe's "Mesmeric Revelation" in *La Liberté de Penser.*

The preface, though short, contains several typical Baudelairean ideas. His claim that able and forceful writers create their own method and interpret nature through their own sensibilities echoes ideas already mentioned in the *Salon of 1846* —a claim developed more fully in later essays.

Even more interesting is the light that the preface throws on the development of Baudelaire's conception of the imagination. At this point in his career Baudelaire obviously views imagination as relatively unimportant and as incomplete in itself. To be "surprising and original," to understand the "mysterious meaning" of things, the writer must possess the "philosophic spirit" in addition to imagination. In later essays, particularly in the *Salon of 1859*, Baudelaire no longer distinguishes between the two, and it becomes obvious that what he here calls the "philosophic spirit" has become an integral part of imagination, that divine faculty which is "related to the infinite" and which teaches man "the moral significance of color, of outline, of sound, and of perfume" (CE, p. 274).

BAUDELAIRE'S PREFACE

Edgar Poe has been much discussed recently, and he deserves to be. With a volume of short stories his reputation has reached across the sea. He has caused astonishment, most of all astonishment, rather than emotion or enthusiasm. That is usually the case with all writers who depend on a method which they themselves have created and which is the natural expression of their temperament. I do not believe that it is possible to find any able writer who has not created his own method, or rather whose native sensibility has not been reflected and transformed into a sure art. Forceful writers are also apt to be philosophers to a greater or lesser extent: Diderot, Laclos, Hoffmann, Goethe, Jean-Paul [Richter], Maturin, Honoré de Balzac, Edgar Poe.[12] Notice that I am taking literary men of every complexion, and the most opposite, as examples. That is true of all of them, even of Diderot, the most audacious and the most adventurous, who applied himself to observe and to control his inspiration, who began by accepting and ended by making a deliberate use of his own enthusiastic, sanguine and boisterous nature. Consider Sterne, whose case is obviously quite different and also quite admirable in a different way. The man made his own method. All these individuals, with tireless effort and good will, translate nature, pure nature.—Which nature?—Their own. Thus they are usually much more surprising and original than those who simply possess imagination, but completely lack the philosophic spirit, and who line up and pile up events without classifying them and without explaining their mysterious meaning. I have said that they were astonishing. I am going to go further and say that they usually aim at astonishment. In the works of several of these men there can be seen a preoccupation with a perpetual supernaturalism. As I have said, that comes from an inherent tendency *to seek*, from the inquisitive mind, the judicial mind, which perhaps has its roots in the most remote impressions of childhood. Others, determined naturalists, examine the

47

soul with a magnifying glass, as doctors examine the body, and wear out their eyes looking for the hidden spring. Others, of a mixed type, try to fuse these two systems in a mysterious unity. Animal unity, the unity of a universal fluid, the unity of original matter, all these recent theories, by a strange coincidence, have somehow entered the minds of poets at the same time that they have entered the minds of scientists.

Thus, finally, there always comes a moment when writers of the type I have been describing become jealous of philosophers, as it were, and then they also set forth their own system of natural philosophy, sometimes even with a certain lack of modesty which has its ingenuousness and its charm. Everyone knows *Séraphitus, Louis Lambert,* and a multitude of passages in other books in which Balzac, a great mind devoured by a legitimate encyclopedic pride, has attempted to harmonize in a unified and definitive system different ideas drawn from Swedenborg, Mesmer, Marat, Goethe and Geoffroy Saint-Hilaire. Edgar Poe was also obsessed by the idea of unity, and he expended as much effort as Balzac on that fond dream. It is certain that when specifically literary minds put themselves to it, they make strange excursions through philosophy. They cut abrupt openings and see sudden vistas on paths which are entirely theirs.

To summarize, I shall say that the three characteristics of *curious* writers are: 1. a *personal* method; 2. *surprise*; 3. a philosophic mania, three characteristics, moreover, which establish their superiority as writers. The selection from Edgar Poe which follows is sometimes based on excessively tenuous reasoning, in other places it is obscure, and now and then it is exceptionally audacious. It is necessary to make the best of it and to digest it just as it is. Above all it is necessary to follow the text literally. Certain things would have become even more obscure. had I chosen to paraphrase the author, instead of holding myself strictly to the letter. I have preferred to use a labored and sometimes baroque French, and to present Edgar Poe's philosophical method in all its truth.

It goes without saying that *La Liberté de Penser* cannot be held responsible for the ideas of the American storyteller, and that it simply believed it could please its readers by offering them this highly interesting scientific curiosity.

❧ PIERRE DUPONT

PREFACE

Baudelaire's first essay on Pierre Dupont is often considered something of an anomaly. His scorn for "the puerile Utopia of the school of *art for art's sake*" and his unequivocal defense of utilitarian art are in flat contradiction to the aesthetic principles that he espoused in his later essays.

It is important to remember, however, that the essay belongs to a period when Baudelaire was imbued with the socialist and democratic ideals that inspired the Revolution of 1848. Fired by enthusiasm for the ideas of Proudhon who, while denouncing Utopian dreamers, was calling for active reform, Baudelaire seems to have adopted, if only for a few short years, a philosophy of action that showed itself both in his life and in his writing. He himself had somewhat incongruously played a minor part in the Revolution of 1848 and had joined with Champfleury and Charles Toubin in publishing a revolutionary newspaper, *Le Salut Public*, which, for lack of financial support, ceased publication after only two issues.

It is not strange then that Baudelaire's socialism should be reflected in his essay of 1851 where he boldly declares that art is "inseparable from morality and utility." If he condemns the shades of René, of Obermann and of Werther, it is only because they are "creations of idleness and solitude," because "the spirit of action no longer leaves room for you among us." Interestingly enough, this admiration for the spirit of action also helps to explain his poem "Le Reniement de Saint Pierre," written during the same socialistic phase of his career and related in many ways to the sentiments expressed in his essay on Dupont. For a world "where action is not the sister of the dream" Baudelaire felt only keen disillusionment, and for a Christ who rejected action and submitted passively to evil and oppression, he professed the most bitter scorn.

It is also important to note that, both before and after his socialistic period, Baudelaire felt for the poor and downtrodden a deep and sincere love that showed itself in such poems as "Les Petites Vieilles," "Le Crépuscule du Soir," "Le Crépuscule du Matin," "La Mort des Pauvres," and in the prose poem "Les Yeux des Pauvres." Dupont's poetry undoubtedly struck a responsive chord in his own heart and awakened memories of the suffering of the working class which he himself had witnessed as a young boy in Lyons.

No doubt also Baudelaire admired Dupont's ability to avoid a stale imitation of the past and to find inspiration in contemporary urban life. To the critic who had so strongly urged modernity in his *Salon of 1846*, Dupont was in literature what Constantin Guys was in art in spite of their utterly different styles. Although both were artists of only secondary importance, both were "in communication with the men of [their] time" and both succeeded in translating their thoughts and emotions in a form that was "sufficiently correct." It is only fair to emphasize that Baudelaire's praise of Dupont was not the result of critical blindness, but rather the result of a transient enthusiasm for ideas and attitudes that Dupont represented and that the critic had temporarily accepted.

The popular sympathies expressed in the article on Dupont were soon to be swept aside, however, by Louis Napoleon's *coup d'état* of December, 1851. On March 5, 1852, Baudelaire wrote to his guardian, Ancelle, that the second of December had "physically de-politized" him. Moreover, the discovery of Joseph de Maistre and of Edgar Allan Poe had already begun to color his political orientation and to turn him to a more aristocratic conception of literature and society.

Baudelaire's second essay on Dupont in 1861 was to be less enthusiastic. Though he had long since rejected the idea of utilitarian art, he did not repudiate his belief that Dupont was a moving writer of songs who, as he had claimed in 1851, had succeeded in making "popular poetry acceptable."

Pierre Dupont (1821–1870), the son of a Lyons blacksmith, came to Paris as a young man and became known as an author of light popular verse and of patriotic songs. Much of what he wrote was inspired by the poverty and want that he himself had known as a child.

He became acquainted with Baudelaire, probably through the painter Emile Deroy, and for a few years was one of the poet's close friends and associates.[13] Baudelaire's essay on Dupont served as a preface to the latter's edition of *Chants et Chansons* (1851).

⧓⧓⧓

I have just carefully re-read the *Chants et Chansons* of Pierre Dupont, and I am still convinced that the success of this new poet is a matter of decided importance not so much because of his own merit, great as it may be, as because of the public sentiments of which this poetry is the symptom, and of which Pierre Dupont has become the echo.

In order to better understand this idea, I beg the reader to consider briefly and in a general way the development of poetry in the recent past. Certainly it would be an injustice to deny the services performed by the so-called Romantic School. It brought us back to the truth of the image, it destroyed academic conventions, and even from the higher point of view of linguistics, it does not deserve the scorn unjustly heaped upon it by certain impotent pedants. But by its very principle the Romantic insurrection was doomed to a short life. By excluding morality

51

and often even passion the puerile Utopia of the school of *art for art's sake* was inevitably sterile. It was flagrantly contrary to the spirit of humanity. In the name of the higher principles that constitute universal life we have the right to declare it guilty of heterodoxy. Assuredly very ingenious men of letters, very learned antiquarians, versifiers who, admittedly, raised prosody almost to a creative level, were associated with this movement and drew some very surprising effects from the means which they had pooled. Some of them were even willing to take advantage of the political climate. Navarin [naval battle of 1827] drew their eyes to the Orient and philhellenism engendered a book [Hugo's *Les Orientales*] as dazzling as an Indian handkerchief or shawl.[14] All the Catholic and Oriental superstitions were sung in skillful and strange rhythms. But to these purely materialistic accents, designed to dazzle the tremulous gaze of children or to caress their sluggish ear, how much more desirable is the lament of that morbid individuality, which from the depths of an imaginary coffin struggled to interest a troubled society in its incurable melancholy [Sainte-Beuve's *Joseph Delorme*]. I am less annoyed by the poet, however egoistic he may be, when he says, "I think . . . , I feel . . ." than by the musician or the indefatigable scribbler who has made a satanic pact with his instrument. The naïve rascality of the one is excusable; the academic effrontery of the other disgusts me.

But even more than the former, I prefer the poet who is in continuous communication with the men of his time and exchanges with them thoughts and emotions translated into a noble language that is sufficiently correct. The poet, situated on one of the points of humanity's circumference, sends back on the same line and in more melodious vibrations the human thought which was transmitted to him; every true poet should be an incarnation, and—to use a recent example which will sum up my thought once and for all—in spite of all those literary works, in spite of all those efforts accomplished outside the law of truth, in spite of all that dilettantism, that *voluptuism* armed with a thousand instruments and a thousand wiles, when there appeared a poet [Barbier], awkward at times, but almost always great, who proclaimed in impassioned language the sacredness of the Revolution of 1830 and sang of the destitution of England and Ireland, despite his defective rhymes, despite his pleonasms, despite his unfinished periods, the question was settled, and art was thereafter inseparable from morality and utility.[15]

The destiny of Pierre Dupont was analogous. Let us recall the last years of the monarchy. How interesting it would be to describe in a dispassionate book the feelings, the doctrines, the external life, the inner life, the styles, and the manners of youth during the reign of Louis-Philippe! Only the mind was excited; the heart had no part in the movement, and the famous phrase: *get rich*, legitimate and true in so far as it implies morality, denied it for the very reason that it did not affirm it. Wealth can be a guarantee of knowledge and morality, provided it is rightly acquired; but when wealth becomes the ultimate goal of all the efforts of the individual, then enthusiasm, charity, philosophy and all that which makes for a common patrimony in an eclectic and capitalistic society, disappear. The history of youth, under the rule of Louis-Philippe, is a history of places of debauchery and of restaurants. In the reign of Louis-Philippe kept women obtained, with less impudence, less extravagance, and with more reserve, a glory and an importance equal to that which they enjoyed during the Empire. From time to time there resounded in the air a great din of speeches similar to those of the Porch [center of the Stoic School in Athens], and the echoes of the Maison d'Or [Restaurant] mingled with the innocent paradoxes of the legislative palace.

Nevertheless, a few fresh and pure songs began to circulate in concerts and in private circles. It was, as it were, a call to order and an invitation on the part of nature; and the most corrupt minds welcomed them as if they were a cooling breeze or an oasis. A few pastorals (*Les Paysans*) had just appeared, and already bourgeois pianos were repeating them with heedless joy.

At this point the Parisian life of Pierre Dupont began in a definite and decided way; but it is useful to go even further back, not only to satisfy a legitimate public curiosity, but also to show the admirable logic that exists in the genesis of material facts and of moral phenomena. The public likes to know about the background of the minds it trusts; one might say that it is inspired in this matter by an indomitable feeling of equality. "You have touched our hearts! You must prove to us that you are only a man and that the same means of improvement exist for us all." To the philosopher, the scholar, the poet, the artist, to all things that are great, to all those who stir and transform it, the public makes the same request. The enormous appetite that we have for biographies springs from a profound feeling of equality.

The childhood and youth of Pierre Dupont resemble the childhood and youth of all men destined to become famous. It is very simple and it explains the years that follow. All the healthy family emotions, love, constraint, rebellious spirit, are mingled together in sufficient quantities to create a poet. The rest is acquired knowledge. Pierre Dupont was born on April 23, 1821, in Lyons, the great city of labor and of industrial marvels. A family of craftsmen, work, order, the daily spectacle of wealth being created, all this was to bear fruit. He lost his mother at the age of four; an aged godfather, a priest, took him into his home and began an education which was to continue in the parochial school of Largentière. On leaving school, Dupont became a silkweaver's apprentice; but soon he was thrust into the stifling atmosphere of a bank. The large sheets of red-lined paper, the hideous green filing cases that belong to notaries and lawyers which are filled with dissensions, hatreds, family quarrels, and often unknown crimes, the cruel, implacable regularity of a business establishment, all these things were well suited to complete the creation of a poet. It is a good thing for each of us to have experienced at some time in his life the pressure of an odious tyranny; he learns to despise it. How many philosophers the seminary has produced! How many rebellious natures have been formed by contact with a cruel and rigid soldier of the Empire! [16] How many songs of liberty we owe to you, O fruitful discipline! One fine morning the poor and noble nature breaks out of its bonds, the satanic charm is broken and there remains only what is needed, a memory of unhappiness, a leaven for the dough.

In Provins there was a grandfather whom Pierre Dupont sometimes visited; there he met M. Pierre Lebrun of the Academy, and shortly afterwards, having drawn lots, he was obliged to join an infantry regiment. By great good fortune, the book *Les Deux Anges* was completed. M. Pierre Lebrun conceived the idea of having many people subsidize the printing of the book; the profits were used to pay for a replacement. Thus Pierre Dupont began what may be called his public life by buying himself out of slavery with his poetry. It is undoubtedly a great honor and a great satisfaction to him to have forced the Muse to play a direct, useful role in his early years.

This same book, incomplete, often incorrect, indecisive in character, nevertheless contains, as is so often the case, the germ of a future talent which could easily have been predicted by a discerning mind. The volume was awarded a prize by the Academy, and from that time on Pierre Dupont held a minor job as an assistant in the work being done on the Dictionary. I readily believe that these duties, however trivial they appeared, served to increase and to perfect in him the taste for beautiful language. Since he was often obliged to listen to stormy discussions on traditional versus modern rhetoric and grammar, to the lively and witty quarrels of M. Cousin with M. Victor Hugo, his mind was strengthened by those gymnastics, and he thus learned to recognize the enormous value of the proper word.[17] This may seem childish to many people, but they have failed to realize the constant work that goes on in the mind of writers and the chain of circumstances necessary to create a poet.

Pierre Dupont finally acted with the Academy as he had done with the banking establishment. He wanted to be free, and he was right. The poet must live by his own efforts; as Honoré de Balzac has said, he must be something of a businessman. He must make a living with his tools. The relationship of Pierre

Dupont and M. Lebrun was always pure and noble and, as Sainte-Beuve has said, if Dupont wanted to be completely free and independent, he was nonetheless grateful for the past.

Then appeared the collection *Les Paysans, Chants Rustiques* in a neat edition, illustrated with rather pretty lithographs, which could boldly show itself in the salons and decently take its place on the pianos of the bourgeoisie. Everyone was grateful to the poet for having finally introduced a little truth and naturalness in these songs destined to delight many an evening party. It was no longer that indigestible mixture of sugar and cream with which uneducated families indiscreetly stuff the memories of their young daughters. It was a truthful mingling of naïve melancholy and boisterous, innocent joy with, here and there, robust accents of working-class virility.

Meanwhile, following his natural bent, Dupont had composed a song more decisive in character and more suited to touch the hearts of the inhabitants of a large city. I still remember the first time that he spoke to me secretly about it with a charming naïveté and as if still undecided and irresolute. When I heard that wonderful cry of melancholy and sorrow (*Le Chant des Ouvriers*, 1846), I was awed and moved. We had been waiting so many years for some solid, real poetry! Whatever the party to which one belongs, whatever the prejudices one has inherited, it is impossible not to be moved by the sight of that sickly throng breathing the dust of the workshops, swallowing lint, becoming saturated with white lead, mercury, and all the poisons necessary to the creation of masterpieces, sleeping among vermin in the heart of districts where the humblest and greatest virtues live side by side with the most hardened vices and with the dregs from prisons—that sighing and languishing throng to which *the earth owes its marvels*, which feels *flowing in its veins an ardent red blood*, which looks long and sadly at the sunshine and shadows of the great parks and, for its only comfort and consolation, bawls at the top of its voice its song of salvation: *Let us love one another. . . .*

From that time on, the destiny of Dupont was assured; he

had only to continue along the path which he had discovered. To recount the joys, the sorrows, and the dangers of each craft, and to illuminate with a consoling philosophy all the particular aspects and all the various horizons of suffering and human toil, such was the duty that devolved on him and that he patiently accomplished. There will come a time when the accents of this workingman's Marseillaise will circulate like a Masonic password, and when the exiled, the abandoned, and the lost, whether under the devouring tropical sky or in the snowy wilderness, will be able to say: I have nothing more to fear, I am in France!, as he hears this virile melody perfume the air with its primordial fragrance:

> Nous dont la lampe le matin
> Au clairon du coq se rallume,
> Nous tous qu'un salaire incertain
> Ramène avant l'aube à l'enclume . . .

The February Revolution quickened this impatient flowering and strengthened its popular inspiration; all the misfortunes and all the hopes of the Revolution echoed in the poetry of Pierre Dupont. The pastoral muse, however, did not yield its hold and, on reading more of his work, one constantly hears the quiet murmur and sees the shimmering of the cool primeval spring that filters from the mountain snows, just as if one were in the midst of a tortuous chain of stormy mountains beside a very ordinary and rough road:

> Entendez-vous au creux du val
> Ce long murmure qui serpente?
> Est-ce une flûte de cristal?
> Non, c'est la voix de l'eau qui chante.

The work of the poet falls naturally into three divisions—the pastoral, the political and socialistic lyrics, and a few symbolic songs which constitute, so to speak, the philosophy of the work. This part is perhaps the most personal; it is the development of a somewhat obscure philosophy, a sort of amorous mysticity. The optimism of Dupont, his unlimited trust in the natural goodness of man, his fanatical love of nature constitute the greatest share of his talent. There is a Spanish play in which a young girl, listening to the excited clamor of the birds in the trees, asks: What is that voice and of what does it sing? And the birds repeat in chorus: love, love! Leaves of the trees, wind in the sky, what do you say, what do you command? And the chorus answers: love, love! The chorus of brooks says the same thing. The series is long and the refrain is always the same.[18] In the work of Dupont that mysterious voice sings unchangingly of the universal remedy. The melancholy beauty of nature has left such an imprint on his mind that if he wishes to compose a funereal song on the abominations of civil war, the first images and the first lines which come to his mind are:

> La France est pâle comme un lys,
> Le front ceint de grises verveines.

No doubt some people will be sorry not to find in those political and martial songs all the tumult and all the glamor of war, all the delirium of ecstasy and hate, the wild call of the bugle, the whistling of the fife mad as the hope of the young who run to conquer the world, the tireless roar of the cannons, the groans of the wounded and all the din of victory, so dear to a military nation like ours. But do not forget that what would be a fault in another becomes a virtue in Dupont. Indeed, how could he contradict himself? From time to time a sharp note of indignation springs from his lips, but it is obvious that he will be quick to pardon at the first sign of repentance, at the first ray of sunlight! Only once, perhaps without realizing it, has Dupont noted the utility of the spirit of destruction; this confession has escaped from him, but notice in what terms:

> Le glaive brisera le glaive,
> Et du combat naîtra l'amour!

In a word, when these songs are carefully re-read, they reveal a special flavor. They stand up well, and they are held together by a common tie—love of humanity.

This last line suggests to me an idea which throws a strong light on the legitimate, though amazing success of our poet. There are periods when the means of execution in all the arts are sufficiently numerous, sufficiently perfected, and sufficiently inexpensive for everyone to be able to appropriate them to himself in almost equal quantity. There are times when all painters know how to cover a canvas more or less quickly and skillfully; the same thing is true of poets. Why is the name of one poet on everyone's lips, while the name of another crawls from one dark pigeonhole to another in a publishing house, or remains shelved in the files of a newspaper office? In short, what is Dupont's great secret and what explains the admiration that surrounds him? This great secret, I can assure you, is very simple; it is neither in his experience, nor his ingenuity, nor in his skill in composing, nor in the greater or lesser number of procedures which he has drawn from the common fund of human knowledge; it is in his love of virtue and humanity and in an indefinable quality that is constantly present in his poetry, something that I should like to call his boundless enthusiasm for the Republic.

There is also something else; yes, there is something else. It is joy!

This joy, which breathes and dominates in the works of a few famous writers, as Champfleury has wisely noted in connection with Honoré de Balzac, is a strange phenomenon. However great the sorrows which befall them, however distressing the human spectacle may be, their good nature gains the upper hand, as does also their great sense of wisdom, which perhaps is something even better. It may be said that they bear within themselves their own consolation. Indeed, nature is so beautiful and man is so great that, from a higher point of view, one can scarcely conceive the meaning of the word: irreparable.[19] When a poet appears who expresses ideas so beautiful and so comforting, how can you have the courage to balk?

59

Take flight then, deceptive shades of René, of Obermann, and of Werther; vanish into the mists of nowhere, monstrous creations of idleness and solitude; like the Gadarene swine, go and plunge yourselves, sheep attacked by the romantic vertigo, into the depths of enchanted forests, whence you were drawn by enemy fairies.[20] The spirit of action no longer leaves room for you among us.

When I glance over the work of Dupont, I am always reminded, probably because of some secret affinity, of the sublime movement of Proudhon, filled with tenderness and enthusiasm.[21] He hears someone humming the Lyonese song:

> Allons, du courage,
> Braves ouvriers!
> Du cœur à l'ouvrage!
> Soyons les premiers.

and he cries: "Go to work with a song, predestined race, your refrain is more beautiful than that of Rouget de Lisle." *

It will be to the eternal credit of Pierre Dupont that he first broke open the door. Axe in hand, he has cut the chains of the drawbridge of the fortress; now popular poetry is acceptable.

Loud imprecations, deep sighs of hope, cries of never-ending encouragement are beginning to create hope. All this will turn into literature, poetry and song, in spite of all resistance.

Great is the destiny of poetry!

Joyous or sad, it always bears in itself a divine Utopian character. It runs the risk of no longer being poetry, if it does not constantly contradict fact. In prison it becomes revolt; in the hospital window the burning hope of being cured; in the dilapidated and dirty attic it adorns itself like a fairy of luxury and elegance; it not only records, but it redeems. Everywhere it becomes the negation of iniquity.

* *Avertissement aux Propriétaires*

Go singing into the future, providential poet; your songs are the luminous reflection of popular hopes and beliefs!

The edition to which this review is appended contains the music for each song, usually composed by the author himself, simple melodies of a pure and free character, but requiring a certain artistry for their proper execution. In order to give a correct idea of this talent, it was indeed helpful to include the musical text, for many of the poems are admirably completed by the song. I, like many others, have often heard Pierre Dupont sing these songs himself, and like them, I think no one has sung them better. I have often heard these rustic or patriotic strains attempted by beautiful voices and yet I have felt only a sense of annoyance. Since this book of songs will go to all those who love poetry and who also want to perform them themselves, either to entertain their family and guests or to enliven the long winter evenings, I shall suggest an idea which struck me when I was seeking the reason for the dissatisfaction which many singers have caused me. It is not enough to have a true or beautiful voice, it is much more important to have feeling. Most of the songs of Pierre Dupont, whether they express a state of mind or take the form of narratives, are lyric dramas whose descriptions constitute the setting and substance. To perform the work well, you *must get right inside* the protagonist, you must become so thoroughly imbued with the emotions that he expresses and feel them so perfectly that the work seems to be your very own. You must assimilate a work in order to express it well; that is certainly one of those banal, often repeated truths that must be repeated again. If you scorn my opinion, look for another secret.

⚜ "AS MAN ADVANCES THROUGH LIFE..."

PREFACE

The following lines, written in an album for Madame Francine Ledoux on August 26, 1851, reflect a personal disillusionment and a spiritual preoccupation that seem strangely grave coming from a young man of thirty. Baudelaire's unhappy liaison with Jeanne Duval, his painful misunderstandings with his mother, his lack of literary success must all have contributed to his mood of sadness and resignation.

If the note expresses a certain disappointment with life, it also reveals the incorrigible idealism that marks the enthusiastic article on Pierre Dupont which he had just written as well as his essay on "The Pagan School" that was soon to appear. The virtue and universal love which Baudelaire mentions in the final lines relate directly to the article on Dupont, and the sympathy that he expresses for old women anticipates such poems as "Les Petites Vieilles" and "Un Cheval de Race."

As man advances through life and as he sees things from a higher vantage point, what the world has agreed to call beauty loses much of its importance, as do sensual delights and many other trifles. To the penetrating eyes of the disillusioned man every season has its value, and winter is not the most forbidding nor the least enchanting. Henceforth beauty will be no more than *the promise of happiness*, as Stendhal, I believe, has said. Beauty will be the form which promises the most kindness, the most fidelity to carry out a promise, the most honesty in fulfilling a pledge, the most subtlety in understanding relationships. Ugliness will be cruelty, avarice, stupidity, deceit. Most young men are unaware of these things and only learn them at their own expense. Some of us know them now, but we know them only for ourselves alone. How could I possibly succeed in convincing a young scatterbrain that no sensual desire is mingled with the irresistible sympathy that I feel for old women, for those creatures who have suffered greatly through their lovers, their husbands, their children, and also through their own mistakes? . . .

If the idea of Virtue and of universal Love is not associated with all our pleasures, all our pleasures will become torture and remorse.

❧ THE RESPECTABLE DRAMA AND NOVEL

PREFACE

The following essay, published November 21, 1851, in *La Semaine Théâtrale,* is a virulent attack on the School of Good Sense and on the popular drama of Emile Augier in particular.

In his essay Baudelaire seems to be moving away from the stand he had taken in his article on Pierre Dupont and to be seeking a position more compatible with his own temperament. He is deeply concerned with "the great and terrible words which incessantly pervade literary controversy: art, beauty, utility, morality" and decries the lack of philosophical wisdom that leads a writer to "seize half of the banner for himself, while maintaining that the other half has no value."

The importance of the essay lies not so much in Baudelaire's criticism of the School of Good Sense as in his solution to the problem of art and beauty versus morality and utility. "Is art useful?" he asks, and answers his own question by saying, "Yes, because it is art." His answer is not entirely a contradiction of the view he had expressed in "Pierre Dupont." He does not dismiss the question of morality in art, but suggests that morality is implicit in all great works of the imagination: "if your novel or your play is well done, no one is going to feel inclined to violate the laws of nature. The first requirement of a healthy art is belief in an integral unity. I defy anyone to show me a single work of the imagination which fulfills all the conditions of the beautiful and which is a pernicious work." The attitude that Baudelaire here expresses will remain fundamentally unchanged throughout his life and lies somewhere between the two extremes of the School of Good Sense and the School of Art for Art's Sake.

The "satanic" decree of Léon Faucher to which Baudelaire refers was issued by the government on October 12, 1851, and authorized prizes for successful moralizing plays "designed for the instruction of the working classes through the propagation of healthy ideas and the spectacle of good examples."

For some time a great craze for respectability has dominated the theater as well as the novel. The puerile excesses of the so-called Romantic School have provoked a reaction which may be charged with unpardonable blundering, in spite of the seemingly pure intentions that prompted it. To be sure, virtue is a good thing, and until now no writer, unless he were a madman, has ventured to maintain that creations of art should violate the great moral laws. The question then is to determine if the so-called virtuous writers are succeeding in making virtue admired and respected, and if virtue is satisfied by the way in which she is being served.

Two examples immediately come to mind. One of the proudest supporters of bourgeois respectability, one of the champions of *good sense*, M. Emile Augier, has written a play, *La Ciguë*, in which a young man, rowdy, drunken, and dissolute, a perfect voluptuary, finally takes a fancy to the pure eyes of a young girl.[22] Great profligates have been known to suddenly cast aside all their luxuries and to seek painful, unknown pleasures in asceticism and in penury. That would be beautiful, although rather commonplace. But that would be too much for M. Augier's virtuous public. I believe he wanted to prove that in the long run we always have to *settle down* and that virtue is very happy to accept the leavings of profligacy.

Let us listen to Gabrielle, the virtuous Gabrielle, as she calculates with her virtuous husband how long a time of virtuous avarice will be required by counting interest and compound interest on capital in order to enjoy ten or twenty thousand pounds of income. Five years, ten years, something like that—I can't remember the *poet's figures*. Then the respectable couple say:

We Shall Afford the Luxury of a Boy!

By the horns of all lewd devils! shades of Tiberius and of the Marquis de Sade! what will they do all that time? Must I dirty my pen by naming all the vices to which they will be obliged to resort in order to accomplish their virtuous program? Or does the poet hope to convince a large audience of ordinary people that the two will live in perfect chastity? Would he, possibly, like to persuade them to take lessons from the thrifty Chinese and from M. Malthus?

No, it is impossible *in good conscience* to write a line filled with such smut. But M. Augier is mistaken, and his error contains his punishment. He has spoken the language of the market place, the language of the rich and fashionable, thinking he has spoken that of virtue. I am told that among the writers of this school there are some felicitous pieces, some good lines, and even a certain amount of verve. In heaven's name, what excuse would there be for the craze, if there were no merit in it of any kind?

But this reaction, this stupid and excessive reaction, is going too far. The brilliant preface to *Mademoiselle de Maupin* jeered at stupid bourgeois hypocrisy, and the insolent smugness of the *School of Good Sense* is wreaking vengeance on romantic excesses. Sad to say, it is indeed a matter of vengeance. *Kean ou Désordre et Génie* [Dumas *père*] seemed to suggest that there is always a necessary relationship between these two terms, and Gabrielle, to avenge herself, calls her husband a poet!

O poète! je t'aime.

A notary! Can you see that *respectable* housewife cooing amorously on her husband's shoulder and looking languishingly at him as in the novels she has read! Can you see all the notaries in the theater applauding the author who treats them as his equals, who avenges them on all those indigent rascals, and who believe that a poet's craft consists in expressing the lyric emotions of the heart in a rhythm determined by tradition! Such is the key to much success.

They began by saying: *poetry of the heart!* Thus the French language is in jeopardy, and harmful literary passions destroy its precision.

In passing it is well to note the parallelism in the stupidity of the two opposite schools and the fact that the same eccentricities of language are found in both. Thus there is a group of poets stupefied by pagan pleasure who constantly use words such as *holy, ecstasy, prayer,* etc., in order to describe persons and things that have nothing holy or ecstatic about them—quite the contrary—thus carrying the worship of women to the point of the most disgusting blasphemy. One of them in a fit of *saintly* eroticism went so far as to cry: *Oh my lovely Catholic darling!* One might as well defile an altar with excrement. It becomes all the more ridiculous, since poets' mistresses are usually rather wretched sluts of whom the least odious are those who cook the meals and do not pay a lover.

Alongside the *School of Good Sense* and its models of vain and proper bourgeois, there has grown up and proliferated a vast, unhealthy multitude of sentimental street girls who likewise bring God into their affairs, Lisettes who are pardoned for everything in the name of French gaiety, prostitutes who have somehow kept an angelic purity, etc. . . . Another form of hypocrisy.

The *School of Good Sense* could now be called the *School of Vengeance.** What has caused the success of *Jérôme Paturot,* that odious offshoot of Courtille in which poets and scholars are spattered with mud and flour by commonplace scamps? The tranquil Pierre Leroux whose numerous works are, as it were, a dictionary of human beliefs, has written sublime and moving pages which the author of *Jérôme Paturot* has perhaps never read. Proudhon is a writer whom Europe will always envy us. Victor Hugo has written some beautiful verses, and I do not believe that the learned M. Viollet-le-Duc is an architect to be laughed at.[23] Vengeance! vengeance! The petty public must be soothed. These works are servile caresses bestowed on the passions of angry slaves.

There are great and terrible words which incessantly pervade literary controversy: art, beauty, utility, morality. A great conflict is taking place, and for want of philosophical wisdom, everyone seizes half of the banner for himself, maintaining that the other half has no value. I shall certainly not air any philosophical claims in so short an article and I do not want to tire people by

* This is the origin of the term: *School of Good Sense.* Some years ago in the offices of the *Corsaire-Satan* in connection with the success of a play of the aforementioned school, one of the editors [Baudelaire] exclaimed in a burst of literary indignation: "There are people who actually believe that comedies are made with good sense!" He meant it is not only with good sense, etc. The editor in chief, who was a rather ingenuous man, thought the remark so excruciatingly funny that he wanted it printed. From that time on the *Corsaire-Satan* and many other papers used the term as an insult and the young men of the aforementioned school picked it up as a banner just as the sans-culottes had done.

attempting any absolute aesthetic demonstrations. I am concerned with what is most important and I speak the language of ordinary people. It is painful to note that we find similar errors in two opposing schools, the bourgeois and the socialistic. Let us moralize! let us moralize! both cry with a missionary's zeal. Naturally the one preaches bourgeois morality and the other socialist morality. Consequently art is nothing more than a question of propaganda.

Is art useful? Yes. Why? Because it is art. Is there a pernicious art? Yes. It is one that falsifies the conditions of life. Vice is attractive, it must be portrayed as attractive; but it brings with it strange maladies and moral sufferings; they must be described. Study every wound like a doctor performing his task in a hospital, and the School of Good Sense, the exclusively moral school, will no longer find anything to seize upon. Is crime always punished and virtue rewarded? No, but nevertheless if your novel or your play is well done, no one is going to feel inclined to violate the laws of nature. The first requirement of a healthy art is belief in an integral unity. I defy anyone to show me a single work of the imagination which fulfills all the conditions of the beautiful and which is a pernicious work.

A young writer [Hippolyte Castille] who has done some good things, but who was carried away on that particular occasion by socialistic sophism, basing himself on a limited point of view, published an article in *La Semaine Théâtrale* attacking Balzac on the score of morality.[24] Balzac, who suffered a great deal from the bitter recriminations of hypocrites, and who attached great importance to this question, took the opportunity to exonerate himself in the eyes of twenty thousand readers. I do not wish to repeat his two articles; they are marvelous in their clarity and in their honesty. He discussed the question thoroughly. He began by adding up, with naïve and comic good nature, all his virtuous characters and all his criminal characters. Virtue came out ahead in spite of the perversity of society "*for which I am not responsible*," he said. Then he pointed out that there are few real scoundrels whose mean souls do not have a better side. After enumerating all the punishments which invariably overtake violators of the moral law and encircle them like an earthy hell, he reprimanded faltering and easily deluded hearts in a sinister and comic way: "Woe unto you, gentlemen, if the fate of the Loustaus and the Luciens inspires you with envy."

Indeed, one must either paint vices as they are or not see them. And if the reader does not bear within himself a philosophic and religious guide who accompanies him in the reading of the book, so much the worse for him.

I have a friend who for several years has trumpeted the name of Berquin in my ears. Berquin, there is a writer for you! a charming, good, consoling, constructive author, a great writer! [25] Having had in my childhood the good fortune, or the misfortune, of reading only books for adults, I didn't know him. One day when I was racking my brain about this fashionable problem of morality in art, fate brought to my attention a volume of Berquin. From the very first I saw that the children in it talked like adults, like books, and that they preached to their parents. That's a false art, I said to myself. As I continued, I noticed that good behavior was always made sickeningly sweet and that wrongdoing was invariably made ridiculous and punished. If you behave, you will get *something nice*—such is the basis of this morality. Virtue is the SINE QUA NON of success. One might question Berquin's Christianity. That is a pernicious art, I said to myself. For when the disciple of Berquin goes out into the world, he will very quickly do the reverse: success is the SINE QUA NON of virtue. Moreover, the label on a successful crime will deceive him and, aided by the precepts of the master, he will go and live at the inn of evil, believing that he is putting up at the sign of morality.

Whether it is Berquin, M. de Montyon, M. Emile Augier or other reputable people, it is one and the same thing. They assassinate virtue, as M. Léon Faucher has just fatally wounded literature with a satanic decree in favor of respectable plays.

Prizes bring misfortune. Academic prizes, prizes for virtue, medals, all those inventions of the devil encourage hypocrisy and chill the spontaneous impulses of a free heart. When I see a man asking for the Cross [of the Legion of Honour], I seem to hear him saying to the sovereign: I have done my duty, it is true; but if you do not inform everyone about it, I swear I will not do it again.

What is there to keep two rascals from getting together in order to win the Montyon prize? [26] The one will feign poverty, the other charity. There is something in an official prize which offends man and humanity and obscures the modesty of virtue. As for me, I should not want to make friends with a man who had won a prize for virtue; I should be afraid of finding in him an implacable tyrant.

As for writers, their prize is to be found in the esteem of their peers and in the cash registers of booksellers.

What in the deuce is the minister meddling with? Does he wish to create hypocrisy in order to have the pleasure of rewarding it? Now the boulevard theater is going to become nothing but a church service. When a writer is several months behind in his rent, he will write a respectable play; when he has a lot of debts, he will write an angelic play. What a fine institution!

I shall return to this subject later and I shall speak of the attempts made by two great French minds, Balzac and Diderot, to rejuvenate the theater.

☙ THE PAGAN SCHOOL

PREFACE

A few weeks after the appearance of "The Respectable Drama and Novel," a second article, "The Pagan School," was published in *La Semaine Théâtrale* on January 28, 1852. In this case the butt of Baudelaire's scorn is Neo-Classicism in both literature and art. He seems to have had in mind some of his friends and acquaintances, among whom were Théodore de Banville, Louis Ménard, Théophile Gautier, Leconte de Lisle, and Victor de Laprade. Although disdain for the works of Ménard and Laprade may have entered into the composition of these pages, Baudelaire's anticlassical attitude was already a deep-seated element of his thinking.

Many of the ideas expressed in the essay relate rather closely to his article on Pierre Dupont and seem to indicate that, in spite of its publication date, it may have been written before the essay on "The Respectable Drama and Novel" or even before "Pierre Dupont."

Baudelaire here condemns the "immoderate love of form" which ignores "the exciting spectacle of an active and hardworking civilization" and excludes all "notions of the just and the true." He maintains that "the frenzied passion for art is a canker which devours all else" and that the "complete lack of the just and the true in art is equivalent to a lack of art."

The Neo-Classicists not only invalidated true art by excluding the useful and true; they were also guilty from a purely literary point of view of producing an art that was "nothing more than a useless and disgusting pastiche." In "Pierre Dupont" he had accused the School of Art for Art's Sake of being sterile since it had excluded morality and often passion. In the present essay he is equally convinced of this sterility: "To dismiss passion and reason is to kill literature. To repudiate the efforts of a preceding society, Christian and philosophic, is to commit sui-

71

cide, to refuse the possibility and the means for improvement."
It seems clear that if Baudelaire believed that Neo-Classic art
was a pastiche, it was in part because it reproduced only the
eternal element of beauty found in the past and that, by divorc-
ing itself from the present, it lacked the element of contingency
which is responsible for the variable, transitory element of
beauty that he had noted in the *Salon of 1846*.

❧❦❧❦❧❦

A very notable incident took place in the year which has
just passed. I do not claim that it is the most important, but
it is one of the most important, or rather one of the most symp-
tomatic.

At a banquet commemorating the February Revolution, a
toast was raised to the god Pan, yes, to the god Pan, by one of
those young men who can be termed educated and intelligent.

"But what has the god Pan to do with the Revolution?" I
said to him.

"What do you mean?" he answered; "why he is the god who
started the Revolution. He is the Revolution."

"And yet hasn't he been dead for a long time? I thought
that a loud voice had been heard soaring over the Mediterranean
and that this mysterious voice, reverberating from the Pillars
of Hercules to the Asiatic shores, had said to the old world:
THE GOD PAN IS DEAD!"

"That's a rumor which has been spread abroad by scandal-
mongers; but there is nothing to it. No, the god Pan is not dead!
the god Pan is still alive," he continued, raising his eyes to the
heavens with a very strange emotion . . . "He is going to return."

He spoke of the god Pan as if he were the prisoner of St.
Helena [Napoleon].

"Well," I said to him, "you must evidently be a pagan?"

"Why of course; don't you know that only Paganism, rightly

understood, properly conceived, can save the world? We must return to the true doctrines, momentarily obscured by the vile Galilean. Moreover, Juno has cast a favorable glance at me, a glance which penetrated to the very depths of my heart. I was sad and melancholy in the midst of the crowd, gazing at the pageant and imploring the beautiful goddess with adoring eyes when one of her kindly and profound glances came to reassure and encourage me."

"Juno looked at you with her cowlike gaze." The poor man must be crazy.

"But don't you see," said a third person, "that it is a question of the ceremony of the fatted ox. He was looking at all those rosy-complexioned women with *pagan* eyes, and Ernestine, who is acting at the Hippodrome and who was playing the role of Juno, gave him a glance full of memories, a veritable *bovine* glance."

"Say whatever you want about Ernestine," said the pagan, somewhat annoyed. "You are trying to disillusion me. But the moral effect has been achieved nonetheless, and I consider this glance a good omen."

It seems to me that such excessive paganism comes from having read without proper understanding too much of Heinrich Heine, whose works are corrupted by materialistic sentimentality.

And since I have mentioned the name of this famous culprit, I may as well tell you right now about a characteristic passage that exasperates me every time I think of it. Heinrich Heine tells in one of his books that, while walking among wild mountains, at the edge of frightening precipices and in the midst of a chaos of ice and snow, he encountered one of those monks who, accompanied by a dog, go in search of lost and dying travelers.[27] A few moments before the author had just given vent to solitary outbursts of Voltairian hatred for priests. He watched for a time this lover of humanity pursuing his sacred task; his proud heart experienced a moment of struggle, and finally after a painful hesitation, he gave up and made a noble resolution: *No! I shall not write against that man!*

What generosity! Sitting by the warm fire, his feet in comfortable slippers, surrounded by the adulation of a pleasure-loving society, the famous gentleman vowed not to defame a poor devil of a monk who would never know his name and his blasphemies and would even have saved him, had the occasion arisen!

No, Voltaire would never have written anything so shameless. Voltaire had too much taste; moreover, he was also a man of action and he loved men.

But to return to Olympus. For some time I have had all Olympus at my heels and it is causing me a great deal of misery; gods have been falling on my head like chimneys. It seems to me that I am having a bad dream, that I am rolling through space and that a multitude of wooden, golden, and silver idols are falling with me, tumbling after me, bumping into me, and breaking my head and back.

Impossible to take a step, to speak a word without stumbling into something pagan.

Should you express fear or sadness on seeing the human race decline, or on seeing public health degenerate through poor hygiene, you will find a poet beside you to answer: "How do you expect women to have beautiful children in a country where they worship a scurvy wretch who was hanged!"—A fine sort of *fanaticism!*

The city is in utter confusion. Shops close. Women hastily lay in their supplies, paved streets are torn up, everywhere hearts are oppressed by the anguish of a great event. The pavement will soon be inundated with blood.—You meet a nasty, complacent fellow; under his arm he is carrying some strange old books in hieroglyphics. "And what about you," you will say, "which side are you on?" "My dear fellow," he answers in a gentle voice, "I have just discovered some very strange new information about the marriage of Isis and Osiris." "May the devil take you! May Isis and Osiris have a lot of children and may they leave us in peace!"

This madness, innocent in appearance, often goes very far.

A few years ago Daumier did a remarkable series of lithographs, *L'Histoire Ancienne*, which was actually the best paraphrase of the famous saying: *Who will deliver us from the Greeks and the Romans?* [28] Daumier pounced brutally upon antiquity and mythology and spit on it. The hot-headed Achilles, the prudent Ulysses, the wise Penelope, that great ninny of a Telemachus, the beautiful Helen who ruined Troy, the burning Sappho, that patroness of hysterical women, all were portrayed with a farcical homeliness that recalled those old carcasses of classic actors who take a pinch of snuff in the wings. Well, I saw a gifted writer weeping before those prints, before that amusing and useful blasphemy.[29] He was indignant, he called it a sacrilege. The poor wretch still needed a religion.

Many people have encouraged with their money and their applause this deplorable craze which tends to turn man into an inert being and the writer into an opium eater.

From the purely literary point of view it is nothing more than a useless and disgusting pastiche. Haven't we made enough fun of the naïve daubers who struggled to copy Cimabue, or of writers enamored of daggers, doublets, and Toledo blades? [30] And you, miserable neopagans, what are you doing if not the same thing? Pastiche, Pastiche! Apparently you have lost your soul somewhere, in some bad spot, since you seem to be running through the past like empty bodies seeking to find another by chance encounter amid the debris of the ancients. What do you expect from heaven or from the stupidity of the public? Enough money to raise altars in your attics to Priapus and to Bacchus? The most logical among you will be the most cynical. They will raise them to the god Crepitus.

Will the god Crepitus make you a soothing drink the day after your stupid ceremonies? Will Venus Aphrodite or the Mercenary Venus assuage the griefs she will have caused you? Will all those marble statues be devoted wives on the day of death, the day of remorse, or the day of helplessness? Do you drink broths made of ambrosia? Do you eat cutlets from Paros? How much can you get on a lyre at the pawnshop?

To dismiss passion and reason is to kill literature. To repudiate the efforts of a preceding society, Christian and philosophic, is to commit suicide, to refuse the possibility and the means for improvement. To surround oneself exclusively with the charms of material art is to run the risk of damnation. For a long time, a very long time, you will be able to see, love and feel only the beautiful, and nothing but the beautiful. I am using the word in a restricted sense. The world will appear to you only in its material form. The springs which make it move will remain hidden for a long time.

May religion and philosophy come one day as if compelled by the cry of a despairing soul! Such will always be the fate of madmen who see in nature only forms and rhythms. Even philosophy will at first appear to them as only an interesting game, as a pleasant form of gymnastics, as fencing in the void. But how great will be their punishment! Every child whose poetic spirit has been overstimulated, whose eyes have not constantly encountered the exciting spectacle of an active and hardworking civilization, who has incessantly heard about glory and pleasure, whose senses have been daily caressed, irritated, frightened, inflamed and satisfied by objects of art, will become the most unhappy of men and will make others unhappy. At twelve years of age he will turn up his nurse's skirt and, if power in crime or in art do not raise him above the average lot, he will die like a dog in the poor house. His soul, constantly excited and unappeased, goes about the world, the busy, toiling world; it goes, I say, like a prostitute crying: Plastic! Plastic! The plastic—that frightful word gives me goose flesh—the plastic has poisoned him, and yet he can live only by this poison. He has banished reason from his heart; and, as a just punishment, reason refused to return to him. The most fortunate thing that can happen to him is for nature to strike him with a terrifying call to order. Indeed, such is the law of life that he who refuses the pure enjoyment of honest activity can feel only the terrible pleasures of vice. Sin contains its own hell, and from time to time, nature says to suffering and poverty: Go and conquer those rebels!

The useful, the true, the good, the really admirable, all

these things will be unknown to him. Infatuated with his tiring dream, he will want to infatuate and to tire others with it. He will not think of his mother, of his nurse; he will vilify his friends or he will love them *only for their form*; if he has a wife, he will scorn and debase her.

Immoderate love of form leads to monstrous and unknown disorders. Absorbed by the fierce passion for the beautiful, the amusing, the pretty, the picturesque—for there are different degrees—notions of the just and the true will disappear. The frenzied passion for art is a canker which devours all else; and since complete lack of the just and the true in art is equivalent to a lack of art, the whole man shrinks; the excessive specialization of one faculty ends in nothingness. I understand the rage of iconoclasts and of Moslems against images.[31] I admit all the remorse of Saint Augustine for the too great pleasure of the eyes. The danger is so great that I excuse the suppression of the object. The folly of art is equal to the abuse of the mind. The creation of one of these two supremacies results in foolishness, hardness of heart and in enormous pride and egoism. I recall having heard an artist, who was a practical joker and who had received a false coin, say on one occasion: I shall keep it for some poor person. The wretch took an infernal pleasure in robbing the poor and in enjoying at the same time the benefit of a reputation for charity. I heard someone else say: Why don't the poor wear gloves to beg? They would make a fortune. And another: Don't give anything to that one; his rags don't fit well; they aren't very becoming to him.

These things should not be dismissed as puerilities. What the mouth is accustomed to say, the heart is accustomed to believe.

I know a considerable number of honest men who, like me, are tired, saddened, grieved, and shattered by this dangerous comedy.

Literature must go and renew itself in a better atmosphere. The time is not distant when it will be understood that every literature that refuses to walk hand in hand with science and philosophy is a homicidal and suicidal literature.

❧ EXPOSITION UNIVERSELLE, 1855

PREFACE

For those interested in the development of Baudelaire's aesthetic ideas, certain excerpts from his essay on the Exposition Universelle are of special interest. The first chapter of the critic's essay, from which the following passages are taken, appeared in *Le Pays* on May 26, 1855. Chapter three, on Delacroix, was published on June 3, and chapter two, on Ingres, after being refused by *Le Pays*, was printed in *Le Portefeuille* on August 12, 1855.

It is in this essay that Baudelaire insists on the impossibility of confining himself to any system of critical thought and that he asserts his independence of all pre-established criteria. Once again he is concerned with the question of beauty. In a passage inspired by Poe who, in turn, had quoted Bacon, he maintains that beauty must always have an element of the strange, and that this strangeness constitutes its individuality. Since the bizarre is, as he says, determined by such varied factors as climate, milieu, race, religion, custom, and the artist's temperament, it is apparent that Baudelaire more or less equates the element of the strange with the transitory or particular element of beauty.

In his stress on the cosmopolitanism required of both critic and spectator if they are to appreciate a beauty that is foreign or strange to their eyes, Baudelaire is indirectly referring to his voyage to the tropics where he had discovered "a new world of ideas" that became an integral part of his experience and accompanied him "in the form of memories to his grave."

In this essay Baudelaire himself demonstrates the quality of cosmopolitanism in his praise of the English painters whose works appeared in the exhibition.

❧❦❧❦❧

CRITICAL METHOD—ON THE MODERN IDEA OF PROGRESS AS APPLIED TO THE FINE ARTS—ON THE SHIFTING OF VITALITY.

. . . What would a modern Winckelmann say (we have any number of them, the nation is teeming with them, the lazy idolize them), were he confronted by a product of China—something strange, bizarre, contorted in form, intense in color, and sometimes so fragile as to be almost evanescent? [32] Yet it is an example of universal beauty; but in order to understand it, the critic, the spectator must effect within himself a mysterious transformation, and by means of a phenomenon of the will acting on the imagination, he must learn by himself to participate in the milieu which has given birth to this strange flowering. Few men possess to the fullest degree this divine grace of cosmopolitanism; but all can acquire it in different degrees. The best endowed in this respect are solitary wanderers who have lived for years in the depths of the forests, in the midst of endlessly rolling plains, with a gun as their only companion, contemplating, analyzing, writing. No scholastic veil, no academic paradox, no pedagogical Utopia has come between them and the complex truth. They know the admirable, the immortal, the inevitable relationship between form and function. Such people do not criticize; they contemplate, they study.

If, instead of a pedagogue, I were to take a man of the world, an intelligent man, and transport him to a distant land, I am sure that, despite the great shock of disembarkation, despite the more or less long and arduous process of adjustment, his sympathy would sooner or later be so keen, so acute, that it would create in him a new world of ideas, a world which would become an integral part of him and which would accompany him, in the form of memories, to his grave. Those strangely shaped buildings which at first annoyed his academic eye (all peoples are academic when they judge others, all peoples are barbaric when they themselves are judged), that flora so disquieting to a mind full of memories of its native land, those

79

men and women whose muscles do not move in the usual manner of his country, whose gait is marked by a different rhythm, whose gaze is not directed with the same magnetism, those perfumes which are no longer those of his mother's boudoir, those mysterious flowers whose deep color enslaves his eye and tantalizes it with its shape, those fruits whose taste misleads and confuses the senses, and reveal to the palate ideas which belong to the sense of smell—this whole world of new harmonies will slowly enter into him, will patiently penetrate him, like the vapors of a perfumed bath; all this unknown vitality will be added to his own vitality; thousands of ideas and sensations will enrich his human dictionary, and it is even possible that, overstepping the line and transforming justice into revolt, he will act like the converted Sicambrian and burn what he had adored, and adore what he had burned.

What would be said, I repeat, what would be written by one of those *narrow-minded modern professors* of aesthetics, as they are called by Heinrich Heine—that delightful writer who would be a genius if he turned more often to the divine—were he confronted by such unfamiliar phenomena? The mad doctrinaire of Beauty would rave on nonsensically, no doubt; confined within the blinding fortress of his system, he would blaspheme life and nature, and his fanaticism, whether Greek, Italian, or Parisian, would induce him to prohibit that impudent people from enjoying, dreaming, or thinking in any way other than his own; with his ink-smeared knowledge, his bastard taste, more barbarous than the barbarians, he has forgotten the color of the sky, the forms of plants, the movement and the smell of animal life, and his stiffened fingers, paralyzed by the pen, can no longer run with agility over the immense keyboard of *correspondences!*

More than once I have tried, like all my friends, to confine myself within a system in order to preach freely. But a system is a kind of damnation which forces us to a perpetual recantation; it is always necessary to invent another, and the exertion required is a cruel punishment. And my system was always beautiful, vast, spacious, convenient, neat, and above all smooth. At least it seemed so to me. And always a spontaneous, unexpected product of universal vitality would come along and give the lie to my childish, antiquated knowledge, that pitiable daughter of Utopia. No matter how much I changed or broadened the criterion, it always fell short of expressing universal man and never caught up with the multiform and multicolored beauty that moves in the infinite spirals of life. Constantly condemned to the humiliation of a new conversion, I made an important decision. To escape the horror of these philosophical apostasies, I proudly resigned myself to modesty: I was content to feel; I sought refuge in an impeccable naïveté. I humbly beg pardon of academic minds of all types who occupy the various workshops of our artistic factory. It is there that my philosophic conscience has found repose; and I can affirm at least, in so far as a man can answer for his virtues, that my mind now enjoys a greater impartiality.

Everyone can easily understand that if the men whose task it is to express the beautiful were to conform to the rules of narrow-minded professors, beauty itself would disappear from the earth, since all types, all ideas, all sensations would be fused into a vast, monotonous, impersonal unity, as immense as boredom and as nothingness. Variety, the *sine qua non* of life, would be effaced from life. So true is it that in the multiple productions of art there is something always new which will forever escape the rules and the analyses of the school! The element of surprise, which is one of the great delights created by art and literature, is due to this very variety of types and sensations.—The *narrow-minded professor*, a sort of mandarin-tyrant, always reminds me of a godless man who substitutes himself for God.

With all deference to the overly proud sophists who have derived their knowledge from books, I shall go even further, and, however subtle and difficult to express my idea may be, I do not despair of succeeding. *The beautiful is always strange.* I do not mean that it is deliberately, coldly strange, for in that case it would be a monster that has jumped the rails of life. I mean

81

that it always contains a little strangeness, an artless, unpremed-
itated, unconscious strangeness, and that it is this strangeness
that gives Beauty its specific character. It is its official stamp,
its characteristic. Reverse the proposition and try to imagine a
commonplace beauty! Now, how could this strangeness—necessary, incompressible, infinitely varied, and determined by milieu,
climate, custom, race, religion, and the artist's temperament—
ever be controlled, improved, rectified by the Utopian rules that
are conceived in some ordinary little scientific temple on this
planet, without mortal danger to art itself? This admixture of
strangeness which constitutes and defines individuality, without
which there can be no beauty, plays in art the role of taste or
of seasoning in foods (may the accuracy of this comparison
excuse its triteness), since, apart from their usefulness or their
nutritional content foods differ from one another only through
the *idea* which they reveal to the palate. . . .

There is another error, very much in fashion, which I wish
to avoid like the Devil himself.—I am referring to the idea of
progress. This dim beacon, an invention of contemporary
philosophism, licensed without the sanction of Nature or God,
this modern lantern casts dark shadows over every object of
knowledge; liberty vanishes; punishment disappears. He who
wishes to see clearly into history must first of all extinguish this
treacherous beacon. This grotesque idea, which has flowered on
the rotten soil of modern folly, has released each man from his
duty, freed each soul from its responsibility, and has liberated
the will from all the bonds imposed on it by the love of the
beautiful. And if this deplorable madness continues for long, the
decadent races will fall into the drivelling sleep of decrepitude
on the pillow of destiny. This infatuation is the symptom of a
decadence that is already too obvious.

Ask any good Frenchman who reads *his* daily paper in a
café what he understands by progress, and he will answer that
it is steam, electricity, and gas lighting, miracles unknown to
the Romans, and that these discoveries clearly testify to our

superiority over the ancients. So great is the darkness in that unfortunate brain and so strangely confused are things of the material and spiritual order! The poor man is so Americanized by zoocratic and industrial philosophers that he has lost all notion of the differences which characterize the phenomena of the physical and moral world, the natural and the supernatural.

If today a nation is more discerning in its understanding of moral issues than it was in the preceding century, there is progress; that is clear enough. If this year an artist produces a work showing more skill or imaginative power than he showed the year before, it is certain that he has made progress. If the products of today are better and cheaper than they were yesterday, that is evidence of indisputable progress in the material order. But where, may I ask, is the guarantee of progress in the future? For that is how the disciples of the philosophers of steam and sulphur matches understand it: progress appears to them only in the form of an indefinite series. Where is that guarantee? It exists, I say, only in your credulity and your self-complacency.

I leave aside the question of determining whether, by refining humanity in proportion to the new enjoyments that it brings it, indefinite progress would not be its most ingenious and its cruelest torture; whether, proceeding by a stubborn negation of itself, it would not be an endlessly renewed form of suicide, and whether, enclosed in the fiery circle of divine logic, it would not resemble the scorpion that stings itself with its own terrible tail, that eternal desideratum which makes its eternal despair.

Transferred into the sphere of the imagination (and this has actually been tried by presumptuous fanatics of logic), the idea of progress looms up with gigantic absurdity, with a grotesqueness which often assumes frightening proportions. The thesis is no longer tenable. The facts are too palpable, too well known. They face the fallacy calmly and laugh at it. In the poetic and artistic order, inventors rarely have predecessors. Every flowering is spontaneous, individual. Was Signorelli really the begetter of Michelangelo? Did Perugino contain Raphael?

The artist depends on himself alone. He promises only his own works to the centuries to come. He stands surety only for himself. He dies childless. He has been *his own king, his own priest, and his own God.* It is in such phenomena that the famous and stormy formula of Pierre Leroux finds its true application.[33]

The same thing is true of nations which cultivate the arts of the imagination with joy and success. Present success is a guarantee that is only temporary, alas, and of very short duration. The dawn began in the East, the light moved toward the South, and now it gleams in the West. France, it is true, by virtue of its central position in the civilized world, seems to be called to garner all the ideas and all the poetry of her neighbors and to return them to other peoples, marvelously wrought and fashioned. But it must never be forgotten that nations, vast collective beings, are subject to the same laws as individuals. In their infancy they wail, stammer, grow heavier and taller. In their youth and maturity they produce wise and bold works. In their old age they fall asleep in the midst of their acquired wealth. Often it happens that the very principle responsible for their strength and development is the one that brings about their decadence, especially when that principle, which was formerly quickened by a zest for conquest, has become for the majority a sort of routine. Then, as I suggested, a moment ago, the vitality of that nation shifts its habitat and goes to visit other lands and other races. Yet it must not be thought that the newcomers inherit everything in full from their predecessors, and that they receive a ready-made doctrine. It often happens (this was true of the Middle Ages) that, everything being lost, everything has to be remade.

✠ SINCE IT IS A QUESTION OF REALISM

PREFACE

Baudelaire's tantalizing notes for an article on Realism were first published by Jacques Crépet in *Mesures* (issue of July 15, 1938) and were reprinted the following year in volume one of *Œuvres Posthumes.*

In the early days of Realism, between 1844 and 1850, Baudelaire had shown some sympathy for the movement. He had been on friendly terms with some of the leaders of the new school, Champfleury, Courbet, and Proudhon, and had spent many hours discussing with them the principles and doctrines of the new movement. It was not long, however, before he lost his enthusiasm for a literature that substituted servile imitation for imagination and concerned itself with the accessory rather than the essential. Encouraged in his aristocratic tastes by his reading of Poe and de Maistre, he soon disassociated himself from his former companions and finally turned his back on the movement completely.

In 1855 Baudelaire found himself in a rather embarrassing situation. Courbet, whose paintings had been refused by the jury of the Exposition Universelle, decided to exhibit the rejected pictures in a private pavilion which he designated the "Pavilion of Realism." [34] Among the paintings he displayed was the large canvas *The Painter's Studio* which portrayed Courbet surrounded by about thirty of his friends, including Champfleury, Proudhon, Max Buchon, and Baudelaire.[35] To make matters worse, Champfleury, in an effort to win support for Courbet and for the cause of Realism, published (September 2) an open letter entitled "Sur M. Courbet, Lettre à George Sand."

Perhaps to divorce himself from a movement whose ideas were so contrary to his own, Baudelaire began work on the article "Since it is a Question of Realism." The title itself was borrowed from a statement made by Courbet and quoted by

85

Champfleury in his letter-manifesto. For one reason or another the article was never finished. From the notes, however, it is clear that the essay was to have been a virulent attack on Champfleury and Courbet who thought only of capturing external reality and of equating impression with expression. In a definition of poetry whose transcendental implications reveal the wide gap that separates his thinking from that of his former associates, Baudelaire can be seen moving toward his conception of imagination—one that will enable the artist to interpret the "hieroglyphics" of this world and to discover "what is completely true only in another world."

❧❧❧❧❧

Champfleury wanted to play a joke on the human race.

Admit, perverse child, that you are enjoying the general confusion and even the fatigue that this article is causing me.

History of the creation of the word.

First visit to Courbet. (At that time, Champfleury attached an inordinate importance to the arts. He has changed.)

What Courbet was at that time.

Analysis of *Courbet* and of his works.

Champfleury poisoned his mind.—He was dreaming of a word, a banner, a *joke*, a watchword or password that would quell the rallying cry: *Romanticism.* He believed there is always need of one of those words with a magic influence whose meaning cannot easily be determined.

Imposing on everyone else *what he believes* to be his method (for he is myopic when it comes to his own nature), he has set off a firecracker and started a great hullabaloo.

As for Courbet, he became the clumsy Machiavelli of this *Borgia* in the historical sense of *Michelet.*

Courbet has theorized about an innocent joke with a compromising grandeur of conviction.

86

Plates with rooster designs.

Puncheon prints.

Domestic themes, villagers of Courbet and of Bonvin.[36]

The translator of Hebbel [Max Buchon].

Pierre Dupont.

Confusion in the public mind.

Once the joke was started, it was necessary to believe in it.

He, the musician of sentiment, turning the crank of his organ in the streets.

Organizing a somewhat flimsy exhibition which had to be constantly buttressed with weak philosophical props [Courbet's exhibition in the Pavilion of Realism].

Therein lies his punishment.

Champfleury bears his realism within him.

Prometheus has his vulture.

(not because he stole fire from heaven, but because he assumed it to be where it is not and wanted to make others believe it).

In the matter of Courbet, observe Préault who perhaps one day . . .[37]

Anger and violent emotions beautiful to observe.

Madame Sand, Castille (Champfleury was afraid of them).

But this silliness is so great.

From that moment, rustic, coarse, dishonest and even boorish Realism.

Champfleury, the poet, ("Les Deux Cabarets d'Auteuil," "La Lettre à Colombine," "Le Bouquet du Pauvre") is a joker at heart. May he remain that way, since he enjoys it, and perhaps it is a part of his talent. Observation in the manner of *Dickens*, the night table of love. If things appear to him in a somewhat fantastic way, it is because of a contraction of his slightly mystical eye.—Since he studies things scrupulously, he thinks he is capturing an external *reality*. Hence, *realism*—he wants to impose what he believes is his method.

However, the question is whether Realism has any meaning at all—serious discussion.

Every good poet was always *realistic*.

Equation between impression and expression.

Sincerity.

Take Banville as an example.

Bad poets are those who . . .

Hackneyed expressions.

Ponsard [popular dramatist].

Besides, Champfleury was after all excusable; exasperated by stupidity, conventionality, the School of Good Sense, he was seeking a standard around which lovers of truth could rally.

But all that turned out badly. Besides, every creator of a school necessarily finds himself in bad company.

The most amusing errors and mistakes have been made. I have been told that they had done me the honor . . . although I have always endeavored to forfeit their esteem.[38]

I would be, however—I give the school fair warning—a sad gift. I completely lack conviction, submissiveness, and stupidity.

For *us*, a joke.—Champfleury, hierophant. But the crowd.

Poetry is what is most real, what is completely true only in *another world*.

This world, a dictionary of hieroglyphics.

Of all this there will remain only a great weariness for the magician, the Vaucanson [39] tormented by his automaton, the unfortunate Champfleury, victim of his cant, of his diplomatic pose, and a large number of dupes whose many and often-repeated errors do not concern literary history any more than the crowd interests posterity.

(*Analysis of Nature, of the talent of Courbet, and of morality*.)

Courbet saving the world.

EDGAR POE,
HIS LIFE AND WORKS

PREFACE

Of the three main essays that Baudelaire wrote about Poe, the first was published in 1852 in two installments of the *Revue de Paris*. The longest literary article he ever wrote, it contains extensive excerpts from "William Wilson" and from the *Narrative of Arthur Gordon Pym*.

Never a puristic or formal critic, Baudelaire believed that biography serves "to explain and to *verify*, so to speak, the mysterious adventures of the brain" and that "in the notes about childhood we find the germ of the strange reveries of the grown man and, better still, of his genius." [40] In the essay itself Baudelaire justified the emphasis he places on biography by reminding the reader that "it is a very great and a very useful pleasure to compare the traits of a great man with his works. Biographies, notes on the manners, habits and physical appearance of artists and writers have always aroused a very legitimate curiosity." [41]

Both the long biographical account, which occupies the greater part of the essay, and the discussion of representative works which follows are marked by the fervor and partisanship which Baudelaire had advocated in the *Salon of 1846*. Although the article gives the impression of being based on firsthand knowledge, the reverse is really the case, as Professor W. T. Bandy has shown. Lacking adequate information for his essay, Baudelaire had turned to an American correspondent in Paris, William Wilberforce Mann, and had obtained from him copies of the *Southern Literary Messenger* containing obituary notices by John R. Thompson (November, 1849) and John M. Daniel (March, 1850). Professor Bandy has pointed out that Baudelaire had translated almost word for word about twenty-five pages of Thompson's article and that he had also borrowed fairly extensively from Daniel.[42]

For the reader interested in the development of Baudelaire's critical ideas the importance of the 1852 essay lies chiefly in his condemnation of utilitarian literature. His position, however, is not as inconsistent with the ideas of the Pierre Dupont article as it may first seem. Like Poe, he denounces utilitarianism in art, but unlike Poe, he restricts his attack to "direct utility." To clarify his position even further he adds: "There can be no doubt that subsequently and consequently poetry may be useful, but that is not its purpose; that comes as something *over and above* its chief function." [43]

In 1856 Baudelaire revised and shortened his study of 1852 and used it as an introduction to the first volume of his Poe translations. As in the preceding essay, he renews his attack on materialism and democracy and bemoans Poe's bad luck, although ten years earlier in "Advice to Young Men of Letters" he had declared that lack of success must be blamed on the author rather than on the apathy and neglect of the public.

Like the essay of 1852, the article is almost entirely biographical; only the last three or four pages are devoted to comments on the character of Poe's work, on its superhuman and unearthly character, on its admixture of the strange and the beautiful.

According to Professor Bandy, the preface to the 1856 translation of Poe's stories "has been without question the most widely read study of Poe that has ever been written." [44] In spite of biographies that are more recent and more scholarly, it has largely determined the European attitude toward Poe for more than a century. Together with the essay of 1857 and the translations of Poe's stories, it helped Baudelaire to accomplish the goal described in a letter to Sainte-Beuve in 1856: "Edgar Poe, who is of little consequence in America, *must* become, that is I want him to become, a great man in *France*." [45]

The best and most thorough study of the question of Poe's fame abroad is Professor Bandy's brochure, *The Influence and Reputation of Edgar Allan Poe in Europe,* published in 1962 by the Edgar Allan Poe Society of Baltimore.

✄✄✄✄✄

. . . Quelque maître malheureux à qui l'inexorable Fatalité a
donné une chasse acharnée, toujours plus acharnée, jusqu'à ce
que ses chants n'aient plus qu'un unique refrain, jusqu'à ce que
les chants funèbres de son Espérance aient adopté ce mélancolique refrain: Jamais! Jamais plus!

Edgar Poe. *Le Corbeau*.[46]

Sur son trône d'airain le Destin, qui s'en raille,
Imbibe leur éponge avec du fiel amer,
Et la Nécessité les tord dans sa tenaille.

Théophile Gautier. *Ténèbres*.[47]

I

Recently there appeared in court an unfortunate man whose
forehead was marked by a rare and strange tattoo: *No luck!* [48]
He bore thus above his eyes the inscription of his life, like the
title of a book, and cross-examination showed that this bizarre
label was cruelly true. In literary history there are similar destinies, real damnations—men who bear the words *bad luck*
written in mysterious characters in the sinuous creases of their
foreheads. The blind angel of expiation has seized upon them
and whips them with all his might for the edification of others.
In vain their lives show talents, virtues, graces; for them Society
has a special curse, and accentuates in them the weaknesses that
its persecution has produced.—What did not Hoffmann do to
disarm destiny and what did not Balzac undertake to charm
fortune?—Is there then a diabolical Providence which prepares
misfortune in the cradle—which *deliberately* thrusts spiritual
and angelic natures into hostile surroundings, like martyrs into
the circus? Are there then *consecrated* souls, destined for the
altar, condemned to march to death and glory through their
own ruins? Will the nightmare of Darkness besiege these exceptional souls eternally?—In vain they struggle, in vain they adapt

themselves to the calculations and tricks of the world; they may be perfect in prudence, they may stop up every opening, they may stuff the windows against the missiles of chance; but the Devil will come in through a keyhole; perfection will be the flaw in their armor, and superlative excellence the germ of their damnation.

> L'aigle, pour le briser, du haut du firmament
> Sur leur front découvert lâchera la tortue,
> Car *ils* doivent périr inévitablement.[49]

Their destiny is written in their whole being, it shines with a sinister brilliance in their eyes and in their gestures, it circulates in their arteries with each drop of blood.

A famous contemporary writer has written a book [*Stello* by de Vigny] to show that the poet cannot find a good place either in a democratic society or in an aristocratic one, no more in a republic than in an absolute or constitutional monarchy. Who has been able to give him a conclusive answer? Today I have a new story to support his thesis, I am adding a new saint to the martyrology; I have to write the history of an illustrious failure, too rich in poetry and passion, who came, after so many others in this base world, to serve the harsh apprenticeship of genius among inferior spirits.

What a grievous tragedy was the life of Edgar Poe! What a horrible ending was his death, the horror of which was increased by vulgar circumstances!—All the documents that I have read lead to the conviction that for Poe the United States was nothing more than a vast prison which he traversed with the feverish agitation of a being made to breathe a sweeter air—nothing more than a great gas-lighted nightmare—and that his inner, spiritual life, as a poet or even as a drunkard, was nothing but a perpetual effort to escape the influence of this unfriendly atmosphere. In democratic societies public opinion is a pitiless dictator; do not ask of it any charity, any indulgence, any elasticity whatever in the application of its laws to the manifold and

complex cases of moral life. It could be said that from the impious love of liberty a new tyranny has been born, the tyranny
of animals, or zoöcracy, which in its ferocious insensibility resembles the Juggernaut.—A biographer will tell us in all seriousness—the good man means well—that if Poe had been willing
to normalize his genius and to apply his creative faculties in
a way appropriate to the American soil, he could have become a
money-making author; another—this one a naïve cynic—that
however beautiful the genius of Poe may have been, it would
have been better for him to have possessed only talent, since
talent always pays off more readily than genius. Another, who
was a newspaper and magazine editor, a friend of the poet, admits that it was difficult to employ him and that it was necessary to pay him less than others, because he wrote in a style
too much above the ordinary level.[50] *What a commercial smell!*
as Joseph de Maistre would say.

Some have gone even further, and joining the dullest incomprehension of his genius to the ferocity of bourgeois hypocrisy, have outdone themselves in insults; and after his sudden
death, they harshly lectured his corpse—especially Mr. Rufus
Griswold who, to recall the bitter remark of Mr. George Graham,
then committed an imperishable infamy.[51] Poe, perhaps feeling
a sinister premonition of his sudden end, had asked Griswold
and Willis to put his works in order, to write his biography and
keep alive his memory. That pedagogical vampire defamed his
friend at great length in a flat and hateful article published as
the introduction of the posthumous edition of Poe's works. Is
there then no ordinance in America which forbids dogs to enter
cemeteries? On the other hand, Willis has shown that kindness
and decency always accompany true intelligence, and that charity towards our fellow men, which is a moral duty, is also one
of the commandments of taste.

Talk to an American about Poe and he will perhaps admit
his genius; perhaps he will even show himself proud of it. But,
with a superior, sardonic tone, which smacks of practicality, he
will speak to you of the irregular life of the poet, of his alco-

holic breath that could have been set on fire with a candle, of his vagabond habits; he will tell you that Poe was an erratic and eccentric person, a stray planet, that he moved constantly from Baltimore to New York, from New York to Philadelphia, from Philadelphia to Boston, from Boston to Baltimore, from Baltimore to Richmond. And if, moved by these preludes of a disheartening story, you suggest that he was perhaps not the only guilty party, and that it must be difficult to think and write readily in a country which has millions of rulers, a country without a great capital and without an aristocracy—then you will see his eyes open and flash lightning, the slaver of outraged patriotism rising to his lips, and you will hear America, through his mouth, hurl insults at Europe, its old mother, and at the philosophy of former times.

I repeat my conviction that Edgar Poe and his country were not on the same level. The United States is a young and gigantic country, naturally jealous of the old continent. Proud of its material development, abnormal and almost monstrous, this newcomer in history has a naïve faith in the omnipotence of industry; it is convinced, like some unfortunate persons among us, that it will succeed in devouring the Devil. Time and money have such a great value there! Material activity, disproportionately emphasized to the point of being a national mania, leaves little room in their minds for things which are not of this world. Poe, who was of good stock and who moreover maintained that the great misfortune of his country was the lack of an aristocracy of birth, since, as he said, among a people without an aristocracy the cult of the Beautiful could only become corrupt, diminish and disappear—who charged his fellow citizens, in their costly and pretentious luxury, with all the symptoms of bad taste characteristic of upstarts—who considered Progress, the great modern idea, as the fatuous dream of simpletons, and who called the alleged *improvements* in houses eyesores and rectangular abominations—Poe was an exceptionally solitary mind. He believed only in the immutable, the eternal, the self-same, and he possessed—cruel privilege in a society enamored of itself—that great

Machiavellian good sense which moves in front of a wise man, like a pillar of fire, across the desert of history.—What would he have thought, what would he have written, unhappy man, if he had heard a sentimental theologian [George Sand] abolish Hell through love for the human race, a philosopher of figures propose a system of insurance (a penny per person) to stop war—and the abolition of capital punishment and spelling, those two related follies!—and how many other sick people who write, *with their ear to the wind*, gyrating fantasies as flatulent as the air that inspires them? [52]—If you add to this impeccable vision of the true, which can be a real weakness in certain circumstances, an exquisite sensitiveness that was distressed by any false note, delicacy of taste that was revolted by anything except exact proportions, an insatiable love of the Beautiful which had become a morbid passion, you will not be surprised that for such a man life should have become hell, and that he should have come to a bad end. You will be astonished that he was able to *endure* such a long time.

II

Poe's family was one of the most respectable in Baltimore. His maternal grandfather had served as quartermaster-general in the Revolutionary War and had won the esteem and friendship of Lafayette. The latter, during his last visit to the United States wished to call upon the widow of the general and to express his gratitude for the services which her husband had rendered. His great-grandfather had married the daughter of the English admiral McBride, who was connected with the most aristocratic families in England. David Poe, the father of Edgar and the son of the general, fell violently in love with an English actress, Elisabeth Arnold, who was famous for her beauty; they eloped. In order to join his destiny more closely to hers, he became an actor and appeared with his wife in various theaters in the principal cities of the United States. They both died at

Richmond, almost at the same time, leaving three young children in the utmost destitution. One of them was Edgar.

Edgar Poe was born in Baltimore in 1813.—I give this date, which is in accordance with his own statement, in contradiction of Griswold who puts his birth in 1811.[53]—If ever the spirit of romance, to use one of his own expressions, presided over a birth—sinister and stormy spirit!—certainly it presided over his. Poe was truly a child of passion and adventure. A rich merchant of the town, Mr. Allan, took a fancy to the pretty orphaned child whom nature had endowed with a charming manner and, since he had no children, he adopted him. Henceforth his name was Edgar Allan Poe. Thus he was brought up in easy circumstances and with the legitimate hope of one of those fortunes that give character a superb certitude. His foster parents took him on a trip to England, Scotland and Ireland, and, before returning home, they left him with Dr. Bransby, who was the director of an important school at Stoke Newington, near London.—Poe himself, in "William Wilson," has described that strange place, built in the old Elizabethan style, as well as the impressions of his school days.

He returned to Richmond in 1822 and continued his studies in America under the best available masters. At the University of Virginia, which he entered in 1825, he distinguished himself not only by a nearly miraculous intelligence, but also by an almost sinister abundance of passions—a truly American form of precocity—which finally led to his expulsion. It is worth noting in passing that already at Charlottesville, Poe had shown a most remarkable aptitude for physical science and mathematics. Later he will make frequent use of it in his strange stories and will draw from it very unexpected technical resources. But I have reason to believe that he did not attach the greatest importance to compositions of this type, and that— perhaps even because of his precocious aptitude—he was inclined to consider them facile tricks compared to works of pure imagination.—Some unfortunate gambling debts brought about a momentary quarrel between him and his foster father, and

Edgar—a most curious fact, and one which proves, whatever one may say, that there was a rather considerable amount of chivalry in his impressionable mind—conceived the idea of taking part in the Greek Revolution and of going away to fight the Turks. He left for Greece.—What became of him in the Orient, what did he do there—did he study the classic shores of the Mediterranean—why do we find him in Saint Petersburg, without a passport—compromised, and in what sort of affair— obliged to call upon the American ambassador, Henry Middleton, in order to escape a Russian sentence and return home?— we do not know; there is a lacuna that only he could fill in. The life of Edgar Poe, his youth, his adventures in Russia and his correspondence have been promised by American magazines for a long time and have never appeared.[54]

Once more in America, in 1829, he expressed the desire to enter West Point; he was admitted, and there as elsewhere showed the signs of an admirably well endowed but undisciplinable intelligence, and after a few months he was dropped.—In his adoptive family there was taking place at the same time an event which was to have the most serious effects on his whole life. Mrs. Allan, for whom he seems to have felt a truly filial affection, died, and Mr. Allan married a very young woman. A domestic quarrel took place—a vague and bizarre story which I cannot tell, because it has not been clearly explained by any biographer. Thus there is no reason to be surprised that he should have broken completely with Mr. Allan, and that the latter, who had children by his second marriage, should have cut him off from his inheritance.

Shortly after leaving Richmond, Poe published a small volume of poems; it was indeed a remarkable beginning. Whoever has a feeling for English poetry will find there already the unearthly accent, the calm melancholy, the delightful solemnity, the precocious experience—I believe I was about to say *innate experience*—which characterizes the great poets.

For a time poverty forced him to become a soldier, and presumably he used the wearisome garrison hours to prepare the material of his future compositions—strange compositions which seem to have been created in order to show us that strangeness is one of the integral parts of the beautiful. Having returned to literary life, the only element in which certain classless beings can breathe, Poe was wasting away in utter destitution, when a happy chance put him on his feet again. The owner of a review had just offered two prizes, one for the best short story, the other for the best poem. An exceptionally beautiful handwriting attracted the eyes of Mr. Kennedy, who was chairman of the committee, and stimulated him to read the manuscripts himself.[55] It turned out that Poe had won both prizes; but he was given only one. The chairman of the jury was curious to meet the unknown writer. The editor of the magazine introduced him to a strikingly handsome young man, in rags, his coat buttoned up to his chin, who had the air of a gentleman as proud as he was hungry. Kennedy treated him well. He introduced Poe to Mr. Thomas White, who was establishing the *Southern Literary Messenger* at Richmond. Mr. White was a bold man, but without any literary talent; he needed an assistant. Quite young then—at the age of twenty-two—Poe found himself the director of a magazine whose destiny depended entirely on him. He created the prosperity which it enjoyed. Since then the *Southern Literary Messenger* has recognized that it was to this wretched eccentric, to this incorrigible drunkard that it owed its circulation and its fruitful notoriety. It was in this magazine that there first appeared *The Unparalleled Adventure of One Hans Pfaall* and several other stories which our readers will see. For nearly two years, Edgar Poe, with a marvelous ardor, astonished his public by a series of compositions of a new type and by critical articles whose liveliness, clearness and reasoned severity were well calculated to attract attention. These articles had to do with books of all sorts, and the excellent education which the young man had had served him well. It is well to remember that this considerable task was done for five hundred dollars, that is to say 2,700 francs a year. *Immediately,*—writes Griswold, by which he means to say: Poe thought himself sufficiently well off, the imbecile!—he married a beautiful and charming young girl, amiable and heroic, but *without a cent*—adds this same Griswold, with a tone of contempt. She was a Miss Virginia Clemm, his cousin.

In spite of the services which he had performed for the magazine, Mr. White quarreled with Poe after about two years. The poet's attacks of hypochondria and drunkenness were apparently the cause of the separation—characteristic occurrences which darkened his spiritual sky, like those ominous clouds which suddenly give the most romantic landscape a seemingly irreparable air of melancholy.—From that time on, we shall see the ill-fated man move his tent, like a nomad of the desert, and carry his portable household gods to the principal cities of the Union. Everywhere he will edit reviews or contribute to them in a brilliant manner. With a dazzling rapidity he will pour out critical and philosophical articles and stories full of magic which were later published under the title: *Tales of the Grotesque and the Arabesque*—a carefully chosen title, for grotesque and arabesque ornaments reject the human figure, and it will be seen that in many respects Poe's writing is outside or above the human. Scandalous and offensive notices appearing in newspapers inform us that Poe and his wife were dangerously ill at Fordham and in absolute poverty. Soon after the death of Mrs. Poe, the poet experienced the first attacks of *delirium tremens*. Suddenly a new assault appeared in a paper—this one more than cruel— which assailed his scorn and his disgust for the world and put him on trial, a real public inquisition, such as he always had to face—one of the most sterile and fatiguing struggles that I know.

Doubtless he was making money, and his literary work almost provided him with a living. But I have proof that he constantly had to overcome humiliating difficulties. Like so many other writers, he dreamed of a journal of his own, he wanted to be *at home*, and he had certainly suffered enough to wish ardently for that definite shelter for his thought. In order to obtain enough money for that purpose, he resorted to giving lectures. You know what they are like—a kind of speculation, the university put at the disposal of literary persons, the author publishing his lecture only after having drawn from it all the revenue that he can. In New York Poe had already given *Eureka*, his cosmogonic poem, as a lecture, and it had even aroused considerable discussion. Now he had the idea of lecturing in his own region, in Virginia. He intended, as he wrote to Willis, to make a tour in the West and South, and he hoped for assistance from his literary friends and from his old college and West Point acquaintances. Accordingly, he visited the principal cities of Virginia, and Richmond once again saw the man whom it had known when he was young, poor and shabby. All those who had not seen Poe since the days of his obscurity came in crowds to see their distinguished fellow citizen. He appeared handsome, elegant, absolutely correct. I even believe that for some time he had gone so far as to join a temperance society. He chose a theme as broad as it was lofty: *The Poetic Principle*, and he developed it with that lucidity which was one of his gifts. He believed, like the true poet that he was, that the purpose of poetry is of the same nature as its principle, and that it should have no object in view other than itself.

The wonderful reception that he received filled his poor heart with pride and joy; he was so delighted that he spoke of settling down in Richmond and ending his days among the places that his childhood had made dear to him. However, he had some business in New York, and he left on the 4th of October, complaining of weakness and chills. On the evening of the 6th, continuing to feel ill on his arrival in Baltimore, he had his baggage sent to the dock from which he was to leave for Philadelphia, and went into a tavern to get a stimulant. There, unfortunately, he met some old acquaintances and stayed late. The next morning, in the pale shadows of dawn, a corpse was found on the street—should it be put that way?—no, a body still living, but already marked by the royal stamp of Death. On the body, whose name was not known, no papers or money were found, and he was taken to a hospital. It was there that Poe died, Sunday evening, October 7, 1849, at the age of 37, defeated by *delirium tremens*, that terrible visitor which had already attacked his mind once or twice.[56] Thus disappeared from the world one of the greatest literary heroes, the man of genius who had written in "The Black Cat" these fateful words: *What disease is like Alcohol!*

This death was almost a suicide—a suicide prepared for a long time. At least, it caused that kind of scandal. There was a great uproar, and *virtue* gave free rein to its pretentious *cant*, openly and voluptuously. The kindest funeral orations could not avoid the inevitable bourgeois moralizing and were quick to seize such an admirable occasion. Mr. Griswold slandered him; Mr. Willis, sincerely grieved, was more than decent. Alas! the man who had scaled the most arduous heights of aesthetics and plunged into the least explored abysses of the human intellect, he who, through a life which resembled an unrelieved tempest, had found new means, unknown techniques to astonish the imagination, to charm minds thirsty for the Beautiful, had just died within a period of a few hours in a hospital bed—what a fate! So much greatness and so much misfortune, to raise a storm of bourgeois phrases, to become the food and theme of virtuous journalists!

Ut declamatio fias! [57]

Spectacles of this sort are not new; it is rare for the newly buried great not to be subjects of scandal. Moreover, Society does not like these mad wretches, and, whether they disturb its festivities or whether it naïvely regards them as scourges, it is undoubtedly right. Who does not recall the declamations in Paris at the time of Balzac's death, in spite of his perfectly natural end?—And still more recently—just a year ago today— when a writer [Gérard de Nerval] admirably honest, highly intelligent, and *who was always lucid*, discreetly, without bothering anyone—so discreetly that his discretion looked like scorn— went away to free his soul in the darkest street that he could find—what disgusting homilies!—what refined assassination! [58] A famous journalist, who will never learn generosity from Jesus, thought the event amusing enough to commemorate in a coarse pun.—In the long list of the *rights of man* which the wisdom of the 19th century keeps increasing so often and so complacently, two rather important ones have been forgotten, the right to contradict oneself and the right to take one's leave. But *Society* considers anyone who kills himself as insolent; it would gladly punish the earthly remains, like the unfortunate soldier, stricken with vampirism, who was exasperated to the point of fury by a cadaver.—And nevertheless, it may be said that, in certain circumstances, after a grave consideration of certain incompatibilities, with a firm belief in certain dogmas and transmigrations—it may be said, without exaggeration and in all seriousness, that suicide is sometimes the most rational act of life.—And thus is formed an already numerous company of phantoms, which haunts us familiarly, and of which each member comes to praise his present repose and to pour out his persuasions.

We must admit, nevertheless, that the lugubrious end of the author of *Eureka* aroused some consoling exceptions, lacking which we would have to despair, and the situation would be unbearable. Mr. Willis, as I have said, spoke decently and even with emotion of the good relations that he had always had with Poe. John Neal and George Graham recalled Mr. Griswold to shame.[59] Longfellow—who is all the more commendable since Poe had cruelly maltreated him—praised his great power as a poet and as a prose writer in a manner worthy of a poet. Someone wrote anonymously that literary America had lost its strongest mind.

But it was Mrs. Clemm whose heart was broken, torn, and pierced by the seven swords. Edgar was both her son and her daughter. It was a hard destiny, Willis says (from whom I borrow these details almost word for word), a hard destiny that she watched over and protected. For Edgar Poe was a disconcerting man; in addition to the fact that he wrote with painstaking care, and *in a style too much above the average intellec-tual level to be well paid*, he was always deep in financial trouble, and often he and his ill wife lacked the necessities of life. One day an old, sweet, serious woman came into Willis' office. It was Mrs. Clemm. She was *looking for work* for her dear Edgar. The biographer says that he was singularly struck, not only by her perfect appreciation, her just appraisal of her son-in-law's talents, but also by her whole outer being—by her sweet and sad voice, by her fine, slightly old-fashioned manners. He adds that for several years he saw this indefatigable servant of genius, poorly and insufficiently dressed, going from office to office in order to sell now a poem, now an article, sometimes saying that *he* was ill—the sole explanation, the sole reason, the invariable excuse that she gave when her son-in-law was momen-tarily stricken by one of those periods of sterility that nervous writers know—never letting a word fall from her lips which could be interpreted as a doubt, as a lessening of confidence in the genius and will of her beloved. When her daughter died, she attached herself to the survivor of the disastrous battle with increased maternal ardor, she lived with him, took care of him, watching over him, defending him against life and against him-self. Assuredly, Willis concludes with lofty and just reasoning, if the devotion of a woman, born of a first love and maintained by human passion, glorifies and consecrates its object, what could one not say in support of a man who inspired a devotion like this, pure, disinterested and as holy as a divine sentinel? The detractors of Poe ought to have realized that there are fascinations so powerful that they can only be virtues.

One can guess how terrible the news was for the unhappy woman. Here are some lines from a letter which she wrote to Willis:

"I have this morning heard of the death of my darling Eddie. . . . Can you give me any circumstances or particulars? . . . Oh! do not desert your poor friend in this bitter affliction. . . . Ask Mr. — to come, as I must deliver a message to him from my poor Eddie. . . . I need not ask you to announce his death and to speak well of him. I know you will. But say what an affectionate son he was to me, his poor desolate mother. . . ."

It seems to me that this woman has more than ancient greatness. Struck by an irreparable blow, she thinks only of the reputation of the person who was everything to her, and she is not content to have it said that he was a genius, it must be known that he was a dutiful and affectionate man. It is clear that his mother—a torch and hearth illuminated by a ray from heaven—has been sent as an example to races who are too careless of devotion, of heroism, and of everything that is beyond duty. Was it not just to inscribe above the works of the poet the name of the woman who was the moral sun of his life? He will preserve in his glory the name of the woman whose love was able to care for his wounds, and whose image will ceaselessly hover over the martyrology of literature.[60]

III

The life of Poe, his manners and morals, his physical being, everything that constituted the whole of his personality, appear to us as something at once dark and brilliant. His person was singular, fascinating, and like his works, marked by an indefinable stamp of melancholy. Moreover, he was remarkably gifted in every way. As a young man he had shown an exceptional skill in every kind of physical exercise, and although he was small, with the feet and hands of a woman, although his whole being had a delicate, feminine character, he was more than robust and capable of wonderful feats of strength. When he was a boy he won a bet for an extraordinary demonstration of swimming. One might say that Nature grants an energetic temperament to those from whom it expects great things, just as it gives a powerful vitality to those trees which symbolize grief and sorrow. Such men, sometimes puny in appearance, are cut in an athletic mold, fit for orgies and for work, inclined to excess and capable of extraordinary sobriety.

There are some things about Edgar Poe concerning which agreement is unanimous, as for example, his great natural distinction, his eloquence and his handsome appearance, of which it is said he was a little vain. His manners, a strange mixture of aloofness and exquisite gentleness, were full of assurance. His face, bearing, gestures, the carriage of his head, all marked him, especially in his best years, as an exceptional person. His whole being breathed an air of intense solemnity. He was really singled out by nature, like those passersby who catch the eye of the spectator and remain in his memory. Even the pedantic and bitter Griswold admits that, when he went to visit Poe, whom he found still pale and ill after the sickness and death of his wife, he was very much struck, not only by the perfection of his manners but also by the aristocratic appearance, the perfumed atmosphere of his apartment, even though it was modestly furnished. Griswold does not realize that, more than anyone else, the poet has the wonderful gift, attributed to Parisian and Spanish women, of being able to adorn himself with nothing, and that Poe, attached to everything that was beautiful, would have found a way to transform a cottage into a new kind of palace. Did he not write, in the most curious and original way, about new conceptions of furniture, about planning country houses, about gardens and reforms in landscape architecture?

There is a charming letter written by Mrs. Frances Osgood, who was one of Poe's friends, and who gives us most interesting details about his manners, his person and his domestic life. This woman, who was herself a distinguished literary person, courageously denies all the vices and faults attributed to the poet. "With men," she tells Griswold, "perhaps he was as you picture him, and as a man you may be right. I think no one could know him—certainly no woman—without feeling the same interest. . . . I have never seen him otherwise than gentle, generous, well bred, and fastidiously refined.

"My first meeting with the poet was at the Astor House. A few days previous Mr. Willis had handed me, at the *table d'hôte*, that strange and thrilling poem entitled 'The Raven,' saying that the author wanted my opinion of it. Its effect upon me was so singular, so like that of 'weird, unearthly music,' that it was with a feeling almost of dread I heard he desired an introduction. . . . With his proud and beautiful head erect, his dark eyes flashing with the elective light of feeling and of thought, a peculiar, and inimitable blending of sweetness and hauteur in his expression and manner, he greeted me, calmly, gravely, almost coldly; yet with so marked an earnestness that I could not help being deeply impressed by it. From that moment until his death we were friends. . . . And in his last words, ere reason had forever left her imperial throne in that overtasked brain, I have a touching memento of his undying faith and friendship.

"It was in his own simple yet poetical home that to me, the character of Edgar Poe appeared in its most beautiful light. Playful, affectionate, witty, alternately docile and wayward as a petted child—for his young, gentle, and idolized wife, and for all who came, he had, even in the midst of his most harassing literary duties, a kind word, a pleasant smile, a graceful and courteous attention. At his desk, beneath the romantic picture of his loved and lost Lenore, he would sit, hour after hour, patient, assiduous, and uncomplaining, tracing, in an exquisitely clear chirography, and with almost super-human swiftness, the lightning thoughts—the 'rare and radiant' fancies as they flashed through his wonderful and ever-wakeful brain. I recollect one morning, toward the close of his residence in this city, when he seemed unusually gay and light-hearted. Virginia, his sweet wife, had written me a pressing invitation to come to them; and I, who could never resist her affectionate summons . . . found him just completing his series of papers, entitled 'The Literati of New York.' 'See,' said he, displaying in triumph several little rolls of narrow papers (he always wrote thus for the press), 'I am going to show you, by the difference of length in these, the different degrees of estimation in which I hold all you literary people. In each of these one of you is rolled up and fully discussed. Come, Virginia, help me.' And one by one they un-

folded them. At last they came to one which seemed inter-
minable. Virginia laughingly ran to one corner of the room with
one end, and her husband to the opposite with the other.
'And whose lengthened sweetness long drawn out is that?' said
I. 'Hear her!' he cried, 'just as if her little vain heart didn't tell
her it's herself.'

"During that year, while travelling for my health, I maintained a correspondence with Mr. Poe, in accordance with the
earnest entreaties of his wife, who imagined that my influence
over him had a restraining and beneficial effect . . . of the
charming love and confidence that existed between his wife and
himself, always delightfully apparent to me, in spite of the many
little poetical episodes, in which the impassioned romance of
his temperament impelled him to indulge; of this I cannot speak
too earnestly—too warmly. I believe she was the only woman
whom he ever truly loved. . . ."

Love never figures in Poe's stories. At least, "Ligeia," and
"Eleanora," are not love stories, properly speaking, since the
central idea on which the work pivots is something quite different. Perhaps he believed that prose was not a language equal
to that strange and almost untranslatable sentiment; for his
poems, in contrast, are strongly saturated with it. In them the
divine passion appears in all its magnificence, like the starry
sky, yet always veiled by an irremediable melancholy. Sometimes he speaks of love in his essays, and even as if it were something whose name makes his pen tremble.

In "The Domain of Arnheim," he declares that the four
fundamental conditions of happiness are: life in the open air,
the love of a woman, detachment from all ambition and the
creation of a new Beauty.—What corroborates the idea of Mrs.
Frances Osgood about Poe's chivalric respect for women is the
fact that, in spite of his prodigious talent for the grotesque and
the horrible, there is not a single passage in all his work which
has to do with lust or even with sensual pleasures. His portraits
of women are, so to speak, aureoled; they shine in the midst of
a supernatural atmosphere and are painted with the emphatic

touch of a worshiper.—As for the *minor romantic episodes*, is it at all surprising that such a high-strung person, whose chief trait was perhaps a thirst for the Beautiful, should sometimes have passionately cultivated gallantry, that volcanic and musk-scented flower for which the seething minds of poets is the natural soil?

I believe that it is possible to get some idea of his strange personal beauty, mentioned in several biographies, by calling up all the vague but nevertheless characteristic notions contained in the word romantic, a word which is generally used to represent the kinds of beauty in which expression is of paramount importance. Poe had a broad, dominating forehead in which certain protuberances revealed the abundant faculties which they are supposed to represent—construction, comparison, causality—and where was enthroned in calm pride the sense of the ideal, the aesthetic sense par excellence.[61] Nevertheless, in spite of these gifts, or even because of these disproportionate favors, his head, seen in profile, did not have an agreeable appearance. As with all things that are excessive in one direction, deficiency can result from abundance, poverty can spring from encroachment. He had large eyes, at once somber and full of light, dark and uncertain in color, tending toward violet, a solid and noble nose, a fine, sad mouth, though slightly smiling, a dark complexion, a pale face, in appearance a little absent-minded and imperceptibly suffused by habitual melancholy.

His conversation was quite remarkable and essentially learned. He was not what is called a glib speaker—a horrible thing—and besides his speech, like his pen, had a horror of the conventional; but vast knowledge, powerful language, serious studies, impressions gathered in several countries made his talk instructive. His eloquence, essentially poetic, full of method, and yet operating outside of all known methods, an arsenal of images drawn from a world little frequented by average minds, a prodigious art of deriving from an evident and absolutely acceptable proposition new and secret perceptions, of opening astonishing perspectives, and in a word, the art of delighting, of stimulating thoughts and dreams, of snatching souls out of the mire of routine, such were the dazzling faculties which many persons remember. But sometimes it happened—so it is said—that the poet, enjoying a destructive caprice, brusquely brought his friends back to earth with a painful cynicism and brutally demolished the spiritual edifice which he had just constructed. Something else to note, moreover, is the fact that he was not at all particular about his auditors, and I believe that the reader will have no difficulty in finding other great and original intelligences in history who were at home in any company. Certain minds, solitary in the midst of crowds, and nourishing themselves on monologues, cannot be particular about their audience. In short, it is a kind of fraternity based on scorn.

As for his drunkenness—publicized and censured with an insistence which could make it appear that all the writers of the United States, except Poe, are angels of sobriety—something should be said. Several explanations are plausible, and none excludes the others. Above all it must be noted that Willis and Mrs. Osgood emphasize how much his whole constitution was upset by a very small amount of alcohol. Moreover, it is easy to understand why such a truly solitary man, profoundly unhappy, who must often have regarded the whole social system as a paradox and a fraud, a man who, harassed by a pitiless destiny, often said that society was nothing but a mob of wretches (Griswold reports this, scandalized as a man who may think the same thing, but who will never say it)—it is natural, I say, to understand why this poet, cast into the hazards of an undisciplined life while still a child, his mind circumscribed by hard and continuous work, should sometimes have sought the pleasure of forgetfulness in intoxication. Literary rancors, the intoxication of the infinite, domestic problems, the indignities of poverty, all of these Poe fled in the blackness of drunkenness as if in a preparatory tomb. But however good this explanation may seem, I do not consider it sufficiently broad, and I am suspicious of it because of its deplorable simplicity.

I am informed that he did not drink as an epicure but

barbarously, with a speed and dispatch altogether American, as if he were performing a homicidal function, as if he had to kill *something* inside of him, a worm that would not die.[62] It is said, further, that one day, when he was about to remarry (the banns had been published, and as he was being congratulated on a marriage which opened the prospect of the greatest happiness and well-being, he had said: you may have seen the banns, but you may be sure I shall not marry), he went about, frightfully drunk, scandalizing the neighbors of his future wife, thus having recourse to his vice in order to shake off a broken promise made to his poor dead wife whose image was always with him, and about whom he had written so well in his "Annabel Lee." I believe, then, that in many cases the important fact of premeditation has been clearly established.

Furthermore, in a long article in the *Southern Literary Messenger*—the magazine whose fortune he had started—I read that this terrible vice never affected the purity or the finish of his style, the lucidity of his thought or his habit of hard work; that the composition of most of his excellent pieces preceded or followed one of his crises; that after the publication of *Eureka* he let himself go very badly; and that in New York, on the very morning that *The Raven* appeared, while everyone was still talking about him, he staggered conspicuously down Broadway. Notice that the words *preceded or followed* imply that drunkenness could be a stimulant as well as a relaxation.

Now there can be no doubt that—like those fleeting and striking impressions, the more striking in their recurrences as they are more fleeting, which sometimes follow an exterior stimulus, a kind of signal such as the sound of a bell, a musical note, or a forgotten perfume, and which themselves are followed by an event similar to an event already known, which occupied the same place in a previously revealed chain—like those strange periodic dreams which frequent our sleep—there exist in drunkenness not only chains of dreams but sequences of reasonings which, to be reproduced, require the setting in which they were born. If the reader has not been horrified, he has already guessed my conclusion: I believe that often, though certainly not always, Poe's drunkenness was a mnemonic means, a method of work, drastic and fatal, but adapted to his passionate nature. The poet had learned to drink, just as a careful writer takes pains to keep notes. He could not resist the desire to recapture the marvelous or frightening visions, the subtle conceptions which he had experienced in a previous exaltation; they were old acquaintances which attracted him imperiously, and in order to renew contact with them, he took the shortest but the most dangerous road. What killed him is a part of that which gives us enjoyment today.

IV

I have little to say about the works of this singular genius; the public will show by its response what it thinks of them. It would be difficult for me, perhaps, but not impossible to disentangle his method, to explain his technique, especially in that portion of his work whose principal effect lies in a well handled analysis. I could introduce the reader to the mysteries of his workmanship, speak at length about that aspect of American genius which makes him delight in a difficulty overcome, an enigma explained, a successful *tour de force*—which leads him to play, with a childish and almost perverse pleasure, in a world of probabilities and conjectures and to create the *hoaxes* which his subtle art has made seem plausible. No one will deny that Poe is a marvelous jongleur, and yet I know that he attached the greatest importance to another aspect of his work. I have some more important, though brief, remarks to make.

It is not by these material miracles, which nevertheless have made his reputation, that he will win the admiration of thinking people; it is by his love of the beautiful, by his knowledge of the harmonic conditions of beauty, by his profound and plaintive poetry, carefully wrought, correct and as transparent as a crystal jewel—by his admirable style, pure and bizarre—as

closely woven as the mesh of chain mail—flexible and painstaking—whose slightest inflection serves to lead the reader
gently toward the desired effect—finally and above all by his
very special genius, by that unique temperament which allowed
him to picture and to explain the *exceptional case in the moral
order* in an impeccable, gripping and terrible manner.—Diderot,
to take one example among a hundred, is a sanguine author;
Poe is a writer who is all nerves, and even something more—
and the best one I know.

In his case every introductory passage has a quiet drawing
power, like a whirlpool. His solemnity surprises the reader and
keeps his mind on the alert. Immediately he feels that something serious is involved. And slowly, little by little, a story unfolds whose interest depends on an imperceptible intellectual
deviation, on a bold hypothesis, on an unbalanced dose of Nature in the amalgam of faculties. The reader, seized by a kind of
vertigo, is constrained to follow the author through his compel-
ling deductions.

No one, I repeat, has told about the *exceptions* in human
life and in nature with more magic—the enthusiastic curiosities
of convalescence; the dying seasons charged with enervating
splendors, hot, humid and misty weather, when the south wind
softens and relaxes one's nerves like the strings of an instrument,
when one's eyes fill with tears which do not come from the
heart;—hallucinations, first appearing doubtful, then convincing
and as rational as a book; the absurd establishing itself in one's
mind and controlling it with a frightful logic; hysteria usurping
the place of the will, contradiction set up between the nerves and
the mind, and personality so out of joint that it expresses grief
by a laugh. He analyzes whatever is most fugitive, he weighs
the imponderable and describes, in a detailed and scientific manner the effects of which are terrible, all that imaginary world
which floats around a high-strung man and leads him into evil.

The fervor with which he throws himself into the grotesque
out of love for the grotesque and into the horrible out of love
for the horrible serves to verify the sincerity of his work and the

harmony between the man and the poet.—I have already pointed out that, in certain men, this fervor was often the result of a vast, unemployed vital energy, sometimes the result of a stubborn chastity, and also of a profound dammed-up sensibility. The unnatural pleasure that a man may feel in watching the flow of his own blood, sudden violent, useless movements, cries uttered for no reason at all, are phenomena of the same kind.

In the midst of the rarefied air of this literature, the mind may feel the vague anguish, the fear close to tears and the uneasiness of heart which exist in vast and strange places. But admiration prevails, and the art is so great! The backgrounds and accessories are appropriate to the feelings of the persons involved. Solitude of nature or agitation of cities, everything is described energetically and fantastically. Like our own Eugène Delacroix, who has raised his art to the level of great poetry, Edgar Poe loves to represent agitated figures against violet or greenish backgrounds in which are revealed the phosphorescence of decay and the smell of storms.[63] So-called inanimate Nature takes on the nature of living beings, and, like them, shudders with a supernatural and convulsive shudder. Opium deepens the feeling of space; opium gives a magical feeling to all tones, and makes all sounds vibrate with a more sonorous significance. Sometimes magnificent vistas, saturated with light and color, suddenly open up in his landscapes, and in the distance are seen oriental cities and buildings, etherealized by the distance, bathed in a golden sunlight.

The characters in Poe, or rather the character in Poe, the man with excessively acute faculties, the man with relaxed nerves, the man whose patient and ardent will hurls defiance at difficulties, he whose gaze is fixed as straight as a sword on objects which increase in importance under his gaze—this man is Poe himself.—And his women, all luminous and sickly, dying of strange diseases, and speaking with a voice which is like music, they are also Poe; or at least, through their strange aspirations, through their knowledge, through their incurable melancholy, they strongly share the nature of their creator. As for his ideal

113

woman, his Titanide, she is revealed in several portraits scattered through his sparse collection of poems, portraits, or rather ways of feeling beauty, which the temperament of the author joins and fuses in a vague but perceptible unity, and in which exists perhaps more delicately than elsewhere that insatiable love of the Beautiful, which is his great title of respect, that is the summation of his claims on the affection and admiration of poets.

Under the title: *Histoires Extraordinaires* we have gathered together various stories chosen from the whole of Poe's work. His work comprises a considerable number of short stories, an equal quantity of critical and miscellaneous articles, a philosophical poem (*Eureka*), poems, and a purely realistic novel (*The Narrative of Arthur Gordon Pym*).

If, as I hope, I should have occasion to speak further of this poet, I shall give an analysis of his philosophical and literary ideas, and in general of works whose complete translation would have little chance of success with a public which much prefers amusement and emotion to the most important philosophical truth.

❀ NEW NOTES ON EDGAR POE

PREFACE

Baudelaire's third essay on Poe served as a preface to his second volume of translations, published in 1857. The essay is one of Baudelaire's most important critical studies, since for the first time it sets forth the principles which form the heart of his aesthetic doctrine. In it he quotes and paraphrases passages from Poe's "The Poetic Principle," often presenting them as if they were his own.

As in his two preceding essays Baudelaire introduces digressions on various topics such as suicide, drunkenness, progress, decadent literature, and the natural perversity of man. Baudelaire was obviously impressed by Poe's notion of perversity which corresponds in many ways to his own belief in original sin. The American writer, who was devoid of any traditional religious convictions, never related his theory of perversity to the Fall, nor did he give it any other theological implications, but Baudelaire seems to have been so elated at his discovery of Poe's conception of the perverse that he ascribed his own beliefs to his literary idol.

Almost all of Baudelaire's favorite ideas are to be found in the essay. Once again he supports Poe in his attack on utilitarian poetry, although he is careful to add that morality is almost inevitably a by-product of poetry—an admission which has no counterpart in "The Poetic Principle." Like Poe, he believes that the short poem is best suited to the requirements of pure poetry. Like him, he also stresses the importance of melancholy, musicality, and strangeness, as well as the need to subject inspiration to discipline. It is in this essay also that Baudelaire modifies his own theory of the relationship of passion to poetry and momentarily accepts Poe's belief that passion is incompatible with pure poetry.

The transcendental implications of poetry that Baudelaire had suggested in "Since it is a Question of Realism" are strengthened by his acceptance of Poe's belief that poetry is human aspiration toward a superior beauty. But perhaps of greatest importance is the fact that Baudelaire seems to have finally arrived at his conception of the imagination which, like Poe, he considers almost a divine faculty. Although he will develop the subject further in the *Salon of 1859*, he has given it here all the importance that it will have in his later essays. His association of the imagination with correspondences and analogies finds no counterpart in "The Poetic Principle"; in fact, the theory of correspondences never seems to have been a part of Poe's literary doctrine. Yet on a number of occasions, such as in the "Purloined Letter" and in "Marginalia" Poe also noted that "the material world abounds with very strict analogies to the immaterial."

Throughout the essay it becomes obvious that Baudelaire found in Poe's literary doctrine a confirmation of his own poetic practices as well as an affirmation of aesthetic ideas he had already accepted and, in some cases, expressed or suggested in his critical essays. It must be acknowledged that he depended too much on Poe for the articulation of those ideas, but in all fairness it must be admitted that the ideas were already inherent in his own work.

In addition to the three long essays, Baudelaire wrote seven short notices which, though very little known, contain a number of interesting observations. Of these the prefaces to "Mesmeric Revelation" and to "Berenice" reveal his antipathy to Realism and his admiration for the visionary artist preoccupied with the problems of "a spiritual man: probabilities, mental illnesses, scientific hypotheses, hopes and considerations about a future life, analysis of the eccentrics and pariahs of this world, directly symbolic buffooneries." [64] These preoccupations would be sufficient to explain Baudelaire's sympathy for a writer whom he considered his spiritual brother and whom he invoked as an intercessor, together with his father and his childhood servant Mariette, in the famous prayer found among the notations in his *Journaux Intimes*.[65]

Yet in spite of his dissatisfaction with Realism and his concern with spiritual reality, Baudelaire recognized some of the possibilities of "representational" expression. A postscript to "Hans Pfaall" (1855) in which he refers to "the capricious hippogriff of *verisimilitude*" indicates that he was conscious of the two-edged character of realistic technique.[66] A few years later (ca. 1863), in a "Translator's Note" that remained unpublished until 1934, Baudelaire was still acclaiming Poe for "the magic of absolute verisimilitude" that he found in his tales.[67] His praise was evidently not the result of a passing whim, for in his analysis of Gautier's poetic stories (1859) he had likewise noted the danger of losing contact with "reality or the magic of verisimilitude." [68]

Among the short and somewhat slight prefaces that Baudelaire wrote in connection with his Poe translations should also be mentioned the introduction to his prose translation of *The Raven*. Once again Baudelaire finds himself in sympathy with Poe's idea that inspiration must be accompanied by will and hard work. Although he admits that Poe deliberately underestimated the importance of inspiration, he agrees that "it will always be useful to show them [the readers] what profit art can draw from deliberation and to make worldly people realize how much labor is required by that object of luxury called Poetry." [69]

I

Decadent literature!—Empty words which we often hear fall, with the sonority of a deep yawn, from the mouths of those unenigmatic sphinxes who keep watch before the sacred doors of classical Aesthetics.[70] Each time that the irrefutable oracle resounds, one can be sure that it is about a work more amusing than the *Iliad*. It is evidently a question of a poem or of a novel, all of whose parts are skillfully designed for surprise, whose style is magnificently embellished, where all the resources of language and prosody are utilized by an impeccable hand. When I hear the anathema boom out—which, I might say in passing, usually falls on some favorite poet—I am always seized with the desire to reply: Do you take me for a barbarian like you and do you believe me capable of amusing myself as dismally as you do? Then grotesque comparisons stir in my brain; it seems to me that two women appear before me: one, a rustic matron, repugnant in her health and virtue, plain and expressionless, in short, *owing everything to simple nature*; the other, one of those beauties who dominate and oppress one's memory, adding all the eloquence of dress to her profound and original charm, well poised, conscious and queen of herself—with a speaking voice like a well-tuned instrument, and eyes laden with thoughts but revealing only what they wish. I would not hesitate in my choice, and yet there are pedagogical sphinxes who would reproach me for my failure to respect classical honor. —But, putting aside parables, I think it is permissible to ask these wise men if they really understand all the vanity, all the futility of their wisdom. The phrase *decadent literature* implies that there is a scale of literatures, an infantile, a childish, an adolescent, etc. This term, in other words, supposes something fatal and providential, like an ineluctable decree; and it is altogether unfair to reproach us for fulfilling the mysterious law. All that I can understand in this academic phrase is that it is shameful to obey this law with pleasure and that we are guilty to rejoice in our destiny.—The sun, which a few hours ago overwhelmed everything with its direct white light, is soon going to flood the western horizon with variegated colors. In the play of light of the dying sun certain poetic spirits will find new delights; they will discover there dazzling colonnades, cascades of molten metal, paradises of fire, a sad splendor, the pleasure of regret, all the magic of dreams, all the memories of opium. And indeed the sunset will appear to them like the marvelous allegory of a soul filled with life which descends behind the horizon with a magnificent store of thoughts and dreams.[71]

But what the narrow-minded professors have not realized is that, in the movement of life, there may occur some complication, some combination quite unforeseen by their schoolboy wisdom. And then their inadequate language fails, as in the case —a phenomenon which perhaps will increase with variants— of a nation which begins with decadence and thus starts where others end.

Let new literatures develop among the immense colonies of the present century and there will result most certainly spiritual accidents of a nature disturbing to the academic mind. Young and old at the same time, America babbles and rambles with an astonishing volubility. Who could count its poets? They are innumerable. Its *blue stockings?* They clutter the magazines. Its critics? You may be sure that they have pedants who are as good as ours at constantly recalling the artist to ancient beauty, at questioning a poet or a novelist on the morality of his purpose and the merit of his intentions. There can be found there as here, but even more than here, men of letters who do not know how to spell; a childish, useless activity; compilers in abundance, hack writers, plagiarists of plagiaries, and critics of critics. In this maelstrom of mediocrity, in this society enamored of material perfections—a new kind of scandal which makes intelligible the grandeur of inactive peoples—in this society eager for surprises, in love with life, but especially with a life full of excitements, a man has appeared who was great not only in his metaphysical subtlety, in the sinister or bewitching beauty of his conceptions, in the rigor of his analysis, but also great and not less great as a *caricature.*—I must explain myself with some care; for recently a rash critic, in order to disparage Edgar Poe and to invalidate the sincerity of my admiration, used the word jongleur which I myself had applied to the noble poet as a sort of praise.[72]

From the midst of a greedy world, hungry for material things, Poe took flight in dreams. Stifled as he was by the American atmosphere, he wrote at the beginning of *Eureka:* "I offer this book to those who have put faith in dreams as in the only realities!" He was in himself an admirable protest, and he made his protest in his own particular way. The author who, in "The Colloquy of Monos and Una," pours out his scorn and disgust for democracy, progress and *civilization,* this author is the same one who, in order to encourage credulity, to delight the stupidity of his contemporaries, has stressed human sovereignty most emphatically and has very ingeniously fabricated hoaxes flattering to the pride of *modern man.* Considered in this light, Poe seems like a helot who wishes to make his master blush. Finally, to state my thought even more clearly, Poe was always great not only in his noble conceptions but also as a prankster.

II

For he was never a dupe! I do not think that the Virginian who calmly wrote in the midst of a rising tide of democracy: "People have nothing to do with laws except to obey them," has ever been a victim of modern wisdom; and: "The nose of a mob is its imagination. By this, at any time, it can be quietly led"—and a hundred other passages in which mockery falls thick and fast like a hail of bullets but still remains proud and indifferent.[73]—The Swedenborgians congratulate him on his "Mesmeric Revelation," like those naïve Illuminati who formerly hailed in the author of the *Diable amoureux* a discoverer of their mysteries; they thank him for the great truths which he has just proclaimed—for they have discovered (O verifiers of the unverifiable!) that all that which he has set forth is absolutely true;—although, at first, these good people confess, they had suspected that it might well have been merely fictitious.[74] Poe answers that, so far as he is concerned, he has never doubted it.—Must I cite in addition this short passage which catches my eye while scanning for the hundredth time his amusing "Marginalia," which are the secret chambers, as it were, of his mind: "The enormous multiplication of books in all branches of knowledge is one of the greatest scourges of this age, for it is one of the most serious obstacles to the acquisition of all positive knowledge." Aristocrat by nature even more than by birth, the Virginian, the Southerner, the Byron gone astray in a bad world, has always kept his philosophic impassibility and, whether he defines the nose of the mob, whether he mocks the fabricators of religions, whether he scoffs at libraries, he remains what the true poet was and always will be—a truth clothed in a strange manner, an apparent paradox, who does not wish to be elbowed by the crowd and who runs to the far east when the fireworks go off in the west.

But more important than anything else: we shall see that this author, product of a century infatuated with itself, child of a nation more infatuated with itself than any other, has clearly seen, has imperturbably affirmed the natural wickedness of man. There is in man, he says, a mysterious force which modern philosophy does not wish to take into consideration; nevertheless, without this nameless force, without this primordial bent, a host of human actions will remain unexplained, inexplicable. These actions are attractive only *because* they are bad or dangerous; they possess the fascination of the abyss. This primitive, irresistible force is natural Perversity, which makes man constantly and simultaneously a murderer and a suicide, an assassin and a hangman;—for he adds, with a remarkably satanic subtlety, the impossibility of finding an adequate rational motive for certain wicked and perilous actions could lead us to consider them as the result of the suggestions of the Devil, if experience and history did not teach us that God often draws from them the establishment of order and the punishment of scoundrels;—*after having used the same scoundrels as accomplices!* such is the thought which, I confess, slips into my mind, an implication as inevitable as it is perfidious. But for the present I wish to consider only the great forgotten truth—the primordial perversity of man—and it is not without a certain satisfaction that I see some vestiges of ancient wisdom return to us from a country from which we did not expect them. It is pleasant to know that some fragments of an old truth are exploded in the faces of all these obsequious flatterers of humanity, of all these humbugs and quacks who repeat in every possible tone of voice: "I am born good, and you too, and all of us are born good!" forgetting, no! pretending to forget, like misguided equalitarians, that we are all born marked for evil!

Of what lies could he be a dupe, he who sometimes—sad necessity of his environment—dealt with them so well? What scorn for pseudophilosophy on his good days, on the days when he was, so to speak, inspired! This poet, several of whose compositions seem deliberately made to confirm the alleged omnipotence of man, has sometimes wished to purge himself. The day that he wrote: "All certainty is in dreams," he thrust back his own Americanism into the region of inferior things; at other times, becoming again the true poet, doubtless obeying the ineluctable truth which haunts us like a demon, he uttered the ardent sighs of *the fallen angel who remembers heaven*; he lamented the golden age and the lost Eden; he wept over all the magnificence of nature *shrivelling up before the hot breath of fiery furnaces*; finally, he produced those admirable pages: "The Colloquy of Monos and Una" which would have charmed and troubled the impeccable de Maistre.

It is he who said about socialism at a time when the latter did not yet have a name, or when, at least, this name was not completely popularized: "The world is infested, just now, by a new sect of philosophers, who have not yet suspected themselves of forming a sect, and who, consequently, have adopted no name. They are the *Believers in everything Old*. Their High Priest in the East, is Charles Fourier—in the West, Horace Greeley; and they are well aware that they are high priests. The only common bond among the members is Credulity:—let us call it Insanity at once, and be done with it. Ask any one of them *why* he believes this or that, and, if he be conscientious (ignorant people usually are), he will make you very much such a reply as Talleyrand made when asked why he believed in the Bible. 'I believe in it first,' said he, 'because I am Bishop of Autun; and, secondly, because I don't know the least thing about it.' What these philosophers call 'argument' is a way they have 'de nier ce qui est et d'expliquer ce qui n'est pas.' " [75]

Progress, that great heresy of decay, likewise could not escape Poe. The reader will see in different passages what terms he used to characterize it. One could truly say, considering the fervor that he expends, that he had to vent his spleen on it, as on a public nuisance or as on a pest in the street. How he would have laughed, with the poet's scornful laugh, which alienates simpletons, had he happened, as I did, upon this wonderful statement which reminds one of the ridiculous and deliberate absurdities of clowns. I discovered it treacherously blazoned in an eminently serious magazine:—*The unceasing progress of science has very recently made possible the rediscovery of the lost and long sought secret of* . . . (Greek fire, the tempering of copper, something or other which has vanished), *of which the most successful applications date back to a* barbarous *and very old period!!!* That is a sentence which can be called a real find, a brilliant discovery, even in a century of *unceasing progress;* but I believe that the mummy Allamistakeo would not have failed to ask with a gentle and discreet tone of superiority, if it were also thanks to *unceasing* progress—to the fatal, irresistible law of progress—that this famous secret had been lost.[76]— Moreover, to become serious about a subject which is as sad as it is laughable, is it not a really stupefying thing to see a nation, several nations, and presently all humanity, say to its wise men, its magicians: I shall love you and I shall make you great if you convince me that we are progressing unconsciously, inevitably— while sleeping; rid us of responsibility, veil for us the humiliation of comparisons, turn history into sophistries and you will be able to call yourselves the wisest of the wise? Is it not a cause for astonishment that this simple idea does not flash into everyone's mind: that progress (in so far as there is progress) perfects sorrow to the same extent that it refines pleasure and that, if the epidermis of peoples is becoming delicate, they are evidently pursuing only an *Italiam fugientem,* a conquest lost every minute, a progress always negating itself? [77]

But these illusions which, it must be added, are selfish, originate in a foundation of perversity and falsehood—meteors rising from swamps—which fill with disdain souls in love with the eternal fire, like Edgar Poe, and exasperate foggy minds like Jean-Jacques [Rousseau], in whom a wounded and rebellious sensibility takes the place of philosophy. That he was justified in his attack on the *depraved animal* is undeniable; but the depraved animal has the right to reproach him for invoking simple nature. Nature produces only monsters, and the whole question is to understand the word *savages.* No philosopher will dare to propose as models those wretched, rotten hordes, victims of the elements, prey of the animals, as incapable of manufacturing arms as of conceiving the idea of a spiritual and supreme power. But, if one wishes to compare modern man, civilized man, with the savage, or rather a so-called civilized nation with a so-called savage nation, that is to say one deprived of all the ingenious inventions which make heroism unnecessary, who does not see that all honor goes to the savage? By his nature, by very necessity itself, he is encyclopedic, while civilized man finds himself confined to the infinitely small regions of specialization. Civilized man invents the philosophy of progress to console himself for his abdication and for his downfall; whereas the savage man, redoubtable and respected husband, warrior forced to personal bravery, poet in the melancholy hours when the setting sun inspires songs of the past and of his forefathers, skirts more closely the edge of the ideal. Of what lack shall we dare accuse him? He has the priest, he has the magician and the doctor. What am I saying? He has the dandy, supreme incarnation of the idea of the beautiful given expression in material life, he who dictates form and governs manners. His clothing, his adornments, his weapons, his pipe give proof of an inventive faculty which for a long time has deserted us. Shall we compare our sluggish eyes and our deafened ears to those eyes which pierce the mist, to those ears *which would hear the grass growing?* And the savage woman with a simple and child-like soul, an obedient and winning animal, giving herself entirely and knowing that she is only half of a destiny, shall we declare her inferior to the American woman whom M. Belle-garigue (editor of the *Grocer's Bulletin!*) thought he was praising by saying that she was the ideal of the kept woman? This same woman, whose overpractical manners inspired Edgar Poe, he who was so gallant, so respectful of beauty, to write the following sad lines: "The frightfully long money-pouches—'like the Cucumber called the Gigantic'—which have come in vogue among our belles—are *not* of Parisian origin, as many suppose, but are strictly indigenous here. The fact is, such a fashion would be quite out of place in Paris, where it is money *only* that women keep in a purse. The purse of an American lady, however, must be large enough to carry both her money and the soul of its owner." [78] As for religion, I shall not speak of Vitzilipoutzli as lightly as Alfred de Musset has done; I confess without shame that I much prefer the cult of Teutatès to that of Mammon; and the priest who offers to the cruel extorter of human sacrifices victims who die *honorably*, victims who *wish* to die, seems to me a quite sweet and human being compared to the financier who immolates whole populations solely in his own interest.[79] Now and then, these matters are still understood, and I once found in an article by M. Barbey d'Aurevilly an exclamation of philosophic sadness which sums up everything that I should like to say about the subject: "Civilized peoples, who keep casting stones at savages, soon you will not deserve to be even idolaters!" [80]

Such an environment—although I have already said so, I cannot resist the desire to repeat it—is hardly made for poets. What a French mind, even the most democratic, understands by a State, would find no place in an American mind. For every intellect of the old world, a political State has a center of movement which is its brain and its sun, old and glorious memories, long poetic and military annals, an aristocracy to which poverty, daughter of revolutions, can add only a paradoxical luster; but That! that mob of buyers and sellers, that nameless creature, that headless monster, that outcast on the other side of the ocean, you call that a State!—I agree, if a vast tavern where the customer crowds in and conducts his business on dirty tables, amid the din of coarse speech, can be compared to a *salon*, to what we formerly called a salon, a republic of the mind presided over by beauty!

It will always be difficult to exercise, both nobly and fruitfully, the profession of a man of letters, without being exposed to defamation, to the slander of the impotent, to the envy of the rich—that envy which is their punishment!—to the vengeance of bourgeois mediocrity. But what is difficult in a limited monarchy or in an ordinary republic becomes almost impossible in a sort of Capernaum where each policeman of public opinion keeps order in the interest of his vices—or of his virtues, for it is all one and the same thing;—where a poet, a novelist of a country in which slavery exists, is a detestable writer in the eyes of an abolitionist critic; where one does not know which is more scandalous—the disorder of cynicism or the imperturbability of Biblical hypocrisy. To burn chained Negroes guilty of having felt their black cheeks sting with the blush of honor, to play with guns in the pit of a theater, to establish polygamy in the paradises of the West, which the savages (this term seems unjust) had not yet soiled with these shameful Utopias, to post on walls, doubtless to sanctify the principle of unlimited liberty, *the cure for nine months' illnesses,* such are some of the salient characteristics, some of the moral examples of the noble country of Franklin, the inventor of a counting-house morality, the hero of a century devoted to materialism. It is good to consider constantly these extraordinary examples of gross behavior in a time when americanomania has become almost a fashionable passion, to the extent that an archbishop has been able to promise us quite seriously that Providence would soon call us to enjoy this transatlantic ideal.

III

Such a social environment necessarily engenders corresponding literary errors. Poe reacted against these errors as often as he could, and with all his might. We must not be surprised then that American writers, though recognizing his singular power as a poet and as a storyteller, have always tended to question his ability as a critic. In a country where the idea of utility, the most hostile in the world to the idea of beauty, dominates and takes precedence over everything, the perfect critic will be the most *respectable,* that is to say the one whose tendencies and desires will best approximate the tendencies and desires of his public— the one who, confusing the intellectual faculties of the writer and the categories of writing, will assign to all a single goal—the one who will seek in a book of poetry the means of perfecting conscience. Naturally he will become all the less concerned with the real, the positive beauties of poetry; he will be all the less shocked by imperfections and even by faults in execution. Edgar Poe, on the contrary, dividing the world of the mind into pure *Intellect, Taste,* and *Moral Sense,* applied criticism in accordance with the category to which the object of his analysis belonged.[81] He was above all sensitive to perfection of plan and to correctness of execution; taking apart literary works like defective pieces of machinery (considering the goal that they wished to attain), noting carefully the flaws of workmanship; and when he passed to the details of the work, to its plastic expression, in a word, to style, examining meticulously and without omissions the faults of prosody, the grammatical errors and all the mass of dross which, among writers who are not artists, besmirch the best intentions and deform the most noble conceptions.

For him, Imagination is the queen of faculties; but by this word he understands something greater than that which is understood by the average reader. Imagination is not fantasy; nor is it sensibility, although it may be difficult to conceive of an imaginative man who would be lacking in sensibility. Imagination is an almost divine faculty which perceives immediately and without philosophical methods the inner and secret relations of things, the correspondences and the analogies. The honors and functions which he grants to this faculty give it such value (at least when the thought of the author has been well understood) that a scholar without imagination appears only as a pseudoscholar, or at least as an incomplete scholar.

Among the literary domains where imagination can obtain the most curious results, can harvest treasures, not the richest, the most precious (those belong to poetry), but the most numerous and the most varied, there is one of which Poe is especially fond; it is the *Short Story.* It has the immense advantage over the novel of vast proportions that its brevity adds to the intensity of effect. This type of reading, which can be accomplished in one sitting, leaves in the mind a more powerful impression than a broken reading, often interrupted by the worries of business and the cares of social life. The unity of impression, the *totality* of effect is an immense advantage which can give to this type of composition a very special superiority, to such an extent that an extremely short story (which is doubtless a fault) is even better than an extremely long story. The artist, if he is skillful, will not adapt his thoughts to the incidents but, having conceived deliberately and at leisure an effect to be produced, will invent the incidents, will combine the events most suitable to bring about the desired effect. If the first sentence is not written with the idea of preparing this final impression, the work has failed from the start. There must not creep into the entire composition a single word which is not intentional, which does not tend, directly or indirectly, to complete the premeditated design.

There is one point in which the short story is superior even to the poem. Rhythm is necessary to the development of the idea of beauty, which is the greatest and the most noble aim of poetry. Now, the artifices of rhythm are an insurmountable obstacle to the detailed development of thought and expression which has *truth* as its object. For truth can often be the goal of the short story, and reasoning the best tool for the construction of a perfect short story. That is why this type of composition, which is not as high on the scale as pure poetry, can provide more varied results, more easily appreciated by the average reader. Moreover, the author of a short story has at his disposal a multitude of tones, of nuances of language, the rational tone, the sarcastic, the humorous, which are repudiated by poetry and which are, as it were, dissonances, outrages to the idea of pure beauty. And that is also why the author who seeks in the short story the single goal of beauty works only at a great disadvantage, deprived as he is of the most useful instrument, rhythm. I know that in all literatures efforts have been made, often successful, to create purely poetic short stories; Edgar Poe himself has written some very beautiful ones. But they are struggles and efforts which serve only to prove the strength of the true means adapted to the corresponding goals, and I am inclined to believe that in the case of some authors, the greatest that can be chosen, these heroic attempts spring from despair.

IV

"*Genus irritabile vatum!* That poets (using the word comprehensively, as including artists in general) are a *genus irritabile*, is well understood; but the *why*, seems not to be commonly seen. An artist *is* an artist only by dint of his exquisite sense of Beauty—a sense affording him rapturous enjoyment but at the same time implying, or involving, an equally exquisite sense of Deformity or disproportion. Thus a wrong—an injustice—done a poet who is really a poet, excites him to a degree which, to ordinary apprehension, appears disproportionate with the wrong. Poets *see* injustice—*never* where it does not exist—but very often where the unpoetical see no injustice whatever. Thus the poetical irritability has no reference to 'temper' in the vulgar sense but merely to a more than usual clear-sightedness in respect to Wrong:—this clear-sightedness being nothing more than a corollary from the vivid perception of Right—of justice—of proportion—in a word, of the beautiful. But one thing is clear —that the man who is *not* 'irritable' (to the ordinary apprehension) is *no poet*." [82]

Thus the poet himself speaks, preparing an excellent and irrefutable apologia for all those of his race. Poe carried this sensibility into his literary affairs, and the extreme importance which he attached to things poetic often led him to use a tone in which, according to the judgment of the weak, a feeling of superiority became too evident. I have already mentioned, I believe, that several prejudices which he had to combat, false ideas, commonplace opinions which circulated around him, have for a long time infected the French press. It will not be useless then to give a brief account of some of his most important opinions relative to poetic composition. The parallelism of error will make their application quite easy.

But above all, I must point out that in addition to the share which Poe granted to a natural, innate poetic gift, he gave an importance to knowledge, work, and analysis that will seem excessive to arrogant and unlettered persons. Not only has he expended considerable efforts to subject to his will the fleeting spirit of happy moments, in order to recall at will those exquisite sensations, those spiritual longings, those states of poetic health, so rare and so precious that they could truly be considered as graces exterior to man and as visitations; but also he has subjected inspiration to method, to the most severe analysis. The choice of means! he returns to that constantly, he insists with a learned eloquence upon the adjustment of means to effect, on the use of rhyme, on the perfecting of the refrain, on the adaptation of rhythm to feeling. He maintained that he who cannot seize the intangible is not a poet; that he alone is a poet who is master of his memory, the sovereign of words, the record book of his own feelings always open for examination. Everything for the conclusion! he often repeats. Even a sonnet needs a plan, and the construction, the armature, so to speak, is the most important guarantee of the mysterious life of works of the mind.

I turn naturally to the article entitled "The Poetic Principle," and I find from the very beginning a vigorous protest against what could be called, in the field of poetry, the heresy of length or of dimension—the absurd importance attributed to bulky poems. "I hold that a long poem does not exist. I maintain that the phrase, 'a long poem,' is simply a flat contradiction in terms." [83] In fact, a poem deserves its title only insomuch as it excites and uplifts the soul, and the real merit of a poem is due to this excitation, to this *uplifting* of the soul. But, from psychological necessity, all these excitations are fugitive and transitory. This strange mood into which the soul of the reader has been drawn by force, as it were, will certainly not last as long as the reading of a poem which exceeds human capacity for enthusiasm.

It is obvious then that the epic poem stands condemned. For a work of that length can be considered poetic only insofar as one sacrifices the vital condition of every work of art, Unity; —I do not mean unity in the conception but unity in the impression, the *totality* of effect, as I said when I had occasion to compare the novel with the short story. The epic poem then appears to us, aesthetically speaking, as a paradox. Bygone ages may have produced a series of lyric poems, later compiled into epic poems; but every *epic intention* obviously is the result of an imperfect sense of art. The time for these artistic anomalies has passed, and it is even very doubtful that a long poem has ever been truly popular in the full meaning of the word.

It must be added that a too short poem, one which does not furnish a *pabulum* that will sustain the excitation created, one which is not equal to the natural appetite of the reader, is also very defective. However brilliant and intense the effect may be, it is not lasting; memory does not retain it; it is like a seal which, placed too lightly and too hastily, has not had time to imprint its image on the wax.

But there is another heresy which, thanks to the hypocrisy, to the dullness, and to the baseness of human minds, is even more formidable and has a greater chance of survival—an error which has a hardier life—I wish to speak of the heresy of *teaching a lesson* which includes as inevitable corollaries the heresy of *passion*, of *truth*, and of *morality*. A great many people imagine that the aim of poetry is a lesson of some sort, that it must now fortify the conscience, now perfect morals, now in short *prove* something or other which is useful. Edgar Poe claims that Americans especially have supported this heterodox idea; alas! there is no need to go as far as Boston to encounter the heresy in question. Even here it attacks and breaches true poetry every day. Poetry, if only one is willing to seek within himself, to question his heart, to recall his memories of enthusiasm, has no other goal than itself; it cannot have any other, and no poem will be so great, so noble, so truly worthy of the name of poetry as that which will have been written solely for the pleasure of writing a poem.

I do not mean that poetry does not ennoble manners—let there be no mistake about it—that its final result is not to raise man above the level of vulgar interests; that would obviously be an absurdity. I say that, if the poet has pursued a moral aim, he has diminished his poetic force; and it is not rash to wager that his work will be bad. Poetry cannot, under penalty of death or failure, be assimilated to science or morality; it does not have Truth as its object, it has only Itself. The means for demonstrating truth are other and are elsewhere. Truth has nothing to do with songs. All that constitutes the grace, the charm, the irresistible attraction of a song, would take from Truth its authority and its power. Cold, calm, impassive, the demonstrative mood rejects the diamonds and the flowers of the Muse; it is then absolutely the inverse of the poetic mood.

Pure Intellect aims at Truth, Taste reveals Beauty, and Moral Sense teaches us what is Right. It is true that taste is intimately connected with the other two, and is separated from Moral Sense only by so slight a difference that Aristotle has not hesitated to include among the virtues some of its delicate operations. Thus, what especially exasperates the man of taste in the spectacle of vice is its deformity, its disproportion. Vice injures the just and the true, revolts the intellect and the conscience; but, as an outrage to harmony, as dissonance, it will wound more particularly certain poetic minds; and I do not think it scandalous to consider every offense against morality, against moral beauty, as a kind of offense against universal rhythm and prosody.

It is that admirable, that immortal instinct for the beautiful which makes us consider the earth and its spectacles as a revelation, as something in correspondence with Heaven. The insatiable thirst for everything that lies beyond, and that life reveals, is the most living proof of our immortality.

It is at the same time by poetry and *through* poetry, by and *through* music that the soul glimpses the splendors beyond the tomb; and when an exquisite poem brings us to the verge of tears, those tears are not the proof of excessive pleasure; they are rather evidence of an aroused melancholy, of a condition of nerves, of a nature which has been exiled amid the imperfect and which would like to take possession immediately, on this very earth, of a revealed paradise.

Thus, the principle of poetry is precisely and simply human

aspiration toward a superior beauty, and the manifestation of this principle is in an enthusiasm, an excitation of the soul—an enthusism altogether independent of passion which is the intoxication of the heart, and of truth which is the food of reason. For passion is *natural*, too natural not to introduce an offensive, discordant tone into the domain of pure beauty, too familiar and too violent not to scandalize the pure Desires, the gracious Melancholies and the noble Despairs which inhabit the supernatural regions of poetry.

This extraordinary elevation, this exquisite delicacy, this accent of immortality which Edgar Poe demands of the Muse, far from making him less attentive to the technique of execution, have impelled him constantly to sharpen his genius as a technician. Many people, especially those who have read the strange poem called *The Raven*, would be shocked if I analyzed the article in which our poet, apparently innocently, but with a slight impertinence which I cannot condemn, has explained in detail the method of construction which he used, the adaptation of the rhythm, the choice of a refrain—the shortest possible and the most suitable to a variety of applications, and at the same time the most representative of melancholy and despair, embellished with the most sonorous rhyme of all (nevermore)—the choice of a bird capable of imitating the human voice, but a bird—the raven—branded with a baneful and fatal character in popular imagination—the choice of the most poetic of all tones, the melancholy tone—of the most poetic sentiment, love for one dead, etc.—"And I shall not place the hero of my poem in poor surroundings," he says, "because poverty is commonplace and contrary to the idea of Beauty. His melancholy will be sheltered by a magnificently and poetically furnished room." [84] The reader will detect in several of Poe's short stories curious symptoms of this inordinate taste for beautiful forms, especially for beautiful forms that are strange, for ornate surroundings and oriental sumptuousness.

I said that this article seemed marred by a slight impertinence. Confirmed advocates of inspiration would be sure to find in it blasphemy and profanation; but I believe that it is for them especially that the article has been written. Just as certain writers feign carelessness, aiming at a masterpiece with their eyes closed, full of confidence in disorder, expecting that words thrown at the ceiling will fall back on the floor in the form of a poem, so Edgar Poe—one of the most inspired men I know—has made a pretense of hiding spontaneity, of simulating coolness and deliberation. "It will not be regarded as a breach of decorum on my part"—he says with an amusing pride which I do not consider in bad taste—"to show that no one point in its composition is referable either to accident or intuition—that the work proceeded, step by step, to its completion with the precision and rigid consequence of a mathematical problem." Only lovers of chance, I say, only fatalists of inspiration and fanatics of *free verse* can find this *attention to detail* odd. There are no insignificant details in matters of art.

As for free verse, I shall add that Poe attached an extreme importance to rhyme, and that in the analysis which he has made of the mathematical and musical pleasure which the mind derives from rhyme, he has introduced as much care, as much subtlety as in all the other subjects pertaining to the art of poetry. Just as he has shown that the refrain is capable of infinitely varied applications, so also he has sought to renew, to redouble the pleasure derived from rhyme by adding to it an unexpected element, the strange, which is the indispensable condiment, as it were, of all beauty. He often makes a happy use of repetitions of the same line or of several lines, insistent reiterations of phrases which simulate the obsessions of melancholy or of a fixed idea—of a pure and simple refrain introduced in several different ways—of a variant refrain which feigns carelessness and inadvertence—of rhymes redoubled and tripled and also of a kind of rhyme which introduces into modern poetry, but with more precision and purpose, the surprises of Leonine verse.[85]

It is obvious that the value of all these means can be proved only through application; and a translation of poetry so studied, so concentrated, can be a fond dream, but only a dream. Poe wrote little poetry; he has sometimes expressed regret at not being able to devote himself, not more often, but exclusively, to this type of work which he considered the most noble. But his poetry always creates a powerful effect. It is not the ardent outpouring of Byron, it is not the soft, harmonious, distinguished melancholy of Tennyson for whom, it may be said in passing, he had an almost fraternal admiration. It is something profound and shimmering like a dream, mysterious and perfect like crystal. I do not need to add, I presume, that American critics have often disparaged his poetry; very recently I found in a dictionary of American biography an article in which it was adjudged esoteric, in which it was feared that this muse in learned garb might create a school in the proud country of utilitarian morality, and in which regret was expressed that Poe had not applied his talents to the expression of moral truths in place of spending them in quest of a bizarre ideal, of lavishing in his verses a mysterious, but sensual voluptuousness.

We are all familiar with that kind of sharp riposte. The reproaches that bad critics heap upon good poets are the same in all countries. In reading this article it seemed to me that I was reading the translation of one of those numerous indictments brought by Parisian critics against those of our poets who are most fond of perfection. Our favorites are easy to guess and every lover of pure poetry will understand me when I say that in the eyes of our antipoetic race Victor Hugo would be less admired if he were perfect, and he has succeeded in having all his lyric genius forgiven only by introducing forcibly and brutally into his poetry what Edgar Poe considered the major modern heresy—*the teaching of a lesson.*

MADAME BOVARY
BY GUSTAVE FLAUBERT

PREFACE

On October 18, 1857, *L'Artiste* published Baudelaire's belated appraisal of *Madame Bovary*. Although the review, as Baudelaire admits, is not so much an attempt to evaluate the novel as to emphasize points that had been neglected or overlooked, it shows remarkable penetration and understanding and anticipates much of the criticism that has appeared since that day.

Recently Robert Kanters has suggested that in his analysis of *Madame Bovary* Baudelaire was following the pattern of rational explication that Poe had used in his article on "The Philosophy of Composition," which purported to "explain" the genesis of *The Raven*.[86] It is an ingenious but not altogether convincing hypothesis. Be that as it may, Flaubert himself was delighted with the review and wrote to the poet: "Your article gave me the *greatest* pleasure. You entered into the arcana of the work as if my brain were yours. It is *deeply* understood and felt. If you find my book suggestive, I can only say that what you have written is no less so." [87]

Margaret Gilman has argued that Flaubert's well known remark, "I am Madame Bovary," may have been made after the novelist had read Baudelaire's article and realized that he had indeed put much of himself into the character of Emma, as the critic had alleged.[88] It is true that while writing the novel Flaubert had insisted that it was completely objective; but it is also true that as late as July, 1852, he had written to Louise Colet: "Passion does not make poetry, and the more personal you are, the weaker you are. I myself have always made that same mistake, because I have always put myself into what I was doing." [89]

Flaubert's enthusiastic response to Baudelaire's review suggests that the poet had judged correctly and that Madame

Bovary was in many respects Flaubert himself. In fact both author and critic must have recognized many of their own traits in the unhappy Emma. Certainly both had known the same dissatisfaction with life and, like her, had often wondered why "everything on which [they] leaned crumbled into rottenness and decay."

It comes as no surprise that Baudelaire was impressed by the fact that Flaubert, unlike most Realists, had succeeded in transforming ugliness into beauty. By softening what was "repugnant and grotesque" with the "opaline nightlight" of poetry, he had succeeded in proving—as had Baudelaire himself—that "all subjects are equally good or bad . . . and that the most commonplace can become the best."

Baudelaire was likewise impressed by Flaubert's refusal to incorporate a moral indictment in his novel. Perhaps nowhere has he better stated his view on the relationship of art and morality: "A true work of art need not contain an indictment. The logic of the work satisfies all the claims of morality, and it is for the reader to draw his conclusions from the conclusion."

That Baudelaire considered Emma to be endowed with what he calls virile virtues—imagination, energy, dandyism, love of domination—may seem somewhat surprising to the reader; yet it is entirely consistent with his belief that woman in general is a "pure animal," devoid of these very characteristics. In various notations in his *Journaux Intimes* he maintains that women are unable to "distinguish between body and soul," since they are guided by instinct or, as he says euphemistically in his review, by "what is called the heart." Woman, he insists, is the contrary of the dandy who, through the discipline of self-purification, can free himself from the natural life of the flesh and turn himself into a work of art.

Baudelaire's belief that imagination is a strictly virile quality is doubtful, to say the least. Yet he was eminently right in noting that Emma was guided not so much by sexual instinct or physical desire as by the "sophisms of her imagination." Motivated by the power of her imagination, she was led to pursue what she naïvely believed to be the ideal.

Baudelaire showed himself equally perceptive in realizing that the famous episode of the operation on the clubfoot and that of Emma's interview with the inept priest were not extraneous, as they had been termed by contemporary critics, but that they served to motivate her actions and to make her more to be pitied than condemned.

Madame Bovary was the only novel of Flaubert that Baudelaire discussed formally. Five years later, after the publication of *Salammbô* (1862), he incisively characterized the somewhat grandiose archaeological novel in a letter to his friend and publisher, Poulet-Malassis:

A beautiful book, full of faults, and one which infuriates all the pests, particularly Babou. *There are those who reproach Flaubert for imitating ancient writers.* What Flaubert has done, he alone was able to do. Entirely too much bric-a-brac, but many splendors, epic, historic, political, even animal. Something astonishing in the gesticulation of all the living beings.[90]

I

In matters of criticism, the position of the laggard writer who follows everyone else permits certain advantages not enjoyed by the prophetic critic who heralds success, who commands it, so to speak, by the authority of bold judgment and disinterested recognition.

M. Gustave Flaubert no longer needs recognition, if indeed he ever needed it. Many writers, including some of the most discriminating and highly respected, have praised and celebrated his excellent book. It only remains for criticism to indicate certain neglected points of view and to insist somewhat more strongly on certain features and highlights which to my mind have not received sufficient praise and comment. Moreover, the position of the belated critic outdistanced by other opinions has, as I was trying to suggest, a paradoxical charm. Freer because, as a straggler he is alone, he seems like one who is summing up the arguments and who, obliged to avoid the vehemence of the prosecution and of the defense, has orders to clear a new way for himself, without other incentive than that of love of Beauty and Justice.

II

Since I have uttered that splendid and terrible word, Justice, allow me—for it gives me great pleasure—to express my thanks to the French court for the shining example of impartiality and good taste that it has set in this case.[91] Incited by a blind and overly violent zeal for morality, by a spirit that mistook its ground, confronted by a novel—and what a novel!—the most impartial, the most honest of novels, the work of a writer unknown until then—by a theme, trite like all themes, lashed and drenched, like nature itself, by every wind and every storm—the court, I repeat, has shown itself as honest and objective as the book which was thrust before it like a burnt offering. And what is even better—if I may be allowed to conjecture from the reasons supporting the judgment—I feel sure that had the judges found anything very reprehensible in the book, they would have overlooked it in recognition of and in gratitude for the BEAUTY with which it is clothed. This remarkable concern for Beauty on the part of men whose intellectual faculties are requisitioned only for the Just and the True is a most moving symptom, when compared with the burning greed of a society which once and for all has abjured all spiritual love and which, disregarding its *former humanity*, heeds only its physical well-being. In short, it may be said that this judgment, through its marked poetic implications, is definitive; that the Muse has been vindicated; and that all writers, at least all those worthy of the name, have been acquitted in the person of M. Gustave Flaubert.

Let us not say then that the book owes its enormous vogue to the lawsuit and the acquittal, as so many others maintain with a touch of unconscious ill-humor. Had the book not been attacked, it would have aroused the same interest, it would have created the same astonishment, the same excitement. For a long time moreover, it had been receiving the acclaim of all men of letters. It had already excited keen interest when it first appeared in the *Revue de Paris*, where indiscreet excisions had destroyed its harmony. The position of Gustave Flaubert, so suddenly made famous, was at once excellent and bad; and I am going to try to give as best I can, the various reasons for the equivocal situation over which his honest and marvelous talent has been able to triumph.

III

Excellent;—for since the disappearance from the scene of Balzac—that prodigious meteor who will cover our country with a cloud of glory, like a strange and extraordinary Eastern sky, like a polar dawn inundating the icy wastes with its magic lights —all interest in the novel had subsided and become dormant. Some striking experiments had been made, it must be admitted. There was M. de Custine, already long famous in an increasingly rarefied society for his *Aloys, Le Monde comme il est,* and *Ethel.*[92] The creator of the plain young girl, that type so envied by Balzac (note *Mercadet*), M. de Custine had published *Romuald ou la Vocation,* a sublimely awkward work in which inimitable pages make one both condemn and excuse its dull and tedious passages. But M. de Custine is a subspecies of genius, a genius whose dandyism rises even to the ideal of negligence. That gentlemanly sincerity, that romantic fervor, that honest raillery, that autocratic and indifferent personality do not appeal to the mob, and this mannered writer had against him all the bad luck that his talent deserved.

M. d'Aurevilly had created a sensation with *Une Vieille*

Maîtresse and *L'Ensorcelée*. This cult of truth, expressed with a frightful intensity, could only displease the crowd. D'Aurevilly, a sincere Catholic, evoking passion in order to conquer it, singing, weeping, and crying out in the midst of the storm, planted defiantly, like Ajax, on a desolate rock, and always seeming to say to his rival—whether man, thunderbolt, god, or matter—: "Destroy me, or I will destroy you!"—was unable to arouse the interest of a dormant species whose eyes are closed to the miracles of the exceptional.

Champfleury, with a charming, youthful spirit, had played very effectively with the picturesque, had trained poetic binoculars (more poetic than he himself believes) at the comic and pathetic mishaps and adventures that occur in the home or in the street; but, whether through originality or through oversight, purposely or unavoidably, he neglected the commonplace, the meeting place of the crowd, the public rendezvous of eloquence.

Still more recently, M. Charles Barbara, a rigorous and logical thinker, eager for intellectual honors, has made some indisputably distinguished efforts; he has attempted to describe, to analyze, exceptional states of mind (an always irresistible temptation) and to deduce the direct consequences of false positions.[93] If I do not express here all the admiration inspired in me by the author of *Héloise* and *L'Assassinat du Pont-Rouge*, it is because he fits into my theme only incidentally as a part of the historical record.

At the opposite pole, Paul Féval, extremely fond of adventure and with a strong gift for the grotesque and the terrible, has followed, like a belated hero, in the footsteps of Frédéric Soulié and Eugène Sue.[94] But the abundant talent of the author of the *Mystères de Londres* and of *Le Bossu* has not succeeded, any more than that of so many outstanding minds, in accomplishing the unexpected and deftly wrought miracle of the poor little provincial adulteress whose whole uncomplicated story is composed of sorrows, disgusts, sighs, and moments of feverish rapture torn from a life cut off by suicide.

I find nothing either to praise or blame in the fact that these writers, some leaning toward Dickens, others modeling themselves after Byron or Bulwer Lytton, too highly gifted perhaps, too contemptuous, have not been able to force their way, like an artless Paul de Kock, over the rickety threshold of Popularity, the only hussy that asks to be violated.[95] At the same time, I am not at all displeased by the fact that M. Gustave Flaubert has accomplished with his first attempt what others seek all their lives. At best, I shall see in it a supererogatory indication of power and I shall attempt to define the reasons which made the author's mind move in one direction rather than in another.

But I have also said that the position of the tardy critic was bad—alas, for a woefully simple reason! For many years the public's interest in spiritual matters had been strangely declining; its fund of enthusiasm had kept steadily shrinking. The last years of Louis-Philippe had witnessed the final explosions of a spirit that could still be stimulated by the play of the imagination; but the new novelist found himself confronting a society that was completely jaded—worse than jaded—degraded and greedy, abhorring only the imaginary and caring only for material possessions.

In such an environment a well nurtured mind, enraptured with the beautiful, but inclined to vigorous fencing, weighing the favorable and unfavorable side of the case, must have said to itself: "What is the surest way of stirring these sluggish old hearts? They don't really know what they like; they have a definite dislike only for what is great; naïve, ardent passion, poetic abandon embarrass and offend them. Let us choose a commonplace subject, since the choice of too lofty a subject is considered presumptuous by the nineteenth century reader. And let us also be careful not to give ourselves away or to speak for ourselves. We shall be as cold as ice in describing those passions and adventures which most people treat with deep feeling; we shall be objective and impersonal, as the [Realistic] school recommends.

"And also, since our ears have been plagued of late with the childish prating of this new school, since we have heard about a certain literary method called *realism*—a repulsive insult flung in the face of every analyst, a vague and elastic word which for the ordinary man signifies not a new means of creation, but a minute description of trivial details—we shall take advantage of the confusion of minds and of general ignorance. We shall cover a commonplace canvas in a style that is vigorous, picturesque, subtle, and exact. We shall introduce the most ardent and the most heated emotions into the most trite love affair. The most solemn, the most decisive words will fall from the most stupid mouths.

"Where is the most stupidity to be found, what milieu is the most stultifying, the richest in absurdities, the most infested with intolerant fools?

"The provinces.

"Who are the most insufferable people there?

"Insignificant persons whose ideas are warped by the petty functions they perform.

"What subject is the most hackneyed, the most prostituted, the most like the hurdy-gurdy's stalest tune?

"Adultery.

"I have no need to make my *heroine* a heroine. If she is sufficiently pretty, has fits of nerves, ambition, and an irrepressible aspiration toward a superior world, she will be interesting. Moreover, the tour de force will be all the more noble, and our sinner will at least have the merit—comparatively quite rare—of being different from the ostentatious chatterboxes of the preceding epoch.

"I have no need to concern myself with style, picturesque arrangement, or with the description of places; these are all things that I can do supremely well; I shall proceed on the basis of analysis and logic, and I shall thus prove that all subjects are equally good or bad, according to the manner in which they are treated, and that the most commonplace can become the best."

And so *Madame Bovary*—a wager, a real wager, a bet, like all works of art—was created.

To accomplish the tour de force in its entirety the author

had only to divest himself (as much as possible) of his sex and to become a woman. The result is a marvel; in spite of all his zeal as an actor, he could not keep from infusing a virile blood into the veins of his creation, and Madame Bovary, in what is most forceful, most ambitious, and also most contemplative in her nature, has remained a man. Just as Pallas Athena sprang full armed from the head of Zeus, so this strange androgynous creature has kept all the attraction of a virile soul in a charming feminine body.

IV

Several critics had said: "this work, truly beautiful in the detail and liveliness of its descriptions, does not contain a single character who represents morality, who expresses the author's inmost thought. Where is the proverbial and legendary character charged with explaining the story and with guiding the reader's understanding? In other words, where is the indictment?"

What nonsense! Eternal and incorrigible confusion of functions and genres! A true work of art need not contain an indictment. The logic of the work satisfies all the claims of morality, and it is for the reader to draw his conclusions from the conclusion.

The adulteress is unquestionably the profound and intimate character of the story; she alone, the dishonored victim, possesses all the graces of the hero.—A moment ago I said that she was almost male, and that the author had endowed her (unconsciously perhaps) with all the virtues of a man.

Let us examine them carefully:

1. Imagination, that supreme and despotic faculty, replacing the heart, or what is called the heart, from which reasoning is usually excluded and which generally dominates in a woman, as it does in an animal;

2. Sudden energetic action, quickness of decision, mystical fusion of reason and passion which characterize men created to act;

3. Excessive taste for seduction, for domination, and even for the most vulgar means of seduction, descending to affectation of dress, perfume, and cosmetics—all of it summed up in two words: dandyism and exclusive love of domination.

And yet, Madame Bovary does give herself; carried away by the sophisms of her imagination, she gives herself magnificently, generously, in an altogether masculine way, to contemptible men who are not her equals, just as poets surrender to contemptible women.

Another proof of the altogether virile quality that flows in her veins is the fact that this ill-fated woman cares less about the visible, external imperfections and the glaring provincialisms of her husband than about that total lack of genius, that spiritual inferiority so clearly demonstrated by the stupid operation on the clubfoot.

And in this connection re-read the pages containing this episode which, though unjustly termed extraneous, really brings the whole character of the person into sharp focus.—A black anger, long repressed, breaks loose in Emma's whole being; doors slam; the astonished husband, who has been unable to give his romantic wife any spiritual enjoyment, is relegated to his room; the ignorant culprit is in disgrace, and Madame Bovary in despair cries out like a lesser Lady Macbeth mated with an incompetent master: "Ah! why couldn't I *at least* be the wife of one of those bald and stooped old scientists whose eyes, shielded by green eyeshades, are always fixed on scientific documents! I could lean on his arm with pride; at least I would be the companion of an intellectual king; but to be chained to this idiot who can't even straighten the foot of a cripple! Oh!"

Truly this woman is very sublime in her way, given her limited environment and the small horizon by which she was bound.

4. Even in her convent education I find proof of Madame Bovary's equivocal temperament.

The good sisters noticed in this young girl an astonishing capacity for life, for getting the best out of life, for suspecting its pleasures; there you have the man of action!

Meanwhile the young girl reveled in the color of the stained glass, in the oriental hues which the tall, elaborately designed windows cast on her convent school prayerbook; she gorged herself on the solemn vesper music and, by a paradox which may be credited to nerves, she replaced the real God in her heart by the God of her imagination, the God of the future and of chance, a picture-book God with spurs and a mustache; and there you have the hysterical poet!

Hysteria! Why couldn't this physiological mystery be made the sum and substance of a literary work—this mystery which the Academy of Medicine has not yet solved and which, manifesting itself in women by the sensation of a lump in the throat that seems to rise (I am mentioning only the chief symptom), shows itself in excitable men by every kind of impotence as well as by a tendency toward every kind of excess?

V

In short, this woman is truly great and above all pitiable. Despite the systematic severity of the author, who has made every effort to remain outside of his book and to assume the role of a manipulator of marionettes, all *intellectual* women will be grateful to him for having raised the female to so high a level —so far from the pure animal and so near to the ideal man— and for having made her share in that combination of calculation and reverie which constitutes the perfect being.

It is said that Madame Bovary is ridiculous. It is true that at one moment she mistakes for a Walter Scott hero a silly gentleman—shall I say a country gentleman?—wearing hunting jackets and flashy suits, and that at still another moment she is in love with a junior clerk in a lawyer's office (who isn't even clever enough to commit a dangerous action for his mistress), and that finally the poor spent creature, a strange Pasiphaë, isolated within the narrow enclosure of a village, pursues the ideal in the low dance halls and the taverns of the prefecture. Yet, what does it matter? We may as well admit it frankly—she is like Caesar at Carpentras, she is seeking the Ideal!

I shall certainly not say, like the Lycanthrope of revolutionary fame [Pétrus Borel]—that rebel who abdicated: "In the face of all the platitudes and stupidities of the present day, don't we still have cigarette paper and adultery?" But I shall maintain that after all, everything considered, even with the most accurate scales, our world is very cruel for having been begotten by Christ, that it is hardly entitled to cast a stone at adultery; and that a few Minotaurized persons more or less will not hasten the rotating speed of the spheres or advance by one second the final destruction of the universe. It is time to put an end to an increasingly contagious hypocrisy and to consider it ridiculous for men and women, deeply corrupted as they are, to denounce an unfortunate author who in modest and reserved language has deigned to cast an aureole over bedroom adventures, always repulsive and grotesque when Poetry does not soften them with the gleam of its opaline nightlight.

If I allowed myself to go on in this analytical vein, I should never have done with *Madame Bovary*; this essentially suggestive book could inspire a volume of observations. For the time being I shall confine myself to pointing out that several of the most important episodes were originally either ignored or abusively attacked by the critics. Examples: the episode of the unsuccessful operation on the clubfoot, and the one, so remarkable, so full of desolation, so truly *modern*, where the future adulteress —for the unhappy woman is still only at the beginning of the downward path!—goes to ask help of the Church, of the divine Mother, of Her who has no excuse for not being always ready, of that Pharmacy where no one has the right to slumber! The good priest Bournisien, concerned only with the scamps in his catechism class, jumping around among the choir stalls and chairs of the church, answers in all innocence: "Since you are ill, Madame, and since M. Bovary is a doctor, *why don't you go and find your husband?*"

What woman confronted by the inadequacy of the priest wouldn't go, like someone released from a madhouse, to plunge her head into the whirling waters of adultery—and who among us in troubled circumstances and at a more unsophisticated age has not inevitably come to know the incompetent priest?

VI

Having at hand two books by the same author (*Madame Bovary* and *La Tentation de Saint Antoine* whose installments have not yet been brought together in book form), I had originally planned to work out a sort of parallel between the two.[96] I wished to establish some equations and correspondences. Under the finely detailed fabric of *Madame Bovary* it would have been easy to find the high qualities of *irony* and *lyricism* which brilliantly illuminate *La Tentation de Saint Antoine*. Here the poet had not disguised himself, and its *Bovary*, tempted by all the demons of illusion and of heresy, by all the lusts of the material world—Saint Anthony in other words, tortured by all the follies which beset us—would have represented him better than his little bourgeois fiction. In this work of which the author has published only extracts, there are some dazzling passages; I am referring not merely to the stupendous feast of Nebuchadnezzar, to the miraculous appearance of the mad little queen of Sheba, a miniature dancing on the retina of the hermit, of the theatrical and turgid scene of Apollonius of Tyana followed by his elephant-driver or rather by his keeper, the idiotic millionaire whom he drags along throughout the world;—I should especially like to call the reader's attention to the sense of suffering, submerged and rebellious, which runs through the whole work, the luminous dark vein—what the English call a *subcurrent*—that serves as a guide through this demon-haunted solitary wilderness.

It would have been easy for me to show, as I have already said, that in *Madame Bovary* M. Gustave Flaubert has deliberately veiled the high lyric and ironic powers revealed without any reserve in *La Tentation,* and that the latter work, which is the secret chamber of his mind, is obviously the more interesting to poets and philosophers.

Perhaps I shall have the pleasure of carrying out this task at some other time.

✺ THÉOPHILE GAUTIER

PREFACE

On March 13, 1859, a rather long-winded and excessively deferential article on Gautier appeared in *L'Artiste.* With a few changes and introduced by a letter which Baudelaire had solicited from Victor Hugo, it was issued as a brochure in November of the same year.

In certain respects the article is disappointing, partly because it lacks the provocative ideas which Baudelaire so often introduced into his essays, partly because it gives heroic stature to a relatively unimportant figure who is chiefly remembered today for having bridged the gap between the Romantic and Parnassian movements and for having introduced into literature the doctrine of Art for Art's Sake.

The sincerity of the praise which Baudelaire lavished on his friend and fellow author has often been questioned, though to the literary public of the day, familiar with Gautier's poetry, short stories, art criticism, and travel books, the praise must have seemed less exaggerated. It is true that the amount of padding suggests that Baudelaire may have been lacking in inspiration. The essay contains two long direct quotations from "New Notes on Edgar Poe," a passage very similar to one used in "The Respectable Drama and Novel," another passage almost identical with one in the *Salon of 1859,* a long digression on the non-artistic nature of the French people, and a penetrating and spontaneous eulogy of Balzac which contrasts with the more studied praise of Gautier. It is also true that Baudelaire's praise of Gautier's art criticism is at variance with the sharply critical attitude he had shown in earlier articles, such as "How a Genius Pays his Debts." Above all, Baudelaire's admission to Victor Hugo that he was "aware of the lacunae in his [Gautier's] astonishing mind" and that he had "dissimulated rather than lied" seems to indicate a rather qualified enthusiasm.[97] His comment may have been prompted in part by his desire to win Hugo's favor and to obtain a letter-preface for his brochure. Yet regardless of the intent, there is no reason to believe that it implies a denial of Gautier's greatness. It may be taken as merely an indication of certain reservations on the part of the critic.

On the other hand, there are many reasons to believe that Baudelaire was completely sincere in his praise. Throughout his entire correspondence he speaks of Gautier only in the most flattering terms. Two of his letters in particular show the extent of his admiration. Writing to his mother in 1857 he expressed the certainty that his own poetry would take its place beside the best poems of Victor Hugo, Théophile Gautier and of Byron, and in his well-known letter of 1866 to Ancelle he included the name of Gautier among those whom he considered the truly great of his time.[98] It is also significant that Baudelaire chose Gautier as the subject of one of the five lectures that he delivered in Brussels.

Baudelaire's admiration for Gautier, moreover, dated back to his youth and was shared by the young poets of his generation. An unpublished poem of Théodore de Banville, one of Baudelaire's closest friends, tells how he and his comrades preferred Gautier to "all others skilled in the art of writing verse." [99] Fifteen years later in the preface to *The Duality of Life*, which had been inspired and corrected by Baudelaire (Crépet describes it as a veritable Baudelairean manifesto), Asselineau called Gautier "the most detached as well as the greatest of the contemporary poets."

Nor was it strange that Baudelaire should have felt profound admiration for the perfection of style and technique and for the harmony of thought and word that characterize the disciplined art of Gautier. In the dedication of *Les Fleurs du Mal* (1857) he had described Gautier as "an impeccable poet, a perfect magician." In his essay of 1859 he is still dazzled by the "evocative magic" of Gautier's masterly handling of words.

Gautier's insistence on the autonomy of art, his belief that "as soon as a thing becomes useful, it ceases to be beautiful" also struck a responsive chord in the younger poet. It is interesting to note that in quoting the passage on utilitarian art from his Poe essay of 1857 Baudelaire retained the statement that the passions are incompatible with the spirituality of pure beauty. In 1857 he had made the claim under the spell of Poe only to go back to his own contrary belief a short time later. In his essay on Gautier the statement remains intact, perhaps because it so well suited the poetry that he was trying to describe.

It is to be expected that Baudelaire would be appreciative of Gautier's use of melancholy, dominated as it was by his obsession with death and even, as in *Albertus*, by his concern with moral evil. Somewhat more surprising is the fact that he saw in Gautier a decipherer and translator of divine hieroglyphics, who showed an "immense innate understanding of universal correspondences and symbols." However, Gautier was not entirely lacking in mystical qualities as becomes evident from his assertion that "spirit is everything, matter exists only in appearance; the universe is perhaps only God's dream or an irradiation of the Word in the vastness of the cosmos." [100]

On the whole Baudelaire's analysis of Gautier is penetrating and sound, although his criticism is generally less interesting than that in many of his other essays. For the reader of today its chief fault lies in the critic's overestimation of Gautier's short stories and art criticism and in his claim that the poet's use of octosyllabic verse had all the majesty of the alexandrine. After all, Gautier himself had maintained in his *Histoire du*

Romantisme, that the alexandrine was "too vast for these modest ambitions."

In the letter-preface to Baudelaire's brochure Hugo thanks the author of *Les Fleurs du Mal* for dedicating to him two new poems, "Les Sept Vieillards" and "Les Petites Vieilles," and succinctly characterizes a particular quality of his verse in the justly famous remark: "You have endowed the sky of art with an indescribable macabre gleam. You have created a new shudder (nouveau frisson)." [101]

⚘⚘⚘

Although we have not given a drink to an old woman, we are in the same position as Perrault's young girl; we cannot open our mouth for a moment without having gold coins, diamonds, rubies, and pearls fall from it; from time to time we would like very much to vomit a toad, a snake, and a red mouse, were it only for a change; but that is not in our power.

Théophile Gautier.—Caprices et Zigzags.

I

I don't know any sentiment more embarrassing than admiration. It resembles love in that it makes one unable to express himself suitably. Where can one find expressions that are strongly enough colored or shadings that are sufficiently delicate to answer the needs of an exquisite sentiment? *Human respect is a scourge in every order of things* according to a book of philosophy which I happen to have at hand; but let no one think that mere human respect is the cause of my embarrassment; my perplexity stems entirely from a fear of not speaking about my subject in a sufficiently exalted manner.

There are biographies that are easy to write—those, for

example, of men whose lives abound in excitement and adventures; in such cases we would merely need to record and to classify the facts and their dates; but in this case there is none of that material diversity that reduces the task of the writer to that of a compiler. Nothing but spiritual greatness. The biography of a man whose most dramatic adventures are played silently inside the bony structure of his skull is a literary work of an altogether different order. As certain heavenly bodies are born with certain functions, so it is with man. Each performs his predestined role magnificently and humbly. Who could imagine a biography of the sun? It is a story which, ever since that planet first gave signs of life, has been filled with monotony, light, and grandeur.

Since, in short, I need only write the story of a *fixed idea* which, moreover, I shall be able to define and analyze, it would matter little, strictly speaking, whether or not I informed my readers that Théophile Gautier was born in Tarbes in 1811. I have had the good fortune of being his friend for many years and I have absolutely no idea whether he revealed his future talents in early childhood through success in school, by winning childish prizes which *sublime children* often cannot win and which, in any event, they are obliged to share with a horde of frightful numskulls singled out by fate. Of these trifles I know absolutely nothing. Théophile Gautier himself may no longer know anything about them, and if by chance he does remember them, I am very sure he would not care to see all this schoolboy rubbish raked up. There is no man who possesses to a greater degree the proud modesty of the true man of letters or who has a greater dread of displaying for the edification of souls enamored of the Beautiful anything that has not been designed, prepared, and perfected for the public. Never expect him to write *memoirs*, or *confessions*, or *recollections*, or anything that does not have a lofty function.

There is one consideration that adds to the happiness I feel in giving an account of a *fixed idea*, and that is to be able finally to speak with as much freedom as I wish about an *unknown* man. All those who have contemplated cases of mistakes or of belated justice on the part of history will understand what the word *unknown* means when applied to Théophile Gautier. It is true that for many years he has made a great stir in Paris and the provinces with his literary articles; it is indisputable that many a reader, interested in everything literary, impatiently awaits his opinion on the plays of the previous week; it is even more indisputable that his reviews of the *Salons,* so dispassionate, so frank and so elevated, are oracles for all the exiles who cannot judge and perceive with their own eyes. For all these various publics, Théophile Gautier is an incomparable and indispensable critic; and yet he remains an *unknown man.* Let me explain my thought.

Imagine yourself *interned* in a *bourgeois* salon having after-dinner coffee with the *man* of the house, the *lady* of the house, and their *young ladies.* Abominable and ludicrous slang which the pen should certainly avoid, just as the writer should forego such irritating company! Before long you will talk about music, perhaps about painting, but most assuredly about literature. Théophile Gautier will eventually come up for discussion. After listening to the banal compliments that will be paid him ("How witty he is, how amusing, how well he writes, and what a *flowing style* he has!"—the prize for a *flowing style* is indiscriminately awarded to every known writer, probably because clear water is the clearest symbol of beauty for people who do not make a profession of thinking), if you presume to point out that they are omitting his chief merit, his incontestable and most striking virtue, that they are forgetting, in other words, that he is a great poet, you will see complete astonishment registered on every face. "To be sure, he has a very poetic style," the shrewdest one in the group will answer, not realizing that it is a question of rhythm and rhymes. All these people have read the Monday articles, but no one in all these years has found either money or time for *Albertus, La Comédie de la Mort,* and *Espagna.* This is very hard for a Frenchman to admit, and if I were not speaking of a writer eminent enough to view all these injustices dispassionately, I think I would have preferred to hide this failing on the part of our public. But that is the way things are. Editions, nevertheless, have multiplied and sold very well. Where did they go? In what closets have these wonderful examples of the purest French Beauty been hidden? I don't know; doubtless in some mysterious region located very far from the quarters of Saint-Germain or of the Chaussée-d'Antin, to speak in the geographical terms used by journalists. I well know that there is no man of letters, no slightly reflective artist, whose memory is not well stocked and embellished with these marvels; but society people, those who are enraptured, or who pretend to be enraptured, with the *Méditations* and the *Harmonies*, are unaware of this new treasure of pleasure and beauty.[102]

I have said that all this was a very painful admission for a French heart; but it is not enough to state a fact, it is necessary to try to explain it. It is true that Lamartine and Victor Hugo have enjoyed for a longer time the favor of a public that was more interested in the activities of the Muse than the public that was already growing torpid when Théophile Gautier finally achieved fame. From that day on, the public has gradually decreased the amount of time that rightfully should be devoted to the pleasures of the mind. But this would be only an inadequate explanation, for—putting aside the poet who is the subject of this study—I observe that the public has carefully gleaned from the works of our poets only those parts which were *made famous* (or besmirched) by some political vignette, a condiment suitable to the nature of its present passions. It has discovered the "Ode à la Colonne," the "Ode à l'Arc de Triomphe," but it does not know the mysterious, the tenebrous, the most charming parts of Victor Hugo. It has often recited Auguste Barbier's *Iambes* on the July Days, but it has not joined the author in pouring out his *Pianto* on a devastated Italy, and it has not followed him on his trip to the *Lazare* of the North.

Now the condiment that Théophile Gautier puts into his works, which for art lovers is exquisitely chosen and intensely pungent, has little or no effect on the palate of the common herd. To be completely popular, must not one consent to deserve popularity, or in other words, isn't it necessary to show oneself a little vulgar in some small secret way, by some little blemish that is scarcely noticeable? In literature, as in morality, there is danger as well as glory in being fastidious. Aristocracy isolates us.

I shall confess quite frankly that I am not among those who see any great harm in this and that I have perhaps shown too much rancor in my treatment of the poor *Philistines*. To recriminate, to protest, and even to demand justice—isn't that being something of a *Philistine* oneself? One constantly forgets that to abuse the rabble is to degrade oneself. Seen from a superior vantage point, every destiny appears to us just. Let us therefore do the contrary and acclaim, with all the respect and enthusiasm that it deserves, this aristocracy which creates a solitude around itself. We note, moreover, that certain faculties are esteemed to a greater or lesser degree according to the century and that throughout the course of the ages there is room for glorious revenges. One can expect anything from human eccentricity, even justice, although it is true that injustice is infinitely more natural to it. Didn't a political writer say the other day that Théophile Gautier has been *overrated!*

II

I can remember very clearly my first interview with this writer, whom the whole world will envy us, as it envies us Chateaubriand, Victor Hugo, and Balzac. I had gone to his home in order to offer him a small volume of verse on behalf of two absent friends.[103] I found him not as imposing as he is today but already stately, at ease, and courteous in his flowing garments. What struck me first of all about his welcome was the complete lack of that curtness, understandable enough, however, among men accustomed by their position to fear visitors.

To describe that manner I should be inclined to use the word good-natured if it were not so trite; in this case it would apply only if it were seasoned and heightened, according to the Racinian recipe, by a fine adjective such as *Asiatic* or *Oriental* in order to express a kind of nature that is, at one and the same time, simple, dignified, and mellow. As for our conversation (what a solemn matter is a first conversation with a famous man who surpasses you in talent even more than he does in age!), it is just as clearly imprinted on my mind. When he saw me with a volume of poetry in my hand, his noble face lit up with an attractive smile; he held out his hand with a sort of childlike eagerness; for in this man who knows how to express everything and who more than anyone else has the right to be blasé it is interesting to note the ready curiosity and the searching glance that he darts at things outside himself. After quickly leafing through the volume, he pointed out that the poets in question indulged too often in the use of the *free* or unorthodox sonnet, readily breaking the rule of the quadruple rhyme. Next he asked, with a curiously suspicious glance and as if to test me, whether I liked to read dictionaries. He said this, moreover, as he says everything—very quietly and in a tone that someone else would have used in asking whether I preferred travel books to novels. Fortunately I had contracted lexicomania when I was very young, and I saw that my answer won his respect. It happened to be in connection with dictionaries that he added *"that a writer was not a writer if he didn't know how to say everything, if he was at a loss and without the means to give form to an idea,* no matter how strange, how tenuous that idea might be, no matter if it were as unexpected as a stone falling from the moon."* Then we talked about hygiene, about the care that the man of letters owes his body and the sobriety that he is obliged to impose on himself. Although he drew some comparisons, as I remember, from the life of dancers and from race horses to illustrate his point, the way in which he treated his subject (sobriety as proof of the respect owed to art and to the poetic faculties) reminded me of what is said in devotional books about the necessity of respecting our body as the temple of God. We also spoke about the great fatuousness of our century and about its mania for progress. In some of the books which he has published since that time I have found a few of the expressions which served to sum up his opinions; for example, this one: "There are three things that a civilized person will never be able to create: a vase, a weapon, a suit of armor." Needless to say, the question in this case is one of beauty and not of utility.—I spoke enthusiastically about the amazing power that he had shown in the comic and the grotesque, but to this compliment he answered frankly that at heart he detested wit and laughter—that laughter which deforms God's creatures! "It is permissible to be witty occasionally, just as it is permissible for the wise man to go on a spree in order to prove to fools that he can be their equal; but it is not necessary."—Since his mind is a cosmopolitan mirror of beauty in which as a consequence the Middle Ages and the Renaissance are very properly and very magnificently reflected, those who might be astonished at this opinion of his have failed to note that he applied himself very early to the study of the Greeks and the Beauty of antiquity, so much so in fact that he baffled those of his admirers who did not possess the real key to his spiritual nature. On this score one can consult *Mademoiselle de Maupin* where Greek beauty was vigorously defended in the very midst of Romantic exuberance.

All this was said clearly and decisively, but without being dogmatic or pedantic, with a great deal of subtlety, but without being too hypercritical. Listening to this eloquent conversation, so far from our century and its violent gibberish, I couldn't help thinking of the lucidity of the Ancients, of an indefinable Socratic echo carried familiarly on the wing of an Eastern wind. I left, won over by so much nobility and kindness, captivated by that spiritual strength for which physical strength serves as a symbol, so to speak, as if to *glorify* once again the true doctrine and to confirm it by a new argument.

How many years with their variegated plumage have taken

wing and fled toward the greedy sky since that happy day in my youth! And yet even now I cannot think of it without a certain emotion. This is the excellent excuse that I can offer to those who may have found me very bold and something of an *upstart* in speaking so familiarly, at the beginning of this work, of my friendship with a famous man. But be assured that if some of us have been on familiar terms with Gautier, it is because, in allowing it, he seemed to wish it. He takes innocent delight in playing the role of an affectionate and understanding father. That is another feature that he has in common with those worthy and celebrated men of antiquity who loved the society of young people and who carried on serious conversations with them under luxuriant green trees, along river banks, or beneath architecture as noble and simple as their souls.

This portrait, sketched in an intimate fashion, needs the assistance of an engraver. Fortunately, Théophile Gautier has served as a critic of the arts and the theater for various periodicals and has thus become one of the most widely known persons in the Parisian world. Almost everyone knows his long, silky hair, his stately, slow gait, and his glance full of feline revery.

III

No French writer, eager for the glory of his country, can fail to look back without a feeling of pride and regret at that period of fruitful crisis when Romantic literature flourished with so much vigor. Chateaubriand, still a powerful figure but like a sun setting on the horizon, seemed a Mount Athos dispassionately contemplating the movement of the plain. Victor Hugo, Sainte-Beuve, Alfred de Vigny had rejuvenated, or better still, had revived French poetry, dead since Corneille. For André Chénier with his languid Louis XVI classicism was not a sufficiently vigorous symptom of revival, and Alfred de Musset, feminine and without a doctrine, could have lived in any period and would never have been more than a prettily gushing idler.

Alexandre Dumas was producing in rapid succession his stormy dramas where volcanic eruption was treated with the dexterity of a skillful irrigator. What fervor there was among the writers of that time and what interest and eagerness on the part of the public! *O vanished splendors! O suns that have disappeared behind the horizon!* [104]—A second phase occurred in the modern literary movement which gave us Balzac, that is to say the real Balzac, Auguste Barbier, and Théophile Gautier. For we must not forget that, although the latter became widely known as a writer only after the publication of *Mademoiselle de Maupin*, his first volume of poetry, bravely launched in the midst of the revolution, dates from 1830. It was, I believe, only in 1832 that *Albertus* was added to these poems. However live and rich the new literary sap may have been up to that time, it must be admitted that one element had been lacking or at least had shown itself only rarely, as for example in *Notre Dame de Paris* (Victor Hugo being a decided exception, owing to the number and the profusion of his talents). I am referring to laughter and to the feeling for the grotesque. *Les Jeunes-France* soon proved that the school had come full circle.[105] However frivolous this work may appear to some, it contains great merits. In addition to *la beauté du diable*, that is to say its youthful charm and impudence, it includes laughter, and the best kind of laughter. At a time when people were being duped, an author clearly established himself as an ironist and proved that he was not a dupe. A healthy good sense saved him from resorting to pastiches and from the religions that were in vogue. "Une Larme du Diable" continued to show this vein of abundant humor to a more marked degree. *Mademoiselle de Maupin* served to make his position even more clear. Many people have long spoken of this work as appealing to puerile passions, as giving pleasure through its subject rather than through the masterly form which distinguished it. Some people must really be obsessed with passion to imagine it everywhere as they do. It is the nutmeg which they use to season everything they eat. With its marvelous style, its correct and studied beauty, pure and ornate, the book was a veritable sensation. It was so considered by Balzac who from that moment wanted to meet the author. To have not only style, but in addition an individual style, was one of the greatest, if not the greatest, ambitions of the author of *La Peau de Chagrin* and *La Recherche de l'Absolu*. In spite of his ponderous and tangled sentences, Balzac was always one of the most discerning and the most fastidious of connoisseurs. With *Mademoiselle de Maupin* there appeared in literature what may be called Dilettantism, which by its exquisite and superlative character is always the best proof of the faculties indispensable to art. This novel, this tale, this picture, this reverie, developed with the persistence of a painter, this hymn to Beauty, so to speak, had above all the important result of establishing once and for all the exclusive love of the Beautiful, the *Fixed Idea*, as the generating condition of works of art.

The things that I have to say on this subject (and I shall say them very briefly) were very well known in other epochs. Later they became obscured and were finally forgotten. Strange heresies have crept into literary criticism. A kind of dark cloud coming from Geneva, from Boston, or from hell has intercepted the lovely rays of the aesthetic sun. The celebrated doctrine of the indivisibility of the Good, the True, and the Beautiful is an invention of pretentious modern philosophizing (strange contagion, which makes one speak the jargon of folly while defining it)! The various objects of spiritual research require faculties which are eternally appropriate to them; sometimes a certain object requires only one, sometimes all of them—the latter occurs only very rarely—but never in the same amount or to the same degree. Again it is necessary to note that the more faculties an object requires, the less noble and pure it is, the more complex it is, the more it contains of the spurious. *Truth* serves as the basis and as the goal of the sciences. Above all it invokes pure intellect. In this case purity of style is desirable, but *beauty* of style may be considered an unnecessary luxury. The *Good* is the basis and the goal of moral research. The *Beautiful* is the only ambition, the exclusive aim of Taste. Although Truth is the goal of history, there is a Muse of history to convey the idea that some of the qualities necessary to the historian depend on the Muse. The Novel is one of the complex genres where a greater or lesser role may be assigned now to Truth, now to Beauty. The part played by Beauty in *Mademoiselle de Maupin* was excessive. It was the author's privilege to give it that importance. The aim of the novel was to express neither the manners nor the passions of an epoch, but rather a single passion of a very special nature, universal and eternal, under the impulse of which the entire book flows, so to speak, in the same river-bed as Poetry, but yet without mingling completely with it, deprived as it is of the double element of rhythm and rhyme. The goal, the objective, the ambition was to portray in an appropriate style not the frenzy of love, but the *beauty* of love and the *beauty* of objects worthy of love, in a word the ecstasy (very different from passion) created by beauty. The complete confusion of genres and of faculties is really a cause for enormous astonishment among those who are not carried away by the errors so much in vogue. Just as different crafts demand different tools, so different objects of spiritual quest require their corresponding faculties.—I presume there are times when it is permissible to quote oneself, especially when it is done to avoid paraphrasing what one has already written. Hence I shall repeat:

"... There is another heresy ... an error which has a hardier life—I refer to the *heresy of teaching a lesson*, which includes as inevitable corollaries the heresy of *passion*, of *truth*, and of *morality*.[106] A great many people imagine that the aim of poetry is a lesson of some sort, that it must now fortify the conscience, now perfect morals, now *prove* something or other which is useful ... Poetry, if only one is willing to seek, however little, within himself, to question his heart, to recall his fervent memories, has no goal other than itself; it can have no other, and no poem will be so great, so noble, so truly worthy of the name of poetry as that which will have been written solely for the pleasure of writing a poem.

"I do not mean that poetry does not ennoble manners—

let there be no mistake about it—that its final result is not to raise man above the level of vulgar interests; obviously that would be an absurdity. I say that if the poet has pursued a moral aim, he has diminished his poetic force; and it is not rash to wager that his work will be bad. Poetry cannot, under penalty of death or failure, be assimilated to science or morality; it does not have Truth as its object, it has only Itself. The means for demonstrating truth are other and are elsewhere. Truth has nothing to do with songs. All the things that constitute the grace, the charm, the irresistible attraction of a song, would take from Truth its authority and its power. Cold, calm, impassive, the demonstrative mood rejects the diamonds and the flowers of the Muse; it is then absolutely the inverse of the poetic mood.

"Pure Intellect aims at Truth, Taste reveals Beauty, and Moral Sense teaches us what is Right. It is true that taste is intimately connected with the other two and is separated from Moral Sense only by so slight a difference that Aristotle has not hesitated to include among the virtues some of its delicate operations. Thus, what especially exasperates the man of taste in the spectacle of vice is its deformity, its disproportion. Vice injures the just and the true, revolts the intellect and the conscience; but as an outrage to harmony, as dissonance, it will wound more particularly certain poetic minds; and I do not think it scandalous to consider every offense against morality, against moral beauty, as a kind of offense against universal rhythm and prosody.

"It is that admirable, that immortal instinct for the beautiful which makes us consider the earth and its spectacles as a revelation, as something in *correspondence* with Heaven. The insatiable thirst for everything that lies beyond, and that life reveals, is the most living proof of our immortality.

"It is at the same time by poetry and *through* poetry, by and *through* music that the soul glimpses the splendors beyond the tomb; and when an exquisite poem brings us to the verge of tears, those tears are not the proof of excessive pleasure; they are rather evidence of an aroused melancholy, of a condition of nerves, of a nature which has been exiled amid the imperfect and which would like to take possession immediately, on this very earth, of a revealed paradise.

"Thus, the principle of poetry is precisely and simply human aspiration toward a superior Beauty, and the manifestation of this principle is in an enthusiasm, an excitation of the soul— an enthusiasm altogether independent of passion, which is the intoxication of the heart, and of truth, which is the food of reason.* For passion is *natural*, too natural not to introduce an offensive, discordant tone into the domain of pure Beauty, too familiar and too violent not to scandalize the pure Desires, the gracious Melancholies and the noble Despairs which inhabit the supernatural regions of poetry."

And elsewhere I said:

"In a country where the idea of utility, the most hostile in the world to the idea of beauty, dominates and takes precedence over everything, the perfect critic will be the most respectable, that is to say the one who will best approximate the tendencies and desires of his public, the one who, confusing the intellectual faculties of the writer and the categories of writing, will assign to all a single goal, the one who will seek in a book of poetry the means of perfecting conscience."

For some years, in fact, a great passion for respectability has gained possession of the theater, of poetry, of the novel, and of criticism.[107] I leave aside the question of understanding what profit hypocrisy can gain from this confusion of functions, or what consolations literary impotence can draw from it. Granting that it is sincerely held, I am satisfied to note and to analyze the error. During the chaotic epoch of Romanticism, the epoch of fervent effusions, people often resorted to the use of this

---

* The imitation of passion, with the search for the Truth and to some extent that of Beauty (not of the Good), are the constituent parts of drama, but it is also the presence of passion that forces drama back to a secondary place in the hierarchy of the Beautiful. If I have neglected the question of the greater or lesser nobility of the faculties, it was to avoid being led too far afield; but the supposition that they are equal does not in the least damage the general theory that I am trying to sketch.

formula: *The poetry of the heart!* Thus passion was fully sanctioned and a sort of infallibility attributed to it. How many absurdities and sophisms an error of aesthetics can impose on the French language! The heart contains passion, the heart contains devotion, crime; Imagination alone contains poetry. But today the error has taken a different course and assumed greater proportions. For example, in a moment of fervent gratitude, a woman says to her husband, a lawyer: *O poet! I love you!* Sentiment encroaching on the domain of reason! Typical reasoning of a woman who doesn't know how to use words correctly! Now all this simply means: "You are an honest man and a good husband; *hence* you are a poet and even more of a poet than those who use meter and rhyme to express ideas of beauty. I shall even maintain," firmly continues this inverted *précieuse*, "that every honest man who can please his wife is a sublime poet. Moreover, I declare, in my bourgeois infallibility, that whoever writes excellent poetry is much less a poet than any honest man who is fond of his home; for the ability to compose verses is obviously detrimental to a husband's faculties, *which are the basis of all poetry!*"

But may the academician who has made this error, so flattering to lawyers, be consoled.[108] He is in a large and distinguished company; for the wind of the century is blowing in the direction of folly, the barometer of modern reason indicates stormy weather. Haven't we recently noted the unanimous applause that greeted a famous writer of the finest repute [Michelet] who situated all poetry not in Beauty but in love!— in a commonplace, domestic and humdrum love!—who in his hatred of all beauty exclaimed: *A good tailor is worth more than three classic sculptors!* and who affirmed that Raymond Lully became a theologian because God punished him for having recoiled before the cancer which was devouring the bosom of a woman with whom he was in love.[109] If he had really loved her, he adds, how greatly this infirmity would have enhanced her in his eyes!—So he became a theologian! Indeed, it serves him right.—The same author advises the husband-in-the-role-of-Providence to beat his wife when she comes as a *suppliant* entreating the *solace of atonement*. And what punishment will he permit us to inflict on an old man lacking in dignity, high-strung and effeminate, playing with dolls, fashioning madrigals in honor of illness, and wallowing ecstatically in the dirty linen of humanity? As for me, I know only one: it is a punishment which leaves a deep and lasting mark, for, as is expressed in the song of our forefathers, those vigorous men who could laugh in all circumstances, even the most irremediable:

> Le *ridicule* est plus tranchant
> Que le fer de la guillotine.[110]

I shall leave this side road where I was led by indignation and return to the main theme. The sensibility of the heart is not entirely favorable to the poetic process. In this case excessive sensibility of the heart can even be harmful. The sensibility of the imagination is of a different nature; it can choose, judge, compare, avoid this, seek that, quickly and spontaneously. It is from that sensibility which is generally called *Taste* that we derive the power of avoiding the *bad* and seeking the *good* in poetic material. As for uprightness of heart, common courtesy requires us to suppose that it is the property of all men, *even poets*. Whether the poet believes or does not believe that it is necessary to give his works the substructure of a pure and proper life concerns only his confessor or the courts. In this respect his situation is entirely like that of all his fellow citizens.

If we limit the meaning of the word *writer* to works that spring from the imagination, it may be seen that, according to my definition of terms, Théophile Gautier is a writer par excellence, because he is a slave to his duty, because he constantly obeys the necessities of his function, because taste for the Beautiful is for him a *fatum*, because he has a fixed idea of his duty. With his luminous good sense (I am referring to the good sense of genius, and not the good sense of ordinary people) he immediately discovered the main path. Each writer is more or less characterized by his chief faculty. Chateaubriand sang the sad glory of melancholy and ennui. Victor Hugo, great, terrible, immense, like a mythical, one might almost say, Cyclopean, creation, represents the forces of nature and their harmonious conflict. Balzac, great, terrible, as well as complex, portrays what is monstrous in a civilization with all its struggles, its ambitions and its passions. With Gautier, it is the exclusive love of the Beautiful and all its subdivisions, expressed in the most appropriate language. And notice that almost all the important writers in each period, those whom we shall call foremen or captains, have beneath them people who are comparable, if not equals, fit to replace them. Thus when a civilization dies, only one poem of a particular genre need be found in order to give an idea of counterparts that have been lost and to permit the critical mind to re-establish the chain of generation without a break. Now through his love for the Beautiful, an immense, fruitful love that is constantly renewed (compare, for example, the last articles on St. Petersburg and the Neva [river] with *Italia* or *Tra los Montes*), Théophile Gautier is a writer whose talent is both *new* and unique. It may be said of him that as yet he has no *understudy*.

To speak adequately of the tool which so well serves this passion for the Beautiful—I am referring to his style—I should have to possess similar resources, that unfailing knowledge of the language, that magnificent dictionary whose leaves, stirred by a divine breath, open at just the right place to produce the right word, the unique word, and finally that sense of order which puts each stroke and each touch in its proper place and which omits no gradations. If one considers that with this marvelous faculty Gautier combines an immense innate understanding of universal *correspondence* and symbolism, that repertory of all metaphor, one will realize why, without fatigue as without fault, he can always define the mysterious attitude which the objects of creation assume in men's eyes. There is in the word, in the *Logos*, something *sacred* which forbids us to turn it into a game of chance. To know how to use a language is to practice a kind of evocative magic. It is then that color speaks like a deep, vibrant voice, that buildings rise and stand out against deep space, that animals and plants, representatives of ugliness and evil, make their unmistakable grimace, that perfume provokes corresponding thoughts and memories, that passion murmurs or roars its eternally changeless language. There is in the style of Théophile Gautier a delightful, amazing precision that recalls those miracles in gambling that result from a profound mathematical knowledge. I remember that when, as a very young man, I savored the works of our poet for the first time, the sensation of exactly the right touch, of the perfectly aimed thrust, made me shiver, and that my feeling of admiration gave me a sort of nervous convulsion. Little by little I became accustomed to perfection and I gave myself up to the movement of this beautiful, undulating, and sparkling style, like a man who is still able to dream while riding a sure-footed horse or who can idly contemplate the magnificent, flawless settings constructed by nature in her hours of genius, while sailing in a boat strong enough to defy unforeseen squalls. It is thanks to these innate faculties which he has so carefully cultivated that Gautier has often been able to sit down at an ordinary table in a newspaper office (as we have all seen) and improvise something, criticism or a novel, which had an irreproachably finished character and which the next day would evoke as much pleasure among readers as the rapidity of its execution and the beauty of its handwriting had caused amazement among the typesetters. Doesn't this speed in solving every problem of style and composition call to mind the strict maxim which he once mentioned to me in a conversation and which he obviously imposed on himself as a constant duty: "Any man who is at a loss to express an idea, however subtle and unexpected that idea may be, is not a writer. The inexpressible does not exist."

IV

This constant concern, involuntary because it was natural, for the beautiful and the picturesque was to drive the author toward a form of the novel suitable to his temperament. The novel and the short story have the advantage of being marvelously flexible. They are suited to all natures, include all subjects, and pursue whatever goals they like. Sometimes it is the pursuit of the passions, at other times the pursuit of truth; one novel appeals to the crowd, another to initiates; this one recounts the life of days gone-by, that one the silent dramas which are played in one man's mind. The novel, which holds so important a place beside poetry and history, is a bastard genre whose domain is really limitless. Like many other bastards, it is a child spoiled by fortune who is successful in everything. It experiences no inconveniences and knows no dangers other than its infinite freedom. The short story, more concentrated, more condensed, enjoys the eternal benefits of constraint; its effect is more intense, and since the time devoted to the reading of a short story is much less than that necessary for the digestion of a novel, the totality of the effect is assured.

The mind of Théophile Gautier, poetic, picturesque, meditative, was to prefer this form, to cherish it, and to dress it in the various costumes most suited to his taste. Therefore, he has fully succeeded in the different kinds of short stories to which he has applied himself. In the grotesque and in the comic he is very powerful. It is, to be sure, the solitary gaiety of a dreamer who, from time to time, opens the floodgates to permit an outpouring of repressed joviality and never loses his *sui generis* charm, who seeks above all to please himself. But where he shows himself the most lofty, where he has displayed the surest and most serious talent, is in the short story which I shall call the poetic *short story*. It may be said that of the innumerable forms of the novel and short story which have occupied or amused the human mind, the most favored has been the novel of manners; it is the one which best suits the general public. Just as Paris likes above all to hear about Paris, so the populace delights in the mirrors in which it sees itself. But when the novel of manners is not enhanced by the natural good taste of the author, it strongly risks being dull and even completely useless, since in matters of art utility may be measured by the degree of nobility. If from this plebeian genre Balzac has made something admirable, invariably strange, and often sublime, it is because he has put his whole being into it. I have often been astonished that Balzac's chief title to fame should be to pass for an observer; it had always seemed to me that his principle merit was that of being a visionary, and an impassioned visionary. All his characters are endowed with the zest for life with which he himself was animated. All his fabrications are as intensely colored as dreams. From the highest ranks of the aristocracy to the lowest dregs of society, all the actors in his *Comédie* are more eager for life, more energetic and cunning in their struggles, more patient in misfortune, more greedy in pleasure, more angelic in devotion than they are in the comedy of the real world. In a word, everyone in Balzac has genius— even the doormen. Every living soul is a weapon loaded to the very muzzle with will. This is actually Balzac himself. And as all beings of the exterior world presented themselves to his mind's eye in strong relief and with a striking grimace, he has made their forms convulsive, he has blackened their shadows and heightened their highlights. His prodigious taste for detail, which stems from an inordinate ambition to see everything and to guess everything as well as to make others see everything and guess everything, forced him, moreover, to give greater emphasis to the main lines in order to maintain the perspective of the whole. He sometimes makes me think of those etchers who are never satisfied with the biting and who transform the main scratches on the plate into veritable ravines. This amazing natural bent has led to marvelous results. But this bent is generally considered a weakness in Balzac. Properly speaking, it is really one of his virtues. But who can boast of being so fortunately endowed and of being able to apply a method that will allow him to clothe the most commonplace things with the splendor of imperial purple? Who can do that? Now, to tell the truth he who does not succeed in doing that, accomplishes very little.

Théophile Gautier's muse lives in a more ethereal world. She cares little—too little some think—about the way M.

Coquelet, M. Pipelet, or M. Tout-le-Monde spend the day, or whether Madame Coquelet prefers the attentions of her neighbor, the bailiff, to the bonbons of the druggist, who in his day was one of the most sprightly dancers at the Tivoli [dance hall].[111] These mysteries do not worry her. She likes to frequent heights less popular than the Rue des Lombards; she loves landscapes that are terrible and forbidding or those that breathe a monotonous charm—the blue shores of Ionia or the blinding sands of the desert. She is fond of occupying richly ornate rooms where floats the fragrance of a choice perfume. Her characters are the gods, the angels, the priest, the king, the lover, the rich, the poor, etc. She loves to bring to life cities that have vanished and to have the dead whom she has restored to youth recount their interrupted passions. She borrows from poetry, not the meter and the rhyme but the splendor or the concise energy of its language. Freeing herself thus from the customary turmoil of present-day realities, she pursues her dream of Beauty without restraint; at the same time she would run the grave risk of not being sufficiently *visible* and *tangible*, were she not so pliant and docile, so much the daughter of a master who can endow everything he sees with life. In a word, to drop the metaphor, the short story that is poetic in nature gains immensely in dignity; it has a more noble, a more universal tone, but it is subject to a grave danger—that of losing a great deal on the side of reality, the magic of verisimilitude. And yet, who doesn't recall the festival of Pharaoh and the dance of the slaves, and the return of the triumphant army in *Le Roman de la Momie?* The imagination of the reader feels itself transported into the real; it breathes the real; it is intoxicated by a second reality created by the sorcery of the Muse. I have not singled out this example; I took the first one that came to my mind; I could have mentioned twenty others.

When one leafs through the works of a powerful master who is always sure of his will and his hand, it is difficult to make a choice, since all the passages that strike the eye or the memory bear a uniform stamp of precision and of finish. Nevertheless,

I would recommend with pleasure the well known story of "Le Roi Candaule," not only as an example of the art of elegant expression but also of mysterious tenderness (for the range of feelings in our author is much more extensive than is generally believed). Most assuredly, it would have been difficult to choose a more trite theme or a drama with a more completely familiar ending, but true writers love such difficulties. All its merit (not taking into account the language) therefore lies in the interpretation. If there is a commonplace, hackneyed sentiment comprehensible to all women, most assuredly it is modesty. But here modesty has a superlative character that makes it resemble religion; it is the cult of woman for herself; it is an archaic, Asiatic modesty having something of the vastness of the ancient world, a veritable flower of the greenhouse, the harem, or the gynaeceum. She is no less defiled by the profane eye than by the mouth or the hand. Contemplation is possession. Candaules has shown the secret beauties of his wife to his friend Gyges; hence Candaules is guilty, he will die. Hereafter Gyges is the only possible husband for a queen so jealous of herself. But hasn't Candaules a powerful excuse? Isn't he the victim of an emotion as imperious as it is fantastic, the victim of the inability of an artist or sensitive man to bear the weight of an immense happiness without confiding it to someone? Certainly this interpretation of the story, this analysis of the emotions which gave rise to the situation is very superior to Plato's fable which makes of Gyges a shepherd, the owner of a talisman by means of which it became easy for him to seduce the wife of his king.

Thus moves in her varied ways this strange muse with her many costumes, this cosmopolitan muse endowed with the versatility of Alcibiades; sometimes with an Oriental mitre girding her brow, with a lofty and sacred air, and with fillets streaming in the breeze; at other times like a festive queen of Sheba, her little copper parasol in her hand, sitting in state on the porcelain elephant that ornamented the mantels of the courtly century. But what she likes above all is to stand on the perfumed banks of the Inland Sea and recount to us with golden words "the glory that was Greece and the grandeur that was Rome"; and then she is indeed "Psyche from the regions which are Holy Land!" [112]

This innate taste for form and for perfection in form was bound to make Théophile Gautier a critic in a class quite by himself. No one has been better able than he to express the happiness given the imagination by the sight of a beautiful object of art, however ruined and terrible it might be. It is one of the astounding prerogatives of Art that the horrible, artistically expressed, becomes beauty and that *sorrow*, when given rhythm and cadence, fills the mind with a serene *joy*. As a critic, Théophile Gautier has known, loved, and explained in his *Salons* and in his admirable travel books, Asiatic beauty, Greek beauty, Roman beauty, Spanish beauty, Flemish beauty, Dutch beauty, and English beauty. When the works of all the artists of Europe were impressively assembled on the Avenue Montaigne [Exposition Universelle] as if in a sort of aesthetic council, who spoke first and who spoke best about that English school which the most informed visitors could scarcely judge except through a few recollections of Reynolds and of Lawrence? Who immediately perceived the varied and essentially new merits of Leslie, of the two Hunts, the one a naturalist, the other the leader of the Pre-Raphaelites, of Maclise, the daring master of composition, so impetuous and sure of himself, of Millais, that meticulous poet, of J. Chalon, the painter of afternoon fetes in the park, as courtly as Watteau, as dreamy as Claude, of Grant, that heir of Reynolds, of Hook, the painter of *Venetian dreams*, of Landseer, whose animals have eyes full of thought, of that strange Paton who makes one think of Fuseli and who embroiders pantheistic conceptions with the patience of another age, of Cattermole, that history painter in water color, and of that other whose name escapes me (Cockerell or Kendall?), an imaginative architect of dreams who builds, on paper, cities whose bridges have elephants as piers, through whose legs pass gigantic three-masters in full sail? [113] Who immediately was able to Britannicize his genius? Who found words suitable to describe the enchanting freshness and the receding depths of English water colors? Wherever there is an artistic product to describe and to explain, Gautier is on hand and always ready.

I am convinced that it is thanks to his innumerable articles and to his excellent descriptions of his travels that all young people (those who possess an innate taste for beauty) have acquired an education that was otherwise lacking. Théophile Gautier has given them a love for painting, just as Victor Hugo had encouraged in them a taste for archaeology. This constant toil, continued with so much patience, was more difficult and more meritorious than it appears at first glance; for let us remember that France, I mean the French public (with the exception of a few artists and writers), is not artistic, naturally artistic; this public is philosophical, moralistic, mechanically-minded, fond of stories and anecdotes, anything but spontaneously artistic. It feels, or rather it judges, part by part, analytically. Other peoples, more favored, grasp everything at once, immediately, and synthetically.

Where one should see only the beautiful, our public seeks only the true. When he should be a painter, the Frenchman becomes a man of letters. One day at the annual Salon I saw two soldiers standing in perplexed contemplation before a picture of a kitchen scene: "But where is Napoleon?" said one (the catalogue had been numbered incorrectly and the kitchen had been given a number that rightly belonged to a famous battle). "Idiot!" said the other; "don't you see that they are preparing the meal for his return?" And they left satisfied with the painter and satisfied with themselves. Such is France. I repeated this anecdote to a general who found in it reason to admire the amazing intelligence of the French soldier. He should have said: the amazing intelligence of all Frenchmen in matters of art! Those soldiers were men of letters!

V

Nor is France any more appreciative of poetry, alas! All of us, even the least *chauvinistic*, have succeeded in defending

France at the dinner table in faraway places; but here, among ourselves, in the family, let us face the facts: France is not poetic; to tell the truth, she even feels a congenital horror of poetry. Among the writers who use verse, those whom she will always prefer are the most prosaic. I really believe—forgive me, true lovers of the Muse!—that I lacked courage at the beginning of this study when I said that, for France, the Beautiful was easy to digest only when seasoned with a political condiment. I should have said the opposite: however political the condiment may be, the Beautiful causes indigestion, or rather the French stomach refuses it immediately. This comes, I believe, not only from the fact that France has been created providentially for the quest of Truth rather than for the quest of Beauty, but also from the fact that the Utopian, communistic, alchemistic character of all her minds permits only one exclusive passion, that of social formulas. Here each person wants to resemble everyone else, but on the condition that everyone resemble him. From this contradictory tyranny there results a conflict which applies only to social forms, leading to a mediocre standard and a general similarity. Hence the destruction and the oppression of any show of originality. Moreover, it is not only in the literary order that real poets appear like strange, fabulous creatures; it may be said that in any field of invention the great man is a monster here. On the contrary, in other countries originality is as profuse and abundant as wild grass. There, custom allows it.

Let us then love our poets secretly and stealthily. Abroad, we shall have the right to boast about them. Our neighbors say: Shakespeare and Goethe! We can answer them: Victor Hugo and Théophile Gautier! Perhaps it will seem surprising that I expatiate less on the genre that does him most credit and that serves as his chief claim to fame than I have on the others. I certainly cannot fully discuss poetics and prosody at this time. Even if our language possessed terms sufficiently numerous and subtle to explain a certain type of poetry, would I be able to find them? It is with poetry as it is with some beautiful women in whom originality and propriety are fused; one doesn't explain them, one *loves* them. *On one hand,* Théophile Gautier has continued the great school of melancholy created by Chateaubriand. His melancholy is even more positive, more sensual in character, bordering at times on the sadness of the ancients. In *La Comédie de la Mort* and among the poems inspired by his stay in Spain, there are some which reveal the giddy sensation and the horror of nothingness. Re-read for example the pieces on Zurbarán and Valdés Leal; the marvelous paraphrase of the maxim inscribed on the dial of the clock of Urrugna: *Vulnerant omnes, ultima necat*; and lastly the prodigious symphony called *Ténèbres*. I say symphony because this poem sometimes makes me think of Beethoven. There are times when this poet, accused of sensuality, falls completely into Catholic terror, so intense is his melancholy. *On the other hand*, he has introduced into poetry, through all the picturesque objects that delight the eye and amuse the mind, a new element which I shall call consolation through the arts. In this sense he has really been an innovator; he has made French verse say more than it had said until now; he has succeeded in adorning it with a thousand high-lighted and prominent details without detracting from the form of the whole or from the general outline. His poetry, at once majestic and precious, moves magnificently, like courtiers in full dress. It is, moreover, characteristic of true poetry to move in a steady flow like great rivers which approach the sea, their death and their infinity, and to avoid haste and abruptness. Lyric poetry soars, but always with a supple and undulating movement. It dislikes everything that is abrupt and broken, and relegates it to the drama and to the novel of manners. The poet whose ability we so passionately admire has a thorough understanding of these important questions, and he has proved it perfectly by systematically and continually introducing the majesty of the alexandrine into the octosyllabic line (*Emaux et Camées*). There especially he achieves the best obtainable results through the fusion of two elements, painting and music, through the breadth of the melody and through the regular and symmetrical dignity of a rhyme that is more than exact.

Shall I recall once again that series of little poems of a few stanzas, elegant or dreamy interludes, some of which resemble sculptures, others flowers, still others jewels, but all of which are clothed in colors finer or more brilliant than the colors of China and India, and are—all of them—purer and sharper in outline than objects of marble or crystal? Whoever loves poetry knows them by heart.

VI

I have tried to express (have I really succeeded?) the admiration inspired in me by the work of Théophile Gautier and to deduce the reasons which justify this admiration. A few, some of them even writers, may not share my opinion. Everyone will soon accept it. In the eyes of the public he is today only a delightful mind; in the eyes of posterity he will be one of the master writers not only of France but also of Europe. In his jesting, his banter, his firm decision never to be a dupe, he is partially French; but if he were completely French, he would not be a poet.

Shall I briefly mention his manners, so unaffected and so affable, his willingness to help, his candor when he feels free, when he is not in the presence of the *Philistine enemy*, his punctuality in performing all his duties? What would be the use? Every writer has been able to appreciate these noble qualities on more than one occasion.

He is sometimes accused of being uninterested in matters of religion and politics. If I wanted to do so, I could write another article which would successfully refute this unjust error. I know—and for me that is enough—that intelligent people will understand me when I say that the need for order with which his splendid mind is imbued suffices to preserve him from any error in political and religious matters, and that he possesses, more than anyone else, the sense of universal hierarchy written from the top to the bottom of nature, at all the steps of the infinite. Others have sometimes spoken of his apparent coldness, of his lack of *humanity*. This criticism again shows shallowness and thoughtlessness. No lover of humanity will ever fail, in certain matters which lend themselves to philanthropic declamation, to quote the famous saying: *Homo sum; nihil humani a me alienum puto.*[114] A poet would have the right to answer: "I have imposed on myself such high duties that *quidquid humani a me alienum puto.* My function is extrahuman!" But without abusing his prerogative Gautier could simply reply (I know that with his kind and tender heart he has the right to do so): "You believe I am cold, and you don't see, oh men of prose and of crime, that I am imposing on myself an artificial calm which your ugliness and barbarity seek constantly to disturb! What you call indifference is only the resignation of despair; he who considers the wicked and the stupid as incurable can only very rarely be moved to pity. It is therefore to avoid the heartbreaking spectacle of your madness and your cruelty that my eyes remain stubbornly turned toward the immaculate Muse."

It is doubtless this same despair of convincing or of correcting anyone that has made Gautier seem to weaken in these last years and to offer a few laudatory words to his Lordship Progress and to her very mighty Ladyship Industry. In such cases we must not be too quick to take him at his word, and there is indeed reason to maintain that *scorn sometimes makes the heart too kind.*[115] For then he keeps his real thought to himself, evincing simply by a slight concession (perceptible to those who know and see clearly in the twilight) that he wishes to live in peace with everyone, even with Industry and Progress, those despotic enemies of all poetry.

I have heard several people express regret that Gautier has never held any official office. It is certain that in many matters, especially in the field of the fine arts, he could have rendered distinguished service to France. But everything taken into consideration, it is better this way. However vast a man's genius may be, however great his good will, an official office always restricts him a little; now his liberty feels its effects, now even his perspicacity. For my part, I prefer to see the author of *La Comédie de la Mort*, of *Une Nuit de Cléopatre*, of *La Morte Amoureuse*, of *Tra los Montes*, of *Italia*, of *Caprices et Zigzags*, and of so many other masterpieces, remain what he has been until now: the equal of the greatest in the past, a model for those who are to come, a diamond more and more rare in an epoch drunk with ignorance and materialism, in other words A PERFECT MAN OF LETTERS.

THE SALON OF 1859

PREFACE

The article on the Salon of 1859, which took the form of a long letter addressed to M. Jean Morel, director of the *La Revue Française*, was published in four installments in June and July of that year. It contains interesting discussions on photography and on such artists as Delacroix, Meryon, Boudin and many others.[116]

The importance of the *Salon*, however, lies not so much in the criticism and discussion of the exhibition, as in the definition and glorification of imagination. Inspired in part by Delacroix, whom he quotes indirectly, Baudelaire views imagination as a visionary and creative faculty to which all other powers are subordinated and from which all great art, whatever its medium, is necessarily derived. It has a destructive and a constructive character: it decomposes all nature and, from the materials that it accumulates and orders, it transcends reality and creates a new world. It allows the artist to avoid the "triteness of actuality" and to achieve the beauty which Baudelaire believed was the goal of all art. In *Paradis Artificiels* (1860), imagination will become one and the same as "the inner eye [which] transforms everything and gives to each thing the complement of beauty which it lacks if it is to be worthy of pleasing." [117]

In his article on Gautier, Baudelaire had maintained that "imagination alone contains poetry." The reason becomes more apparent in the *Salon of 1859*. Because imagination is "the queen of truth," because it "has a definite relationship with the infinite," it becomes the means by which the poet is able to discover "what is most real, what is completely true only in *another world*." The *Salon of 1859* thus becomes the key to Baudelaire's critical thought and the point at which all his aesthetic ideas converge.

THE QUEEN OF FACULTIES

In recent years we have heard it said in a thousand different ways: "Copy nature; copy only nature. There is no greater delight, no finer triumph, than an excellent copy of nature." And this doctrine, so inimical to art, was alleged to apply not only to painting but to all the arts, even to the novel, even to poetry. To these doctrinaires so satisfied with nature, an imaginative man would certainly have had the right to answer: "I consider it useless and tiresome to portray things as they are, because nothing that exists satisfies me. Nature is ugly, and I prefer the monsters of my imagination to the triteness of actuality." It would have been more philosophical, however, to ask these dogmatists, first whether they are really certain of the existence of external nature, or in case this question seemed too well calculated to please their caustic humor, whether they are quite certain of knowing *all nature*, all that is contained in nature. A "yes" would have been the most boastful and the most absurd of answers. If I have correctly understood these strange and degrading divagations, the doctrine meant, at least I am doing it the honor of believing that it meant: The artist, the true artist, the true poet, should paint only in accordance with what he sees and what he feels. He should be *really* true to his own nature. He should avoid, like death itself, borrowing the eyes and emotions of another man, however great that man may be; for in that case his productions would be lies, so far as he is concerned, and not *realities*. But if the pedants of whom I am speaking (there is pedantry even in what is contemptible) and who have representatives everywhere—since this theory flatters impotence and indolence alike—if these pedants did not wish the matter to be understood in this way, let us simply believe that they meant: "We have no imagination, and we decree that no one shall have any."

How mysterious is this queen of faculties! It affects all the other faculties; it rouses them, it sends them into combat. Sometimes it resembles them to the point of confusion, and yet it is always very much itself, and the persons who are not stirred by it are easily recognizable by an indefinable curse which withers their productions like the fig tree of the Gospel.

It is analysis, it is synthesis; and yet men who excel in analysis and who are fairly apt in summarizing may lack imagination. It is that, and it is not altogether that. It is sensitivity, and yet there are very sensitive persons, too sensitive perhaps, who are devoid of it. It is imagination that has taught man the moral meaning of color, of outline, of sound, and of perfume. In the beginning of the world it created analogy and metaphor. It decomposes all creation, and from the materials, accumulated and arranged according to rules whose origin is found only in the depths of the soul, it creates a new world, it produces the sensation of the new. Since it has created the world (this can really be said, I believe, even in a religious sense), it is only right that it should govern it. What do people say about a warrior without imagination? That he may make an excellent soldier, but that if he is put in command of armies, he will make no conquests. The case is like that of a poet or a novelist who might take the command of his faculties away from his imagination to give it, for example, to his knowledge of the language or to his observation of facts. What is said of a diplomat without imagination? That he may know all about the history of treaties and alliances in the past, but that he will not sense the treaties and alliances that may evolve in the future. Of a scholar without imagination? That he has learned everything that could be learned from what he was taught, but that he will not discover laws that have not yet been conceived. Imagination is the queen of truth, and the possible is one of the provinces of truth. It has a definite relationship with the infinite.

Without it, all the faculties, however sound or keen they may be, are seemingly nonexistent, whereas the weakness of certain secondary faculties, when excited by a vigorous imagination, is a secondary misfortune. None of the faculties can do without it, and it can even replace some of the others. Imagination often guesses, boldly and simply, what the secondary faculties seek and find only after successive trials of several methods unadapted to the nature of things. Lastly, it plays a powerful role even in morality; for if I may be so bold as to ask —what is virtue without imagination? You might as well speak of virtue without pity, virtue without heaven; it is something hard, cruel, sterilizing, which in certain countries has become bigotry and in certain others, Protestantism.

In spite of all the magnificent qualities that I attribute to the imagination, I shall not insult your readers by explaining to them that the more it is helped, the more powerful it becomes, and that the strongest weapon in our battles with the ideal is a fine imagination with a vast store of observations at its disposal. However, to come back to what I was saying a moment ago about its power to supplement other faculties, a power which it owes to its divine origin, I wish to cite an example, a very small example, at which I hope you will not scoff. Do you believe that the author of *Antony*, of *Comte Hermann*, of *Monte-Cristo*, is a scholar? You don't think so, do you? Do you think he is well versed in the arts, that he has made a careful study of them? You don't believe that either. That would even be antipathetic to his nature, in my opinion. Well, he is an example who proves that imagination, although unassisted by practice and knowledge of technical terms, is incapable of uttering heretical nonsense in a matter which, for the most part, comes under its province. Not long ago I was traveling on a train and I was pondering over the article that I am now writing; I was reflecting especially about that strange reversal of things which has permitted man to scorn the most honorable and the most useful of the moral faculties—in a century, it is true, in which, by way of punishment, everything has been permitted him— when I saw lying on a nearby cushion a stray copy of *L'Indépendance Belge*. In it Alexandre Dumas had taken it upon himself to write a review of the works appearing in the Salon. The incident aroused my curiosity. You can imagine my joy when I saw my reflections fully verified by an example that chance had brought to my attention. What a fine occasion for surprise, you will say, that this man, who seems to represent universal vitality, should praise so magnificently a period abounding in life, that the creator of Romantic drama should exalt, in a tone not without grandeur, I assure you, those happy days when, alongside the new school of literature there flourished a new school of painting: Delacroix, the Devérias, Boulanger, Poterlet, Bonington, etc. That is certainly to be expected! *Laudator temporis acti!* But that he should praise Delacroix so wittily, that he should explain so clearly the nature of his opponents' madness, that he should even go so far as to point out the failings of the best of today's most famous painters, that he, Alexandre Dumas, so careless and facile, should demonstrate so well, for example, that Troyon lacks genius and even what he lacks in simulating genius—tell me, my dear friend, do you find that so simple? All this, to be sure, was written in that dramatic, *slipshod* manner which he has adopted in talking to his innumerable audience; but yet, how much charm and spontaneity in the expression of truth! You have already anticipated my conclusion: If Alexandre Dumas, who is not a scholar, had not had the good fortune to possess a rich imagination, he would only have written nonsense; he has said some very sensible things and he has said them well, because . . . (I must conclude this digression), because imagination, thanks to its compensatory nature, contains the critical spirit. There remains, nevertheless, one dodge for those who wish to contradict me, and that is to claim that Alexandre Dumas is not the author of his *Salon*. But this insult is so old, and this expedient so commonplace that it should be left to those who are fond of trumpery and to journalistic *hacks* and *reporters*. If they have not already picked it up, they will do so.

THE RULE OF THE IMAGINATION

Yesterday evening, after having sent you the last pages of my letter, in which I had written, not without a certain diffidence: *Since imagination has created the world, it governs it,* I was scanning *The Night Side of Nature* and I came across these lines which I am quoting solely because they are a paraphrase justifying the line that was worrying me: "By imagination, I do not simply mean to convey the common notion implied by that much abused word, which is only *fancy*, but the *constructive* imagination, which is a much higher function, and which, in as much [sic] as man is made in the likeness of God, bears a distant relation to that sublime power by which the Creator projects, creates, and upholds his universe." I am not at all ashamed but, on the contrary, very happy to be in agreement with the excellent Mrs. Crowe, in whom I have always admired the capacity for belief which is as fully developed in her as is the capacity for distrust in many others.[118]

I was saying that long ago I had heard a man [Delacroix], truly scholarly and profoundly learned in his art, express the most comprehensive and yet the most simple ideas on this subject. When I met him for the first time, I had no experience other than that which comes from an overwhelming love and no other reasoning save instinct. It is true that this love and this instinct were fairly keen, for from my earliest youth, my eyes, filled with paintings or engravings, could never be satiated, and I think that worlds could come to an end, *impavidum ferient*, before I would become an iconoclast. Evidently he wanted to be very kind and obliging, for at first we talked of commonplaces, that is to say, of the most comprehensive and the most profound questions—about nature, for example. "Nature is only a dictionary," he would often say. To properly understand the full meaning implied in this statement, one should keep in mind the many ordinary uses of the dictionary. In it one seeks the meaning of words, the genealogy of words, the etymology of words; in short, one extracts from it all the elements that compose a sentence and a narrative. But no one has ever considered the dictionary as a composition in the poetic sense of the word. Painters who obey their imagination seek in their dictionary the elements which suit their conception; yet, in adapting these elements with a certain art, they give them an altogether new physiognomy. Those who lack imagination copy the dictionary. The result is a very great fault, the fault of banality, which is especially true of those painters whose specialty brings them into closer contact with exterior nature—landscape painters, for example, who generally consider it a triumph not to show their personality. Through too much looking, they forget to feel and to think. . . .

I have no fear that anyone will find it absurd to suppose that the same education is applicable to a host of different individuals. For it is evident that systems of rhetoric and prosody are not arbitrarily invented tyrannies, but rather a collection of rules required by the very nature of the spiritual being. And systems of prosody and rhetoric have never kept originality from showing itself clearly. The contrary—namely, that they have aided the development of originality—would be infinitely more true.

To be brief, I am obliged to omit numerous corollaries resulting from my principal formula, in which is contained, so to speak, the entire formulary of the true aesthetic, and which may be expressed thus: The whole visible universe is but a storehouse of images and signs to which imagination will give a relative place and value; it is a sort of food which the imagination must digest and transform. All the powers of the human soul must be subordinated to the imagination, which commandeers them all at one and the same time. Just as knowing the dictionary well does not necessarily imply a knowledge of the art of composition, and just as the art of composition does not itself imply a universal imagination, so a good painter may not be a great painter. But a great painter is inevitably a good painter, because a universal imagination includes the understanding of all means of expression and the desire to master them.

𝕏 PHILOSOPHIC ART

PREFACE

An unfinished article, "Philosophic Art," composed about 1859, was published posthumously ten years later in the volume of literary and art criticism entitled *L'Art Romantique*.

Baudelaire had planned to write such an essay for several years and had evidently given it a great deal of thought. He is primarily concerned with contrasting his conception of pure art with the rationalistic tendencies of philosophic or didactic art, particularly as represented by Chenavard and the German School.[119]

The article is significant, if only for its succinct definition of pure art—an art which, through the fusion of external and internal elements, aims to create a magical effect for the reader or spectator. The definition is revelatory of Baudelaire's own poetic theory and practice and furnishes a key to some of the finest works of the Symbolist School and to modern art in general.

It is worth noting that Baudelaire's attitude toward what he calls philosophic art remains what it was in 1846 when he reviewed Louis Ménard's play, *Prometheus Unbound*.

᷒᷒᷒᷒

What is the modern conception of pure art? It is the creation of a suggestive magic containing both the object and the subject, the world outside the artist and the artist himself.

What is philosophic art according to Chenavard and the German School? It is plastic art that aims to replace books or, in other words, to compete with the printing press in teaching history, morality, and philosophy.

There are, to be sure, periods of history in which plastic art is destined to paint the religious beliefs and the historic archives of a nation.

But for several centuries there has been developing a more and more marked separation of powers in the history of art; there are subjects which belong to painting, others to music, others to literature.

Is it the inevitable result of decadence that today each art manifests a desire to encroach on its neighbor, that painters introduce the musical gamut into painting, sculptors introduce color into sculpture, writers introduce plastic means into literature, and that other artists—those with whom we are concerned today—introduce a sort of encyclopedic philosophy into plastic art itself?

All good sculpture, all good painting, all good music suggests the emotions and the dreams which it wishes to suggest.

But reasoning and deduction belong to books. . . .

Philosophical art is not as foreign to French nature as one might suppose. France loves myths, morality, the rebus; or, to be more exact, a country of reason, she loves intellectual endeavor.

It is the Romantic School which reacted against these rationalistic tendencies and won acceptance for the glory of pure art.

❦ RICHARD WAGNER AND TANNHÄUSER IN PARIS

PREFACE

The years 1859–1861 find Baudelaire at the height of his critical powers. His articles on the Salon of 1859, on Wagner, and on Constantin Guys are the final steps in the evolution of his artistic thought. Fascinating as the essays are from the standpoint of general aesthetic ideas, they are also superb examples of the application of those ideas.

Baudelaire's essay on Wagner was his only excursion into musical criticism. Although he had made no formal study of music, he was sensitive to its beauty and was often carried away by its sweeping power: "Music often engulfs me like the sea." In a letter to Wagner and on several other occasions he mentions his fondness for Beethoven and Weber, and in his famous evocation of Delacroix's paintings ("Les Phares") he compares his gloomy skies in which strange fanfares sound to a stifled sigh from Weber.

Baudelaire may first have become interested in Wagner through Gérard de Nerval and Champfleury who were both ardent admirers of the German composer. As early as 1849 he had written in a letter (July 13) that Wagner would be "the most illustrious of the masters." It was only in 1860, however, that Baudelaire's enthusiasm for Wagner was transformed into a passionate admiration comparable to that which he felt for Poe and Delacroix. In 1860 Wagner himself had come to Paris to direct his music which until then had been heard only twice in Paris—in 1850 and again in 1858. The three concerts which he gave at the Salle Ventadour created a furor reminiscent of the reception given *Hernani* thirty years earlier. For the most part the critics were hostile, but Baudelaire who sensed the greatness of the music, rushed to the defense of Wagner and wrote an enthusiastic letter expressing his intense admiration. The letter (included below as a preface to his article) may be considered a spontaneous, though very abbreviated, first draft of the article which he was to write a year later after witnessing a performance of the opera *Tannhäuser*.

The essay on Wagner, dated March 18, appeared April 1 in the *Revue Européenne* about two weeks after the opening night (March 13, 1861). Baudelaire had evidently written the major part of the essay before he had actually seen the opera; the last pages were composed after the first performance when the opera had already been declared a failure. The article, together with a postscript dated April 8, was published as a brochure on May 4, 1861.

Though Wagner never fully realized Baudelaire's genius, he was deeply appreciative of his encouragement and praise and sought out the critic to express his personal gratitude. Six years later Wagner is said to have been grieved to learn of the death of his admirer and defender. On his side, Baudelaire never lost his enthusiasm for the German composer. One of his greatest joys during the last bleak years of his life, and especially during his illness, was to hear the music of Wagner played for him by sympathetic friends.

Baudelaire's criticism of Wagner is intended not so much for professional students of music as for the "poetic readers" to whom he had referred in the *Salon of 1846*. Along with his own comments, however, he includes extensive quotations and paraphrases from Wagner, Liszt, and Berlioz which supply technical information that he lacked.

Although the poet had renounced the idea of being guided by a "system," he did have a natural way of approaching every form of artistic expression. As early as 1846 he had stressed the need for a critic to see a work of art through his own temperament in order to make a meaningful translation of his experiences. Not until 1861, however, did he call attention to the role that intelligence had played in his criticism. Wagner's music—which he describes as "a revelation"—was a challenge to his powers of expression that forced him into a definition of his whole critical purpose: "I resolved to discover the why and the wherefore and to transform my pleasure into knowledge. . . ." Baudelaire goes on to argue that every truly creative artist becomes a critic, at least of his own work. Not surprisingly, he believes that the creative artist is the best critic.

In this essay, as in many others, certain key ideas recur. The discussion of music, which suggests colors and visual experiences to his mind, gives him an opportunity to emphasize synaesthetic correspondences (with which he had long been concerned) by anonymously quoting two quatrains from his sonnet, "Correspondances." In another chapter he calls attention to the spiritual analogies that are revealed in human myths. Elsewhere, the importance of suggestion is stressed; through imagination the auditor must complete the lacunae left in the music, just as a reader or spectator must finish a poem or a painting. Every significant work of art, he adds, is "an inexhaustible source of suggestions." The statement is a logical development of his conviction stated in several earlier essays that "the poetry of a picture lies in the soul of the spectator, and genius consists in awakening it." [120]

Wagner's compositions excited Baudelaire because of their "modern" and "Romantic" qualities, their "passion," their "concentration and nervous intensity," and also because of the "satanic" and "diabolical" elements that they contained. He applauds Tannhäuser's aspiration to suffering and his "joy in damnation."

Yet he was equally stirred by the opposed "celestial" aspects of Wagner's music. Baudelaire's evocation of the overture to *Lohengrin*, to cite but one example, could only have been written by an idealistic poet. It reveals the aesthetic and spiritual exaltation and the "suggestive magic" of poems such as "Elévation," "Correspondances," and "Les Phares."

The essay itself is remarkable evidence of the validity of the method which its author describes. It shows both his imagination and his intelligence at work—the imagination of a creative artist evoking and re-creating an aesthetic experience; the curiosity of an analytical mind seeking the means by which the composer's genius finds expression.

[LETTER FROM BAUDELAIRE TO WAGNER]

Friday, February 17, 1860

Sir,

I have always imagined that no matter how accustomed to fame a great artist might be, he would not be insensible to a sincere compliment, when that compliment was an expression of gratitude, as it were, and I have likewise imagined that such a compliment could have a *special* value coming from a Frenchman, that is to say from a man little prone to enthusiasm and born in a country where poetry and painting are scarcely any better understood than music. First of all, I want to tell you that I owe you *the greatest musical enjoyment that I have ever experienced.* I have reached an age when one scarcely finds pleasure in writing to famous men, and I would have hesitated even longer to express my admiration by letter, had I not noticed every day outrageous, ridiculous articles in which every possible effort is made to defame your genius. You are not the first man, Sir, who has given me occasion to suffer and to blush for my country. In short, indignation has impelled me to express my gratitude. I said to myself: I want to be distinguished from all those idiots.

The first time I went to the Théâtre des Italiens to hear

your works I was not favourably disposed and, to tell the truth, I was even badly prejudiced; but I deserve to be excused; I have been duped so often; I have heard so much music by insufferably pretentious charlatans. By you I was conquered at once. What I felt is indescribable, and if you will be kind enough not to laugh, I shall try to express it to you. At first it seemed to me I was familiar with that music, and later in thinking about it, I understood how this illusion came about; it seemed to me that the music was *mine*, and I recognized it as every man recognizes the things he is destined to love. To anyone except an intelligent man, this sentence would seem utterly ridiculous, especially coming from someone who, like me, *does not know music*, and whose whole musical education is restricted to having heard (with great pleasure, to be sure) some beautiful works of Weber and Beethoven.

Next, the quality which most impressed me was that of grandeur. It possesses greatness and it makes one experience greatness. I have encountered everywhere in your works the solemnity of the great sounds, the great aspects of Nature, and the solemnity of the great passions of man. One feels himself immediately carried away and subjugated. One of the strangest parts and one which gave me a new musical sensation is that which is intended to portray religious ecstasy. The effect produced by the "Entry of the Guests into the Wartburg" and by the "Wedding Chorus" is tremendous. I felt all the majesty of a life that is more ample than our own. And something else: I often had a feeling, somewhat strange in nature, of pride and of joy in understanding, in being possessed, in being overwhelmed, a truly sensual pleasure like that of rising in the air or being tossed on the sea. And at the same time the music now and again breathed pride of life. Generally those profound harmonies seemed to me like stimulants which accelerate the pulse of the imagination. Finally, I also felt, and I beg you not to laugh, sensations which probably derive from my bent of mind and from my habitual preoccupations. Throughout, there is something exalted and exalting, something aspiring to mount higher, something excessive and superlative. For example, to use comparisons borrowed from painting, I imagine before my eyes a vast expanse of dark red. If this red represents passion, I see it pass gradually, through all the transitions of red and rose to the incandescence of a fiery furnace. It would seem difficult, even impossible to achieve anything more intense; and yet a final flash appears, cutting an even whiter streak than the white that serves as a background. It is, if you like, the supreme cry of a soul in a paroxysm of ecstasy.

I had begun to write a few thoughts on the passages from *Tannhäuser* and *Lohengrin* which we had heard; but I realized the impossibility of saying everything.

I could continue my letter indefinitely. If you have been able to read this far, I thank you. I have only a few more words to add. From the day I first heard your music, I have said to myself constantly, especially in my bad moments: *If only I could hear a little Wagner this evening.* There are doubtless other men like me. In short, you must have been satisfied with the audience whose instinct was far superior to the poor knowledge of the journalists. Why could you not give additional concerts and include some new compositions? You have given us a foretaste of new pleasures; have you the right to deprive us of the rest?—Once again, Sir, I thank you; in an hour of discouragement you have recalled me to my real self and to the truly great.

Ch. Baudelaire

I am not adding my address, because you might think I have a favour to ask of you.

⊱⊰⊱⊰⊱⊰

I

Let us go back thirteen months in time, if you will, to the beginning of the debate; and I trust that you will allow me, in my appraisal, to speak often in personal terms. The *I*, rightly considered impertinent in many cases, implies nevertheless a great modesty; it confines the writer within the strictest limits of sincerity. By reducing his task, it makes it easier. Finally, it is not necessary to be a master of probability to be sure that sincerity will find friends among fair-minded readers; there is a good chance that the ingenuous critic, who reports only his own impressions, will also report those of some unknown partisans.

Thirteen months ago, then, there was a great furor in Paris. A poor, unknown German composer who, without our being aware of the fact, had made a living among us for a long time by petty jobs, but whom the German public had been acclaiming as a genius for fifteen years, returned to the place of his earlier misfortunes in order to submit his works to our judgment. Until then Paris had heard little of Wagner; there was a vague awareness that the question of a reform in musical drama was being debated on the other side of the Rhine and that Liszt had enthusiastically adopted the ideas of the reformer. M. Fétis had launched a kind of indictment against him, and those who may be interested in leafing through issues of *La Revue et Gazette Musicale de Paris* will be able to discover once again that the writers who pride themselves on expressing the most judicious and the most moderate opinions, hardly pride themselves on discretion and temperateness, or even on ordinary courtesy, in the criticism of opinions that are contrary to their own.[121] The articles by M. Fétis are hardly more than distressing diatribes, but the irritation of the venerable dilettante only served to prove the importance of the works that he consigned to anathema and ridicule. For thirteen months, moreover, during which public curiosity has not died down, Richard Wagner has been subjected to many other insults. Nevertheless, some years ago, returning from a visit to Germany, Théophile Gautier, who had been very much moved by a performance of *Tann-häuser*, translated his impressions in *Le Moniteur* with the plastic sureness that gives an irresistible charm to all of his writings. But these various documents, appearing at long intervals, had escaped the attention of the crowd.

As soon as the posters announced that Richard Wagner was going to have some fragments of his compositions played in the concert hall on the Boulevard des Italiens, there occurred one of those amusing incidents such as we have seen before, which prove that the French have an instinctive and impatient need to take a stand about everything without deliberation or examination. Some spoke of marvels, and others began a shocking denigration of works that they had not yet heard. Today this ridiculous situation still continues, and it may be said that there has never been so much discussion about an unknown subject. In short, the Wagner concerts promised to be a veritable battleground of doctrines, one of those solemn crises in art, one of these mêlées in which artists, critics and public usually enter into confused and violent discussions; fortunate crises that indicate health and richness in the intellectual life of a nation, and that we had forgotten, so to speak, since the great days of Victor Hugo. I am taking the following lines from the review by M. Berlioz (February 9, 1860): "The lobby of the Théâtre Italien was an interesting spectacle on the evening of the first concert. There were arguments, cries, rages that always seemed on the point of degenerating into acts of violence." Had it not been for the presence of the Emperor, the same scandalous situation might have occurred at the Opéra a few days ago, especially since there were *more connoisseurs* in the audience. At the end of one of the dress rehearsals, I recall having seen one of the most eminent critics in Paris ostentatiously planted in front of the box office, blocking the exit of the crowd, laughing like a maniac, like one of those unfortunate persons who, in asylums, are called *overstimulated*. Believing that his face was known to everyone, the poor man seemed to be saying: "See how I laugh, I, the famous S. . . . [Scudo]! Be sure that your judgement conforms with mine." [122] In the review that I mentioned a moment ago, M. Berlioz, who nevertheless showed much less warmth than one might have expected from him, added: "The profusion of nonsensical remarks, absurdities and even lies that were bandied about that evening was prodigious and proves clearly that, among us at least, when it comes to appreciating music different from what is usual, passion and prejudice take the floor and keep good sense and good taste from speaking."

Wagner had been daring: the program of his concert did not include instrumental solos, or songs, or any of the showy numbers so dear to a public that is fond of virtuosos and their *tours de force*. Nothing but ensembles, choruses or symphonies. There was a violent struggle, it is true, but the public, left to itself, was excited by some of the irresistible passages whose meaning was more clear to them, and Wagner's music triumphed through its own power. The overture of *Tannhäuser*, the stately march in the second act, the overture of *Lohengrin* especially, the "Wedding Chorus" and the "Epithalamium" were magnificently applauded. To be sure, many things remained unclear, but fair-minded listeners said: "Since these compositions are designed for the theater, we must wait; the staging will clarify the things that are insufficiently defined." Meanwhile, it was firmly established that, as a composer of symphonies, as an artist capable of translating the tumult of the human soul by a thousand combinations of sound, Richard Wagner was on the highest level, as great certainly as the greatest.

I have often heard it said that music cannot boast of being able to translate anything with the certainty of literature or painting. To a certain extent that is true, but it is not altogether true. It translates in its own way and by its own means. In music, as in painting and even in literature, which is nevertheless the most concrete of the arts, there is always a lacuna that is filled by the imagination of the auditor.

Doubtless these are the reasons that led Wagner to consider dramatic art, that is the union, the coincidence of several arts, as the pre-eminent art, the most synthetic and the most perfect.

Now, if we put aside for a moment the plastic elements, the stage sets, the use of ideal performers, and even the libretto, it is still undeniable that the more eloquent the music, the more swift and true its suggestiveness, the greater the chance that sensitive persons will conceive ideas in harmony with those that inspired the artist. As an example there immediately comes to mind the famous overture of *Lohengrin* of which M. Berlioz has written a magnificent eulogy in technical language. However, I shall confine myself to illustrating its value by the suggestions that it offers.

In the program given to the audience at the Théâtre Italien at that time I read:

From the first measures, the soul of the pious, solitary man who is waiting for the sacred vase *plunges into infinite spaces*. He sees a strange apparition which gradually takes on a shape and a form. This apparition becomes still more precise, and *the miraculous host of angels*, bearing the sacred chalice in their midst, passes before him. The holy procession approaches; the heart of the man elected by God is slowly exalted; it expands, it dilates; ineffable aspirations are aroused in him; *he yields to an increasing beatitude*, finding himself closer and closer to *the luminous apparition*, and when finally the Holy Grail itself appears in the midst of the sacred cortège, *he abandons himself to an ecstatic adoration, as if the whole world had suddenly disappeared*. Meanwhile the Holy Grail bestows its blessings on the praying saint and consecrates him as its knight. Then *the burning flames gradually lose their brilliance*; with holy joy, the host of angels, smiling at the earth which they are leaving behind, regains the celestial heights. It has left the Holy Grail in the hands of pure men whose *hearts have been filled by the divine liqueur*, and the august host vanishes *into the depths of space* in the same way in which it appeared.

The reader will soon understand why I have underlined certain phrases. Now I take Liszt's book, and I open it at the page where the illustrious pianist (who is an artist and a philosopher) translates the same passage in his own way: [123]

This introduction contains and reveals *the mystic element*, always present and always concealed in the piece . . . In order to make us realize the inexpressible power of this secret, Wagner first shows us the *ineffable beauty of the sanctuary*, inhabited by a God who avenges the oppressed and asks only *love and belief* from the faithful. He introduces us to the Holy Grail; he makes shimmer before our eyes the temple of incorruptible wood, with its sweet-smelling walls, its *golden* doors, its *asbestos* beams, its *opal* columns, its *cymophane* partitions, whose splendid porticoes are approached only by those with pure hands and exalted hearts. He does not make us see it in its real and imposing structure, but allowing for the weakness of our senses, as it were, he first reveals it to us reflected in some *azure waves* or reproduced by *some iridescent cloud*.

At the beginning there is a *vast dormant expanse* of melody, *a vaporous ether that spreads out* as a background for the sacred tableau that appears before our profane eyes, an effect assigned exclusively to the violins, divided into eight different groups which, after several measures of harmonics, continue in the highest notes of their registers. Then the motif is repeated by the softest wind instruments; the horns and the bassoons join in and prepare the entry of the trumpets and trombones, which repeat the melody for the fourth time, with *a dazzling flash of color*, as if at that very moment the sacred edifice *had shone* before *our blinded eyes in all its luminous and radiant magnificence*. But *the vivid sparkling*, gradually brought to *the intensity of solar radiance*, quickly fades like a *celestial light*.

The *transparent mist* of clouds closes, the vision slowly disappears in the same *variegated* incense in the midst of which it had appeared, and the passage ends with the six first measures, which have become *even more ethereal*. Its quality of *ideal mysticity* is made especially perceptible by the constant *pianissimo* of the orchestra that is interrupted only for a brief moment when the *brass accentuates* the marvelous lines of the single motif of the introduction. Such is the image presented to our excited senses when we listen to this sublime *adagio*.

May I be allowed to explain and express in words the inevitable translation that my imagination made of the same passage when, with closed eyes, I heard it for the first time, and when I felt as if I were being lifted up above the earth?

Certainly I would not dare to speak complacently about my *reveries*, if it were not useful to compare them with the *reveries* just mentioned. The reader knows what we are trying to do: to show that true music suggests analogous ideas to different minds. Besides, it would not be ridiculous in this connection to argue *a priori*, without analysis and without comparisons; for what would be really surprising would be that sound *could not* suggest color, that colors could not convey a melody, and that sound and color were unsuited to translating ideas, things always having been expressed by a reciprocal analogy since the day when God created the world as a complex and indivisible whole.

> La Nature est un temple où de vivants piliers
> Laissent parfois sortir de confuses paroles;
> L'homme y passe à travers des forêts de symboles
> Qui l'observent avec des regards familiers.
>
> Comme de longs échos qui de loin se confondent
> Dans une ténébreuse et profonde unité,
> Vaste comme la nuit et comme la clarté,
> Les parfums, les couleurs et les sons se répondent.[124]

To continue, I remember that, from the first measures, I experienced one of those happy impressions that almost all imaginative men have known in dreams when they were asleep. I felt myself freed from *the bonds of weight,* and in memory I recaptured the extraordinary *pleasure* which floats about *heights* (we may note in passing that I did not know the program cited above). Next, involuntarily, I imagined to myself the delightful state of a man gripped by a great dream in an absolute solitude, but a solitude with *an immense horizon* and filled with a *vast diffused light; an immensity* with no décor except itself. Soon I experienced the sensation of a brighter *light, of an intensity of light* increasing so quickly that none of the nuances furnished by the dictionary would suffice to express *this always renascent increase of brilliance and whiteness.* Then I had the full realization of a soul moving in a luminous milieu, of an ecstasy *composed of pleasure and knowledge,* and soaring above and far away from the natural world.

You will easily be able to note the differences among these three translations. Wagner speaks of *a host of angels bearing a sacred vessel;* Liszt sees *a miraculously beautiful building* which is reflected in a hazy mist. My reverie is less defined by material objects: it is more vague and more abstract. But the important thing here is to emphasize the similarities. If there were only a few, they would still constitute sufficient proof; but fortunately they are far more numerous and striking than is necessary. In the three translations we find the sensation of *physical and spiritual beatitude;* of *isolation;* of the contemplation of *something infinitely great and infinitely beautiful;* of *an intense light* that delights *the eyes and makes the soul faint with rapture;* and finally the sensation of *space extended to the uttermost conceivable limits.*

No composer excels Wagner in *painting* space and depth, both material and spiritual. That is an observation that some of the best minds could not help making on several occasions. He possesses the art of translating by fine gradations everything that is excessive, immense, aspiring in the natural and spiritual life of man. Listening to this passionate and despotic music, it sometimes seems that one is observing the vertiginous conceptions stimulated by opium that are painted on a background of darkness torn by reverie.

From that moment, that is to say from the first concert, I was obsessed by a desire to penetrate more deeply into the understanding of these singular works. I had experienced (at least that was what it seemed to me) a spiritual operation, a revelation. The pleasure that I had felt was so strong and so terrible that I could not help wishing to return to it constantly. Doubtless much of what I had already learned from Weber and Beethoven entered into what I had felt, but there was also something new that I was powerless to define, and that impotence aroused in me anger and curiosity mingled with a strange delight. For several days, for a long time, I kept saying to myself, "Where shall I be able to hear some of Wagner's music this evening?" Those of my friends who owned pianos were martyrs on more than one occasion. Soon, as with all novelties, symphonic passages from Wagner resounded in casinos for the benefit of crowds eager for vulgar pleasures. The flashing majesty of that music fell like thunder in an evil place. The word spread quickly, and we often observed the comic spectacle of serious and refined men subjecting themselves to contact with unwholesome crowds for the sake of enjoying the solemn march of the "Entry of the Guests into the Wartburg" or the stately nuptial music of *Lohengrin*.

Nevertheless, frequent repetitions of the same melodic phrases, in passages drawn from the same opera, implied mysterious intentions and a method that were unknown to me. I resolved to discover the why and the wherefore and to transform my pleasure into knowledge before an operatic performance appeared and supplied me with a perfect clarification. I questioned friends and enemies. I masticated the indigestible and wretched pamphlet by M. Fétis. I read Liszt's book, and finally, lacking *L'Art et la Révolution* and *L'Œuvre d'Art de l'Avenir*, works that have not been translated, I found a copy of the book entitled *Opéra et Drame* in an English translation.

II

The French kept on joking, and vulgar journalism relentlessly continued its habitual childish comments. Since Wagner had always insisted that dramatic music should *reveal* feeling, should adapt itself to feeling with the same precision as words, though obviously in a different way, that, in other words, it should express the undefined part of feeling that words, which are too specific, cannot render (here he was saying nothing that was not accepted by all sensible minds), a great many people, convinced by journalistic wits, imagined that the master believed music had the power of expressing the concrete form of things and that he was thus inverting roles and functions. It would be useless and boring to enumerate all the gibes based on that false judgment which, coming sometimes from malice and sometimes from ignorance, had led public opinion astray beforehand. But in Paris more than anywhere else, it is impossible to stop a writer who thinks he is amusing. Public curiosity having been aroused by Wagner, many articles and pamphlets were published that informed us about his life, his long-continued struggles and all his anguish. Among the documents that are familiar today, I wish to select only those that seem to me useful in clarifying and defining the character and nature of the master. He who wrote that *the man who from birth was not endowed by a fairy with the spirit of discontent about everything that exists will never succeed in discovering anything new,* unquestionably must have found in the conflicts of life more pain than anyone else. I find the explanation of Wagner's revolutionary opinions in that capacity for suffering that is common to all artists and that is all the greater as their instinct for the just and the beautiful is more pronounced. Embittered by so many disappointments, disillusioned by so many shattered dreams, impelled by an error that is understandable in such an excessively tense and sensitive mind, there came a time when he felt obliged to postulate a spiritual complicity between bad music and bad governments. Possessed by the supreme desire of seeing routine conquered once and for all by the ideal in art (it is an essentially human illusion), he brought himself to hope that political revolutions would promote the cause of revolution in art. Wagner's very success disproved his expectations and his hopes; for it took the order of a *despot* in France to get the revolutionary's work performed. We have already seen the romantic revolution in Paris encouraged in the same way by the monarchy, while the liberals and republicans remained stubbornly attached to the routines of so-called classic literature.

From the information that he has published about his youth, I note that when he was a child, he lived in the heart of the theater, frequented the wings and composed plays. The music of Weber, and later that of Beethoven, acted on his mind with an irresistible force, and soon, as years and studies multiplied, he found it impossible not to think in a dual manner, poetically and musically. He perceived every idea simultaneously in two forms, one of the two arts beginning to function where the other reached its limits. The dramatic sense, which was one of his most dominant faculties, was bound to impel him to revolt against all the frivolities, the platitudes and the absurdities of musical drama. Thus Providence, which presides over revolutions in art, ripened in a youthful German brain the problem that had been so much discussed in the eighteenth century. Anyone who has read attentively the *Lettre sur la Musique,* which serves as a preface to *Quatre Poèmes d'Opéras Traduits en Prose Française,* can have no doubts about the matter. In it he often cites the names of Gluck and of Méhul with a passionate enthusiasm. With all due respect to M. Fétis, who insists on establishing for eternity the predominance of music in lyric drama, the opinion of minds such as Gluck, Diderot, Voltaire and Goethe is not to be disdained. If the last two subsequently disowned their favorite theories, it was in their case only an expression of discouragement and despair. Leafing through the *Lettre sur la Musique,* I felt coming back to life in my mind, as if through a mnemonic echo, various passages in Diderot which affirm that true musical drama cannot be anything other than the cries and sobs of passion expressed in notes and rhythm. The same scientific, poetic and artistic problems keep recurring through the ages, and Wagner does not profess to invent, but simply to confirm an old idea which, on more than one occasion, will doubtless be vanquished and victorious in turn. Indeed, all these questions are extremely simple, and it is rather surprising to see a revolt against the theories of *the music of the future* (to use an expression as inexact as it is generally accepted) among the very persons whom we have so often heard complaining about the tortures inflicted on every reasonable mind by the routine character of the usual operatic libretto.

In the same *Lettre sur la Musique,* in which the author gives a very brief and very lucid analysis of his three earlier works, *L'Art et la Révolution*, *L'Œuvre d'Art de l'Avenir* and *Opéra et Drame*, we find a very lively concern with the Greek theater that is quite natural, even inevitable in a dramatist-composer who was to seek in the past the justification of his disgust for the present. We also find suggestions that are useful in the establishment of new conditions for the lyric drama. More than a year ago now, in his letter to Berlioz he said:

I asked myself what should be the conditions of art that could inspire inviolable respect in the audience and, to avoid too much hazardous speculation about that question, I sought my point of departure in ancient Greece. First I noted the pre-eminent artistic form, the *drama*, in which the idea, however profound it may be, can make itself manifest with the greatest clarity and in the most universally intelligible manner. Today we are rightly astonished that thirty thousand Greeks should have been able to follow performances of the tragedies of Aeschylus with sustained interest; but if we look for the means by which these results were achieved, we find that it was through an alliance of all the arts joined for the same purpose, that is for the production of the most perfect and the only true work of art. That led me to study the relations of the various branches of art to one another and, after having grasped the relation that exists between the *plastic* and the *mimetic*, I examined that which exists between music and poetry: from that examination there suddenly sprang up clarifications that completely dissipated the darkness which had troubled me up to that time.

I recognized, indeed, that precisely where one of the arts reaches its impassable limits, the other immediately began to function in its sphere of action with the most rigorous exactitude; and that consequently, through the intimate union of these two arts, one could express with the most satisfying clarity that which neither could express by itself; that, on the contrary, every attempt to render by means of one of them what could be rendered only by the two together, was inevitably bound to lead first to obscurity and confusion, and then to the degeneration and to the corruption of each art in particular.

And in the preface of his latest book, he returns to the same subject in these terms:

In a few rare artistic creations I had found a real base on which to rest my dramatic and musical ideal; now, in its turn, history offered me the model and type of ideal relations between the theater and public life as I conceived them. I found the model I was looking for in the ancient Greek theater: there the theater functioned only on certain solemn occasions when a religious festival was accompanied by the pleasures of art. The most distinguished political leaders took a direct part in these solemn events as poets or directors; they appeared like priests before the eyes of the people gathered together from the city and the countryside, and that assembly was filled with such a lofty expectation of sublimity in the works that were to be enacted that the most profound poems, those of an Aeschylus and of a Sophocles, could be presented to the people and were assured of being perfectly understood.

The destiny of Wagner was determined by this absolute, despotic taste for a dramatic ideal in which everything, from a declamation marked and underlined by the music with so much care that the singer cannot omit a single syllable—a veritable arabesque of sounds delineated by passion—to the most painstaking care about staging and sets, in which, as I say, all the details should at all times contribute to the totality of the effect. With him, that was in effect a permanent postulation. Since the day when he freed himself from the old routines of the libretto and when he courageously repudiated his *Rienzi*, an opera of his youth which had been honored by a great success, he has marched straight ahead, without the slightest deviation, toward this imperious ideal. Therefore I was not at all surprised to find in those works that have been translated, particularly in *Tannhäuser*, *Lohengrin* and *The Flying Dutchman*, an excellent method of construction, a spirit of order and division that recalls the architecture of ancient tragedies. But the phenomena and the ideas which occur periodically through the ages always take

on at each resurrection the complementary character of variance
and circumstantiality. The radiant ancient Venus, the Aphrodite
born from the white foam of the sea, has not traversed the hor-
rifying darkness of the Middle Ages with impunity. She no
longer dwells on Mount Olympus or on the banks of the sweet-
smelling archipelago. She has retired into the depths of a cave,
magnificent to be sure, but lighted up by fires which are not
those of the benign Phoebus. By descending beneath the earth,
Venus has come close to hell and doubtless, at certain abominable solemnities, she proceeds to pay homage to the Archfiend,
prince of the flesh and lord of sin. Likewise, the poems of
Wagner, although they reveal a sincere taste for and a perfect
understanding of classic beauty, also contain a considerable
amount of the Romantic spirit. If they evoke the majesty of
Sophocles and Aeschylus, at the same time they compel our
minds to recall the medieval *Mystery Plays*, developed when
the plastic arts dominated Roman Catholic expression. They are
comparable to those great visions which the Middle Ages
painted on the walls of churches or wove into magnificent
tapestries. Their general aspect is definitely legendary: *Tannhäuser*, legend; *Lohengrin*, legend; *The Flying Dutchman*, a
legend. And it is not merely an inclination natural to every
poetic mind that led Wagner to this apparent specialty; it is a
formal, deliberate decision determined by the study of the conditions most favorable to lyric drama.

He himself has carefully explained the question in his
books. The fact is that not all subjects are equally suited to
provide the basis for a comprehensive drama endowed with a
universal character. Obviously there would be great danger in
translating the most delightful and the most perfect genre
picture into a fresco. It is above all in the universal heart of man
and in the history of that heart that the dramatic poet will find
pictures that are universally intelligible. In order to be perfectly
free to construct an ideal drama, it will be wise to eliminate all
the difficulties that might arise from technical, political or even

too specific historic details. I shall let the master himself speak:

The only picture of human life that may be called poetic is that in which the motives that have meaning only to abstract intelligence are replaced by the purely human impulses which govern the heart. This tendency (which relates to the finding of a poetic subject) is the sovereign law that controls poetic form and presentation. . . . The rhythmic arrangement and the almost musical ornament of rhyme are for the poet the means of giving lines and musical phrases a power that is as dominating as a spell and that governs feeling as it wishes. This tendency, so essential to the poet, leads him to the limits of his art, limits which directly border on music; and, consequently, the most complete work of the poet should be that which in its final realization would be perfect music.

Hence I found myself led necessarily to designate *myth* as the ideal material for the poet. Myth is the original and anonymous poem of the people, and in every age we find it revived, recast once again by each succeeding generation of great poets in cultivated periods. Myth, indeed, almost completely strips human relations of their conventional form, intelligible only to abstract reason; it reveals what is truly human in life, what is eternally comprehensible, and reveals it in that concrete form, free of all imitation, which gives to all true myths their individual character, recognizable at the first glance.

And elsewhere, returning to the same theme, he says:

Once and for all I abandoned the terrain of history and established myself on that of legend. . . . I was able to put aside all the detail necessary to describe and represent historic fact and its accidents, all the detail that is required for the complete understanding of a remote and special period of history, and that contemporary writers of historical plays and novels deduce, for that reason, in such a circumstantial manner. . . . Legend, regardless of the period or nation to which it belongs, has the advantage of including nothing except what is purely human in that period or nation, and of presenting it in a form that is strikingly original and therefore intelligible at the first glance. A ballad, a popular song suffice to represent in an instant this character in its most fixed and its most striking features. . . . The character of the scene and the tone of the legend together contribute to cast the mind into that *dream* state which soon carries it to the point of full *clairvoyance,* and the mind then discovers a new relationship among the phenomena of the world that its eyes had not been able to perceive in the ordinary waking state.

How could Wagner fail to understand admirably the sacred, divine character of myth, he who was at once a poet and a critic? I have heard many persons draw from the very range of his faculties and from his high critical intelligence a reason to distrust his musical genius, and I think that this is a propitious occasion to refute a very common error whose principal root is perhaps the ugliest of human feelings, envy. "A person who reasons so much about his art cannot produce beautiful works in a natural way," say some, who thus deprive genius of its rationality and assign to it a purely instinctive and practically vegetable function. Others are disposed to consider Wagner as a theoretician who produced operas solely to verify *a posteriori* the value of his own theories. That is not only completely false, since the master began when he was quite young, as we know, by producing various kinds of poetic and musical composition, and only gradually succeeded in creating an ideal of the lyric drama for himself, but it is even something that is absolutely impossible. It would be a very novel occurrence in the history of the arts for a critic to become a poet—a reversal of all psychic laws, a monstrosity; on the other hand, all great poets naturally and inevitably become critics. I feel sorry for poets who are guided by instinct alone; I consider them incomplete. In the spiritual life of the former a crisis invariably develops in which they wish to analyze their art, to discover the obscure laws by virtue of which they have created, and to draw from this study a series of precepts whose divine goal is infallibility in poetic production. It would be a miracle if a critic became a poet, and it is impossible for a poet not to contain within himself a critic. Therefore the reader will not be surprised that I consider the poet as the best of all critics. The people who reproach the musician Wagner for having written books on the philosophy of his art, and who for this reason suspect that his music is not a natural, spontaneous product, should likewise deny that da Vinci, Hogarth and Reynolds could have produced good paintings simply because they deduced and analyzed the principles of their art. Who discusses painting better than our great Delacroix? Diderot, Goethe, Shakespeare—all creative writers, all admirable critics. Poetry was the first to exist, to assert itself, and it has engendered the study of rules. Such is the undisputed history of human endeavor. Now, since everyone is the whole world in miniature and since the history of an individual mind represents the history of the universal mind on a small scale, it would be just and natural (lacking the proofs that exist) to suppose that the development of Wagner's thoughts has been analogous to the work of humanity in general.

III

Tannhäuser represents the struggle of the two principles that have chosen the human heart as their chief battlefield—flesh against spirit, hell against heaven, Satan against God.[125] And this duality is represented immediately, in the overture, with an incomparable skill. What has not already been written about this passage? Nevertheless, we may be sure that it will still provide material for many arguments and eloquent commentaries; for it is characteristic of truly artistic works to be an inexhaustible source of suggestions. The overture then, as I say, sums up the thought of the drama in two songs, the religious song and the voluptuous song which, to use Liszt's expression, "are placed here like two mathematical terms and which, in the finale, find their equation." The "Pilgrims' Chorus" comes first, with the authority of a supreme law, as if to indicate immediately the true meaning of life, the goal of the universal pilgrimage, that is God. But since the intimate sense of God is soon drowned in every soul by the lusts of the flesh, the song that represents holiness is gradually overwhelmed by the sighs of pleasure. Already the true, the terrible, the universal Venus stands out in every imagination. And whoever has not yet heard the marvelous overture of *Tannhäuser* should not imagine a song of ordinary lovers dallying beneath arbors, or the accents of a drunken band defying God in the language of Horace. It is something quite different, at once more true and more sinister. Languors, delights mingled with fever and cut short by anguish, constant returns toward a pleasure that promises to quench, but never quenches thirst; wild palpitations of the heart and senses, imperious commands of the flesh, all the onomatopoetic dictionary of love is heard here. Finally, little by little, the religious theme slowly and gradually regains control and absorbs the other in a peaceful victory, as glorious as that of the irresistible being over the sickly and profligate being, of Saint Michael over Lucifer.

At the beginning of this study, I noted the power with which Wagner, in the overture of *Lohengrin*, had expressed the ardors of mysticism, the yearning of the spirit for an incommunicable God. In the overture of *Tannhäuser*, in the struggle between the two opposed principles, he has not shown himself less subtle or less powerful. Whence has the master drawn that raging song of the flesh, that absolute knowledge of the diabolical side of man? From the first measures our nerves vibrate in unison with the melody; every creature of flesh endowed with memories begins to tremble. Every well balanced mind bears within it two infinites, heaven and hell, and in every image of one of these infinites he suddenly recognizes half of himself. The satanic titillations of a vague love are soon followed by enticements, dazzling displays, cries of victory, moans of gratitude, and then savage roars, the reproaches of victims and the impious hosannas of executioners, as if barbarity always has to have its place in the drama of love, and sensual enjoyment has to lead, by an inescapable satanic logic, to the delights of crime. When the religious theme, cutting across the unchained evil, returns little by little to re-establish order and to regain the ascendant, when it rises again in all its solid beauty above this chaos of dying pleasures, the whole soul experiences a kind of relief, the beatitude of redemption; an ineffable feeling that will recur at the beginning of the second tableau when *Tannhäuser,* having escaped from the cave of Venus, finds himself once again restored to true life, with the religious sound of the bells of home, the simple song of the shepherd, the hymn of the pilgrims and the cross planted on the road, the emblem of all the crosses that must be borne on all roads. In this last incident there is a power of contrast which has an irresistible effect on the mind and which recalls the breadth and ease of Shakespeare. A moment ago we were in the depths of the earth (Venus, as we have said, lives close to hell), breathing an air that is perfumed but suffocating, illuminated by a rose-colored light that does not come from the sun; we were like the chivalric Tannhäuser himself who, surfeited with enervating pleasures, *aspires to suffering!* A sublime cry that all the avowed critics would admire in Corneille, but that none of them will perhaps consent to recognize in Wagner. At last we are back on earth, we breathe its fresh air, we accept its joys with gratitude, its sorrows with humility. Poor humanity has returned to its home.

A moment ago, in trying to describe the voluptuous part of the overture, I urged the reader to put aside any thought of commonplace love songs such as a gallant in an amorous mood might conceive; the fact is that there is nothing commonplace here; there is rather the overflowing of an energetic nature, which pours into evil all the forces owed to the cultivation of the good; it is frenzied love, immense, chaotic, elevated to the height of a counterreligion, of a satanic religion. Thus the composer, in his musical translation, escaped the vulgarity that too often accompanies the portrayal of the most popular sentiment —I was about to say the most coarse—and to do that, it was enough for him to paint excess in desire and in energy, the immoderate, ungovernable ambition of a tender soul that has gone astray. Likewise, in the plastic presentation of the idea, he has happily avoided a wearisome number of victims, of innumerable Elvires. The pure idea, embodied in the unique Venus, speaks much more effectively and much more eloquently. Here we do not see an ordinary libertine *flitting from one beauty to another* but general, universal man living morganatically with the absolute Ideal of pleasure, with the Queen of all the she-devils, of all the female fauns and of all the female satyrs who had been relegated to the underworld since the death of the great Pan, in other words, with the indestructible and irresistible Venus.

A hand better trained than mine in the analysis of musical works will provide the reader, in these same columns, with a complete and technical review of this strange and misunderstood *Tannhäuser;* consequently, I should limit myself to general views which, however sketchy they may be, are nonetheless useful.* For certain minds, moreover, isn't it more convenient to stand on a height in order to judge the beauty of a landscape than to follow, one by one, all the paths that furrow its surface?

I am only anxious to remind the reader that, to the great credit of Wagner, in spite of the very proper importance that he gives to the dramatic text, the overture of *Tannhäuser,* like that of *Lohengrin,* is completely intelligible, even to a person who does not know the libretto; and further, that the overture not only contains the central idea, the psychic duality that constitutes the drama, but also the principal phrases, clearly accentuated, which are destined to paint the general feelings expressed in the course of the work, as is demonstrated by the insistent repetitions, whenever the action demands it, of the diabolically voluptuous melody and of the religious motif or "Pilgrims' Chorus." As for the great march in the second act, it has long since won over the most recalcitrant minds, and one may apply to it the same praise that has been given to the two overtures I have mentioned, namely, that it expresses in the clearest, most vivid and most representative way what it wishes

---

* The first part of this study appeared in the *Revue Européenne* for which M. Perrin, former director of the Opéra Comique, whose sympathy for Wagner is well known, is the music critic.

to express. Who indeed, on hearing those tones, so rich and so bold, that stately, elegantly measured rhythm, those regal fanfares, could imagine anything other than a feudal ceremony, a procession of heroic men in brilliant costumes, all of them tall, all of them endowed with a powerful will and simple faith, as magnificent in their pleasures as they were terrible in their wars?

What shall we say of Tannhäuser's aria, of his journey to Rome, in which the literary beauty is so admirably supported and completed by the recitative that the two elements fuse in an inseparable whole? There was some apprehension about the length of this passage, and yet as we have seen, the aria possesses an invincible dramatic power. The sadness, the depression of the sinner during his arduous journey, his joy at seeing the supreme pontiff who absolves our sins, his despair when the latter reveals the irreparable nature of his crime, and finally the almost inexpressible feeling, so terrible it is, of joy in damnation; all of this is said, expressed, translated in words and music in such a concrete way that it is almost impossible to imagine any other way of saying it. Then the auditor understands that such a misfortune can be rectified only by a miracle, and he excuses the unlucky knight for seeking once again the mysterious path that leads him to the cave, in order that he may at least experience the charms of hell with his diabolical bride.

The drama of *Lohengrin*, like that of *Tannhäuser*, possesses the sacred, mysterious and yet universally intelligible character of legend. A young princess, accused of a dreadful crime—the murder of her brother—has no way of proving her innocence. Her case is to be judged by an ordeal. No knight who is present offers to enter the lists for her, but she has confidence in a strange vision: an unknown warrior appears to her in a dream. He is the knight who will defend her. In fact, at the final moment, when everyone believes her guilty, a small boat approaches the bank, drawn by a swan harnessed with chains of gold. Lohengrin, knight of the Holy Grail, protector of the innocent, defender of the weak, has heard her appeal in the depths of the marvelous hiding place where he carefully guards the divine cup, twice consecrated by the Last Supper and by the blood of our Lord which Joseph of Arimathea had caught in it as it streamed from his wound. Lohengrin, the son of Parsifal, steps out of the boat, clad in silver armor, helmeted, with a shield on his shoulder and a small golden horn at his side, resting on his sword. "If I win the victory for you," Lohengrin says to Elsa, "will you consent to accept me as your husband? . . . If you consent to consider me your husband, Elsa, you must promise never to question me, never to inquire about my country, my name or my nature." And Elsa says: "I shall never ask you that question, my lord." And as Lohengrin solemnly repeats the formula of the promise, Elsa replies: "My shield, my angel, my savior! You who believe firmly in my innocence, could there be a more criminal doubt than not having faith in you? Just as you defend me in my distress, so I shall faithfully abide by the law that you impose upon me." And Lohengrin, embracing her, exclaims: "Elsa, I love you!" There is here a beauty of dialogue that occurs frequently in Wagner's dramas, imbued with primitive magic, magnified by ideal sentiments, and whose solemnity does not in the least lessen its natural grace.

Lohengrin's victory establishes the innocence of Elsa. Frédéric and the sorceress Ortrude, two wicked persons anxious to see Elsa condemned, succeed in arousing her feminine curiosity, in blighting her joy with doubts, and in tormenting her until she breaks her vow and asks her husband to acknowledge his origin. Doubt has destroyed faith, and lost faith carries happiness away with it. Lohengrin kills Frédéric in punishment for an attempted ambush and, before the king, the warriors and the assembled people, announces his true origin: ". . . Whoever is chosen to serve the Grail is immediately endowed with a supernatural power; even he who is sent by it to a far country, charged with the mission of defending the rights of virtue, is not deprived of his sacred strength as long as his being the knight of the Grail is unknown; but the nature of this virtue of the Holy Grail is such that, once it is revealed, it immediately flees profane eyes; that is why you should entertain no doubts about its knight; if he is recognized by you, he is obliged to leave you at once." Now listen to his response to the forbidden question! "I was sent to you by the Grail; my father, Parsifal, wears its crown; I, its knight, am named Lohengrin." The swan reappears at the bank to return the knight to his miraculous country. The sorceress, carried away by her hate, reveals that the swan is none other than Elsa's brother on whom she has cast a spell. Lohengrin enters the boat after having addressed an earnest prayer to the Holy Grail. A dove takes the place of the swan, and Godfrey, Duke of Brabant, reappears. The knight has returned to Mount Salvat. Elsa who doubted, Elsa who wished to know, to examine, to verify, Elsa has lost her happiness. The ideal has taken flight.

Doubtless the reader has noticed in this legend a striking analogy with the myth of the ancient Psyche, who also was a victim of demonic curiosity and, unwilling to respect the incognito status of her divine spouse, lost all her happiness by penetrating the mystery. Elsa listened to Ortrude, as Eve listened to the serpent. The eternal Eve falls into the eternal trap. Can it be that nations and races transmit fables to each other as men bequeath inheritances, patrimonies, and scientific secrets? One would be tempted to believe it, so striking is the moral analogy which stamps the myths and legends that have grown up in different lands. But this explanation is too simple to appeal to a philosophical mind for long. The allegory created by a people cannot be compared to the seeds given with brotherly affection by one farmer to another who wishes to acclimatize them in his country. Nothing of that which is eternal and universal needs to be acclimatized. The moral analogy of which I spoke is, as it were, the divine stamp on all popular fables. It may be considered, if you wish, the sign of a single origin, the proof of an irrefragable relationship, but on the condition that this origin be sought only in the absolute principle and the common origin of all beings. One myth may be considered the brother of another in the same way that a Negro is called the brother of the white man. I do not deny either fraternity or filiation in certain cases; I merely believe that in many others the mind could be misled by surface resemblances or even by moral analogy and, to resume our botanical metaphor, that myth is a tree which grows everywhere, in any climate, beneath any sun, spontaneously and without being grown from grafts. Religions and poetry from the four corners of the earth furnish us superabundant proof in this matter. Just as sin is everywhere, so redemption is everywhere; myth is everywhere. There is nothing more cosmopolitan than the Eternal. Please excuse this digression which carried me along in an irresistible way. I am returning to the author of *Lohengrin*.

One might say that Wagner has a special enthusiasm for feudal ceremonies, Homeric gatherings which represent a concentration of vital forces, excited crowds that are reservoirs of human electricity, from which the heroic style springs with a natural impetuosity. The nuptial music and the epithalamium of *Lohengrin* make a worthy pendant to the introduction of the guests to the Wartburg in *Tannhäuser*, which is perhaps even more majestic and more vehement. Nevertheless the master, always exercising good taste and careful about nuances, has not represented here the turbulence that a crowd of commoners would normally manifest in such circumstances. Even at the apogee of its most violent tumult, the music expresses no more than the excitement of well-bred persons; it is a court that is enjoying itself, and its liveliest drunkenness still preserves the rhythm of good manners. The excited joy of the crowd alternates with the soft, tender and solemn epithalamium; the tempestuous public celebration is contrasted several times with the sober and touching hymn that solemnizes the marriage of Elsa and Lohengrin.

I have already mentioned certain melodic phrases whose constant return, in different passages of the same work, had insistently intrigued my ear when Wagner's first program was performed in the concert hall on the Boulevard des Italiens. We have noted that, in *Tannhäuser*, the recurrence of the two principal themes, the religious motif and the song of pleasure,

216

served to arouse the attention of the public and to put it in a mood analogous to that in the drama. In *Lohengrin*, this mnemonic system is given a much more detailed application. Each person is, so to speak, blazoned by the melody that represents his moral character and the role that he is called upon to play in the story. Here I humbly allow Liszt to speak, and I take this opportunity to recommend his book (*Lohengrin et Tannhäuser*) to all lovers of this profound and refined art. In spite of the somewhat strange language that he uses, a kind of dialect made up of borrowings from several languages, he is able to translate all the rhetoric of the master with an infinite charm:

"The spectator, forewarned and willing to forego *those unrelated passages which, cogged to each other along the thread of some plot, form the substance of our usual operas*, will find it strangely interesting to follow throughout three acts the profoundly studied, astonishingly skillful and poetically intelligible arrangement with which Wagner, *by means of several leading musical phrases*, has tightened the *melodic knot* which constitutes his whole drama. The turns that these phrases make, clinging to and intertwined with the words of the poem, create an effect that is deeply moving. But if, after having been struck and impressed by it in the theater, one still wishes to better understand what has been so effectively accomplished and to study the score of this work in such a new genre, one will remain astonished by all the intentions and nuances that cannot be grasped immediately. Is it not necessary to study the plays and epics of the great poets at length in order to master all of their meaning?

"By means of a method that he applies in a quite unexpected way, Wagner succeeds in extending the dominion and the claims of music. Dissatisfied with the power that it exercises over our hearts in arousing the whole gamut of human emotions, he makes it capable of stimulating our ideas, of appealing to our minds, of stirring our reflections, and he endows it with a moral and intellectual meaning. . . . He draws the character of his personages and of their main passions melodically, and the melodies appear *in the lyrics or in the accompaniment* each time that the passions and the sentiments that they express are involved. This systematic recurrence is joined to an art of arrangement which would offer, through the subtlety of its psychological, poetic and philosophical insights, an exceptional interest even for those to whom quavers and semiquavers are meaningless hieroglyphics. Merely by forcing our minds and memories to constant exertions, Wagner lifts the action of music above the realm of vague emotions and adds to its charms some of the pleasures of the mind. By this method, which complicates the facile enjoyment obtained by *a series of songs rarely related to each other*, he demands an unusual amount of attention from the audience; but at the same time he prepares more perfect emotions for those who know how to enjoy them. His melodies are, in a sense, *personifications of ideas*; their return signals the particular feelings which the words do not explicitly indicate. It is to them that Wagner entrusts the responsibility of revealing all the secrets of the heart. There are phrases, for example like those in the first scene of the second act, which move through the opera like a poisonous snake, winding itself around its victims and then fleeing from their holy defenders; there are other phrases, like those in the introduction, which return only rarely with the final and divine revelations. The important situations and characters are all described musically by a melody which becomes their constant symbol. Now since the melodies have a rare beauty, we shall say for the benefit of those who, in studying a score, confine themselves to judging the relations between quavers and semiquavers, that even if the music of this opera were deprived of its beautiful text, it would still be a first class production."

Indeed, without poetry, Wagner's music would still be a poetic work, endowed as it is with all the qualities that constitute well made poetry; self-explanatory in that all of its elements are so well combined, united, adapted to one another, and—if one may use a barbarism to express a superlative quality —scrupulously concatenated.

The Phantom Vessel or The Flying Dutchman is the very popular story of the wandering Jew of the Ocean for whom, nevertheless, a helpful angel has obtained a means of redemption: If the captain, who goes ashore every seven years, meets a faithful woman, he will be saved. The ill-fated man, driven back by a storm every time that he tried to sail around a dangerous cape, had once cried out: "I shall break through that impassable barrier even if I have to struggle through all eternity!" And eternity had accepted the challenge of the daring navigator. Since that time the doomed ship had appeared here and there, on different coasts, sailing headlong into storms with the despair of a warrior seeking death; but the storms always spared him, and even pirates fled before him, making the sign of the cross. The Dutchman's first words after arriving at an anchorage, are solemn and ominous: "The time has expired, seven more years have passed! The sea casts me ashore in disgust. . . . Proud Ocean! in a few days you will have to bear me again! . . . Nowhere is there a tomb, nowhere is there death, such is the terrible sentence of my damnation . . . The final day of judgment, when will it shine in my night? . . ." Beside the terrible vessel a Norwegian ship has cast anchor; the two captains meet, and the Dutchman asks the Norwegian "to shelter him in his home for a few days . . . to give him a new country." He dazzles him with the offer of immense wealth and, finally, says bluntly: "Do you have a daughter? . . . Let her be my wife! . . . I shall never reach home. What good is it to amass all these riches? Be persuaded, consent to this marriage and take all of my treasures."—"I do have a daughter who is beautiful, utterly faithful, loving and devoted to me."—"May she always keep that love for her father, may she be faithful to him; she will also be faithful to her husband."—"You are giving me jewels, pearls of inestimable value; but the most precious jewel is a

faithful wife."—"It is you who are giving that jewel! . . .
Shall I see your daughter today?"

In the Norwegian's quarters several girls are talking about
the Flying Dutchman, and Senta, possessed by a fixed idea, her
eyes fastened on a mysterious portrait, is singing the ballad that
describes the damnation of the navigator: "Have you encountered at sea the ship with the blood-red sail and black mast? On
board a pale man, the shipmaster, keeps a ceaseless vigil. He
sails in endless flight, without respite, without rest. Yet someday he may find deliverance, if he finds on earth a woman who
will be faithful to him unto death . . . Pray heaven that soon
a woman will keep faith with him! Long ago, wishing to sail
around a cape against heavy winds in a raging storm, he uttered
a blasphemy in his mad folly: In all eternity I will not give up!
Satan heard him and took him at his word! And now he is condemned to wander across the seas, ceaselessly, without rest! . . .
But so that the ill-fated man might yet find deliverance on
earth, an angel of God revealed a means of salvation to him.
May you find it, pale navigator! Pray to heaven that soon a
woman will keep faith with him!—Every seven years he casts
anchor and goes ashore to seek a wife. Every seven years he
pleads his suit, and never yet has he found a faithful woman
. . . Hoist the sails! Raise the anchor! False love, false vows! Be
quick! Set sail! without respite, without rest!" And suddenly,
emerging from a deep reverie, Senta cries out in a flash of inspiration: "May it be I who will deliver you through my fidelity!
May the angel of God make me known to you! It is through me
that you will achieve salvation!" The mind of the girl is magneti-
cally attracted by misfortune; the condemned captain, who can
find redemption only through love, is her true fiancé.

At length the Dutchman appears and is introduced by
Senta's father; he is indeed the man in the portrait, the legendary
figure suspended on the wall. When the Dutchman, like the terrible Melmoth who was moved by the fate of his victim Im-
malea, tries to dissuade her from a too perilous devotion, when
the doomed man, full of pity, rejects the instrument of salvation,

when, quickly returning to his ship, he wishes to leave her to the joys of family life and commonplace love, she refuses and insists on following him: "I know you well! I know your destiny! I knew you when I saw you for the first time!" And he, hoping to frighten her, replies: "Ask the seas in every latitude, ask the sailors who have furrowed the sea in every direction; they know this ship, the terror of pious souls: I am called the Flying Dutchman!" Pursuing the disappearing ship with her devotion and her cries, she answers: "Glory to your liberating angel! Glory to his law! Look, and see that I am faithful to you unto death!" And she throws herself into the sea. The ship sinks. Two aerial forms rise above the waves: the Dutchman and Senta have been transfigured.

To love an unfortunate person for his misfortune is an idea too great to enter any but an ingenuous heart, and to have made the redemption of a damned soul dependent on the passionate imagination of a girl is surely a beautiful thought. The whole drama is done with a sure hand, in a direct manner; each situation is faced squarely; and a character such as Senta has in it a supernatural and romantic grandeur that delights and terrifies. The extreme simplicity of the poem increases the intensity of effect. Everything is in its place, everything is well ordered and well proportioned. The overture that we heard at the concert in the Théâtre Italien is lugubrious and profound, like the ocean, the wind and the darkness.

I am obliged to limit this study, and I believe that I have said enough (today at least) to enable the unprejudiced reader to understand Wagner's tendencies and dramatic form. In addition to *Rienzi, The Flying Dutchman, Tannhäuser* and *Lohengrin,* he has composed *Tristan and Isolde,* and four other operas that form a tetralogy, whose subject is drawn from the Nibelungenlied, as well as numerous critical works. Such are the accomplishments of this man whose person and ideal aspirations have so long been the subject of puerile conversation in Paris, and who has been the victim of facile jokes every day for more than a year.

IV

One can always momentarily disregard the element of system that every great self-conscious artist inevitably introduces into all his works; in this case we have still to seek and to verify what personal, characteristic qualities distinguish him from others. An artist, a man truly worthy of that great name, should possess something essentially *sui generis*, thanks to which he is *he* and no one else. From this point of view, artists may be compared to various flavors, and the repertory of human metaphors is perhaps not vast enough to provide an approximate definition of all known artists and of all *possible* artists. We have already noted, I believe, two men in Richard Wagner, the man of order and the man of passion. Here we are concerned with the passionate man, the man of feeling. His personality is so vividly inscribed in the slightest passage of his work that the search for his chief quality will not be very difficult. From the beginning one thing had struck me very forcibly: in the voluptuous and orgiastic portion of the overture of *Tannhäuser*, the artist had put as much force and had developed as much energy as he had in painting the mysticism that characterizes the overture of *Lohengrin*. The same aspiration in the one as in the other, the same titanic ascent and also the same refinements, the same subtlety. That which especially marks the music of this master in an unforgettable way, it seems to me, is its nervous intensity, its violence of passion and of will. With the sweetest or the most strident voice, this music expresses all the innermost secrets of the heart of man. It is true that an ideal aspiration presides over all of his compositions; but if, in his choice of subjects and in his dramatic method, Wagner resembles antiquity, by the passionate energy of his expression, he is today the truest representative of modern nature. And all the knowledge, all the efforts, all the studied arrangements of this rich mind are, to tell the truth, only the very humble and very zealous servants of that irresistible passion. The result, regardless of the subject that he uses, is a superlative solemnity of tone. By means of that passion he adds

something superhuman to everything; by means of that passion
he understands everything and makes everything understood.
Everything that is implied in the words: *will, desire, concentration, nervous intensity, explosion,* is felt and is sensed in his
works. I do not believe that I am deceiving either myself or
anyone else in affirming that I see therein the principal characteristics of the phenomenon that we call *genius;* or at least
that we find the above mentioned characteristics in the analysis
of everything that until now we have rightly called *genius.* In
matters of art, I confess that I do not hate excess; moderation
has never seemed to me the sign of a vigorous artistic nature. I
like the superabundant health, the overflowing will that are
inscribed in works of art like the flaming coals of a volcano and
that, in everyday life, often characterize those periods, filled
with delight, that follow a great moral or physical crisis.

As for the reform which the master wishes to introduce by
combining music and drama, what will come of that? It is impossible to make any precise prediction. In a vague and general
manner, one may say with the Psalmist that, late or soon, those
who have been cast down will be exalted, that those who have
been exalted will be humbled, but one can say nothing more
than what is equally applicable to the familiar course of all
human affairs. We have seen many things, once considered
absurd, that later became models adopted by the crowd. Everyone today remembers the energetic resistance that at first greeted
the plays of Victor Hugo and the paintings of Eugène Delacroix. Besides, we have already pointed out that the quarrel
which now divides the public was a forgotten quarrel, suddenly
revived, and that Wagner himself had found in the past the
first elements of the *base on which to establish his ideal.* What
is quite certain is that his doctrine is well designed to unite
intelligent people, wearied for a long time by the errors of the
Opera, and it is not surprising that men of letters in particular
have shown themselves sympathetic to a musician who prides
himself on being a poet and a dramatist. In the same way the
writers of the eighteenth century acclaimed the works of

Gluck, and I cannot help seeing that the persons who are repelled by Wagner's works also show a decided antipathy to his
precursor.

Finally, the success or failure of *Tannhäuser* can prove
absolutely nothing; it cannot determine in the slightest degree
the favorable or unfavorable outcome in the future. If *Tannhäuser* were an execrable work, it could still be *praised to the
skies*. If it were perfect, it could still be found revolting. As a
matter of fact, the question of the reform of the opera is not
settled, and the battle will continue; after dying down, it will
begin again. Recently I heard it said that if Wagner achieved a
brilliant success with his drama, it would be a purely individual
happening, and that his method would not have any subsequent
influence on the destinies and transformations of musical drama.
I believe that I am justified by the study of the past, that is the
eternal, to predict the very opposite, namely, that a complete
failure would not in any way destroy the possibility of new
attempts in the same direction, and that in the very near future
we may well see not only new composers but even very well
established men, profit in some measure from the ideas propagated by Wagner and pass happily through the breach which he
has opened. In what history has anyone ever read that great
causes were lost in a single battle?

March 18, 1861

A FEW MORE COMMENTS

"The trial is over! The *music of the future* has been buried!"
joyfully cry all the scoffers and schemers. "The trial is over!"
repeat all the inane journalists. And all the idlers respond in
unison, quite innocently, "The trial is over!"

Indeed, a trial has taken place which will be repeated many
thousands of times before the world comes to an end; first of all,
it is a fact that no great and serious work can enter human
memory or take its place in history without lively disputes.

Furthermore, ten stubborn persons with the help of shrill whistles can unnerve the actors, destroy the receptivity of the audience, and with their noisy protests interfere with the tremendous voice of the orchestra, even if that voice equals the Ocean in power. Finally, a most curious obstacle has come to light: annual subscription tickets create a kind of aristocracy which, at any given moment, for any reason or excuse, can exclude the general public from any share in judging a work. If the same system were used in other theaters, at the Comédie Française for instance, we should soon see the same dangers and the same scandals develop there. A limited group would be able to deny the vast Parisian audience the right to appraise a work, the judgment of which belongs to everyone.

We can assure the people who believe they are rid of Wagner that they have rejoiced too soon. I strongly urge them to celebrate less loudly a triumph which is after all not especially honorable and even to resign themselves to future disappointments. The truth is that they do not understand very well the seesaw of human affairs, the ebb and flow of passions. Nor do they realize what patience and stubbornness Providence has always bestowed on those to whom she has entrusted a function. Today the reaction has begun; it was born on the very day when malice, stupidity, routinism, and envy combined in an effort to bury the work. The immensity of the injustice engendered a thousand sympathies, which are now evident on all sides.

To persons far removed from Paris who may be fascinated and intimidated by this monstrous heap of stones and men, the unexpected fate of *Tannhäuser* must seem an enigma. It would be easy to explain it by the unfortunate coincidence of several causes, some of which have nothing to do with art. Let us at once admit the principal, dominating reason: Wagner's opera *is a serious work* that demands sustained attention; it is easy to imagine all the unfavorable odds that this fact implies in a country where traditional tragedies succeeded above all because of the facile distractions that they offered. In Italy, the audience eats sherbets and gossips during the intermissions when fashion does not require applause; in France, people play cards. "If you expect me to give uninterrupted attention to your work, you are being very impertinent," the recalcitrant listener cries; "give me a digestive pleasure and not something that strains my mind." To this main reason must be added others that are well known to everyone, at least in Paris. The Imperial command, which does great honor to the prince and for which one may sincerely thank him, I believe, without being accused of obsequiousness, stirred up against the artist many envious persons and many of those idlers who always think they are being independent when they bay in unison. The decree which had just granted some freedom of speech and press released a natural turbulence, long repressed, which threw itself like a wild animal on the first passer-by. The passer-by was *Tannhäuser*, authorized by the sovereign and openly sponsored by the wife of a foreign ambassador.[126] What an admirable occasion! For several hours a French audience amused itself at the expense of this woman. And, something less known, Madame Wagner herself was insulted during one of the performances. A prodigious triumph!

A stage setting that was worse than inadequate, designed by a former vaudevillist (can you imagine *Les Burgraves* staged by M. Clairville?); a limp and incorrect performance from the orchestra; a German tenor of whom much was expected and who kept singing out of tune with an unfortunate insistence; a sleepy Venus dressed in a clutter of white chiffon who no more had the effect of coming from Mount Olympus than of being born in the sparkling imagination of a medieval artist; all the seats taken, for two performances, by a crowd of persons who were hostile, or at least indifferent, to every ideal aspiration; all of these things should likewise be taken into consideration. This is the appropriate time to thank Mademoiselle Sax and Morelli who alone bravely faced the storm. It would not be proper to praise only their talent; it is also necessary to recognize their gallantry. They resisted the rout; without flinching for a moment, they remained faithful to the composer. With admirable Italian flexibility, Morelli humbly adapted himself to the taste and style of the author, and persons who have often had an opportunity to hear him, say that this docility was useful to him and that he never appeared to such advantage as in the role of Wolfram. But what shall we say of M. Niemann, of his weaknesses, of his swoons, of his childish bad temper, we who have seen theatrical storms in which men like Frédérick and Rouvière, and Bignon himself (although less justified by fame) openly defied public incomprehension, played with more zeal as the audience showed itself more unjust, and constantly made common cause with the author?—Finally, the question of a ballet, magnified to the level of a vital question and debated for several months, contributed a good deal to the commotion. "An opera without a ballet! What is that?" said the old fogies. "What is that?" said the stage door Lotharios. "Take care!" the anxious minister himself said to the composer. To satisfy them, it was decided to have some Prussian regiments in short skirts maneuver on the stage with the mechanical gestures of a military school; seeing all those legs and confused by a poor stage set, some of the spectators said: "That is a poor ballet, and the music is not suitable for a dance." Common sense replied: "It isn't a ballet; but it should be a bacchanal, an orgy, as the music suggests, like those sometimes staged at the Porte-Saint-Martin, the Ambigu, the Odéon, and even at lesser theaters, but such as the Opera cannot conceive, since it doesn't know how to do anything at all." Thus, it was not a literary reason, but simply the incompetence of the stage crew that necessitated the suppression of a whole tableau (the second appearance of Venus).

That men who are able to afford the luxury of a mistress among the dancers at the Opera should wish to see displayed as often as possible the talents and beauties which they have purchased is surely an almost paternal feeling that everyone understands and easily excuses; but it is intolerable that these same men, without concern for public curiosity and the pleasures of others, should make impossible the performance of a work that displeases them, because it does not satisfy the demands of their protectorate. Keep your harem and religiously preserve its traditions; but give us a theater where those who don't think as you do may find other pleasures better suited to their tastes: Thus we shall be rid of you, and you of us, and everyone will be satisfied.

There was some hope of snatching the victim away from these fanatics by presenting the opera on a Sunday, that is on a day when the season-ticket holders and Jockey Club members gladly yield the theater to the crowds who wish to take advantage of their leisure and of the unoccupied seats. But they had reasoned quite correctly: "If we allow a success today, the management will consider it a sufficient excuse to inflict the work on us for a month." And so they attacked again, fully armed, that is with homicidal instruments prepared in advance. The audience, the whole audience, struggled through two acts, and in its good will, augmented by indignation, it applauded not only the irresistibly beautiful passages but even the passages that were surprising and disconcerting, either as the result of a confused performance or because, to be appreciated, they needed a composure that was impossible. But these storms of anger and enthusiasm immediately led to a reaction that was no less violent and much less tiring for the opponents. Then this same audience, hoping that the disturbance could be overcome by quiet, became silent, wishing above all to listen and judge. But a *few* whistles *courageously* continued, *without excuse and without interruption*; the admirable "Rome Narrative" could not be heard (I don't know whether it was even sung) and the whole third act was submerged in the uproar.

In the press no opposition, no protest, except that of M. Franck Marie in *La Patrie*.[127] M. Berlioz avoided giving his opinion; negative courage. Let us thank him for not having added to the universal insults. And then an immense whirlwind of imitation carried all pens away, stimulated a delirium of talk, like the strange spirit that inspires a crowd to alternate miracles of gallantry and pusillanimity, collective courage and collective cowardice; French enthusiasm and Gallic panic.

Tannhäuser had not even been heard.

So now there are complaints from all sides; everyone would like to see Wagner's work, and everyone protests against high-handed treatment. But the management has yielded to a few conspirators and is already refunding the money paid for later performances. And so, incredible as it may seem—if indeed there can be anything more scandalous than what we have just witnessed—we now see a defeated management which, in spite of public encouragements, has abandoned the idea of continuing very profitable performances.

It seems, moreover, that the example is spreading and that the public is no longer considered the final judge of theatrical presentations. As I write these lines, I am informed that a fine play, admirably constructed and written in an excellent style, is going to close within a few days in another theater where it was brilliantly produced despite the efforts of a certain impotent caste which was formerly called the literary class and which today is inferior in intelligence and in refinement to a seaport audience.[128] Truly, the author is very foolish to think that these people would show enthusiasm for anything as impalpable, as nebulous as *honor*. The best they can do is to *bury* it. What are the mysterious reasons for this eviction? Would success embarrass the future plans of the director? Could unintelligible official considerations have overridden his good will, violated his interests? Or rather is it necessary to imagine something monstrous, that it to say a director who, to push himself forward, pretends to want good plays and, having finally achieved his purpose, quickly returns to his true taste, which is that of idiots and which is obviously the most profitable? What is even more inexplicable is the weakness of the critics (some of whom are poets), who cherish their greatest enemy and who, if they sometimes criticize his commercialism in a fleeting moment of courage, still continue in many cases to encourage his business by all sorts of favors.

During all this uproar, faced by the deplorable gibes in the papers that made me blush like a refined man at the sight of some vile action, a cruel idea obsessed me. Although I have always carefully stifled in my heart the excessive patriotism whose fumes can cloud the brain, I remember having experienced, on distant shores, in dining rooms filled with the most varied human beings, a horrible pain when I heard voices (just or unjust, what does it matter) ridiculing France. At such moments all my filial emotion, suppressed for intellectual reasons, would burst forth. Some years ago when, in his reception speech, an unfortunate academician [Ponsard] took it into his head to include an appreciation of the genius of Shakespeare, to whom he referred familiarly as old *Williams* or the good *Williams* —an appreciation that was really worthy of a janitor at the Comédie Française—I shuddered at the harm this illiterate pedant was going to inflict on my country. In fact, for several days all the English papers made fun of us, and in the most distressing way. According to them, French writers did not even know how to spell Shakespeare's name; they understood nothing of his genius, and France, grown stupid, recognized only two authors, Ponsard and Alexandre Dumas *fils, the two favorite poets of the new Empire,* added *The Illustrated London News.* Notice that political hatred joined outraged literary patriotism.

Now, during the scandals stirred up by Wagner's work, I asked myself: "What is Europe going to think of us, and what will they say about Paris in Germany? A handful of noisy people is disgracing the whole country!" But no, that won't happen. I believe, I know, I swear that among literary men, artists and even among society people there are still many well-bred persons, endowed with a sense of justice, whose minds are always generously open to the new things that are presented to them.

Germany would be wrong to believe that Paris is full of rascals who blow their noses with their fingers in order to wipe them off on the back of a great man who is a visitor. Such a supposition would not be completely fair. As I have said, a reaction is developing on all sides; the most unexpected expressions of sympathy have appeared, encouraging the author to persist in his destiny. If things continue in this way, we may suppose that many regrets will soon be effaced and that *Tannhäuser* will reappear, but in a place where the season-ticket holders will not be interested in harassing it.[129]

The idea has finally been launched, a breach has been made; that is the important thing. More than one French composer will wish to take advantage of the salutary ideas propagated by Wagner. Regardless of the short time during which the work appeared before the public, the Emperor's command, which enabled us to hear it, has been extremely beneficial to the French mind, a logical mind, fond of order, that will easily continue in its own evolution. Under the Republic and the first Empire, music was raised to a height which made it, in place of a faltering literature, one of the glories of the period. Was the leader of the second Empire only curious to hear the work of a man who was being discussed among our neighbors, or was he stirred by a more patriotic and a more comprehensive thought? In any case, his simple curiosity will have been profitable to all of us.

April 8, 1861

REFLECTIONS ON SOME
OF MY CONTEMPORARIES

The ten articles (of which four have been put in the appendix) grouped together under the rubric "Reflections on Some of my Contemporaries" were written between 1859 and 1861 for *Les Poètes Français*, an anthology edited by Eugène Crépet. First published in *La Revue Fantaisiste* in the summer of 1861, they appeared in volume four of the anthology in 1862. Of the articles submitted for publication Crépet rejected those on Barbier, Borel, and Moreau. On the other hand, he accepted an essay on Banville which he had not originally commissioned.

In spite of sharp political and literary differences of opinion that led to a quarrel between the editor and the critic, Crépet never lost his admiration for the poet and in 1887 produced an important pioneer work, *Charles Baudelaire, Œuvres Posthumes et Correspondance Inédite*. It was his son, Jacques Crépet, who in turn published the definitive edition of Baudelaire's works between 1922 and 1953.

Baudelaire began the series of criticisms in 1859, but progressed rather slowly, taking as long as a year to complete the article on Hugo. To Crépet he complained that he had put "an enormous amount of effort" into writing the essays and maintained that only the editor's "blindness" kept him from realizing their value. "What I write is good and irrefutable," he once wrote to Crépet in a moment of exasperation.[130] More often than not, his claim has proved to be surprisingly true.

VICTOR HUGO

PREFACE

Baudelaire's interesting essay on Victor Hugo is characteristically personal, biographical, philosophical, and generalizing. At the time he wrote the essay his acquaintance with the exiled poet was very slight. In a letter to Hugo in 1859 he admitted having seen him only twice some twenty years earlier. Later he was to be a frequent guest at his home in Brussels and to become a warm friend of Madame Hugo who at first had seemed only ridiculous to him. Toward Hugo himself, Baudelaire's attitude remained somewhat ambivalent. While sincerely admiring much of his work, he was infuriated by his republicanism, his belief in progress and in the alliance of art and morality, his pontifical attitude and his conception of himself as a second Christ who could presume to give advice even to God himself (*Conseils à Dieu*).

In his correspondence and *Journaux Intimes* Baudelaire often gave free vent to his hostility. In a passage of the Journals he refers to Hugo as so "lacking in elegiac and ethereal qualities that he would horrify even a notary." In still another passage he describes him as priestlike, with his head always bent—"too bent to see anything except his navel."

To one reading between the lines of his letter to Ancelle (February, 1865), it is clear that his animosity was further increased by his own poverty and obscurity: "One can be both a *wit* and a *boor*—just as one can possess *a special genius* and be a *fool* at the same time. Victor Hugo has indeed proved that to us.—By the way, he is coming to live in Brussels. He has bought a house in the Leopold quarter. It seems that he and the Ocean have quarreled. Either he hasn't had the strength to endure the Ocean, or the Ocean *itself* has become bored with him.—It was hardly worthwhile to carefully fit out a palace on a rock! As for me, alone, forgotten by everyone, I shall sell my mother's little house only in the last extremity.—But I have even more pride than Victor Hugo, and I feel, I know that I shall never be as stupid as he." [131]

In his public statements Baudelaire was much more restrained, except during his earlier years when he sometimes showed himself sharply critical. He had credited Delacroix rather than Hugo with being the real leader of the Romantic movement and he had not hesitated to condemn his excessive use of antithesis and conscious symmetry.[132] Even when he was most critical, however, he never failed to recognize Hugo's amazing technique and versatility.

The praise that Baudelaire accorded Hugo beginning in 1859 may have been partly inspired by selfish reasons, but it was also the result of a genuine admiration for the poet's later works.[133] The enthusiasm for *La Légende des Siècles*, expressed in a letter to his mother, is much too convincing to be questioned.

In his essay on Hugo, Baudelaire is sometimes blamed for having resorted to a certain amount of vague and conventional praise and for having failed to mention that part of Hugo's work which ran counter to his most cherished aesthetic beliefs and ideas. To have been completely frank, however, would undoubtedly have resulted in the rejection of his article. It should be remembered that Crépet refused to accept the excellent but outspoken essay on Auguste Barbier, one of the best of the series, and that elsewhere Baudelaire had often expressed his distaste for belief in progress and utilitarian art.

In spite of a tendency to gloss over Hugo's more obvious faults, Baudelaire succeeded admirably in revealing the true greatness of Victor Hugo. That he should note his universality, his virtuosity, his taste for the excessive and the immense, his phenomenal success in creating the modern epic, is not particularly surprising. Of much more significance is his awareness of the greatness of Hugo as a metaphysical poet, his perception of Hugo's ability to express the mystery of life with the "indispensable obscurity" essential to all great art. It is here that

Baudelaire anticipates the present day revaluation of Hugo by recognizing the cosmic power, the epic strength, and the sense of mystery that characterize his later work. In the eyes of the critic it was this aspect of Hugo which above all made him into a translator and decipherer who, drawing "from the inexhaustible storehouse of *universal analogy*," gave himself up to "all the reveries suggested by the infinite spectacle of life on earth and in the heavens."

⧗⧗⧗⧗⧗

I

For many years now Victor Hugo has no longer been in our midst. I remember the time when his figure was one of those most frequently encountered among the crowds, and many times I wondered, seeing him appear so often amid holiday excitement or in the silence of some lonely spot, how he could reconcile the needs of his incessant work with the sublime but dangerous taste for strolling and for reverie. This apparent contradiction is evidently the result of a well ordered life and of a strong spiritual constitution which permits him to work while walking, or rather to be able to walk while he is working. At all times, in all places, under the light of the sun, in the surging crowds, in the sanctuaries of art, beside dusty bookstalls exposed to the wind, Victor Hugo, serene and thoughtful, seemed to say to external nature: "Fix yourself in my eyes so that I may remember you."

At the time of which I am speaking, a time when he exercised a real dictatorship in literary matters, I occasionally encountered him in the company of Edouard Ourliac, through whom I also met Pétrus Borel and Gérard de Nerval. He seemed to me very affable, very powerful, always in control of his feelings, and relying on a restricted wisdom made up of a few irrefutable axioms. For a long time he had shown, not only in his books but also in the adornment of his personal life, a great taste for the monuments of the past, for picturesque furniture, china, engravings, and for all the mysterious and brilliant décor of earlier times. The critic whose eye overlooks this detail would not be a real critic; for not only does this taste for the beautiful and even for the strange as expressed through the plastic, confirm the literary character of Victor Hugo; not only did it confirm his revolutionary, or rather regenerative doctrine, but also it appeared as the indispensable complement of a universal poetic character. It is all very well that Pascal, fired by asceticism, should have persisted in living thereafter within four bare walls furnished with cane chairs, and that a priest of Saint-Roch (I no longer remember which one) should have had all his furniture sold at auction, to the horror of all prelates fond of comfort; that is all beautiful and great. But if I see a man of letters who is not oppressed by poverty neglect things that delight the eye and entertain the imagination, I am tempted to believe that he is a very incomplete man of letters, to say the least.

Today when we glance over the recent poetry of Victor Hugo, we see that he has remained what he was, a thoughtful wanderer, a solitary man, yet in love with life, a contemplative and inquiring mind. But it is no longer in the wooded and flowering outskirts of the great city, on the rough embankments of the Seine, in paths swarming with children that he sets his feet and eyes to wander. Like Demosthenes, he talks with the wind and the waves; formerly he roamed alone in places seething with human life; today he walks in solitudes peopled with his thoughts. And so he is perhaps even greater and more remarkable. The colors of his dreams have taken on a solemn hue and his voice has grown deeper in rivaling that of the Ocean. But there as here, he still seems to us like a statue of Meditation in movement.

II

In the days, already so distant, of which I was speaking, happy days when men of letters formed a society sorely missed by its survivors, who will never again find its equal, Victor Hugo was the one to whom everyone turned, seeking the watchword. Never was royalty more legitimate, more natural, more acclaimed by gratitude, more confirmed by the impotence of rebellion. When one recalls what French poetry was before he appeared, and what a rejuvenation it has undergone since he came; when one imagines how insignificant it would have been without him, how many mysterious and profound sentiments that have been given expression would have remained unvoiced, how many intellects he has discovered, how many men made famous by him would have remained obscure, it is impossible not to consider him as one of those rare, providential minds who bring about the salvation of all men in the literary order, as others do in the moral order and still others in the political order. The movement created by Victor Hugo still continues under our eyes. That he has received powerful support no one will deny; but if today mature men, young people, and society women have a feeling for good poetry, for poetry that is profoundly rhythmic and intensely colored, if the public taste has again risen to pleasures it had forgotten, it is Victor Hugo to whom the credit belongs. It is, moreover, through his powerful instigation that erudite and enthusiastic architects are repairing our cathedrals and preserving our ancient monuments of stone. No one will hesitate to admit this except those for whom justice is not a pleasure.

I can speak only very briefly in this article about his poetic faculties. Doubtless, in some matters I shall merely be summarizing many excellent things that have already been said; perhaps I shall have the good fortune to give them greater emphasis.

Victor Hugo was, from the outset, the man who was best endowed and most obviously chosen to express in poetry what

I shall call *the mystery of life.* Nature which lies before us, no matter where we turn, and which envelops us like a mystery, shows herself under several simultaneous aspects, each of which, to the extent that it is more intelligible, more perceptible to us, is reflected more intensely in our hearts: form, attitude and movement, light and color, sound and harmony. The music of Victor Hugo's verses is adapted to the profound harmonies of nature; as a sculptor, he carves into his stanzas the unforgettable form of things; as a painter, he illuminates them with the right color. And the three impressions penetrate the reader's mind simultaneously, as if they came directly from nature. From this triple impression comes *the morality of things.* No artist is more universal than he, more suited to put himself in contact with the forces of universal life, more inclined to bathe ceaselessly in nature. Not only does he express precisely and translate literally what is clearly and distinctly visible, but he expresses with an *indispensable obscurity* what is obscure and vaguely revealed. His works abound in extraordinary features of the kind which we could call *tours de force,* if we did not know that they are essentially natural to him. The poetry of Victor Hugo can translate for the human soul not only the most direct pleasures that it draws from visible nature but also the most fleeting, the most complicated, the most moral (I am purposely using the word moral) sensations which are transmitted to it by visible substance, by inanimate or what is called inanimate nature; it can translate not only the form of substance exterior to man, vegetable or mineral, but also its aspect, its expression, its sadness, its tenderness, its exultant joy, its repulsive hate, its charm or its horror; in short, in other words, all that is human in every imaginable thing and also all that is divine, sacred, or diabolic.

Those who are not poets do not understand these things. Fourier appeared one day, a little too pompously, to reveal to us the mysteries of *analogy.*[134] I do not deny the importance of some of his small discoveries, although I believe that his mind was too attached to material accuracy not to make mistakes and to attain straight off the moral certitude of intuition. With the same care he could have revealed to us all the excellent poets whose works educate the reading public as much as the contemplation of nature. Moreover, Swedenborg, who possessed a much greater soul, had already taught us that *heaven is a very great man;* that everything, form, movement, number, color, perfume, in the *spiritual* as well as in the *natural* world, is significant, reciprocal, converse, *corresponding.*[135] Lavater, limiting the demonstration of universal truth to man's facial conformation, had translated for us the spiritual meaning of contour, of form, of dimension. If we broaden the demonstration (not only have we the right, but it would be infinitely difficult to do otherwise), we arrive at this truth that everything is hieroglyphic, and we know that symbols are only relatively obscure, that is to say according to the mind's purity, good will, or native insight. Now, what is a poet (I am using the word in its broadest sense) if not a translator, a decipherer? Among the best poets, there are no metaphors, comparisons, or epithets which are not adapted with mathematical exactitude to the particular circumstance, because these comparisons, metaphors, and epithets are drawn from the inexhaustible storehouse of *universal analogy* and cannot be found elsewhere. Now let me ask if, after a careful search, one will find, not in our history only but in the history of all peoples, many poets who, like Victor Hugo, contain so magnificent a repertory of human and divine analogies. I have read in the Bible about a prophet who was asked by God to devour a book.[136] I do not know in what world Victor Hugo has previously consumed the dictionary of the language which he was called upon to speak, but I see that the French lexicon, as he uses it, has become a world, a colorful, melodious, and moving universe. Through what sequence of historical circumstances, philosophical destinies, sidereal conjunctions this man was born among us, I haven't the least idea, and I do not think it is my duty to examine it here. Perhaps it is simply because Germany had Goethe, and England Shakespeare and Byron, that Victor Hugo was rightfully owed to

France. I see from the history of peoples that each in its turn is called to conquer the world; perhaps the same thing is true of poetic domination as is true of rule by the sword.

From his ability to absorb the life around him, unique in its amplitude, as well as from his powerful faculty of meditation, Victor Hugo has become a very extraordinary poetic character, questioning, mysterious, and, like nature itself, vast and detailed, serene and agitated. Voltaire did not see mystery in anything, or at least in very few things. But Victor Hugo does not cut the Gordian knot of things with Voltaire's military dispatch; his keenly perceptive senses reveal abysses to him; he sees mystery everywhere. And indeed, where doesn't it exist? From it derives the sense of fright that penetrates several of his most beautiful poems; from it come those turbulent verses that rise and fall, those masses of stormy images carried along with the speed of a fleeing chaos; from it come those frequent repetitions of words, all destined to express the captivating shadows or the enigmatic countenance of mystery.

III

Thus Victor Hugo possesses not only greatness but universality. How varied is his repertory and, although always *one* and compact, how many-sided it is! I don't know if, among art lovers, there are many like me, but I can't help being extremely annoyed when I hear people speak of a landscapist (however perfect he may be), of a painter of animals or a painter of flowers with the same enthusiasm that might be used in praising a universal painter (that is to say a real painter) such as Rubens, Veronese, Velásquez or Delacroix. It seems to me, in fact, that he who does not know how to paint everything can not be called a painter. The renowned men whom I have just named express perfectly everything that each of the specialists expresses and, in addition, they possess an imagination and a creative faculty which speaks vigorously to the minds of all men.

The moment you wish to give me the idea of a perfect artist, my mind does not stop at perfection in one genre, but it immediately conceives the necessity of perfection in all genres. The same thing is true of literature in general and of poetry in particular. He who is not capable of painting everything, palaces and hovels, feelings of tenderness and of cruelty, circumscribed family affection and universal charity, the charm of plant life and the miracles of architecture, all that which is most pleasant and all that which is most horrible, the inner meaning and the external beauty of every religion, the moral and physical aspect of every nation, everything in short from the visible to the invisible, from heaven to hell—such a person, I say, is not really a poet in the broadest sense of the word and according to the heart of God. You say of one: he is a poet of the *home* or of the family; of another: he is a poet of love; and of another: he is a poet of glory. But by what right do you thus limit the range of each artist's talent? Do you mean to say that he who has extolled glory is *for that very reason* unsuited to celebrate love? You thereby invalidate the universal meaning of the word *poetry*. If you do not merely want to suggest that circumstances which have nothing to do with the poet have thus far confined him to one speciality, I shall always believe that you are speaking of a poor poet, of an incomplete poet, however clever he may be in *his* genre.

Ah! in the case of Victor Hugo we do not have to point out these distinctions, for his genius is without limits. Here we are dazzled, enchanted, and enveloped as if by life itself. The transparent air, the domed sky, the outline of a tree, the gaze of an animal, the silhouette of a house are painted in his books with the brush of an accomplished landscapist. In everything he puts the palpitation of life. If he paints the sea, no *seascape* will equal his. The ships which furrow its surface or which cut through its foam will have, more than those of any other painter, the appearance of fierce combatants, the character of will and of animality which mysteriously emerges from a geometric and mechanical apparatus of wood, iron, ropes and canvas; a monstrous animal created by man to which the wind and the waves add the beauty of movement.

As for love, war, family pleasures, the sorrows of the poor, national splendors, all that which is peculiar to man and which constitutes the domain of the genre painter and of the history painter, what have we seen that is richer and more concrete than the lyrical poetry of Victor Hugo? If space allowed, this would doubtless be the occasion to analyze the moral atmosphere which hovers and moves through his poems and which derives very obviously from the author's own temperament. It seems to me that it is unmistakably characterized by a love which makes no distinction between what is very strong and what is very weak, and that the attraction exercised over the poet by these two extremes stems from a single source, which is the very strength, the primordial vigor with which he is endowed. Strength delights and intoxicates him; he approaches it as if it were a brother: fraternal affection. Thus he is irresistibly attracted to every symbol of the infinite, the sea, the sky; to all the ancient representatives of strength, Homeric or Biblical giants, paladins, knights; to enormous and fearful beasts. He makes child's play of fondling what would frighten weaker hands; he moves about in immensity without vertigo. On the other hand, but through a different tendency, whose source is, however, the same, the poet always shows warm compassion for all that is weak, lonely, sorrowful, for all that is fatherless: a paternal attraction. The man of strength, who senses a brother in all that is strong, sees his children in all that has need of protection or consolation. It is from strength itself and from the certainty that it gives to one who possesses it that the spirit of justice and of charity is derived. Thus in the poems of Victor Hugo there constantly occur those notes of love for fallen women, for the poor who are crushed in the cogwheels of society, for the animals that are martyrs of our gluttony and despotism. Few people have noticed the magic charm which kindness adds to strength and which is so frequently seen in the works of our poet. A smile and a tear on the face of a colossus is an almost divine form of originality. Even in his short poems devoted to sensual love, in those verses so voluptuous and so melodious in their melancholy, may be heard, like the continuous accompaniment of an orchestra, the deep voice of charity. Beneath the lover one senses a father and a protector. It is not a matter here of that sermonizing morality which, with its pedantic air and its didactic tone, can spoil the most beautiful piece of poetry but of an implicit morality which slips unnoticed into poetic matter like imponderable fluids into the machinery of the world. Morality does not enter into this art as its avowed purpose; it is intermingled with it and lost sight of, as in life itself. The poet is unintentionally a moralist through the abundance and plenitude of nature.

IV

The excessive, the immense are the natural domain of Victor Hugo; he moves in it as if in his native atmosphere. The genius which he has always displayed in painting *all the monstrosity* surrounding man is truly prodigious. But it is especially in recent years that he has experienced the metaphysical influence emanating from all these things; the curiosity of an Oedipus obsessed by innumerable Sphinxes. Who does not remember "La Pente de la Rêverie," done so long ago? A large part of his recent work seems to be the natural yet vast development of the faculty which gave birth to this fascinating poem. One might say that from that time on the poet's reverie has been interrupted more and more frequently by questioning and that in his eyes all aspects of nature are constantly bristling with problems. How has the father who is *one* been able to engender duality, and how has he been finally metamorphosed into endless numbers? Mystery! Must or can the infinite totality of numbers be again concentrated into the original unity? Mystery! The suggestive contemplation of the heavens occupies an immense and dominant place in the most recent works of the poet.

Whatever the subject treated, the heavens dominate and rise above it like a changeless dome where mystery and light hover together, where mystery scintillates, where mystery invites curious reverie, where mystery dispels discouraged thought. Ah, even today, in spite of Newton and in spite of Laplace, astronomical certainty is not so great that reverie cannot find a place for itself among the vast lacunae still unexplored by modern science. Very rightly the poet lets his thought wander in an intoxicating labyrinth of speculations. There is not a problem that has been discussed or attacked, no matter when or by what philosophy, that has not inevitably come to demand its place in the works of the poet. Are the world of the stars and the world of souls finite or infinite? Is there a continuous bringing forth of beings in the vast cosmos as there is in the finite world? Would that which we are tempted to take for an infinite multiplication of beings be only a circulatory movement bringing these same beings back to life at times and under conditions marked by a supreme and all-embracing law?

Would matter and movement be only the respiration and inspiration of a God who brings forth worlds and then calls them back in turn to his bosom? Will all that which is multiple become one and will our universe and all those which we see suspended around us come to be replaced one day by new universes springing forth from the thought of Him whose sole happiness and sole function are to create unceasingly? And will not conjecture on the moral significance, on the intended purpose of all these worlds, our unknown neighbors, also naturally take its place in the immense domains of poetry?

Heavenly bodies, stars, suns, constellations, with your germinations, blossomings, flowerings, eruptions that are successive, simultaneous, slow or sudden, progressive or complete, are you simply forms of the life of God, or habitations prepared by his goodness or his justice for souls whom he wishes to educate and to gradually bring near himself? Worlds eternally studied, unknown perhaps forever, speak, have you your paradises, hells, purgatories, prisons, villas, palaces, etc.? . . . Would there be anything so *extravagant*, so monstrous, so exceeding the rightful limits of poetic conjecture in believing that there may spring forth from the limbo of the future new systems and clusters of planets which will assume unexpected forms, adopt unforeseen combinations, undergo unrecorded laws, imitate all the providential vagaries of a geometry too vast and too complicated for understanding? I insist on the word *conjecture* which serves to define fairly satisfactorily the extrascientific character of all poetry. In the hands of a poet other than Victor Hugo, such themes and such subjects could too easily have taken on a didactic form, which is the greatest enemy of true poetry. To recount in verse *known* laws governing the movement of the moral or sidereal world is to describe what has been discovered and what falls completely under the scientist's telescope or compass; it is to confine oneself to tasks pertaining to science, to encroach on its functions, and to encumber its traditional language with the superfluous and, in this case, dangerous embellishment of rhyme; but to give oneself up to all the reveries suggested by the infinite spectacle of life on earth and in the heavens is the legitimate right of anyone, consequently of the poet who is empowered to translate into a magnificent language, other than prose and music, the eternal conjectures of inquiring humanity. In describing what is, the poet is degraded and descends to the level of the professor; in recounting the possible he remains faithful to his function; he is a collective soul who questions, who weeps, who hopes and who sometimes finds the answer.

V

A new proof of the same infallible taste is revealed in the latest work which Victor Hugo has offered for our pleasure. I am referring to *La Légende des Siècles*. Except at a nation's dawn, when poetry is both the expression of its soul and the repertory of its knowledge, history put into verse is a deviation from the laws which govern the two genres, history and poetry; it is an outrage against the two Muses. In periods of great culture there comes about in the spiritual world a division of work which strengthens and perfects each part; and he who then tries to create an epic poem as it was understood by younger nations, runs the risk of diminishing the magic effect of poetry, if only through the intolerable length of the work, and of robbing history of a part of the wisdom and sobriety which older nations demand of it. Usually it results in nothing more than tedious nonsense. In spite of all the well meaning efforts of a French philosopher [Edgar Quinet] who believed that, without long-standing talent and without prolonged study, one could suddenly put poetry at the service of a poetic thesis, Napoleon, even today, is too much a part of history to be made into a legend. It is no more permissible than it is possible for man, even a man of genius, to artificially move back the centuries in that way. Such an idea could occur only to a philosopher, a professor, in other words to a man withdrawn from life. When in his first poems Victor Hugo tries to show us Napoleon as a legendary character, he is still a Parisian speaking, a contemporary who is deeply moved and lost in dreams; he evokes the legend that is *possible* in the future; he does not reduce it by his own authority to a past state.

Now, to come back to *La Légende des Siècles*, Victor Hugo has created the only epic poetry that could have been created by a man of his time for the readers of his time. First, the poems composing the work are usually short, and even the brevity of some is no less extraordinary than their power. This is already an important consideration, which is evidence of a complete understanding of all the possibilities of modern poetry. Next, wishing to create a modern epic poem, in other words a poem that has its source or rather its pretext in history, he carefully refrained from borrowing anything from history except that which it can rightfully and profitably lend to poetry. I am referring to legends, myths, fables which are, as it were, condensations of national life, deep reservoirs where sleep the blood and tears of peoples. Finally, he has not celebrated any particular nation or the passion of any particular century in his verse; he has risen at once to one of those philosophical heights from which the poet can survey the whole evolution of humanity with a glance that is impartially curious, angry, or compassionate. The majesty with which he has made the centuries pass before us like ghosts emerging from a wall, the complete command with which he has set them in motion—each with its correct costume, its true appearance, its authentic behavior—is something which we have all seen. The sublime and subtle art, the terrible familiarity with which this magician has made the Centuries speak and gesticulate, would not be impossible for me to explain; but what I am especially anxious to point out is that this art could only move comfortably in a legendary milieu and that (putting aside the talents of the magician) it is the choice of the terrain that has facilitated the unfolding of the spectacle.

From his distant exile, toward which our eyes and ears are turned, the beloved and venerated poet has announced new poems. In recent years he has proved to us that the domain of poetry, however limited it may be, is nonetheless, by the law of genius, almost limitless. In what order of things, by what new means will he renew his proof? Will he wish hereafter to borrow unknown delights, for example, from buffoonery, (I am choosing at random), from immortal gaiety, from joy, from the supernatural, from the magical and from the marvelous, endowed by him with that immense, superlative character with which he can endow all things? It is not in the province of criticism to say; but what criticism can affirm without fear of being mistaken, because it has already seen successive proofs, is that he is one of those rare mortals, even more rare in the literary world than in any other, who draw new strength from the years and who, through an endlessly repeated miracle, continue growing younger and more vigorous until death.

✳ AUGUSTE BARBIER

PREFACE

In his 1851 essay on Pierre Dupont, Baudelaire had expressed his admiration for the poetic genius of Barbier in spite of certain faults that marred his verse. Carried away by the revolutionary spirit, he had approved Barbier's utilitarian conception of poetry and had concluded that "art was forever inseparable from morality."

By 1861 Baudelaire had long since rejected utilitarianism which, like Poe, he considered the great modern heresy. In his essay on Gautier (1859) he had already hinted that his admiration for Barbier was subject to certain reservations. The essay of 1861 leaves no doubt as to his position. He is obviously still under the spell of Barbier's deeply moving verse. He still admires his vigor, his natural eloquence, his ability to arouse the emotions of the reader. But he is adamant in his objection to the poet's association of art and morality. In the preceding essay on Hugo, Baudelaire had praised the exiled poet for the implicit morality of his best works and had reminded the reader (and incidentally Hugo himself) of his objection to the use of explicit moralizing—"that sermonizing morality which, with its pedantic air and its didactic tone, can spoil the most beautiful piece of poetry." In his analysis of Barbier, Baudelaire lays aside all restraint and frankly criticizes the poet for arbitrarily imposing a moral purpose on his art. By so doing, Barbier had corrupted his "superb poetic power" and had substituted "platitudinous solemnity" for "forceful simplicity."

Despite the validity of the criticism, the essay was rejected by Crépet whose democratic sympathies were closely allied to those of Barbier. Baudelaire refused to make any changes in his article, and the essay was finally published elsewhere (in *La Revue Fantaisiste*) on July 15, 1861.

Baudelaire continued to feel a sincere admiration for Barbier despite his faults. On January 31, 1862 in writing to Flaubert he included Barbier's name among those who represented "pure literature."

Auguste Barbier (1805–1882) is best known for his first volume of poems, *Iambes* (1832), which has to do with the Revolution of 1830. Another work, *Il Pianto* (1833), presents a nostalgic picture of Italy, and *Lazare* (1837) reflects the desolation associated with the Industrial Revolution in England.

❧❦❧❦❧

If I should say that the goal of Auguste Barbier has been the quest of beauty, his exclusive and primary quest, I believe he would be annoyed, and obviously he would have the right to be. However magnificent his poetry may be, *poetry* in itself has not been his chief love. He had evidently set for himself a goal which he thinks is of a higher and nobler nature. I have neither enough authority nor enough eloquence to undeceive him; but I shall take advantage of the opportunity which is offered me to treat once again this tiresome question of the alliance of the Good with the Beautiful, a question which has become muddled and uncertain only through the enfeeblement of minds.

I write without any sense of embarrassment because, on the one hand, he has attained fame as a poet and will not be forgotten by posterity and because, on the other hand, I myself have a great and long-standing admiration for his ability. He has written some superb poetry; he is naturally eloquent; he carries the reader away with the emotions that fill his heart to overflowing. His language, vigorous and picturesque, has almost the charm of Latin. It flashes with sublime brilliance. His first compositions are still remembered by everyone. His fame is justly deserved. All this is indisputable.

But the source of this fame is not *pure*, for it sprang from circumstances. Poetry is sufficient unto itself. It is eternal and ought never to require exterior aids. Now, a part of Auguste Barbier's fame comes to him from the circumstances in which he produced his first poems. What makes them admirable is the lyric movement which animates them and not, as he doubtless believes, the noble ideas that they are intended to express. *Facit indignatio versum*, said an ancient poet, who, however great he may be, was speaking from a personal motive.[137] That is true enough, but it is also quite certain that poetry written for the mere love of poetry has a greater chance of being beautiful than poetry written out of *indignation*. The world is full of very indignant people who, however, will never write beautiful verse. And so we note at the outset that if Auguste Barbier has been a great poet, it is because he possessed the faculties, or some of the faculties, which make a great poet, and not because he expressed the indignation of respectable people.

In this misapprehension on the part of the public there is, in fact, a confusion that is very easy to explain. Such and such a poem is beautiful and moral, but it is not beautiful *because* it is moral. Another is beautiful and immoral, but its beauty does not come from its immorality, or rather, to speak plainly, what is beautiful is no more moral than it is immoral. Usually it happens, I know, that truly beautiful poetry transports the soul toward a celestial world; beauty is something so powerful that it can only ennoble souls; but this beauty is absolute, and the odds are that if you as a poet wish to impose a moral goal on yourself in advance, you will considerably diminish your poetic power.

The same thing is true of morality imposed on works of art as is true of that other condition, no less ridiculous, imposed on them by other people, namely, the expression of thoughts or *ideas* drawn from a world foreign to art—scientific *ideas*, political *ideas*, etc. Such is the point of departure of those who are given to false reasoning or, to say the least, of those who, because they are somewhat lacking in poetic power, wish to make poetry into something rational. The idea, they say, is the most important thing (they should say: idea and form are one); naturally and inevitably they soon say: Since the idea is of primary importance, form, which is less important, may be neglected without danger. The result is the destruction of poetry.

Now in the case of Auguste Barbier, a born poet and a great poet, the constant and exclusive concern for expressing moral or useful ideas has gradually led to a slight disdain for correctness, polish, and finish, which in itself would be enough to constitute a kind of decadence.

In "La Tentation" (his first poem, eliminated in the later editions of his *Iambes*), he had shown from the very beginning a grandeur, a dignity of manner which is his real distinction and which he has never discarded even in the moments when he has proved most disloyal to the purely poetic idea. This innate grandeur and this lyric eloquence were brilliantly displayed in all the poetry relating to the Revolution of 1830 and to the spiritual or social disturbances that followed it. But these poems, I repeat, were *applied* to circumstances and, beautiful though they are, they are marked by the unfortunate quality of occasionality and of fashion. "*Mon vers, rude et grossier, est honnête homme au fond,*" cries the poet; but was it really as a poet that he drew inane, moral commonplaces from bourgeois conversation? Or was it as a respectable man that he wanted to bring back to our stage the white-robed Melpomene (what has Melpomene to do with respectability?) and to suppress the dramas of Victor Hugo and of Alexandre Dumas? [138] I have noticed (I say this in all seriousness) that people who are too fond of utility and morality willingly neglect grammar, like persons who are carried away by their emotions. It is a sad thing to see so highly gifted a poet suppress articles and possessive adjectives, whenever those monosyllables or disyllables inconvenience him, and employ a word in a sense contrary to usage simply because that word has the right number of syllables. In such a case I do not believe in a lack of ability; I blame rather the natural indolence of those who depend on inspiration. In his songs about the decadence of Italy and about the poverty of England and Ireland (*Il Pianto* and *Lazare*) there are as usual, I repeat, sublime accents; but the same affectation of utility and morality appears and spoils the most noble impressions. If I were not afraid of slandering a man so worthy of respect in every way, I would say that this somewhat resembles a grimace. Can you imagine a *Muse* making a *grimace?* In addition, a new fault, a new mannerism is apparent here which has nothing to do with careless rhyme or the suppression of articles. I am referring to a certain platitudinous solemnity or to the use of certain solemn platitudes which was formerly passed off as majestic and forceful simplicity. There are fashions in literature, as there are in painting and in dress; there was a time in poetry and in painting when there was a great quest of the *naïve*, a new kind of preciosity. Platitudes were glorified, and I remember that Edouard Ourliac laughingly quoted to me this line of his own composition as a model of the genre:

Les cloches du couvent de Sainte-Madeleine

Many similar instances will be found in the poems of Brizeux, and I should not be surprised if Barbier's friendship with Antony Deschamps and with Brizeux has helped to encourage him in this Dantesque grimace.[139]

Throughout all his work we recognize the same faults and the same virtues. Everything seems unexpected and spontaneous; the vigorous touch, in the Latin manner, stands out constantly among feeble lapses and awkward lines. There is no need for me to point out, I presume, that *Pot-de-vin, Erostrate, Chants Civils et Religieux* are all works which have a moral purpose. I shall pass over the small volume *Odelettes*, which is merely a painful attempt to achieve the charm of the ancients, and come to *Rimes Héroïques*. Here, to speak frankly, all the folly of the century appears, resplendent in its unconscious nakedness. Under the pretext of writing sonnets in honor of great men, the poet has celebrated the lightning rod and the weaving loom. The prodigious absurdities to which this confusion of ideas and functions could lead us is obvious. One of my friends has worked on an anonymous poem about an invention made by a dentist; indeed the lines may well have been good and the author full of conviction.[140] Yet who would dare say that even in that case it would have been poetry? I confess that whenever I see such a waste of rhymes and rhythms, I feel a great sadness that is in proportion to the greatness of the poet. Judging by numerous symptoms I believe that today one could affirm without fear of ridicule the most monstrous, the most absurd, and the most untenable of errors, to wit that *the goal of poetry is to enlighten people and, with the help of rhyme and harmony, to fix scientific discoveries more easily in the memory of men.*

If the reader has followed me attentively, he will not be surprised if I summarize this article, written more in sadness than in jest, in this way: *Auguste Barbier is a great poet and justifiably he will always pass as such. But he has been a great poet in spite of himself, so to speak; he has tried to spoil superb poetic powers by a false idea of poetry; fortunately, these powers were great enough to resist even the poet who sought to diminish them.*

❧ PÉTRUS BOREL

PREFACE

Baudelaire's essay on Pétrus Borel is in many ways more interesting for what it reveals about the critic than for its evaluation of the Lycanthrope. Baudelaire himself was somewhat perplexed by the attraction that he felt for the strange creature who was "one of the stars in the somber Romantic sky."

It is apparent that his appreciation was based as much on personal sympathy as on his admiration for the occasional flashes of genius that illuminate the work of his contemporary. Baudelaire may have recognized in Borel certain traits of character and temperament similar to his own and identified himself to some extent with the subject of his essay. In any case, his psychological portrayal of the Lycanthrope often gives the impression of being autobiographical.

Moreover, as Enid Starkie has pointed out, Borel had exerted a certain amount of influence on Baudelaire's aesthetic ideas. According to Miss Starkie, the verse prologue of *Madame Putiphar* anticipates Baudelaire's late poetry, and *Champavert* may have suggested the idea of treating physical love with an unaccustomed dignity and grandeur.

Pétrus Borel (1805–1859) was a poet and novelist who became the leader of a group of stormy young Romantic writers called *bousingos*, presumably because of the wide brimmed sailor-like hat which they affected. He is best known for his novel, *Madame Putiphar*; a volume of stories, *Champavert, contes immoraux*; and a collection of poems entitled *Rhapsodies*. He also translated the novel *Robinson Crusoe*. His works are marked by melodrama, violence, and misanthropy. It is thought that the saying "Man is a wolf to man" inspired him to adopt the name "the Lycanthrope."

For the best study of this little-known figure see Enid Starkie, *Pétrus Borel*, London, 1954.

✄✄✄✄✄✄

There are names that become proverbs and adjectives. When in 1859 a small newspaper wants to express all the disgust and contempt that it feels for a poem or a novel of a gloomy and extravagant character, it utters the words: Pétrus Borel!

and nothing more needs to be said. Judgment has been pronounced and the author is demolished.

Pétrus Borel, or Champavert the Lycanthrope, author of
Rhapsodies, of *Contes Immoraux* and of *Madame Putiphar*,
was one of the stars in the somber Romantic sky. Forgotten or
extinct, who remembers that star today and who is familiar
enough with it to presume to talk of it so formally? "*I*," I shall
gladly say, like Medea, "*I, I say, and that is enough!*" [141]
Edouard Ourliac, his comrade, did not hesitate to laugh at him,
but Ourliac was a small-town Voltaire who detested anything
excessive, especially an excessive love for art. Théophile Gautier
alone, whose open-mindedness delights in the universality of
things, and who, even if he wished, could not neglect anything
interesting, subtle, or picturesque, smiled with pleasure at the
strange lucubrations of the Lycanthrope.

Lycanthrope was a good name for him! Man-wolf or were-
wolf, what fairy or what demon cast him into the somber
forests of melancholy? What evil spirit bent over his cradle and
said to him: *I forbid you to please?* In the spiritual world there
is something mysterious which is called *Ill Luck*, and none of us
has the right to argue with Fate. She is the goddess who is least
comprehensible and who possesses, more than any pope or
lama, the privilege of infallibility. I have very often wondered
how and why a man like Pétrus Borel, who had shown a truly
epic talent in several scenes of his *Madame Putiphar* (especially
in the opening scenes where the savage and Northern drunkenness of the heroine's father is portrayed; in the scene where the
favorite horse brings back to the mother, ravished years before,
but still full of hate at her dishonor, the corpse of her beloved
son, poor Vengeance, a courageous boy who had fallen at the
first encounter and whom she had so carefully schooled for
vengeance; finally in the portrayal of the hideous sights and the
tortures of the dungeon, which compare in power to Maturin);
I have wondered, I say, how the poet who produced the strange
poem—with its brilliant sonorousness and its color almost
primitive in its intensity—which serves as a preface to *Madame*

Putiphar, could also show awkwardness in so many places, could encounter so many stumbling blocks and obstacles, and fall into such abysmally *bad luck*. I haven't any specific explanation to give; I can only point out symptoms, symptoms of a morbid nature in love with contradiction for the sake of contradiction and always ready to swim against every current without calculating either its strength or his own. Everyone, or almost everyone, inclines his handwriting to the right; Pétrus Borel slanted his completely to the left, so much so that all the letters, though carefully formed, looked like lines of soldiers thrown back by grapeshot. Moreover, writing was such a painful task that the slightest, most commonplace letter, an invitation, forwarding money, cost him two or three hours of tiring meditation, not counting the erasures and corrections. Finally, the strange spelling which is flaunted in *Madame Putiphar*, as a deliberate outrage to the visual habits of the public, is a feature which completes this caricature-like portrait. It is certainly not a simplified spelling like that of M. Erdan or that of Voltaire's cooks, but on the contrary, a spelling, more than picturesque, that takes advantage of every opportunity to ostentatiously call attention to etymology.[142] I can't picture, without feeling sympathetic pain, all the exhausting battles that the author must have had with the typesetters entrusted with printing his manuscripts in order to realize his typographical dreams. Thus, not only did he like to violate the moral habits of the reader, but also he liked to baffle and torment the eye by the graphic expression.

More than one person will doubtless ask why we make room in our gallery for a mind which we ourselves consider so incomplete. It is not only because this mind, however ponderous, shrill, incomplete it may be, has sometimes struck a dazzling and true note, but also because in the history of our century he has played a role not without importance. His specialty was Lycanthropy. Without Pétrus Borel there would be a lacuna in Romanticism. In the first phase of our literary revolution, poetic imagination turned especially toward the past; it often adopted the melodious and moving tone of regret. Later on, melancholy assumed a more decided, more savage, more worldly accent. A misanthropic republicanism joined the new school, and Pétrus Borel was the most presumptuous and the most paradoxical expression of the spirit of the *Bousingots* or of *Bousingo;* for in the spelling of these words, which are the products of fashion and of circumstances, a certain amount of hesitation is always permissible. This spirit, both literary and republican, contrary to the democratic and bourgeois passion which later so cruelly oppressed us, was excited both by an aristocratic hatred, unbounded, unrestricted, pitiless, directed against kings and the bourgeoisie, and by a general sympathy for all that which in art represented excess in color and in form, for all that which at one and the same time was intense, pessimistic and Byronic; a strange sort of dilettantism which can be explained only by the odious circumstances encompassing bored and turbulent youth. If the Restoration had turned into a period of glory, Romanticism would not have parted company with royalty; and this new sect, which professed equal scorn for the moderate political opposition, for the painting of Delaroche or the poetry of Delavigne, and for the king who directed the development of the middle of the road policy, would have found no reason to exist.[143]

As for me, I sincerely confess, even if it seems absurd, that I have always had some sympathy for this unfortunate writer whose abortive genius, full of ambition and of awkwardness, succeeded in producing only painstaking drafts, stormy flashes, figures whose native grandeur was impaired by something too bizarre in their dress or in their voice. He has, in short, a color all his own, a flavor *sui generis;* if he had nothing more than the attraction of willfulness, that is already a good deal. But he loved literature fiercely, and today we are overrun with pretty and docile writers all ready to sell the Muse to escape the potter's field.

Last year as we were finishing these notes, too severe perhaps, we learned that the poet had just died in Algeria where, discouraged or scornful, he had withdrawn far from the literary scene, without having published the *Tabarin* which had been announced a long time before.

❧ THÉODORE DE BANVILLE

PREFACE

Baudelaire's article on Banville is noteworthy not only for its keen analysis of the poet's works, but because it introduces some of his own general aesthetic ideas. His admiration for his friend and fellow poet was undeniably genuine in spite of vast differences in their style, inspiration, and standards. In a sonnet written in 1842 Baudelaire had applauded Banville's "disciplined audacity" and precocious genius; twenty years later he still appreciated the exuberance and brilliant lyric talent of his art.

Baudelaire was well aware that Banville stood apart from "the essentially demoniac tendency" of modern art, so apparent in Maturin, Byron, Poe, and himself. Whereas writers such as these "cast resplendent, dazzling rays on the latent Lucifer hidden in every human heart," Banville had the boldness and the originality to be a "perfect classicist" in a "satanic and Romantic atmosphere." He was content to effect "a return to the lost Eden," as Baudelaire himself had done in some of his loveliest poems, and to "translate the beautiful hours of life, those hours when one feels happy to think and to be alive."

Certain passages of the essay describe its author as much as they do Banville. The contention that the lyric poet can descend from "ethereal regions" and create "a new kind of delight" from ugliness and stupidity seems to be a justification of Baudelaire's own achievement.

Théodore de Banville (1823–1891) achieved success at an

early age for his faultlessly contrived poetry which anticipated that of the Parnassians. Throughout his life he was a close friend of Baudelaire except for a brief estrangement caused by the latter's jealousy over the actress, Marie Daubrun. Baudelaire's admiration for Banville remained unchanged until his death. It is true that Banville was one of those at whom the critic scoffed in his essay "The Pagan School"; but elsewhere, whether in his correspondence or in his literary criticism, Baudelaire speaks of him only with the highest praise.

On his side, Banville was a great admirer of the poet and critic. After Baudelaire's death in 1867, it was Banville who pronounced the moving funeral oration and it was he who helped Asselineau to prepare the posthumous edition of Baudelaire's works. Many of his prose works contain reminiscences of his association with the author of *Les Fleurs du Mal*.

Among his best poetical works are: *Les Stalactites* (1846), *Le Sang de la Coupe* (1857), and *Les Exilés* (1867). He also wrote essays, two plays, tales of Parisian life, and a treatise on French poetry (*Petit Traité de Poésie Française*).

⊰⊱⊰⊱⊰⊱

Théodore de Banville was famous while still a very young man. *Les Cariatides* dates from 1841.[144] I remember the amazement with which people perused that volume which contained an accumulation of so many riches, a little confused and a little jumbled. The author's age was repeated over and over, and few persons were willing to accept such extraordinary precocity. At that time Paris was not what it is today, a chaos, a bedlam, a Babel peopled with idiots and good-for-nothing creatures, not overly fastidious about their way of killing time and completely averse to literary enjoyment. At that time *all Paris* was composed of a select few whose task it is to mould the opinions of others and who, when a poet happens to be born, are always the first to know about it. They naturally hailed the author of *Les Cariatides* as a man who had a long career ahead of him. Théodore de Banville seemed to be one of those marked men for whom poetry is the easiest language to speak and whose thought flows of itself in a rhythmic pattern.

The qualities most apparent to the eye were brilliance and wealth of expression; but the numerous and unconscious imitations, the very variety of tone, according as the young poet underwent the influence of this or that predecessor, contributed in no small way to distract the reader's mind from the principal merit of the author, from that which was later to be his great originality, his claim to glory, his trademark. I am referring to sureness in lyric expression. I do not deny, mind you, that *Les Cariatides* contains some admirable pieces which the poet could be proud to sign even today. I wish only to point out that the ensemble of the work, with its brilliance and variety, did not reveal at the outset the special nature of the author, whether that nature was not fully *developed*, or whether the poet was still under the fascinating charm of all the poets of the great era.

But in *Les Stalactites* (1843–1845) the thought seems clearer and better defined; the object of the quest can be better surmised. The color, less lavish, shines nevertheless more brightly, and the form of each object stands out in a sharper silhouette. *Les Stalactites* represents, in the growth of the poet, a particular phase where it could be said that he tried to react against his original tendency toward an effusiveness that was too prodigal, too undisciplined. Several of the best pieces in this volume are very short and suggest the restrained elegance of ancient pottery. Yet it is only later, after reveling in a thousand difficulties, in a thousand gymnastic exercises, which only true lovers of the Muse can appreciate at their true value, that the poet, combining in perfect harmony the exuberance of his original nature and the experience of his maturity, was to produce, one serving the other, poems of consummate skill and of a *sui generis* charm, such as "La Malédiction de Vénus," "L'Ange Mélancolique," and above all certain sublime stanzas which have no title, but which will be found in the sixth volume of his complete poems—stanzas worthy of Ronsard in their boldness, their elasticity, and their breadth, and whose opening lines, full of grandiloquence, presage superhuman transports of pride and joy.

> Vous en qui je salue une nouvelle aurore,
> Vous tous qui m'aimerez,
> Jeunes hommes des temps qui ne sont pas encore,
> O bataillons sacrés!

But what is this mysterious charm which the poet himself knew he possessed and which he intensified until he made of it an enduring virtue? If we cannot define it exactly, perhaps we shall find some words to describe it, perhaps we shall be able to discover in part the sources from which it derives.

I once said, I no longer remember where: "The poetry of Banville represents the beautiful hours of life, those hours when one feels happy to think and to be alive." [145]

I read a statement by a critic: "To divine the heart of a poet, or at least his chief preoccupation, let us seek in his works the word or words that appear there with the greatest frequency. The word will explain the obsession." [146]

If my feelings did not deceive me (as will soon become obvious) when I said: "Banville's talent represents the beautiful hours of life," and if I find in his works a word which, by its frequent repetition, seems to indicate a natural propensity and a fixed purpose, I shall have the right to conclude that this word can serve, better than any other, to characterize the nature of his talent as well as the sensations contained *in the hours of life when one feels most alive.*

This word is the word *lyre*, which for the author evidently possesses a prodigiously comprehensive meaning. *Lyre* expresses that almost supernatural state, that intensity of life when the heart *sings*, when it is *constrained to sing*, like the tree, the bird, and the sea. By a reasoning which perhaps errs in recalling mathematical methods, I come to the conclusion that the poetry of Banville, by suggesting first of all the idea of *beautiful hours,* then by constantly presenting to the eye the word *lyre* (*lyre* being expressly used to convey the *beautiful hours,* the ardent spiritual vitality, the hyperbolical man, in a word), the talent of Banville is essentially, decidedly, and deliberately lyric.

There is, in fact, a lyric manner of feeling. The most ill-favored men, those to whom fortune gives the least leisure, have sometimes experienced impressions of this kind, so rich that the soul is, as it were, illuminated by them, so intense that it is, as it were, exalted. In those marvelous moments the whole inner being, too light, too expansive, soars into the air as if to attain a higher region.[147]

Inevitably there also exists a lyric manner of speaking, and a lyric world, a lyric atmosphere, landscapes, men, women, animals who all have something of the character preferred by the Lyre.

First of all let us state that hyperbole and apostrophe are forms of expression which are not only the most pleasant to it but also most necessary, since these forms derive naturally from a heightened state of vitality. Next we observe that every lyric mood that we experience compels us to consider things not under their specific, exceptional aspect but in their principal, general, universal features. The lyre gladly shuns all the details in which the novel delights. The lyric soul takes strides as vast as syntheses; the mind of the novelist revels in analysis. It is this consideration which serves to explain what convenience and what beauty the poet finds in mythology and in allegories. Mythology is a dictionary of living hieroglyphics, hieroglyphics known by everyone. Here, landscape is clothed in the same hyperbolic magic as the figures; it becomes *setting.* Woman is not only a creature of a supreme beauty, comparable to that of Eve or Venus; in order to express the purity of her eyes, not only will the poet borrow comparisons from every limpid, dazzling, transparent object, from all the finest reflectors and all the most beautiful crystallizations of nature (in this connection let us note Banville's predilection for precious stones), but also he will have to endow woman with a kind of beauty such as the mind can conceive as existing only in a superior world. Now, I remember that in three or four places our poet, wishing to ascribe an incomparable and unsurpassable beauty to women, says that they have heads like *those of children*. That is an especially lyric stroke of genius, which reveals itself by a taste for the superhuman. That expression obviously implies the idea that the most beautiful of human faces is one whose radiance has never been dimmed or marked by the wear and tear of life, by passion, anger, sin, anguish, or care. Every lyric poet, by virtue of his nature, inevitably effects a return to the lost Eden. Everything in the lyric world—men, landscapes, palaces—is, so to speak, apotheosized. Now, through the infallible logic of nature, the word *apotheosis* is one of those that unfailingly appears under the pen of the poet when he has to describe (and you may be sure that he does not fail to enjoy it) a mingling of glory and light. And if the lyric poet has occasion to speak of himself, he will not depict himself bent over a table scrawling horrible little black symbols on a white page, fighting against intractable lines or struggling against the obtuseness of the proofreader, any more than he will show himself in a poor, wretched, or disorderly room; nor, if he wishes to appear dead, will he show himself rotting beneath his linen shroud in a wooden casket.[148] That would be lying. Horrors! That would be contradicting the true *reality*, in other words his own nature. The dead poet does not find himself too well served by nymphs, houris, and angels. He can rest only in the green Elysian fields, or in palaces more beautiful and profound than the architecture built of mist by the setting sun.[149]

> Mais moi, *vêtu de pourpre, en d'éternelles fêtes,*
> Dont je prendrai ma part,
> Je boirai le nectar au séjour des poètes,
> A côté de Ronsard.

Là, dans ces lieux, *où tout a des splendeurs divines*
Ondes, lumière, accords,
Nos yeux s'enivreront de formes féminines
Plus belles que des corps;
Et tous les deux, parmi des spectacles *féeriques,*
Qui dureront toujours,
Nous nous raconterons nos batailles *lyriques*
Et nos belles amours.

I like that; I find in this love of luxury carried beyond the grave a confirmation of grandeur. I am touched by the marvels and the magnificence that the poet decrees in favor of anyone who plays the lyre. I am happy to see the poet's complete apotheosis stated flatly, bluntly, and without undue modesty, and I should even consider the poet who differs from my opinion in this matter as guilty of bad taste. But I confess that to be so bold as to venture this *Declaration of Rights* of the poet one must be completely lyric, and few persons have the right to be so bold.

But after all, you will say, lyric as the poet may be, can he never descend from the ethereal regions, can he never feel the flow of ambient life around him, never see the spectacle of life, the everlasting absurdity of the human animal, the nauseating silliness of women, etc.? . . . Why yes indeed! the poet can descend into life; but be assured that if he consents to do so, it is not without purpose, and that he will be able to profit from his journey. From ugliness and stupidity he will create a new kind of delight.[150] But here again his buffoonery will retain something of the hyperbolic; excess will destroy its bitterness, and satire, by a miracle springing from the very nature of the poet, will rid itself of all its hate in an explosion of mirth, innocent because it is carnival-like.

Even in idealistic poetry the Muse can associate with the living without being cheapened. It can gather new ornaments everywhere. Modern tinsel can add exquisite grace, a new mordancy, (a pungency, as they used to say) to her goddess-

like beauty. Phaedra in hoop skirts has delighted the most refined minds of Europe; even more easily Venus, who is immortal, can set down her chariot in the Luxembourg Gardens
when she wishes to visit Paris. Why do you suspect that this
anachronism is an infraction of the rules that the poet has
imposed on himself, of what we may call his lyric *convictions?*
For can one commit an anachronism when dealing with things
that are eternal?

To tell the whole truth as we see it, Théodore de Banville
must be considered an original poet of the highest type. Indeed,
if one glances over contemporary poetry and its best representatives, it is easy to see that it has reached a mixed state of a very
complex nature; plastic genius, philosophical ideas, lyric enthusiasm, satiric wit, are combined and intermingled in infinitely
varied amounts. Modern poetry is related at one and the same
time to painting, music, sculpture, decorative art, satiric philosophy, and to the analytic spirit; and, however happily and skillfully blended it may be, it emerges with obvious indications of a
subtlety borrowed from various arts. Some could perhaps see in
this symptoms of depravity of taste. But that is a question which
I do not wish to discuss here. Banville alone, as I have already
said, is purely, naturally, and intentionally lyric. He has returned
to the means of poetic expression used by earlier writers, finding
them no doubt entirely adequate and perfectly adapted to his
purpose.

But what I said about the choice of means applies no less
aptly to the choice of subjects, to the theme considered in itself.
Up to a rather advanced point in modern times, art, poetry, and
especially music has sought only to delight the mind by offering
it pictures of bliss in contrast with the horrible life of contention
and struggle in which we are plunged.

Beethoven began to stir the worlds of melancholy and incurable despair amassed like clouds in man's inner sky. Maturin
in the novel, Byron in poetry, Poe in poetry and in the analytical
novel—the one in spite of his prolixity and his verbiage so
detestably imitated by Alfred de Musset; the other in spite of

his annoying terseness—have admirably expressed the blasphemous side of passion; they have cast resplendent, dazzling rays on the latent Lucifer hidden in every human heart. I mean that modern art has an essentially demoniac tendency. And it seems that this satanic side of man, which man takes pleasure in explaining to himself, increases every day, as if the devil, like one who fattens geese, enjoyed enlarging it by artificial means, patiently force-feeding the human race in his poultry yard in order to prepare for himself a more succulent dish.

But Théodore de Banville refuses to be drawn toward these blood-filled marshes, these abysses of mud. His art, like that of the ancients, expresses only what is beautiful, joyous, noble, great, rhythmic. Consequently, in his works you do not hear the dissonant, discordant music of the witches' sabbath, any more than the yelping of irony, that vengeance of the conquered. In his verse everything has a festive, innocent air, even sensual pleasure. His poetry is not only regret and nostalgia for the Paradisiac state, but even a very deliberate return to it. From this point of view we can then consider him an original writer of the bravest type. In a completely satanic or Romantic atmosphere, in the midst of a chorus of imprecations, he has the audacity to sing the goodness of the gods and to be a perfect *classicist*. I intend this word to be understood in its most noble meaning, in the truly historic sense.

✺ PIERRE DUPONT

PREFACE

Baudelaire's second essay on Dupont is not so different from the first as is often believed. He had, of course, long since rejected the idea of utilitarian art which he had advocated in 1851 and which he had used to justify his favorable attitude toward Dupont's verse. In the 1861 essay there is no mention of utilitarianism except for a passing reference to Dupont's "too obvious tendency toward didactic categories and divisions." The emphasis is rather on the fact that Dupont's poetry had served as a healthy reaction to Neo-Classicism.

On the whole Baudelaire's judgment remains what it had been ten years earlier. He is more severe in his criticism of the poet's careless and slovenly style, but he tempers his severity by praising his natural charm, his spontaneity and, rather surprisingly, his ability to express the "immortal freshness of nature."

The article reveals a warmth of affection and a nostalgia for the past seldom noted in the critical essays. Yet it is clear that, in Baudelaire's eyes, Dupont is no more than a minor poet, a singer of songs filled with tenderness and compassion. By associating him with those "who owe infinitely more to nature than to art," the critic separates him from those whom he considers truly great, such as Poe, Gautier, and Hugo, and relegates him to the lesser rank of Barbier and Madame Desbordes-Valmore.

❧❦❧❦❧❦

After 1848 Pierre Dupont attained great glory. Lovers of a disciplined and carefully wrought literature may have found that glory too great; but today they are only too well avenged, for at present Pierre Dupont is neglected more than is proper.

In 1843, '44, and '45 an immense, endless cloud, which did not come from Egypt, swept down over Paris. This cloud spewed forth the Neo-Classicists who were certainly the equivalent of several legions of locusts. The public was so weary of Victor Hugo, of his indefatigable powers, of his indestructible beauties, so annoyed at always hearing him called *the just*, that it had long since decided in its collective mind to accept as an idol the first blockhead who might appear on the scene. The conspiracy of everything stupid in favor of mediocrity always makes a good story; but actually there are cases when, however veracious one may be, he cannot expect to be believed.

This new infatuation of the French for classical nonsense threatened to last a long time; fortunately, vigorous symptoms of resistance made themselves felt from time to time. Already Théodore de Banville had produced, though fruitlessly, *Les Cariatides*; all the beauties they contained were of a type which the public was momentarily to reject, since they were the melodious echo of the powerful voice that it wished to stifle.

Pierre Dupont then brought his bit of help; and this modest assistance was immensely effective. I appeal to all those friends of ours who were beginning their literary careers at that time and felt distressed by the newly revived heresy; and I think they will admit with me that Pierre Dupont was an excellent distraction. He was a veritable dike which served to avert the flood until it finally spent itself and dried up.

Up to that time our poet had remained undecided, not in his sympathies but in his way of writing. He had published a few poems of a judicious, moderate taste, giving evidence of serious study, but in a mongrel style which did not aim much higher than that of Casimir Delavigne. Suddenly he was inspired; he remembered the emotions of his childhood, the latent poetry of childhood, formerly so often stimulated by what may be called anonymous poetry, the song—not that of the so-called man of letters bent over an official desk and using a bureaucrat's leisure time, but the song of the man in the street, of the laborer, the mason, the wagoner, the sailor. The album of *Les*

Paysans was written in a clear, firm style, fresh, picturesque and unpolished; and the lines, like a rider carried by his horse, were borne by artless melodies, easy to remember and composed by the poet himself. Its success is still remembered. It was very great, it was universal. Men of letters (I am speaking of the real ones) found in it food for the mind. Society was not insensible to that rustic charm. But the great advantage that the Muse drew from it was to bring the public mind back to true poetry, which, it appears, is more troublesome and difficult to like than the routine and the old-fashioned. The bucolic was rediscovered; like the pseudobucolic of Florian, it had its charms, but above all it possessed a penetrating, profound accent drawn from the theme itself and tending to develop rather quickly into melancholy.[151] Its charm was natural and not an artificial veneer like that used by the painters and writers of the eighteenth century. A few coarse expressions even served to make more apparent the refinement of the rough characters whose joys and sorrows were recounted in these poems. A peasant who shamelessly admits that the death of his wife would distress him less than the death of his oxen does not shock me any more than clowns who show more affection and more paternal and kindly interest for their horses than for their children. Beneath the horrible jargon of each profession is found the poetry of the profession; Pierre Dupont has succeeded in discovering it, and he has often expressed it in a brilliant manner.

In 1846 or 1847 (I rather think it was '46) during one of our long, happy strolls (in those days when we were not yet writing with one eye fixed on the clock; do you remember, my dear Pierre, those joys of a prodigal youth?) Pierre Dupont told me about a short poem which he had just composed and about whose value he was very uncertain. He sang to me, with that charming voice which he possessed at that time, the magnificent *Chant des Ouvriers.* He was really quite uncertain, not knowing exactly what to think of his work; he will not be angry with me for publishing this detail, amusing enough in its way. The fact is that it was a new vein for him; I say *for him,* because a mind more practiced than his in following its own evolution could have guessed, after the Album, *Les Paysans*, that he would soon be drawn into singing the sorrows and joys of all the poor.

However much of a rhetorician one must be, however much of a rhetorician I am, and however proud I am to be one, why should I blush to admit that I was deeply moved?

> Mal vêtus, logés dans des trous,
> Sous les combles, dans les décombres,
> Nous vivons avec les hiboux
> Et les larrons amis des ombres.
> Cependant notre sang vermeil
> Coule impétueux dans nos veines;
> Nous nous plairions au grand soleil
> Et sous les rameaux verts des chênes!

I know that the works of Pierre Dupont are not of a consummate and perfect taste; but he has the instinct, if not the reasoned sense, of perfect beauty. Here indeed is an example of it: what is more ordinary, more trite than wealth as seen by poverty? But here, the feeling is complicated by poetic pride, by partly glimpsed pleasures of which one feels oneself worthy; it is a veritable stroke of genius. What a prolonged sigh! What yearning! *We too, we understand the beauty of palaces and parks! We too, we can imagine the art of being happy!*

Was this song one of those volatile atoms floating in the air which, massed together, turn into storms, tempests, grave events? Was it one of those premonitory signs seen at that time in the intellectual atmosphere of France by many perspicacious men? I do not know; but the fact remains that shortly afterwards, very shortly, that resounding hymn was admirably appropriate to a general revolution in politics and to political applications. It became, almost immediately, the rallying cry of the disinherited classes.

Day by day the poet's mind was fired by the movement of

this revolution. All its events are echoed in his verses. But I must point out that if the instrument of Pierre Dupont is of a nobler nature than that of Béranger, it is not, however, one of those warlike trumpets which nations like to hear on the eve of great battles. It does not resemble

> . . . Ces trompes, ces cymbales,
> Qui soûlent de leurs sons le plus morne soldat,
> Et le jettent, joyeux, sous la grêle des balles,
> Lui versant dans le cœur la rage du combat.*

Pierre Dupont is a sensitive soul, given to Utopian ideas and, in that respect, truly bucolic. Everything in him revolves around love; and war, as he conceives it, is only a way of preparing for universal reconciliation:

> Le glaive brisera le glaive,
> Et du combat naîtra l'amour!

Love is stronger than war, he says again in the *Chant des Ouvriers.*

There is in his spirit a certain strength which always implies goodness; and his nature, little disposed to resign itself to the eternal laws of destruction, wishes to accept only those consoling ideas in which it can find analogous elements. Instinct (a very noble instinct his!) dominates his power of reasoning. Dealing with abstractions repels him and he shares with women that unusual privilege whereby all his poetic virtues, like his poetic faults, come to him from sentiment.

It is to that charm, to that feminine sensitivity that Pierre Dupont owes his best songs. By great good fortune, the revolutionary activity which at that time fired almost all hearts, did not turn him completely away from his *natural* bent. No one has expressed in gentler and more penetrating terms the small joys and the great sorrows of the common people. The collection of his songs depicts a whole little world where man utters

* Pétrus Borel. Preface in verse of *Madame Putiphar.*

more sighs than laughter, and where nature, whose immortal freshness is admirably felt by our poet, seems intended to comfort, to appease, and to lull the poor and the forsaken.

Everything belonging to the category of gentle and tender emotions is expressed by him with an accent rejuvenated and renewed by the sincerity of the feeling. But to the feeling of tenderness, of universal love he adds a sort of contemplative spirit which until then had remained foreign to French song. The contemplation of the immortal beauty of things is constantly mingled in his little poems with the sorrow caused by man's stupidity and poverty. He possesses, without being aware of it, a certain turn of pensiveness which makes him resemble the best didactic English poets. Gallantry itself (for there is gallantry, even of a subtle kind, in this bard of rustic life) has a pensive and compassionate character. In many a composition he has shown, by unexpected rather than skillfully modulated accents, how sensitive he is to the eternal charm emanating from a woman's lips and eyes:

> La nature a filé sa grâce
> Du plus beau fil de ses fuseaux!

And elsewhere, forgetting revolutions and social wars, the poet sings with a delicate and voluptuous accent:

> Avant que tes beaux yeux soient clos
> Par le sommeil jaloux, ma belle,
> Descendons jusqu'au bord des flots,
> Et détachons notre nacelle.
>
> L'air tiède, la molle clarté
> De ces étoiles qui se baignent,
> Le bruit des rames qui se plaignent,
> Tout respire la volupté.
> O mon amante!
> O mon désir!
> Sachons cueillir
> L'heure charmante!

De parfums comme de lueurs
La nacelle amoureuse est pleine;
On dirait un bouquet de fleurs
Qui s'effeuille dans ton haleine;
Tes yeux, par la lune pâlis,
Semblent emplis de violettes;
Tes lèvres sont des cassolettes!
Ton corps embaume comme un lis!

Vois-tu l'axe de l'univers,
L'étoile polaire immuable?
Autour, les astres dans les airs
Tourbillonnent comme du sable.
Quel calme! que les cieux sont grands,
Et quel harmonieux murmure!
Ma main dedans ta chevelure
A senti des frissons errants!

Lettres plus nombreuses encor
Que tout l'alphabet de la Chine,
O grands hiéroglyphes d'or,
Je vous déchiffre et vous devine!
La nuit, plus belle que le jour,
Ecrit dans sa langue immortelle
Le mot que notre bouche épèle,
Le nom infini de l'Amour!
    O mon amante!
    O mon désir!
    Sachons cueillir
    L'heure charmante!

Thanks to a mental process peculiar to lovers when they are poets, or to poets when they are lovers, woman is embellished with all the charms of the landscape, and the landscape occasionally profits from the charms which the beloved unsuspectingly imparts to the sky, the earth, and the sea.[152] It is another of those frequent touches which characterize the manner of Pierre Dupont when he plunges confidently into surroundings which are favorable to him and when he yields to the free development of his nature without concern for the things which he cannot really call *his*.

I should have liked to dwell at greater length on the virtues of Pierre Dupont who is and always will remain one of our most valued poets, in spite of a too obvious tendency toward didactic categories and divisions—in poetry often a sign of indolence, since the natural lyric development should contain all the necessary didactic and descriptive elements—in spite of much carelessness of language and really inconceivable *slovenliness* of form. I have heard it said by many very competent people that finish, richness, in short perfection, repelled them and prevented them from having *confidence*, so to speak, in the poet. This strange opinion (strange to me) is very apt to make us resigned to corresponding incompatibilities in the poet's mind and in the reader's temperament. So let us enjoy our poets on the condition, however, that they possess the most noble, the most indispensable qualities, and let us take them as God has made them and given them to us, since we are assured that one quality is increased only by the more or less complete sacrifice of another.

I am obliged to be brief. To conclude in a few words, Pierre Dupont belongs to that natural aristocracy of minds who owe infinitely more to nature than to art and who, like two other great poets, Auguste Barbier and Madame Desbordes-Valmore find, only in the spontaneity of their heart the expression, the song, the cry destined to be eternally impressed in the memory of all.

❧ LECONTE DE LISLE

PREFACE

Baudelaire's essay on Leconte de Lisle, unfortunately rather short, is not only one of his best critical essays but also one of the best analyses ever made of the verse of the Parnassian poet. His description of Leconte de Lisle conforms in many ways to his ideal of dandyism, just as that of Moreau had contradicted it. He deeply admires the highly disciplined art of the Creole poet, his avoidance of Romantic effusion and sentimentality, his intellectual aristocracy and scorn for all that was not superior.

But though Baudelaire makes no mention of dandyism in connection with Leconte de Lisle, he does point out the similarities of his style and thought to those of Gautier and Renan in a brilliant comparison that reveals his critical penetration. At the same time he notes that the poet's interest in the pagan past was a means of escape, a means of fleeing the transitory values of an age that he hated and of evoking the immutable aspects of eternal nature.

Where Baudelaire shows himself most astute, however, is in recognizing that Leconte de Lisle's real originality lay in his portrayal of the "powerful, crushing forces of nature" and in the evocation of the primitive grandeur and the "majesty of animals in movement and in repose." Baudelaire's judgment has been confirmed by posterity, and later critics have agreed that "Here, Leconte de Lisle is a master and a great master."

On his side, Leconte de Lisle had certain reservations about the author of *Les Fleurs du Mal*, as is plainly indicated by his notations: "Very intelligent and orginal but limited in imagination, lacking inspiration. An art that is too often clumsy." [153]

※≪※≪※≪

I have often wondered, without ever being able to find an answer, why Creoles, generally speaking, have not introduced any originality, any power of conception or of expression into their literary productions. They might be considered feminine souls, made solely to contemplate and to enjoy. The very fragility, the slenderness of their bodies, their velvety eyes which look without seeing, the strange narrowness of their brows, strikingly high, everything that is so often charming about them, suggest that they are enemies of work and of thought. Languor, graciousness, a natural ability to imitate, which, by the way, they share with Negroes, and which almost always gives a certain provincial air to a Creole poet, however distinguished he may be, these are the things we have generally observed in the best of them.

M. Leconte de Lisle is the first and only exception I have encountered. Even if we assume that there are others, he will unquestionably remain the most astonishing and the most vigorous. If descriptions, too well done, too intoxicating not to have been moulded on childhood memories, did not occasionally reveal to the critic's eye the origin of the poet, it would be impossible to discover that he was born on one of those volcanic and perfumed islands where the human soul, gently lulled by all the pleasurable sensations of the atmosphere, gradually loses the power of thought. Even his physical appearance belies the customary idea of the Creole that we have formed. A heavy brow, a broad and massive head, clear and cold eyes at once give the impression of strength. Beneath these dominant features, the first to attract our attention, play smiling lips animated by incessant irony. Finally, to complete the contradiction in the spiritual as well as in the physical realm, his conversation, substantial and serious, is constantly seasoned by that raillery which is a confirmation of strength. Thus, not only is he erudite, not only has he given much time to meditation, not only has he that poetic eye which can extract the poetic character from everything, but also he has wit, a rare quality in poets—wit in the popular sense and in the highest sense of the word. If this power of raillery and of buffoonery does not appear (distinctly, I mean) in his poetic works, it is because it wishes to be hidden, because it has understood that it was its duty to hide. Since he is a real poet, serious and thoughtful, Leconte de Lisle abhors the confusion of genres, and he knows that art obtains its most powerful effects only through sacrifices adapted to the rarity of its goal.

I shall try to define the place held in our century by this serene and powerful poet, one of our dearest and most prized. The distinctive character of his poetry is a feeling of intellectual aristocracy, which would be sufficient in itself to explain the unpopularity of the author, if, on the other hand, we didn't know that in France unpopularity attends everything that approaches any kind of perfection. Through his innate taste for philosophy and through his power of picturesque description he rises far above those melancholy drawing-room poets, those makers of albums and keepsakes where everything, philosophy and poetry, is adapted to the emotions of young girls. We might just as well compare the vapidity of Ary Scheffer or the commonplace pictures in our missals with the strong figures of Cornelius.[154] The only poet to whom Leconte de Lisle could be compared, without absurdity, is Théophile Gautier. These two minds take equal delight in travel; these two imaginations are naturally cosmopolitan. Both like a change of scene and both like to dress their thought in the variable fashions that time scatters through eternity. But Théophile Gautier gives detail sharper relief and heightened color, while Leconte de Lisle is more concerned with the philosophic armature. Both love the Orient and the desert; both admire repose as a principle of beauty. Both flood their poetry with a warm light, more sparkling in Théophile Gautier, more restful in Leconte de Lisle. Both are equally indifferent to all human deceits and succeed, without effort, in never being dupes. There is still another man, though in a different category, with whom Leconte de Lisle may be compared, and that is Ernest Renan. In spite of the differences separating the two, all discerning minds will detect a similarity. In the poet, as in the philosopher, I find that lively yet objective interest in religions and that same spirit of universal love, not for humanity taken in itself but for the various forms, depending on the era and the climate, with which man has clothed beauty and truth. In neither one is there ever any absurd impiety. To paint in beautiful verse, luminous and serene in nature, the various ways in which man, until now, has worshipped God and sought the beautiful, such has been, as far as one can judge from his most complete collection, the goal which Leconte de Lisle has assigned to his poetry.

His first pilgrimage was to Greece; and from the very first his poems, with their echo of classic beauty, were singled out by connoisseurs. Later, he did a series of imitations of Latin poems, which I for my part value infinitely more. But to be entirely fair, I must confess that my liking for the subject may well influence my judgment in this case, and that my natural predilection for Rome prevents me from feeling all the enjoyment that I should in the reading of his Greek poems.

Little by little his taste for travel drew him towards worlds of more mysterious beauty. The role that he has given to Asiatic religions is enormous, and it is there that he has poured out in majestic torrents his natural dislike for transitory things, for the frivolous things of life, and his infinite love for the immutable, for the eternal, for *divine nothingness*. At other times, with what seems capricious suddenness, he turned to the snows of Scandinavia and told us of the Northern gods, overthrown and dispelled, like the mist, by the radiant child of Judea. But whatever the majesty of manner and the soundness of reason displayed by Leconte de Lisle in these varied subjects, what I prefer in his works is a certain vein that is completely new, which belongs to him and to him alone. The poems of this type are few, and it may be that he neglected this genre the most, because it was the most natural to him. I am referring to the poems where, without preoccupation with religion and the successive forms of human thought, the poet described beauty as it appeared to his original and individual eye—the powerful, crushing forces of nature, the majesty of animals in movement or in repose, the charm of woman in sunny regions, and lastly the sublime calm of the desert or the fearful magnificence of the ocean. Here, Leconte de Lisle is a master and a great master. Here, triumphant poetry has no goal other than itself. True lovers of poetry know that I am referring to such poems as "Les Hurleurs," "Les Eléphants," "Le Sommeil du Condor," etc., and above all to "Le Manchy" which is an incomparable masterpiece, a true evocation, where glisten with all their mysterious charm the beauty and magic of the tropics, which no beauty, Southern, Greek, Italian, or Spanish can equal.

I have little to add. Leconte de Lisle has the ability to control his ideas; but that would mean almost nothing if he didn't also have the ability to handle his tools. His language is always noble, firm, strong, without shrill notes, without false modesty; his vocabulary vast; his linking of words is always distinguished and conforms perfectly with the nature of his mind. He employs rhythm with breadth and sureness, and his instrument has the mellow but full and deep tone of the viola. His rhymes, always exact without being too finical, fulfill the conditions that beauty requires and always comply with that contradictory and mysterious love of the human mind for surprise and symmetry.

As for that unpopularity which I mentioned at the beginning, I think I am echoing the poet's own thought when I say that it causes him no sadness and that the contrary would add nothing to his satisfaction. It is enough for him to be popular among those who are themselves worthy of pleasing him. Furthermore, he belongs to that family of minds which has for all that which is not superior a scorn so quiet that it doesn't even deign to express itself.

❧ LES MISÉRABLES
BY VICTOR HUGO

PREFACE

Victor Hugo believed *Les Misérables* to be one of his greatest achievements, possibly the very greatest. Although critical opinion, both French and Anglo-Saxon, has generally been in sharp disagreement, the recent centennial colloquium (December, 1961), convened at the University of Strasbourg to revaluate the novel, has taken a much more favorable view.

An enormously long novel divided into five parts and forty-eight books, *Les Misérables* was composed over a period of thirty years. Despite many deeply moving incidents and scenes of truly epic grandeur, it is often nothing more than a vehicle for the social views of its author, touching as it does on almost every imaginable subject from the battle of Waterloo to the sewers of Paris.

Baudelaire's review of *Les Misérables*, published in *Le Boulevard*, April, 1862, has been accused of being insincere and hypocritical. It is true that he heartily disliked the novel, as Asselineau has testified, and that he wrote to his mother: "The book is disgusting and idiotic. I have shown in this connection that I can be a skillful liar. He [Hugo] wrote an absolutely ridiculous letter to thank me. This proves that a great man can be a fool." [155]

On close examination, however, the review is less hypocritical than it first appears. Baudelaire begins his article with a long quotation from his previous essay on Hugo in which he had praised the poet for not making morality—"a sermonizing morality"—"the avowed purpose" of *Les Contemplations* and *La Légende des Siècles*. Without further comment he adds that morality is indeed "the avowed purpose" of *Les Misérables* and he cites as proof Hugo's own defense: "so long as ignorance and poverty exist on earth, books such as this cannot be useless."

With only the briefest hint of disbelief in Hugo's optimism, Baudelaire goes on to acclaim "the marvelous talent" with which the novelist had attracted public attention to "the bottomless chasms of social misery." The informed reader, aware of Baudelaire's contempt for utilitarian literature, cannot fail to notice that the critic's praise is directed not at the literary value of the novel but rather at its power as a purely social document. Baudelaire goes on to admit that a mature writer who remained unmoved by poverty would be "completely monstrous." Such a writer does not exist, he affirms; and the reader is at once mindful of the critic's own preoccupation with poverty and suffering. What is important, he concludes, is "to know if a work of art should have a goal other than *art*, if art should express devotion only to *itself*, or if a goal, more noble or less noble, inferior or superior, can be imposed on it." Had he answered his own question, Baudelaire would have only antagonized Hugo and his many admirers. Moreover, he had already stated his position fully and clearly in several previous essays.

Turning to the "literary form" of Les Misérables, Baudelaire points out that the characters are powerful and living abstractions, ideal figures representing ideas necessary to his thesis. At the same time by singling out the chapter "Tempête sous un Crâne," he shows his preference for the moral struggle which inevitably makes the character in question more than a mere abstraction.

In the last section of his review Baudelaire resorts to clever innuendo in order to say what he might otherwise have left unsaid. Les Misérables, he maintains, is "a book of charity, a call to order." But even while agreeing with Hugo that "books such as this are never useless" he discredits the validity of the novel even as a social document by a passing reference to the "intentional deception or unconscious bias" of the author in stating the terms of the problem. The reader is left with the impression that Hugo may have succeeded in proving his thesis only by building a case to fit.

And finally Baudelaire cannot resist ending the article with an affirmation of his own belief in original sin. Not, however, before he subtly shows Hugo's inconsistency in accepting a philosophy that maintains the goodness of Man, yet fails to accuse God of cruelty and malice in allowing the innocent to suffer.

✄✄✄✄

I

A few months ago, in connection with the great poet, the most vigorous and most popular in France, I wrote the following lines which in a very short period of time were to find an application even more obvious than *Les Contemplations* and *La Légende des Siècles*.

If space allowed, this would doubtless be the occasion to analyze the moral atmosphere which hovers and moves through his poems and which derives very obviously from the author's temperament. It seems to me that it is unmistakably characterized by a love which makes no distinction between what is very strong and what is very weak, and that the attraction exercised over the poet by these two extremes stems from a single source, which is the very strength, the primordial vigor with which he is endowed. Strength delights and intoxicates him; he approaches it as if it were a brother: fraternal affection. Thus he is irresistibly attracted to every symbol of the infinite, the sea, the sky; to all the ancient representatives of strength, Homeric or Biblical giants, paladins, knights; to enormous and fearful beasts. He makes child's play of fondling what would frighten weaker hands; he moves about in immensity without vertigo. On the other hand, but through a different tendency, whose source is, however, the same, the poet always shows warm compassion for all that is weak, lonely, sorrowful, for all that is fatherless: a paternal attraction. The man of strength, who senses a brother in all that is strong, sees his children in all that has need of protection or consolation. It is from strength itself and from the certainty that it gives to one who possesses it that the spirit of justice and of charity is derived. Thus in the poems of Victor Hugo there constantly occur those notes of love for fallen women, for the poor who are crushed in the cogwheels of society, for the animals that are martyrs of our gluttony and despotism. Few people have noticed the magic charm which kindness adds to strength and which is so frequently seen in the works of our poet. A smile and a tear on the face of a colossus is an almost divine form of originality. Even in his short poems devoted to sensual love, in those verses so voluptuous and so melodious in their melancholy, may be heard, like the continuous accompaniment of an orchestra, the deep voice of charity. Beneath the lover one senses a father and a protector. It is not a matter here of that sermonizing morality which, with its pedantic air and its didactic tone, can spoil the most beautiful piece of poetry but of an implicit morality which slips unnoticed into poetic matter like imponderable fluids into the machinery of the world. Morality does not enter into this art as its avowed purpose; it is intermingled with it and lost sight of, as in life itself. The poet is unintentionally a moralist through the abundance and plenitude of nature.

There is only a single line here that must be changed; for morality does enter directly into *Les Misérables* as its *avowed purpose,* as is evident, moreover, from the poet's own admission, printed as a preface at the beginning of the book:

So long as there exists, as a result of laws and customs, a social damnation artificially creating hells, in the very midst of civilization, and complicating divine destiny with human fate . . . so long as ignorance and poverty exist on earth, books such as this cannot be useless.

"So long as . . . !"Alas, you might as well say *ALWAYS!* But this is not the place to analyze such questions. We merely wish to do justice to the marvelous talent with which the poet has seized public attention and bent it, like the recalcitrant head of a lazy schoolboy, toward the bottomless chasms of social misery.

II

In the exuberance of his youth the poet can take special pleasure in singing the pomp and glory of life; for the eye of youth is especially attracted by all the splendor and riches of life. Maturity, on the other hand, turns curiously and anxiously toward problems and mysteries. There is something so utterly strange in that black spot made by poverty on the sun of riches or, if you prefer, in that bright spot made by wealth on the vast darkness of poverty, that a poet, a philosopher, a writer would have to be completely monstrous not to be moved and mystified at times to the point of anguish. Certainly such a writer does not exist; he cannot exist. Hence all that distinguishes one from another, the sole difference, is to know if a work of art should have a goal other than *art*, if art should express devotion only to *itself*, or if a goal, more noble or less noble, inferior or superior, can be imposed on it.

It is especially, I say, in their full maturity that poets become fascinated by certain problems, sinister and obscure in character, which attract them like a strange abyss. Yet one would be very much mistaken to include Victor Hugo in the category of creators who waited a long time before plunging into those questions that concern universal conscience in the highest degree. From the beginning, we may say, at the very outset of his brilliant career, we find in him that preoccupation with the weak, the outcast, and the damned. The idea of justice is revealed quite early in his works by a taste for rehabilitation. "Oh! n'Insultez jamais une Femme qui Tombe!," "Un Bal à L'Hôtel de Ville," *Marion de Lorme, Ruy-Blas, Le Roi s'Amuse,* are poems which offer sufficient proof of this already well established tendency, we might almost say this obsession.

III

Is it really necessary to analyze *Les Misérables* in detail, or rather the first part of *Les Misérables*? The work is now in everyone's hands, and everyone knows its plot and structure. To me it seems more important to note the method used by the author in bringing to light the truths of which he has made himself the servant.

This book is a book of charity, that is to say a book intended to excite, to stimulate a charitable spirit; it is a book that raises questions, that poses complex social problems, agonizing and terrible in nature, that says to the reader's conscience: "Well, what do you think about this? What is your conclusion?"

As for the literary form of the book, a poem, it should be added, rather than a novel, we find a premonitory indication in the preface to *Marie Tudor*, which furnishes new proof of the unchanging character of the moral and literary ideas held by the illustrious author:

. . . . The danger of the true is the petty; the danger of the great is the false. . . . Wonderful omnipotence of the poet! He makes things loftier than we are, which live as we do. Hamlet, for example, is as real as any of us, and greater. Hamlet is colossal and yet real. The fact is that Hamlet is not you, he is not I, he is all of us. Hamlet is not a man, he is Man.

To constantly extract the great from the true, the true from the great, is, in the eyes of the author of this drama, the purpose of the poet in the theater. And these two words, *great* and *true*, include everything. Truth contains morality, the great contains the beautiful.

It is quite evident that in *Les Misérables* the author wanted to create living abstractions, ideal figures, each of which, representing one of the principal types necessary to the development of his thesis, was raised to epic heights. It is a novel constructed in the manner of a poem in which each character is an exception only through the exaggerated manner in which he represents a *generality*. The way in which Victor Hugo has conceived and constructed this novel and the way in which he has cast the rich elements usually employed in special works (the lyric sense, the epic sense, and the philosophical sense) into an indefinable amalgam in order to make a new Corinthian metal, confirms once again the fatality which led him as a young man to partially transform the ancient ode and ancient tragedy into the poems and dramas that we know.

Thus Monseigneur Bienvenu represents hyperbolic charity, endless faith in self-sacrifice, absolute confidence in Charity considered as the most perfect means of moral instruction. In the painting of this type there are observations and touches of wonderful delicacy. It is apparent that the author took delight in perfecting this angelic model. Monseigneur Bienvenu gives away everything that he has and knows no other pleasure than that of sacrificing himself endlessly, without respite, without regret, to the poor, the weak, and even the guilty. Bowing humbly before dogma, but not attempting to fathom it, he has dedicated himself to the practice of the Gospel. "Gallican rather than ultramontanist," as well as a man of fashionable society, and endowed, like Socrates, with the power of irony and wit. I have been told that in an earlier period a certain priest of Saint Roch, who was prodigal in sharing his goods with the poor and who was taken unawares one morning by further demands, suddenly sent all his furniture, his pictures, and his silver to be sold at auction.[156] In character Monseigneur Bienvenu is exactly like that. But I am also told—to continue the story of the priest of Saint Roch—that the talk about this action, very simple in the eyes of the man of God, but too beautiful in terms of worldly morality, soon spread and reached the ears of the king, and that finally this dangerous priest was sent to the archbishop to be gently scolded. For this type of heroism could be considered an indirect criticism, as it were, of all priests too weak to raise themselves to that height.

Valjean is the naïve, innocent brute; he is the ignorant proletarian, guilty of an offense we would all doubtless excuse (the theft of a loaf of bread), but which, legally punished, casts him into the school of Evil, that is to say into Prison. There, his intelligence is developed and sharpened in the oppressive thoughts of imprisonment. At length he leaves, cunning, formidable, dangerous. He has repaid the Bishop's hospitality with a second theft, but the latter saves him by a white lie, convinced that Pardon and Charity are the only lights that can dissipate all the darkness. The awakening of that conscience does indeed take place, but not quickly enough to prevent animal habit, which is still present in the man, from dragging him into a new lapse. Valjean (now M. Madeleine) has become honest, rich, and powerful. He has enriched, almost civilized, a once poor community of which he is mayor. He has made for himself a wonderful cloak of respectability; he is protected and armored by good works. But a fatal day arrives when he learns that a false Valjean, closely resembling him, stupid and despicable, is going to be condemned in his place. What is to be done? Is it really true that the inner law, Conscience, orders him to demolish all that hard won and glorious structure of his new life, by revealing his own identity? Is "the light that every man brings into this world at birth" sufficient to illumine these complex and dark mysteries? M. Madeleine emerges victorious—but after what fearful struggles!—from this sea of anguish and through his love of Truth and Justice becomes Valjean once again. The chapter which recounts minutely, slowly, analytically this struggle of the man with himself ("Tempête sous un Crâne"), with its hesitations, its mental qualifications, its paradoxes, its false consolations, its desperate attempts to cheat, contains pages in which not only French literature but even the literature of thinking Humanity may forever take pride. It is glorious for Rational Man that these pages should have been written! One would have to look a great deal and a long time, a very long time, to find elsewhere pages equal to those which expose in so tragic a manner all the appalling Casuistry inscribed from the Beginning in the heart of Universal Man.

In this gallery of suffering and catastrophic events there is a horrible, repugnant figure—the gendarme, the police sergeant, strict, inexorable justice, uncritical justice, the law that is not interpreted, savage intelligence (can it be called intelligence?) that has never understood attenuating circumstances, in a word the Letter without the Spirit, the abominable Javert. I have heard some fairly sensible people say of Javert: "After all, he is a decent fellow; and he has his own greatness." This is certainly the time to say with de Maistre: "I don't know what an honest man is." [157] At the risk of being considered guilty ("those who tremble feel themselves guilty," said that madman Robespierre), I confess that for me Javert seems an incorrigible monster, as starved for justice as a wild animal for raw flesh, the absolute Enemy in a word.

And then in this connection I should like to make a small criticism. However enormous, however emphatic in outline and movement the ideal figures of a story may be, we must suppose that they had a beginning, like people in real life. I know that man may be more than zealous in every profession. He becomes a hunting dog, a fighting dog in everything that he does. That is certainly a form of beauty that has its origin in the passions. Thus one can be a policeman *with enthusiasm*; but does one join the police as *a result of enthusiasm*, and is it not, on the contrary, one of those professions which one may enter only under the pressure of certain circumstances and for reasons that have nothing to do with fanaticism?

I assume that it is not necessary to recount and explain all the tender, heartbreaking beauty which Victor Hugo has lavished on the character of Fantine, the fallen shopgirl, the modern woman, caught between the fatality of poorly paid work and the fatality of legal prostitution. We have long known how skillful he is in expressing the cry of passion in the abyss, the groans and furious tears of the lioness deprived of her young! Here, by a very natural liaison, we are led to recognize once again the sureness and lightness of touch with which this vigorous painter, this creator of colossi, colors the cheeks of childhood, enlivens their eyes, and describes their lively and ingenuous movements. You might say Michelangelo taking delight in vying with Lawrence or Velásquez.

IV

Les Misérables is then a book of charity, an astounding call to order of a society too enamored of itself and too little concerned with the immortal law of brotherhood; a plea for the wretched (those who suffer from poverty and are degraded by it), uttered by the most eloquent lips of our day. In spite of any possible intentional deception or any unconscious bias in the manner—in the eyes of strict philosophy—in which the terms of the problem are stated, we believe, just as does the author, that books such as this are never useless.

Victor Hugo is for Man, and yet he is not against God. He trusts in God, and yet he is not against Man.

He spurns the frenzy of rebellious Atheism, and yet he does not approve the bloodthirsty gluttony of the Molochs and the Teutatès.

He believes that Man is born good, and yet even in the face of the constant disasters that befall him he does not accuse God of cruelty and malice.

I believe that even for those who find in orthodox doctrine, in pure Catholic theory, an explanation, if not complete, at least more comprehensive, of all the disturbing mysteries of life, Victor Hugo's new book should be Bienvenu [welcome] (in keeping with the name of the bishop whose triumphant charity it relates); it is a book to be applauded and to be appreciated. Is it not useful for the poet, the philosopher, to take egoistic Happiness by the hair from time to time and say to it while rubbing its nose in blood and dung: "See your handiwork and swallow it"?

Alas, even after all the progress that we have been promised for so long, there will always remain enough traces of Original Sin to establish its everlasting reality!

℀ THE PAINTER OF MODERN LIFE

PREFACE

"The Painter of Modern Life," written in 1859–1860 and published in *Le Figaro* late in 1863, was Baudelaire's last important critical work. Stimulated by the drawings of Constantin Guys whose sense of modernity was in certain respects analogous to his own, he composed a series of reflections on nature, fashion, art, dandyism, cosmetics, military life, and other themes that had obsessed him for many years. Several chapters are felicitous descriptions of groups of drawings done by Guys; others set forth some of the critic's maturely considered aesthetic ideas relating to modernity, artifice, and genius.

In his last essay, as in his earliest *Salons*, he insists on the artistic possibilities of contemporary life and on the dual character of beauty with its inextricable mingling of "the transitory" and "the eternal." It has sometimes been argued that in choosing Guys as the subject of so long an essay (sixty-one pages), Baudelaire was guilty of a mistake in critical judgment and was exaggerating the importance and the merit of the artist. It is perfectly clear from the very first paragraphs that, on the contrary, he recognized Guys as one of the *poetae minores* whose works revealed a "circumstantial beauty" that he found "good, sound and delightful." [158] It was because Guys exemplified so well his idea of transitory beauty that Baudelaire chose him as the subject of his essay. Although he sincerely admired his modernity, his elegance, his lightness of touch, he obviously does not rank him with men of genius such as Delacroix, Poe, and Wagner.

The essay on Guys echoes the early *Salons* not only in its discussion of modernity but also in its development of other questions that had been more or less briefly touched upon. In his early critical writing Baudelaire had viewed naïveté as one of the prime requisites of the creative artist; in "The Painter of Modern Life" he goes a step further and equates genius with the fresh impressions of youth which the mature and thoughtful artist can transform into art with the aid of imagination and memory. Genius thus becomes childhood recovered through an act of will—a fusion of imagination and analytical intelligence.

In contrast to the more conventional view of nature with which he had begun in the 1840's, Baudelaire now asks (1863), "Who would dare to assign to art the sterile function of imitating nature?" The discussion of nature leads him far afield and into the area of moral philosophy. Apparently guided by Joseph de Maistre and the Marquis de Sade (as well as by his own temperament), the critic makes a vigorous attack on the whole eighteenth-century conception of the goodness of nature and of man.[159] Nature is fundamentally evil, he says, but it may be redeemed by art.

Constantin Guys (1805–1892), a modest artist who refused to allow Baudelaire to use his full name, did drawings of fashionable life, genre pictures and records of the events of his day. During the Crimean War he was employed by the *Illustrated London News* as a pictorial reporter. His cosmopolitanism and varied interests appealed to Baudelaire, who had an important share in creating the vogue for Guys that still continues.

⚔⚔⚔

[EXCERPTS]

BEAUTY, FASHION AND HAPPINESS

There are people in the world, and even in the world of artists, who go to the Louvre, walk quickly past many interesting, though *second-rate* pictures, without giving them as much as a glance, and then stand musing before a Titian or a Raphael, one of those most popularized by engravings; afterwards they leave quite satisfied, with more than one saying to himself: "I know my museum." There are also people who, having once read Bossuet and Racine, think they have a thorough knowledge of the history of literature.

Fortunately there appear on the scene from time to time redressers of wrongs, critics, art lovers, inquisitive minds who maintain that everything is not to be found in Raphael or in Racine, that there is much that is good, sound and delightful in the *poetae minores*; and that, finally, having so much love for general beauty, which is expressed by the classic poets and artists, is no excuse for neglecting particular beauty, circumstantial beauty, and pictures of manners.

I should add that in recent years people have improved somewhat in this respect. Today the value attached by art lovers to the charming colored engravings of the last century proves that there has been a needed reaction among the public. Debucourt, the Saint-Aubins, and many others have entered the dictionary of artists worthy of being studied. But these artists portray the past; now it is to the painting of contemporary manners that I wish to pay particular attention today. The past is interesting not only for the beauty distilled from it by the artists for whom it was the present, but also because it is the past, because of its historical value. The same thing is true of the present. The pleasure we derive from the portrayal of the present comes not only from the beauty with which it may be clothed but also from its essential quality of being the present. . . .

This is indeed a good opportunity to establish a rational and historical theory of beauty in opposition to the theory of an absolute and unique beauty, to show that beauty, although it produces a single impression, always and inevitably contains two elements; for the difficulty of discerning the variable elements of beauty within this unity of impression in no way invalidates the necessity of variety in its composition. Beauty is composed of an element that is eternal, invariable, and exceedingly difficult to measure, and of another element that is relative and circumstantial, such as period, fashion, morality, emotion, taken either one by one or all together. Without this second element which is, so to speak, the amusing, titillating, appetizing icing on the divine cake, the first element would be indigestible, inappreciable, unadapted and unsuited to human nature. I defy anyone to discover any example whatsoever of beauty that does not contain these two elements.

I will choose, if I may, from the two extreme limits of history. In hieratic art, the duality is immediately obvious; the element of eternal beauty becomes manifest only with the consent and under the control of the religion to which the artist adheres. In the most frivolous work of a sophisticated artist belonging to one of the periods that we are vain enough to call civilized, the duality is equally clear; the eternal portion of beauty will be both veiled and expressed, if not as a result of fashion, at least through the particular temperament of the author.

The duality of art is the inevitable result of the duality of man. The eternal element may be considered the soul of art, if you wish, and the variable element its body. That is why Stendhal—an impertinent, teasing, and even repellent intellect, whose impertinences, nevertheless, are useful in provoking thought—came closer to the truth than many others when he said that *Beauty is only the promise of happiness*.[160] To be sure, this definition goes too far; it subjects beauty far more than it should to the infinitely variable ideal of happiness; it is too ready to divest beauty of its aristocratic character. But it has the great merit of firmly avoiding the mistake of the academicians.

I have explained these things on more than one occcasion; these lines will suffice for those who are fond of these games of abstract thought; but I know that, in general, French readers do not especially enjoy them, and I am anxious to begin a discussion of the concrete and specific part of my subject.

THE ARTIST

MAN OF THE WORLD, MAN OF THE CROWD AND CHILD

Thus, in order to understand Mr. G., you should remember from the outset that *curiosity* may be considered as the starting-point of his genius.

Do you recall a picture (it is indeed a picture!), created by the most powerful pen of our day [Poe], which is entitled "The Man of the Crowd"? From behind the window of a café, a convalescent, contemplating the crowd with delight, mingles in thought with all the thoughts pulsating around him. Having just escaped from the shadows of death, he joyfully breathes in all the germs and emanations of life; having been on the point of forgetting everything, he now remembers and ardently wishes to remember everything. Finally, he rushes into the crowd in search of an unknown person whose face, glimpsed momentarily, had fascinated him. Curiosity has become a fatal, irresistible passion.

Imagine an artist whose state of mind would always be like that of the convalescent, and you will have the key to the character of Mr. G.

Now, convalescence is like a return to childhood. Like the child, the convalescent enjoys to the utmost the faculty of taking a lively interest in things, even those that seem the most commonplace. Let us return, if possible, by a retrospective effort of the imagination toward our earliest, our most youthful impressions, and we shall recognize that they are strangely related to the intensely colored impressions that we felt on recovering from a physical illness, provided that the illness had left our spiritual faculties pure and untouched.

Everything the child sees is *new*; he is in a constant *state of rapture*. Nothing more closely resembles what is called inspiration than the joy with which a child absorbs form and color. I shall venture even further and maintain that inspiration is related to *cerebral congestion* and that every sublime thought is accompanied by a more or less violent shock that is felt even in the brain. The nerves of a man of genius are strong; those of a child are weak. In the one, reason plays a considerable role; in the other, sensibility dominates almost the whole being. But genius is simply *childhood recovered* at will, childhood now endowed, in order to express itself, with virile organs and with an analytical mind that enables it to order and arrange all the materials accumulated involuntarily.

It is this profound and joyful curiosity that explains the fixed and animal-like ecstasy of children's faces in the presence of something *new*, whether it be a face or a landscape, light, gilding, colors, shimmering materials, or the magic of a woman's beauty enhanced by her dress. A friend of mine once told me that, as a small child, he watched his father getting dressed, and that he noticed with delight and surprise the muscles of his arms, the gradations of his skin coloring tinged with pink and yellow, and the bluish network of veins. The spectacle of external life was already filling him with awe and making a deep impression on his mind. Already he was becoming obsessed and dominated by form. Predestination was precociously showing its face. His *doom* was sealed. Need I tell you that this child is today a famous painter?

A moment ago I asked you to think of Mr. G. as an eternal convalescent; to complete your conception, consider him also as a child-man, as a man in constant possession of the genius of childhood, that is as a genius for whom no aspect of life has been *dulled*.

I said that I was reluctant to call him a pure artist and that he himself disclaims the title with a humility that is tinged with an aristocratic modesty. I would gladly call him a *dandy*, and I should have some good reasons for doing so, for the word *dandy* implies a perfect character and a subtle understanding of the whole moral mechanism of this world. But on the other hand, the dandy aspires to insensibility, and in that respect Mr. G., who is dominated by an insatiable passion to see and to feel, definitely cuts himself off from dandyism. *Amabam amare*, said Saint Augustine. "I am passionately in love with passion," Mr. G. might well say. The dandy is blasé, or he pretends to be, as a matter of policy and for reasons of caste. Mr. G. has a horror of people who are blasé. He is a master of the difficult art (discerning minds will understand me) of being *sincere without being ridiculous*. I might well bestow on him the title of philosopher, a name that he would merit in more than one respect, if his excessive love of things that are visible, tangible, concentrated in plastic form, did not inspire in him a certain aversion for those things that form the impalpable realm of the metaphysician. Let us relegate him then to the rank of a pure pictorial moralist, like La Bruyère.

MODERNITY

Modernity is the transitory, the fugitive, the contingent, the half of art, of which the other half is the eternal and the immutable. Every painter of the past had his own modernity; most of the beautiful portraits that remain to us from bygone days depict the costumes of their period. They are perfectly harmonious because the costume, the coiffure, and even the gesture, the glance and the smile (every period has its own mien, its own glance, its own smile) form a whole that is completely alive. As for this transitory, fleeting element whose metamorphoses are so frequent, you have no right either to scorn it or to ignore it. By suppressing it, you are bound to fall into the emptiness of an abstract and indefinable beauty, like that of the one woman before the first sin. . . . In a word, if any particular modernity is to be worthy of becoming antiquity, it is necessary to extract from it the mysterious beauty that human life involuntarily gives it. . . .

Woe unto him who seeks in antiquity anything other than pure art, logic, and general method! By plunging too deeply into the past, he loses sight of the present; he renounces the values and privileges provided by circumstances; for almost all our originality comes from the stamp that *time* imprints upon our feelings.

IN PRAISE OF MAKE-UP

There is a song so trite and absurd that it can scarcely be quoted in a work that claims to be serious, but which clearly reveals in comic style the aesthetic views of people who fail to think. *Nature enhances beauty!* Had he been able to speak French, it may be supposed that the "poet" would have said: *simplicity enhances beauty!* which is equivalent to a truth of an altogether unexpected kind: that which does *not exist* enhances that which exists.

Most of the errors about beauty spring from the eighteenth century's false conception of morality. At that time nature was considered as the basis, source, and type of every possible form of the good and the beautiful. The denial of original sin had not a little to do with the general blindness of that period.[161] If, however, we are willing to leave the matter simply to the obvious facts, to the experience of all ages and to the *Gazette des Tribunaux* [police reports], we shall see that nature teaches nothing, or almost nothing; that, in other words, it *compels* man to sleep, to drink, to eat, and to protect himself as best he can against the hostile elements. It is nature also that drives him to kill his neighbor, to eat him, to imprison him, to torture him; for, as soon as we turn from the category of needs and necessities to that of luxuries and pleasures, we see that nature can counsel only crime. It is this same infallible nature that has created parricide and cannibalism, and a thousand other abominations which modesty and good taste prevent us from mentioning. It is philosophy (I mean good philosophy) and religion that bid us care for our poor and sick kinsmen. Nature (which is nothing more than the voice of our self-interest) orders us to beat them to death. Examine, analyze everything that is natural, all the actions and desires of the purely natural man; you will find nothing but the horrible. Everything that is beautiful and noble is the result of reason and thought. Crime, for which the human animal acquires a taste in his mother's womb, is of natural origin. Virtue, on the contrary, is *artificial* and supernatural, since at all times and in all nations it has taken gods and prophets to teach it to bestialized humanity, and since man *by himself* would have been powerless to discover it. Evil is done without effort, *naturally*, inevitably; good is always the product of an art. Everything that I have said about nature as an evil counselor in matters of morality, and about reason as a true reformer and redeemer may be applied to the world of beauty. I am thus led to consider personal adornment as one of the signs of the primeval nobility of the human soul. The races that our confused and debased civilization calls savage (with an altogether laughable pride and complacency) understand as well as the child the lofty spirituality of dress. By their naïve eagerness for all that sparkles, for parti-colored plumage and shimmering materials, for the superlative grandeur of artificial forms, the savage and the baby show their dissatisfaction with the real and, unwittingly, prove the immateriality of their souls. Woe unto him who, like Louis XV (the product not of a true civilization but of a return to barbarism), carries depravity to the point of no longer enjoying anything except *simple nature.**

Hence fashion must be considered a symptom of the taste for the ideal which surmounts everything coarse, earthly and foul accumulated by natural life in the human brain; as a sublime deformation of nature; or rather as a lasting and continuous effort to transform nature.[162] Thus—without knowing why—people have sensibly pointed out that all fashions are charming, that is to say, relatively charming, each one being a new effort, more or less successful, to achieve beauty, to approximate an ideal the desire for which endlessly excites the unsatisfied human

---

* It is known that when Mme. Du Barry wished to avoid receiving the king, she was careful to put on rouge. That was sufficient indication. She thus closed her door. By embellishing herself she drove away the royal disciple of nature.

mind. But if you really wish to enjoy fashions, they must not be considered lifeless objects. You might as well admire old clothes hanging, as slack and inert as the skin of Saint Bartholomew, in a second-hand dealer's shop. They must be imagined vivified, brought to life by the beautiful women who wore them. That is the only way in which their meaning and spirit can be understood. So if the aphorism, *all fashions are charming*, strikes you as being too absolute, you need only say that all had their own rightful charm, and you will not be mistaken.

Woman is perfectly right, and is even fulfilling a kind of duty, when she strives to appear magical and supernatural; she must astonish, she must charm; an idol, she must adorn herself in order to be worshipped. She must borrow from all the arts the means to rise above nature in order to captivate hearts and create a striking effect.[163] It matters very little that her ruse and artifice are recognized by everyone if their success is sure and the effect always irresistible. It is for these reasons that the philosophical artist will readily find the justification of all the practices employed by women at all times to strengthen and to deify, so to speak, their fragile beauty. The enumeration of these practices would be endless; but if we restrict ourselves to what our day and age ordinarily calls *make-up*, who does not see that the use of face powder, so foolishly criticized by naïve philosophers, has as its purpose and result the removal from the complexion of all the blemishes that nature has disrespectfully strewn over it and the creation of an abstract unity in the texture and color of the skin, a unity which, like that produced by tights, immediately makes a human being similar to a statue, that is to say, similar to a superior and divine being? As for the artificial black which outlines the eye and the rouge which marks the upper part of the cheek, although their use is based on the same principle, on the need to surpass nature, the result is designed to satisfy a quite opposite need. The red and the black represent life, a superabundant and supernatural life; the black frame makes the glance more penetrating and strange, emphasizes the eye and gives it the appearance of a window opened on the infinite; the red, which heightens the color of the cheeks, still further increases the brightness of the pupil and adds to a beautiful feminine face the mysterious passion of a priestess.

Hence, if I am making my meaning clear, cosmetics should not be used with the ordinary but inadmissible purpose of imitating beautiful nature and of rivaling youth. It has been pointed out, moreover, that artifice does not enhance ugliness and can serve only beauty. Who would dare to assign to art the sterile function of imitating nature? Make-up does not need to hide itself, to avoid being noticed; on the contrary, it can display itself, if not ostentatiously, at least with a kind of ingenuousness.

Those who are too solemn to seek beauty even in its slightest manifestations are free to laugh at my reflections and to criticize their puerile gravity; their austere judgment does not affect me in the least; I will be satisfied to appeal to true artists and to the women who, at birth, have received a spark of the sacred fire with which they would like to illuminate their whole being.

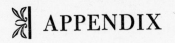

APPENDIX

NORMAN STORIES AND IDLE TALES
BY JEAN DE FALAISE

PREFACE

The following one-page review, published anonymously in an obscure magazine, *Le Corsaire-Satan,* in 1845, suggests that Baudelaire's attitude toward nature was more traditional at the beginning of his career than it came to be later on. At the same time there is a somewhat more characteristic stress on the value of naïveté, that is, on a fresh, spontaneous response to experience.

Jean de Falaise was in reality Philippe de Chennevières who, with Prarond, Le Vavasseur and Buisson, was a member of the so-called Norman School. Many years later, when Chennevières had become Director of Fine Arts, Baudelaire was to write him, before leaving for Brussels, asking that he give special attention to the hanging of the paintings submitted to the Salon by Manet and Fantin-Latour.[1]

For his part Chennevières greatly admired Baudelaire's genius, in spite of his distaste for the satanism and preoccupation with evil that marked much of the poet's work.

Those who love and are concerned with true literature will read these two small, modest volumes with the keenest interest. The author is one of those men, too rare today, who early in their career have familiarized themselves with every stylistic device. The peculiar expressions, so frequently found in the first of these volumes, those strange sentences, often marked by bold and picturesque provincialisms, give it a new and somewhat audacious charm but one which the author has used with extraordinary skill.

The special merit of *Norman Stories* is its complete freshness and the naïveté of its impressions, a sincere love of nature and the Epicureanism of a gentleman. Whereas today every author tries to assume a personality and a way of feeling that is not his own, Jean de Falaise has remained completely himself and has very quietly succeeded in producing an original work.

Endowed with so mild and so amusing an eccentricity, the author makes a mistake in taking such pains to imitate the letters of Mme. de Scudéry.[2] On the other hand, M. de Balzac offers few pictures of manners as vivid as "Un Souvenir de Jeunesse d'un Juré de Calvados," and Hoffmann could claim "Le Diable aux Iles" without shame.—And all this is not saying too much. Listen and judge for yourselves.

❦ HOW A GENIUS PAYS HIS DEBTS

PREFACE

In the following bit of literary journalism published on November 24, 1845, in *Le Corsaire-Satan*, Baudelaire lampoons Balzac's use of ghost writers as a means of increasing his literary earnings.

Eugène Crépet believes that the attack, so inconsistent with Baudelaire's lifelong admiration for the novelist, stemmed from his indignation at Balzac's willingness to debase his genius.[3] What seems even more likely is that the article had the same sort of commercial basis that its writer was criticizing in Balzac. Like the author of *La Comédie Humaine*, Baudelaire was always desperately in need of money.

The attack may also have served as a form of rationalization on the part of Baudelaire. That Balzac, despite his great genius, had had to prostitute his art in order to pay his debts may have served as an excuse in Baudelaire's mind for his own lack of financial success as a writer.

The final paragraph, which tends to soften the irony, was added as a sort of afterthought when the article was re-published a year later (August 23, 1846) in a small newspaper known as L'Echo.

※※※※※

I was told the following story with the request not to repeat it to anyone; that is why I want to tell everyone.

. . . He was sad, to judge by his frown, his wide mouth less distended and thick-lipped than usual, and by his abrupt pauses as he strode along through the Opera Arcade. He was sad.

It was really he, the keenest business and literary mind of the nineteenth century; he whose poetic brain is covered with figures like the office of a financier; it was really he, the man of the mythological bankruptcies, of the hyperbolic and phantasmagoric ventures who always forgets the most important thing; the eager pursuer of dreams, ever in *search of the absolute*; he, the most extraordinary, the most ludicrous, the most comic, the most interesting, and the most vainglorious of all the characters in *La Comédie Humaine*; he, that eccentric, as unbearable in real life as he is delightful in his writings, that overgrown child puffed up with genius and pride, who has so many merits and so many faults that one hesitates to take some away for fear of losing the others and of thus spoiling this incorrigible and predestined monstrosity!

What was making the great man so gloomy as he walked along with his head hanging down and his forehead wrinkled into a *Peau de Chagrin* [grained leather]? [4]

Was he dreaming of pineapples at four sous, of a suspension bridge made of tropical vines, of a stairless villa with boudoirs draped in muslin? Had some princess nearing forty cast him one of those profound glances which beauty owes to genius? Or was his brain, absorbed in an idea for some industrial machine, being tortured by all *Les Souffrances d'un Inventeur?*

No, alas! No, the great man's sadness was ordinary, down-to-earth, low, shameful, and ridiculous; he found himself in the embarrassing situation known to us all in which every fleeting minute carries away on its wings a chance of salvation; in which, with eyes fixed on the clock, the inventive genius feels the need of doubling his strength, of tripling it, or even increasing it tenfold as time grows shorter and the fatal hour quickly approaches. The illustrious author of the *Théorie de la Lettre de Change* had a promissory note of twelve hundred francs that was due the next day, and it was already late in the evening.

In cases like this it sometimes happens that the mind, harassed, overburdened, pressed, and crushed under the piston of necessity, suddenly escapes from its prison in an unexpected and triumphant flash.

This may have been what happened to the great novelist. For a smile replaced the contraction which distorted the proud lines of his mouth; his eyes left the ground, and calm and serene, he proceeded toward the Rue Richelieu with a majestic and measured step.

He entered a house where a rich and prosperous businessman was resting from his day's work, enjoying a cup of tea beside an open fire; he was received with all the honors due his great name, and after a few moments he revealed the purpose of his visit in the following words: "Would you like to have for the day after tomorrow two long feature articles on 'Les Français Peints par Eux-mêmes,' written and signed by me in *Le Siècle* and *Les Débats?* [5] This is a golden opportunity for you."

The publisher, different in this respect from his colleagues, apparently considered the reasoning reasonable, for the bargain was concluded at once.

The latter, on second thought, insisted that the fifteen hundred francs be paid on the appearance of the first article, whereupon the writer placidly returned to the Opera Arcade.

After a few moments he noticed a small young man with a lively, cantankerous expression, who had recently written for him an amazing preface to *La Grandeur et Décadence de César Birotteau*, and who was already known among journalists for his comic and almost impious verve; pietism had not yet clipped his claws, and bigoted journals had not put their blessed candle snuffers to work.[6]

"Edouard, would you like to have one hundred and fifty francs tomorrow?—Well, what do you say, come and have some coffee."

The young man drank a cup of coffee which immediately stimulated his small Southern frame.

"Edouard, tomorrow morning I have to have three long columns on 'Les Français Peints par Eux-mêmes'; tomorrow morning, you understand, and very early, for the entire article must be recopied by my hand and signed with my name; that is very important."

The great man uttered these words with that admirable pomposity and that arrogant tone which he sometimes uses to friends whom he is unable to receive: "I am very sorry, my dear, not to invite you in; I am entertaining a princess whose honor is in my hands, and you understand . . ."

Edouard shook hands with him as if with a benefactor and rushed off to his work.

The great novelist ordered a second article on the Rue de Navarin.[7]

The first article appeared two days later in *Le Siècle*. Oddly enough, it was signed neither by the little man nor by the great man, but by a third person well known at that time in Bohemian circles as a lover of tomcats and of the Opéra-Comique.[8]

The second friend [9] was, and still is, fat, lazy, and sluggish; what is more, he has no ideas and can only string words together like the beads of an Indian necklace,[10] and since it takes longer to cram three long columns with words than to write a volume filled with ideas, his article did not appear until several days later. It was not printed in *Les Débats*, but in *La Presse*.

The promissory note of twelve hundred francs was paid; everyone was perfectly satisfied, except the publisher, who was almost satisfied. And that is the way one pays his debts . . . when one is a genius.

Should anyone maliciously take this for the *scoffing* of a petty journalist or for an attack on the fame of the greatest man of our century, he would be shamefully mistaken; I have merely wanted to show that the great writer could find a solution for a financial problem as easily as for the most mysterious and the most complicated novel.

❧ PROMETHEUS UNBOUND
BY L. DE SENNEVILLE

PREFACE

Baudelaire's clear-cut ideas, analytical sense and incisive style are all evident in this amusing and devastating review of a verse play written by Louis Ménard, a former school companion, who had adopted the pen name of Louis de Senneville. The satiric quality of the opening dialogue, reminiscent of Diderot, paves the way for a more serious discussion in which for the first time Baudelaire expresses a marked antipathy for Neo-Classicism and philosophic art. Later articles will show a growing distaste for what he considers the false assumptions of both schools of thought.

Several thoroughly Baudelairean conceptions make their appearance in the course of the essay: the spectator creates the poetry of a picture; poetry cannot be deliberately philosophical; rationalism is shallow; and religion is something to be respected.

Of greatest interest to the present-day reader, however, is the fact that Baudelaire can be seen moving toward the conception of the imagination which was to become the basis of his aesthetics: "Never confuse the phantoms of reason with the phantoms of imagination; the former are equations, the latter are beings and memories."

Louis Ménard, who was later to become the distinguished Greek scholar of the Parnassian movement, did not soon forget the remarks of his former schoolmate. Eleven years later, in 1857, he sought to even the score by calling the author of *Les Fleurs du Mal* an awkward boy who, suffering from arrested development, was trying to pass himself off as a devil with forked feet.[11] For Ménard (1822–1901), see Henri Peyre's excellent study, New Haven, Yale University Press, 1932.

꠸꠸꠸꠸

This is philosophical poetry.—What is philosophical poetry?—Who is M. Edgar Quinet?—A philosopher?—Hm! Hm!—A poet?—Oh! Oh![12]

And yet, M. Edgar Quinet is a man of genuine merit.— Well, so is M. de Senneville!—Explain yourself.—I am quite ready to do so. When a painter says to himself: I am going to do a painting that will be as poetic as can be! Ah, poetry! . . . —he produces a cold painting in which intention shines at the expense of the work:—*Le Rêve du Bonheur* or *Faust et Marguerite.*—And yet, MM. Papety and Ary Scheffer are not devoid of talent;—but! . . . the fact is the poetry of a picture should be made by the spectator.[13]

—Just as the philosophy of a poem should be made by the reader.—You've got the point. That's it exactly.

—Then poetry isn't something philosophical?—Poor reader, how you take the bit in your teeth when you are put on the right track!

Poetry is essentially philosophical; but as it is above all *inevitable*, it must be involuntarily philosophical.

—And so philosophical poetry is a false genre?—Yes— Then why talk about M. de Senneville?

—Because he is a man of considerable merit.—We shall speak of his book as we would of a tragedy containing a few witticisms.

Besides, he has made a good choice—the broadest and *most infinite* subject, the greatest circumference, the most universal of all *Protestant* themes—*Prometheus Unbound!*—humanity in revolt against phantoms! the discoverer banished! reason and liberty crying: justice!

—The poet believes they are going to obtain justice, as you will see:

The scene takes place in the Caucasus in the late hours of the night. Prometheus in chains, at the mercy of the vulture, is singing his eternal lament and summoning suffering humanity to the splendor of the forthcoming liberty. The chorus—humanity—relates its sad story to Prometheus: first, the barbarous worship of the distant past, the oracles of Delphi, the false consolations of the Sages, the opium and laudanum of Epicurus, the great orgies of the decadence, and finally the redemption through the blood of the lamb.

> Mais le symbole tutélaire
> Dans le ciel, qu'à peine il éclaire,
> Jette en mourant ses derniers feux.

Prometheus continues to *protest* and to promise a new life; Harmonia, *the most beautiful of the Muses*, comes to console him and summons before him *the spirit of heaven, the spirit of life, the spirit of earth and the spirit of the meteors,* who speak to Prometheus in a rather rambling style about the mysteries and secrets of nature. Prometheus declares he is the king of heaven and earth.

> Les dieux sont morts, car la foudre est à moi.

Which means that Franklin has dethroned Jupiter. Io, that is to say Mary Magdalene or Mary, that is to say love, comes in turn to philosophize with Prometheus; the latter explains to her why her love and her prayers were only pure Epicureanism, sterile and miserly works:

> Pendant que tes genoux s'usaient dans la prière,
> Tu n'as pas vu les maux des enfants de la terre!
> Le monde allait mourir pendant que tu priais.

Suddenly the vulture is pierced by a mysterious arrow. Hercules appears, and human reason is freed by force—an appeal to insurrection and to *evil passions!* Harmonia orders the ancient prophets, Manou, Zoroaster, Homer, and Jesus Christ, to come and pay homage to the new God of the Universe; each one sets forth his doctrine, and Hercules and Prometheus in turn undertake to prove to them that the Gods, whoever they may be, reason less well than man, or humanity, as the socialists would say; and so with Jesus Christ himself returning to uncreated night, there remains nothing more for new humanity except to sing the praises of the new regime, based solely on knowledge and on power.

Sum total: Atheism.

That is all very well, and we would ask nothing better than to subscribe to it, if it were gay, pleasant, attractive, and satisfying.

But nothing of the kind; M. de Senneville has shunned the cult of Nature, that great religion of Diderot and Holbach, the sole ornament of atheism.[14]

That explains why we reach this conclusion: Of what use is philosophical poetry, since it is worth neither an article in the *Encyclopédie* nor a song by Désaugiers? [15]

Just one more word:—the philosophical poet needs Jupiter at the beginning of his poem to represent a certain number of ideas; at the end, Jupiter is suppressed.—Evidently the poet didn't believe in Jupiter!

Now great poetry is essentially *naïve*, it *believes*, and that is what constitutes its grandeur and its power.

Never confuse the phantoms of reason with the phantoms of imagination; the former are equations, the latter living beings and memories.

The first Faust is magnificent, and the second bad.—M. de Senneville's style is still rambling and imprecise; he knows nothing about strongly colored rhymes, those lanterns which light the path of the idea; he also knows nothing about the effects that can be drawn from a certain number of words that are variously combined. M. de Senneville is nevertheless a man of ability who, at times in his *treatise*, has been carried to fairly great heights by a firm belief in reason and by modern pride, but who has inevitably experienced the drawbacks of the genre he has adopted. A few noble and great lines are proof that had M. de Senneville wished to develop the pantheistic and naturalistic side of the question, he might have obtained some beautiful effects where his talent would have shone with a more fluent brilliance.

ADVICE TO YOUNG MEN OF LETTERS

PREFACE

The following article, published under the signature Baudelaire-Dufays, in *L'Esprit Public* in 1846, sums up Baudelaire's views during the confident years of his youth and offers advice which unfortunately he himself did not always follow. Contrary to the opinions expressed in the Poe essays, he maintains that there is no such thing as bad luck, that "guignon" is more the fault of the artist than of the public. Contrary to his own practice, he affirms that "inspiration is the sister of daily work" and that effort and will can overcome the many obstacles which beset a young author.

The Baudelaire of the later years can be recognized in his insistence on the supremacy of poetry as a literary genre and in the importance that he attaches to conscientious workmanship.

Twenty years later in Brussels, after having suffered a stroke, Baudelaire still struggled to correct proofs with the same meticulous care that had characterized him from the beginning of his career.

⅋⅋⅋⅋⅋

The precepts that you are about to read are the fruit of experience; experience implies a certain number of foolish mistakes; since everyone has made them—if not all of them, at least most of them—I hope my experience will be verified by that of everyone else.

The aforesaid precepts have no claim other than that of a *vade mecum*, no usefulness other than that of *Common Courtesy.*—Enormous usefulness! Imagine rules of courtesy written by an understanding and kind-hearted Madame de Warens, imagine the art of dressing oneself properly taught by a mother! [16]—In much the same way I shall inject a very fraternal affection into these precepts dedicated to young writers.

I

BEGINNERS' LUCK AND BAD LUCK

Young writers who speak of a young confrere with a note of envy and say: "That's a splendid beginning; he has had rare good luck!" do not stop to think that every beginning has always been preceded by prior efforts and that it is the result of twenty other beginnings of which they are unaware.

313

I do not know whether in matters of reputation there has ever been such a thing as success coming like a stroke of lightning; I am inclined to believe that success results—in an arithmetical or geometrical ratio depending on the ability of the author—from previous successes often invisible to the naked eye. There is a slow aggregation of molecular successes; but miraculous and spontaneous generations, never!

Those who say: "I have no luck," are those who have not yet had enough success and who do not realize it.

I am taking into account the thousand circumstances which envelop the human will and which themselves have their legitimate causes; they form a circumference within which the will is enclosed; but this circumference is moving, living, turning, and it changes its circle and its center every day, every minute, every second. Thus, impelled by it, all human wills which are cloistered therein vary their reciprocal play from one moment to another, and that is what constitutes liberty.[17]

Liberty and fatality are two opposites: seen close at hand or from a distance, they are a single will.

That is why there is no such thing as bad luck. If you are unlucky, it is because you lack something: learn to know this something and study the play of neighboring wills in order to displace the circumference more easily.

One example among a thousand. Several people whom I love and respect are angered by the popularity of certain contemporary writers—logogriphs in action; but the talent of these people, however trifling it may be, does exist nonetheless, and the indignation of my friends does not exist, or rather it *exists to a lesser degree,* for it is wasted time, the least valuable thing in the world.[18] The question is not to know whether literature of the heart or of form is superior to that in vogue. That is only too true, at least in my opinion. But it is only half true as long as you do not have as much talent in your chosen field as Eugène Sue has in his. Arouse the same amount of interest with different means; possess a power that is equal and superior, but directed in an opposite direction; double, triple, quadruple the dose until it reaches the same concentration and you will no longer have the right to slander the *bourgeois*, for the *bourgeois* will be with you. Until then, *vae victis!* for nothing is true except power, and power is the supreme justice.

II

PAYMENT

However beautiful a house may be, it is first of all—before we consider its beauty—so many feet high and so many feet wide. Likewise, literature, which is the most priceless material, is first of all the filling up of so many columns, and a literary architect, whose name in itself is not a guarantee of profit, has to sell at all kinds of prices.

There are young men who say: "Since it pays so little, why give oneself so much trouble?" They could have produced *better work*; and had they done so, they would have been robbed only by their present needs, by the law of nature; they have robbed themselves;—poorly paid, they could still have found honor therein; poorly paid, they have dishonored themselves.

I shall summarize everything I could write on this subject in this final maxim which I offer as food for thought to all philosophers, all historians, and all businessmen: It is only through fine sentiments that one can make a fortune!

Those who say: "Why *kill oneself* for so little!" are the ones who later, after achieving distinction, want to sell their books in serial form at 200 francs an installment, and who, when rejected, come back the next day and offer them at a loss of 100 francs.

The reasonable man is the one who says: "I believe that this is worth so much because I have genius; but if I must make some concessions, I shall make them in order to have the honor of being published by you."

315

III

ON LIKES AND DISLIKES

In love as in literature, preferences are involuntary; nevertheless they need to be confirmed, and reason plays an ulterior role in the matter.

Sympathies that are genuine are excellent, for they are dual —those that are false are odious, for they only add up to one, minus initial indifference, which is better than hate, the inevitable consequence of deception and disillusionment.

That is why I accept and admire fellowship in so far as it is based on essential relations of reason and temperament. It is one of the sacred manifestations of nature, one of the many applications of that sacred proverb: union makes strength.

The same law of candor and naïveté should govern antipathies. There are people, however, who court hatred as rashly as they do admiration. That is most imprudent; it is equivalent to making an enemy for oneself—without benefit or profit. A blow which misses its mark may nonetheless deeply offend the rival for whom it was intended, not to mention the fact that it may accidentally strike one of the bystanders.

One day during a fencing lesson a creditor came to disturb me; I pursued him down the stairway with thrusts of my foil. When I returned, the fencing master, a peaceful giant who could have knocked me over like a feather, said to me: "How lavish you are with your dislikes! A poet! A philosopher! For shame!"—I had wasted enough time for two fencing matches, I was winded, ashamed, and scorned by one more man—a creditor, whom I had not really harmed.

Indeed, hate is a precious liquor, a poison more costly than that of the Borgias, for it is made of our blood, our health, our sleep, and two-thirds of our love! We must be chary of it!

IV

ON RIDICULE

Ridicule should be practiced only against agents of error. If you are strong, you will ruin yourself by attacking a strong man; even if you disagree on certain points, there will always be certain times when he will be on your side.

There are two methods of ridicule: by the curved line or by the straight line, which is the shortest path.

You will find plenty of examples of the curved line in the articles of J. Janin.[19] The curved line amuses the gallery, but is not instructive.

The straight line is now being used successfully by a few English journalists; in Paris it has fallen into disuse; M. Granier de Cassagnac himself seems to have forgotten it.[20] It consists in saying: "Mr. X . . . is a dishonest man, and what is more he is an idiot; that is what I am going to prove,"—and to prove it! —primo, secundo, tertio, —etc. I recommend this method to all those who have confidence in reason and a strong fist.

Ridicule that misses its mark is a deplorable mishap; it is an arrow which reverses its course or at least skins the hand that shoots it, a bullet whose ricochet can kill you.

V

CONCERNING METHODS OF COMPOSITION

Today it is necessary to produce a great deal; hence one must work quickly, make haste slowly, and make every blow count; not even one hit must be useless.

To write quickly one must have thought a great deal; one must have mulled over a subject constantly—while walking, bathing, eating, or even making love. E. Delacroix once said to me: "Art is something so ideal and so fleeting that the tools are never adequate enough or the means sufficiently expeditious."

317

The same thing is true of literature—hence I do not believe in erasing and crossing out; it disturbs the mirror of thought.

Some of the most distinguished and the most conscientious writers—Edouard Ourliac for example—begin by filling up a lot of paper; they speak of this as covering their canvas.—The aim of this chaotic procedure is not to lose anything. Then each time that they recopy, they prune and they trim. The result, even when excellent, is a waste of time and talent. To cover a canvas is not to load it with colors, but to sketch with a thin glaze, to lay out masses in light and transparent tones.—The canvas should be covered—in the writer's mind—at the moment that he picks up his pen to write down the title.

It is said that Balzac scribbles notations all over his copy and proofs in the most fantastic, disorderly way. A novel thus passes through a series of geneses which destroy not only the unity of the sentences but also of the work. It is doubtless this poor method which often makes his style somewhat verbose, bungling, and muddled—the only fault of this great storyteller.

VI

ON DAILY WORK AND INSPIRATION

Debauchery is no longer the sister of inspiration: we have annulled that adulterous relationship. The rapid enervation and weakness of certain finely endowed persons bear sufficient testimony against this odious notion.

A very substantial and regular diet is all that a productive writer requires. Inspiration is decidedly the sister of daily work. These two opposites are no more mutually exclusive than any other opposites found in nature. Inspiration is obedient, like hunger, like digestion, like sleep. There is undoubtedly a kind of divine mechanics of the mind of which we should not feel ashamed, but which we should rather use to the best advantage, just as doctors use the mechanics of the body. If one is willing to live in a stubborn contemplation of tomorrow's work, daily

318

perseverance will serve inspiration—just as legible writing helps to clarify thought, and as calm and profound thought aids in writing legibly; for the time of bad handwriting has passed.

VII

CONCERNING POETRY

As for those who devote themselves or have devoted themselves successfully to poetry, I advise them never to give it up. Poetry is one of the arts which yields the best profits; but it is a sort of investment that pays deferred, though very high, dividends.

I challenge the envious to cite any good poetry which has ruined a publisher.

From the moral point of view, poetry establishes such a line of demarcation between minds of the first and second order that the most bourgeois public does not escape its despotic influence. I know people who read the articles of Théophile Gautier only because he has written *La Comédie de la Mort*; it may be that they do not feel all the charms of this work, but they know he is a poet.[21]

There is nothing surprising about this, however, since every healthy man can do without food for two days—but without poetry, never!

The art which satisfies the most imperious need will always be the most honored.

VIII

ON CREDITORS

Doubtless you remember a play entitled *Désordre et Génie*.[22] The fact that disorder has sometimes accompanied genius simply proves the great power of genius; unfortunately, for many young people this title expresses not so much a co-incidence as something inevitable.

I very much doubt that Goethe had creditors; Hoffmann himself, the unbusinesslike Hoffmann sought constantly to escape the clutches of need in which he was caught, and more-over he died at the moment when a more ample life was be-ginning to offer freer rein to his genius.

Never have any creditors; pretend to have them, if you wish; that is my only admonition.

IX

CONCERNING MISTRESSES

If I observe the law of contrasts which governs the moral and the physical order, I am obliged to classify the *respectable woman*, the blue stocking and the actress as women who are dangerous to writers;—the *respectable woman* because she be-longs necessarily to two men and because she is poor food for the despotic soul of a poet; the blue stocking, because she is an abortive man; the actress, because she has a smattering of literature and uses slang—in short, because she is not a woman in the full sense of the word, since her public means more to her than love.

Can you imagine a poet in love with his wife and obliged to see her play a man's part? I should think he would want to set the theater on fire.

Can you imagine this same poet obliged to write a part for a wife who has no talent?

Or another struggling to express to the audience by means of his epigrams the pain which this audience has inflicted on him through the being most dear to him—that being whom Orientals imprisoned behind triple locks before they came to study law in Paris? It is because all true men of letters abhor literature at certain times that I accept for them—free, proud souls, tired minds always in need of rest on the seventh day—

only two possible classes of women: prostitutes or stupid women, love or Alice sit-by-the-fire.[23] My brothers, do I need to explain the reasons?

❧ STORIES BY CHAMPFLEURY

PREFACE

Baudelaire's review of Champfleury's three volumes of stories, all published in 1847, appeared in *Le Corsaire-Satan*, January 18, 1848.

The review is one of Baudelaire's most uninspired—the result, it would seem, of an attempt to write sympathetically, yet objectively, about something for which he had little enthusiasm. The flat, photographic realism of Champfleury, devoid of imagination, of poetry, and of beauty, was completely alien to Baudelaire's temperament, even in 1848 when, because of his friendship with Courbet, Champfleury, and Dupont, he was more kindly disposed to Realism and to the utilitarian conception of literature than at any other time in his life. "Sensible, simple, and natural" can hardly be viewed as high praise coming from one who believed that criticism should be "biased, impassioned, partisan." It is only when he praises Balzac, "a great man in every sense of the word . . . a creator of a method . . . the only method worth studying," that Baudelaire seems to feel at ease and to speak with conviction.

Champfleury (1821–1889), pseudonym of Jules Husson, was a novelist, critic, and art historian. Today he is best known as the author of *Le Réalisme* (1857), one of the first studies of the movement.

❧❧❧❧❧

CHIEN-CAILLOU, PAUVRE TROMPETTE, FEU MIETTE

There appeared one day a very small, very modest, very simple volume, in short something of importance, *Chien-Caillou*, the simple, clear, bluntly told story—or rather record —of a poor, very eccentric print maker, so poverty stricken that he lived on carrots, with a rabbit and a prostitute as his only companions—and produced masterpieces! [24] That is what Champfleury ventured in his first attempt: contenting himself with nature and having boundless confidence in it.

The same volume contained other remarkable stories, among them: *M. le Maire de Classy-les-Bois,* and in connection with this story I shall ask the reader to note how very well Champfleury knows the provinces, that inexhaustible treasury of literary elements, so triumphantly demonstrated by our great H. de Balzac and also—in his small corner where the public will have to seek him out—by another very unassuming and retiring person, the author of *Norman Stories* and of *Idle Tales,* Jean de Falaise (Philippe de Chennevières), a worthy soul entirely dedicated to work and to the religion of nature, like Champfleury, and like him brought up on newspapers far removed from the terrible dysenteries of MM. Dumas, Féval and their cohorts.

Next comes *Carnaval,* or some valuable observations on that itinerant sight, that sad spectacle decked out in ribbons and gaudy colors, laughed at by idiots but respected by Parisians.

The second volume contained *Pauvre Trompette,* or the sad story of a very selfish, drunken old woman who ruins her son-in-law and her daughter in order to gorge her little dog on Curaçao and Anisette. The son-in-law, completely exasperated, poisons the dog by indulging its appetite for liqueur and the cruel mother hangs a sign in the shop window which doomed her son-in-law to the scorn and hatred of the public.—A true story like those that precede it.—Now it would be a serious mistake to believe that all these short stories were intended only to amuse and entertain. One cannot possibly imagine how much genuine sorrow and sadness Champfleury has been able to put, or rather, to see, in them.

The day he wrote M. *Prudhomme au Salon* he was jealous of Henri Monnier.[25] We know that he who can do more can do less. Hence, though this story is written in a very refined and a very amusing way, to tell the truth the author is capable of better things, and he has better things to do.

Grandeur et Décadence d'une Serinette. Here he creates in an altogether delightful manner a child, a musical child, either a little boy or a little girl, one cannot be too sure. This short story clearly reveals the long-standing affinity of the author with certain German and English writers, melancholy spirits endowed like him with an involuntary and persistent irony. There should be noted, also, as I mentioned above, an excellent description of provincial meanness and stupidity.

Une Religion au Cinquième. This is the story, the description of how a modern religion is concocted, the realistic portrayal of some of those wretches, such as we have all known, who think that one begets a doctrine as one begets a child, on a straw mattress with the *Compère Mathieu* in one's hand—and that there is nothing more to it than that.[26]

The last volume is dedicated to Balzac. It would be impossible to put more sensible, simple, and natural works under a more august patronage. The dedication is excellent, excellent in style, excellent in ideas. Balzac is in reality a novelist and a scholar, an inventor and an observer, a naturalist who understands equally well the law governing the generation of ideas and of tangible beings. He is a great man in every sense of the word; he is a creator of method and the only one whose method is worth studying.

And in my opinion this is not one of the least favorable omens for the literary future of Champfleury.

This last volume contains *Feu Miette*, the story, true to life as usual, of a famous charlatan of the Quai des Augustins.— *Fuenzès*, a beautiful idea, a fatal picture which brings misfortune to those who buy it!

Simple Histoire d'un Rentier, d'un Lampiste et d'une Horloge,—an admirable piece, an account of the eccentricities that develop inevitably in the stagnant and lonely life of the provinces. It is difficult to better portray and to better delineate ambulant automatons whose very brains take on the character of lamps and clocks.

Van Schaendel, Père et Fils: You fanatical naturalistic painters who live on carrots in order to paint them better and wear feathers in order to paint a parrot correctly, read and re-read these important lessons colored by a powerful German irony.

Up to this point I have said nothing about style. One can easily imagine what it is like. It is bold, abrupt, blunt, poetic, like nature. Nothing turgid or excessively literary. Just as the author strives to see people and their faces clearly, always strange to those who can see clearly, so too he strives to catch the cry of their animality, and from this there results a kind of method, all the more striking, as it is, so to speak, elusive. I may be explaining my thought badly, but all those who have felt the need of creating an aesthetic for their own use will understand me.

The only thing for which I might reproach the author is his tendency not to realize his own potentialities, not to work over his material sufficiently, to have too much confidence in his readers, and to fail to draw conclusions or exhaust his subject, all of them reproaches which can be reduced to a single one and which derive from the same principle. But perhaps I am wrong; one must not force anyone's destiny; large sketches are more beautiful than confused pictures, and it may be that he has chosen the best method, one which is simple, short and old.

The fourth volume, which will soon appear, is at least as good as the preceding ones.

Finally, by way of conclusion, these stories are essentially entertaining and belong to a very high order of literature.

❦ JULES JANIN AND THE TWELFTH-NIGHT CAKE

PREFACE

The following fragment, written early in 1848 and left unfinished, remained unpublished until the twentieth century. Offering nothing new so far as Baudelaire's critical ideas are concerned, it is further evidence of his distaste for lack of originality and of self-discipline.

Many years later in an open letter to Janin, which was also left unfinished, Baudelaire answers the article that the latter had had published in *L'Indépendance Belge* of February 11, 1865. Infuriated by Janin's attack on the German poet Heine and by his belief that Happiness was the real Muse of France, Baudelaire reproaches the academic critic for his "disgusting love of joy," reminds him that Byron, Tennyson and Poe represent the "melancholy sky of modern poetry," and asks with obvious annoyance: "Why shouldn't sadness have its own beauty? And horror also? And everything? And anything whatever?" [27]

Jules Janin (1804–1874) was a popular literary critic, especially known for his weekly articles on the theater in the *Journal des Débats*.

❦❦❦❦

FRAGMENT

To give the reader, uninitiated in *the mysteries* of literature and uninformed about the genesis of reputations, some idea of the real literary importance of these little books replete with wit, poetry, and observations, let me say that the first one, *Chien-Caillou, Fantaisies d'Hiver*, was published simultaneously with another small book written by a very famous man who had conceived the idea of these quarterly publications at the same time as Champfleury. Now for those minds which are more demanding, dealing every day, as they do, with the production of books, Champfleury's first volume swallowed up that of this famous man.

All those of whom I speak knew *The Twelfth-Night Cake*; they knew it because it is their business to know everything. *The Twelfth-Night Cake*, a sort of Christmas book or *Livre de Noël*, was primarily a clearly affirmed effort to draw from language all the effects that a transcendant instrumentalist draws from his instrument—to play infinite variations on the dictionary.[28] Misplaced effort! The error of a weak mind!

In this strange book ideas quickly follow each other, rush along with the swiftness of sound, resting haphazardly on infinitely tenuous connections; they are held together by an extremely fragile thread, according to a method of thought exactly like that of people locked up in insane asylums; a vast stream of involuntary ideas, a steeplechase, an abnegation of the will.

This strange feat was accomplished by a man whose one special faculty is a lack of self-discipline, a man of chance encounters and of *blind luck!*

Certainly, there was talent there; but how he abused it! how profligate he was with it! And besides how tiresome and how painful!

No doubt one should show a little respect or at least a little grateful compassion for the indefatigable fluttering about of an aging ballerina; but alas! what hackneyed devices, what feeble methods and what tiresome smirking! The ideas of the man in question are like silly old women who have danced too much, who have displayed and tossed their legs too much. *Sustulerunt saepius pedes.* Where is the heart, where is the soul, where is the sense in all this?

❧ THE DUALITY OF LIFE
BY CHARLES ASSELINEAU

PREFACE

Baudelaire's review of *The Duality of Life* appeared in *L'Artiste* on January 9, 1859. A collection of short stories, the book had been published in 1858 by Charles Asselineau, Baudelaire's closest and most loyal friend.[29] Writer, bibliophile, and during the last years of his life director of the Bibliothèque Mazarine, Asselineau possessed a fine, sensitive mind and a kindly self-effacing nature that endeared him to his many literary friends. Introduced to Baudelaire in 1845 by the painter Deroy, he came to know and understand the poet better than anyone else, including his mother. With Banville he edited the posthumous edition of Baudelaire's works (1868–1870) and at the same time published a moving biography (1869) of the unhappy poet.

Baudelaire's close association with Asselineau may have tended to make him somewhat more kindly in his review than might otherwise have been the case. The last paragraphs clearly indicate that it was the choice of subject, far more than the style, that appealed to the critic. The duality of man was a perennial theme in his own writing, and there is no doubt that the poet and critic frequently glimpsed his own image in the "mirror" that Asselineau held up to "the thoughtful reader, the *homo duplex*." In his analysis Baudelaire often seems to be characterizing himself: "minds that are always dual, torn between action and intention, dream and reality, with one half always harming the other or usurping the other's place." Or again, the remarkably self-revelatory description of the hero of "The Lie" who "will remain poor and alone, but faithful to himself, and will persist in drawing from his mind the only embellishment of his life."

Baudelaire likewise shared Asselineau's interest in dreams which for him were a "language of hieroglyphics whose key I do not possess." A letter that the poet wrote to Asselineau in 1856, describing a strange dream from which he had just awakened, constitutes a fascinating document for those interested in the psychological factors motivating his complex and often baffling personality.[30] In his book *L'Echec de Baudelaire* Dr. René Laforgue has used this same dream in analyzing Baudelaire's personality and his work. More recently Michel Butor has discussed the dream in his *Histoire Extraordinaire—Essai sur un Rêve de Baudelaire.*

Of considerable interest is the fact that Baudelaire does not mention the preface, although it contains a number of typically Baudelairean ideas. Its thought and often even its phraseology are so characteristic of Baudelaire's critical essays that it is obviously the result of conversations and discussions between the two friends. Perhaps the critic felt too closely associated with the preface to comment on ideas already expressed in essays such as "The Respectable Drama and Novel" and "Philosophic Art."

There seems little doubt, however, that the actual writing was done by Asselineau, for in 1934 Yves Le Dantec discovered proof sheets of the preface containing marginal notations in which Baudelaire makes sharply critical observations and corrections in regard to style and syntax.

≈≈≈≈≈

Eleven short stories are presented under the general title: *The Duality of Life.* The reading of some of the pieces that make up this elegant and eloquent volume clearly reveals the meaning of the title. There is a chapter in Buffon which is entitled *Homo Duplex* whose contents I can no longer remember very precisely, but whose brief, mysterious title, so provocative of thought, has always plunged me into reverie, and which even now, when I wish to give you an idea of the spirit that animates M. Asselineau's work, comes unexpectedly to my mind, challenges it, and confronts it like a fixed idea. Who among us is not a *homo duplex?* I am speaking of those whose minds from childhood have been "touched with pensiveness," minds that are always dual, torn between action and intention, dream and reality, with one half always harming the other or usurping the other's place. There are some who travel to distant places while seated by the fire, unmindful of its quiet comfort; others, ungrateful for the adventures that Providence has granted them, cherish the dream of a sheltered life enclosed within the most narrow confines. Intentions left along the wayside, dreams forgotten in an inn, projects that are thwarted by obstacles, illness and misfortune springing up from success like poisonous plants from rich, uncultivated soil, regret mingled with irony, backward glances like those of a vagabond who stops for a moment to collect his thoughts, the incessant mechanism of earthly life constantly pulling and tearing the fabric of ideal life—such are the chief elements of this exquisite book which, through its spontaneity, its genial informality, and its suggestive sincerity, has something of the nature of the monologue and the personal letter sent to far-off lands.

Most of the pieces which comprise the whole are examples of human misfortune contrasted with the happiness of dreams. Note for example *Le Cabaret des Sabliers* in which two young people regularly go a few miles from the city to seek consolation for the grief and cares which make it intolerable to them, forgetting, in the horizontal landscape of the rivers, the tumultuous life of the streets and the anguish within a desolate home. Note also *L'Auberge:* a traveler, a scholar, after inspiring so strong a liking in his hostess that she offers him her daughter in marriage, returns suddenly to the circle in which his destiny imprisons him. On receiving that generous and ingenuous offer, the learned traveler had at first broken into heartless laughter, which certainly would have scandalized the good Jean-Paul [Richter], always so angelic in spite of his mockery.[31] But I can well imagine that, on his return journey and back in his routine, the thoughtful and philosophic traveler became more sober and may have said to himself with a little remorse, a little regret, and the apathetic sigh of skepticism, always tempered with a slight smile: "After all, the good innkeeper was perhaps right; the elements of human happiness are fewer and simpler than the world and its perverse doctrines would lead us to believe." —Note also *Les Promesses de Timothée*, the abominable struggle between a swindler and a dupe; the confidence man, that peculiar type of thief, is very properly punished, I assure you, and I am very grateful to M. Asselineau for finally showing us his dupe saved and reconciled to life by a man of bad repute. This sort of thing often happens, and the *deus ex machina* of the happy ending is, more often than we wish to admit, one of those whom the world calls a ne'er-do-well, or even a scoundrel. *Mon Cousin Don Quixote* is one of the most remarkable pieces, constructed so as to reveal the two great virtues of the author—the sense of moral beauty and the irony arising from the spectacle of injustice and stupidity. This *cousin*, whose head is bubbling with plans for education, for universal happiness, whose ever youthful blood is fired by devouring enthusiasm for the Greeks, this despot of heroism who wishes to mould and does mould his family in his own image, is more than interesting; he is appealing; he lifts our heart by making it ashamed of its daily cowardice. The lack of common ground between this new Don Quixote and the soul of the century produces a decided comic effect mingled with pathos; although, to tell the truth, laughter provoked by a sublime fault is almost an indictment of the one who laughs; and the universal Sanchos by whom the magnanimous eccentric is beset, do not inspire less scorn than the Sancho of the novel.—More than one old woman will read with a smile, and perhaps a tear, *Le Roman d'une Dévote*, a love of fifteen years standing, unconfessed, unshared, unrealized, and forever unknown to the object of that love—a pure mental monologue.

Le Mensonge represents in a form both artful and natural the general idea of the book, which could be called: *On the Art of Escaping from Daily Life.* Wealthy Turks sometimes order from our artists décors that represent apartments adorned with sumptuous furniture opening on imaginary horizons. These strange dreamers thus receive magnificent drawing rooms on canvas, rolled up like a picture or a map. The hero of *Le Mensonge* does likewise; and he is a hero much less rare than one might think. A perpetual lie adorns and clothes his life. It results in a few troubles and mishaps during the course of his daily life, but we have to pay for our happiness. One day, however, in spite of all the disadvantages of his deliberate and systematic folly, happiness, true happiness, offers itself to him, wishing only to be accepted and requiring no persuasion; to merit it, however, he would have to satisfy one small condition—he would have to confess a lie. To destroy a fabrication, to contradict himself, to demolish an ideal structure, even at the price of actual happiness, is an impossible sacrifice for our dreamer! He will remain poor and alone, but faithful to himself, and will persist in drawing from his mind the only embellishment of his life.

One of M. Asselineau's great talents is his ability to understand well and to depict well the legitimacy of the absurd and the improbable. He seizes upon and reproduces, sometimes with rigorous fidelity, the strange reasonings of dreams. In passages of this type, his forthright manner, as plain and straightforward as a report, achieves great poetic effect. I shall quote as an example a few lines drawn from an extremely strange short story, *La Jambe.*

"What is surprising in the life of a dream is not so much finding oneself transported into fantastic regions, where all customs are confused and all accepted ideas are contradicted, where often even the impossible (something that is still more frightening) is mingled with the real. What strikes me even much more, is the assent given to these contradictions, the ease with which the most monstrous fallacies are accepted as very natural things, so as to make us believe in powers or ideas of an extraordinary nature, alien to our world.

"I dreamed one day that I was in the midst of a dense

throng in the central lane of the Tuileries attending the execution of a general. A solemn, respectful silence reigned in the crowd.

"The general was brought in a coach. He came out at once, in full uniform, bareheaded, and chanting a funereal song in a low voice.

"Suddenly a war horse, saddled and caparisoned, was seen caracoling on the terrace at the right, near the Place Louis XV.

"A policeman approached the condemned man and respectfully handed him a loaded gun. The general aimed, fired, and the horse fell.

"The crowd drifted away and I myself withdrew, inwardly quite convinced that *when a general was condemned to death, it was customary for him to be saved, should his horse appear at the place of execution and be killed by him.*"

Hoffmann, in his usual vein, would not have defined an abnormal state of mind any better.

The two most important pieces, *La Seconde Vie* and *L'Enfer du Musicien*, are faithful to the basic thought of the volume. To believe that *to wish is to be able*, to take the exaggeration of the proverb literally, leads a dreamer from disappointment to disappointment and finally to suicide. By a special favor from beyond the grave, all the powers that he has so ardently desired and longed for, are suddenly accorded him, and armed with all the genius granted him in this second birth, he returns to earth. A single sorrow, a single obstacle that he had not foreseen soon makes life impossible for him and forces him to seek refuge in death once again—sorrow caused by all the troubles, all the annoyances, all the misunderstandings resulting from the disparity thenceforth created between him and the terrestrial world. Equilibrium and equation are destroyed, and like an Ovid too wise for his former fatherland, he can say:

Barbarus hic ego sum, quia non intelligor illis.[32]

L'Enfer du Musicien portrays that dreadful case of hallucination in which a composer finds himself condemned to hear all his compositions performed simultaneously, well or badly, on all the pianos in the world. He flees from city to city, seeking sleep like a promised land, until mad with despair, he reaches the other hemisphere where night, taking the place of day, finally gives him some respite. In that distant land, moreover, he finds love which, like a potent medicine, restores all his faculties and calms his disturbed physical organism. "The sin of pride has been redeemed by love."

The analysis of a book is always an armature without flesh. Yet, for an intelligent reader, this analysis can be enough to make him sense the inquiring mind that animates the work of M. Asselineau. It has often been said: *The style is the man;* but could it not be said with equal justice: *The choice of subject is the man?* Of the flesh of the book, I can say that it is good, soft, elastic to the touch; but it is the inner soul above all that deserves to be studied. This charming little book, personal, extremely personal, is like a winter monologue, murmured by the author as he warms his feet before the fire. It has all the charm of a monologue, the manner and the sincerity of a confidence, and even that feminine casualness which is a part of sincerity. Will you maintain that you still like, that you still adore, those books whose thought, strained to the limit, makes the reader fear that it will break at any moment and fills him with nervous trepidation, so to speak? This book is intended to be read as it was written, in a dressing gown, seated before the fire. Happy the author who is not afraid to show himself in informal attire! And in spite of the eternal humiliation that man experiences in the confessional, happy is the thoughtful reader, the *homo duplex* who, able to recognize his mirror in the author, is not afraid to exclaim: "Thou art the man!" [33] Here is my confessor!

✻ MARCELINE
✻ DESBORDES-VALMORE

PREFACE

Baudelaire's critical versatility is evident in his graceful
essay on Marceline Desbordes-Valmore.[34] One might have supposed *a priori* that the critic would have felt little enthusiasm
for the unsophisticated and somewhat sentimental verse of
Madame Desbordes-Valmore. The whole tone of the article
makes one wonder if Baudelaire's appreciation of her poetry was
not something of an acquired taste, if his respect for Sainte-
Beuve, who had edited and prefaced a collection of her poems
in 1842, had not helped to encourage his interest in an artist to
whom he might otherwise have felt more or less indifferent.

Not that Baudelaire can be accused of insincerity. He freely
praises the natural charm and the spontaneity of her verses, but
he also frankly admits his dislike for the negligence which often
characterized her style. One feels that the lovely prose poem in
which he compares the poet's verse to an old English garden is
not so much an example of the "poetic criticism" of which he
had spoken in the *Salon of 1846* as it was a means of extending
the remarks that he had already made.

It seems fairly obvious that Baudelaire's comments about
other women authors were directed against George Sand. Although he fails to mention her name, his caustic remarks bear
a close resemblance to certain passages in his *Journaux Intimes*
where he speaks of Sand with far less restraint.

Of especial interest to the present-day reader is Baudelaire's reference to his own use of symbolism: "I have always
liked to seek in the exterior and visible world examples and
metaphors which may help me to characterize the joys and impressions of a spiritual order." Consciously or unconsciously, he
is describing the method on which many of his greatest poems
are based—that of discovering in nature symbols which translate

the emotions and the "état d'âme" of the author. (See Lloyd Austin's *L'Univers Poétique de Baudelaire*.)

Marceline Desbordes-Valmore (1786–1859) began her career as an actress but, after 1839, settled down in Paris where she struggled to support her family through her writing. She is best known for her lyrical poems, especially those which are a nostalgic evocation of her childhood. Admired by many of the writers of the day—Balzac, Hugo, Lamartine, Alexandre Dumas—she was encouraged by Sainte-Beuve who remained a faithful friend until her death.

In 1884 Verlaine included Madame Valmore in his gallery of *Poètes Maudits*.

Haven't you been told more than once by a friend to whom you were confiding one of your preferences or enthusiasms: "That's strange, that is completely inconsistent with your doctrine and with all your other enthusiasms?" And you would answer: "That may be, but that's the way it is. I like it; I like it probably because it is in violent contradiction with my whole nature."

Such is my position in regard to Madame Desbordes-Valmore. If the cry, if the sincere sigh of a rare soul, if the desperate aspiration of the heart, if unexpected, spontaneous powers, if all that which is gratuitous and God-given suffice to make a great poet, Marceline Valmore is and always will be a great poet. It is true that if you take time to notice how lacking she is in everything acquired through work, her greatness will be strangely diminished; but at the very moment when you feel the most impatient and saddened by the carelessness, the unevenness, and the confusion which you, a serious-minded and responsible man, consider deliberate indolence, a sudden, unexpected, imcomparable beauty emerges, and you are irresistibly carried away to the heights of the poetic heaven. Never was a poet more natural; never was anyone less artificial. No one has been able to imitate this charm, because it is entirely original and innate.

If ever a man desired the gifts and honors of the Muse for his wife or daughter, he couldn't wish for others than those bestowed on Madame Valmore. Among the rather large number of women who have plunged into literary work today, there are very few whose works haven't been, if not an affliction for their family or even for their lovers (since the least modest men like modesty in the object of their affection), at least a blemish resulting from some form of those masculine absurdities which in women assume the proportions of a monstrosity. We have known the philanthropist woman author, the systematic priestess of love, the republican poetess, the poetess of the future, Fourierist or Saint-Simonean; and our eyes, enamoured of the beautiful, have never succeeded in becoming accustomed to all this studied ugliness, to all this impious villainy (there are even poetesses of impiety), to all these sacrilegious imitations of the masculine mind.

Madame Desbordes-Valmore was a woman, always a woman, nothing but a woman; but to an extraordinary degree she was the poetic expression of all the natural loveliness of women. Whether she sings the languishing desires of the young girl, the forlorn grief of a forsaken Ariadne, or the warm raptures of maternal love, her song always keeps the delightful accent of a woman; no borrowing, no meretricious embellishment, nothing but the *eternal feminine*, as the German poet says. It is then in her sincerity itself that Madame Valmore has found her recompense, that is to say, a fame which we think is as secure as that of the most perfect artists. That torch which she waves before our eyes in order to illuminate the mysterious groves of sentiment, or which she holds over our most intimate memories of amorous or filial love in an effort to revive them, that torch has been lighted in the innermost recesses of her own heart. Victor Hugo has expressed magnificently, as always, the beauties and delights of family life; but only in the poems of the ardent Marceline will you find that warmth lavished by a mother on her brood which a few sons, less ungrateful than others, long remember with pleasure.[35] If I were not afraid that a comparison with the animal world might be taken as lack of respect for this exquisite woman, I would say that I find in her the grace, the anxious concern, the suppleness, the violence of the female animal, the cat or the lioness, full of love for its young.

It has been said that Madame Valmore, whose first poems date back to 1818, has been quickly forgotten in our time. Forgotten by whom, may I ask? By those who, not feeling anything, cannot remember anything. She has outstanding and solid merits which remain fixed in one's memory, powerful impacts that unexpectedly reach our hearts, magical bursts of passion. No author catches more easily than she the exact turn of phrase for expressing emotions, the sublime that is overlooked. Just as taking the simplest and easiest pains constitutes an invincible obstacle to that impetuous and spontaneous pen, so, on the other hand, that which for everyone else is the object of a laborious search comes very naturally and effortlessly to her; there is a never-ending series of felicitous discoveries. She pens the most admirable things as casually as she would write a note to a friend. A charitable and passionate soul as she describes herself so well, although unintentionally, in this line:

> Tant que l'on peut donner, on ne veut pas mourir!

A too sensitive soul on whom the harshness of life left an ineffaceable imprint, it was especially proper that she cry out in her desire to find Lethe:

> Mais si de la mémoire on ne doit pas guérir,
> A quoi sert, ô mon âme, à quoi sert de mourir?

Certainly no one had more right than she to write on the title page of a recent volume:

> Prisonnière en ce livre une âme est contenue!

When death came to remove her from this world, where she so well knew how to suffer, and to bear her to the heaven whose peaceful joys she so fervently desired, Madame Desbordes-Valmore, indefatigable priestess of the Muse, who knew not how to still the cries and songs which filled her heart to overflowing, was preparing still another volume whose proofs came one by one to lie scattered on her bed of pain which she had not left for two years. Those who piously helped her in the preparation of this farewell told me that we would find in it the full radiance of a vitality which never felt itself so much alive as in affliction. Alas! this book will be a posthumous crown to add to all those, already so dazzling, which are to adorn one of our most flower-bedecked tombs.

I have always liked to seek in the exterior and visible world examples and metaphors which may help me to characterize the joys and impressions of a spiritual order. I think back to what the poetry of Madame Valmore made me feel when I scanned it with youthful eyes which, in highly-strung men, are both so ardent and so discerning. This poetry seems to me like a garden; but it does not have the grandiose formality of Versailles, nor does it have the vast and dramatic picturesqueness of an ingenious Italy which knows so well the art of *constructing gardens (aedificat hortos)*; not even, no, not even *La Vallée des Flûtes* or *Le Ténare* of our old Jean-Paul [Richter].[36] It is a simple English garden, romantic and fanciful. Clusters of flowers represent the many expressions of sentiment. Pools, limpid and motionless, which reflect everything resting upside down on the inverted vault of the heavens, represent profound resignation all strewn with memories. This charming garden of another age lacks nothing, neither a few Gothic ruins hidden in a rustic spot nor the unknown mausoleum which, at the turn of a path, takes our heart by surprise and enjoins it to think of eternity. Winding and shaded lanes lead to unexpected horizons. Thus the poet's thought, after meandering capriciously, opens onto the vast perspectives of the past or future; but these skies are too vast to be everywhere pure, and the temperature of the climate too warm not to brew storms. The idle passer-by, who contemplates these areas veiled in mourning, feels tears of hysteria come to his eyes. The flowers droop, vanquished, and the birds sing only in subdued tones. After a first flash of lightning comes the roll of thunder; it is a lyric explosion; finally an inevitable flood of tears restores to all these things, prostrate, suffering, and disheartened, the freshness and the vigor of a new youth!

THÉOPHILE GAUTIER

PREFACE

The short essay on Gautier contains little that Baudelaire had not already said in previous articles. Once again he emphasizes Gautier's mastery of language and style and commends his belief that idea and expression are one. Significant also is his claim that, from a grotesque or ugly object, Gautier was able to extract a mysterious and symbolic beauty.

Of chief interest, however, is Baudelaire's contention that Gautier, despite his concern for form, was not lacking in feeling as "fatuous critics" had so often maintained.

It was Gautier who wrote the notice on Baudelaire for Crépet's *Les Poètes Français*. Baudelaire seems to have been pleased with the result and in a note dated August 4, 1862, expressed his appreciation: "It is the first time that I have been praised as I have wanted to be."

A cry from the heart is always absurd, but it is sublime because it is absurd. *Quia absurdum!*

> Que faut-il au républicain?
> Du cœur, du fer, un peu de pain!
> Du cœur pour se venger,*
> Du fer pour l'étranger,
> Et du pain pour ses frères!

That is what *La Carmagnole* says; it is a cry both absurd and sublime.

Do you wish the exact analogue in another order of sentiments? Open Théophile Gautier: the young girl, courageous and intoxicated with her love, wishes to carry off her cowardly, hesitant lover who resists and protests that the desert is without shade and without water and the flight full of peril. How does she answer? In a tone of pure sentiment:

> Mes cils te feront de l'ombre!
> Ensemble nous dormirons
> Sous mes cheveux, tente sombre,
> Fuyons! Fuyons!
>
> Sous le bonheur mon cœur ploie!
> Si l'eau manque aux stations,
> Bois les larmes de ma joie!
> Fuyons! Fuyons!

It would be easy to find in the same poet other examples of the same type:

> J'ai demandé la vie à l'amour qui la donne!
> Mais vainement. . . . .

cries Don Juan, who is asked by the poet in the land of the dead to explain the enigma of life.

---

* Variant: *Pour le danger—Pour se venger* is better suited to the tone of this song, which Goethe could have called, more fittingly than *La Marseillaise*, the hymn of the rabble.

Now I wanted first of all to prove that Théophile Gautier possessed, quite as much as if he were not a perfect artist, that famous quality which fatuous critics persist in denying him: feeling. How many times and with what magical language he has expressed the greatest subtleties of love and melancholy! Few people have deigned to study these marvelous flowers— I don't exactly know why, and I don't see any reason other than the natural repugnance of the French for perfection. Among the innumerable prejudices of which France is so proud, let us note this idea which is prevalent and which is naturally foremost among the precepts found in commonplace criticism, namely, that a work which is *too well* written *must* be lacking in feeling. Feeling, because of its popular and intimate character, appeals exclusively to the crowd, which has been steered as far away as possible from well written works by its customary teachers. In any case, let us admit at once that Théophile Gautier, a very reputable writer of feuilletons, is little known as a novelist, badly appreciated as a travel writer, and almost *unknown* as a poet, especially if the slight popularity of his poetry is weighed against its brilliant and vast merits.

Victor Hugo, in one of his odes, pictures Paris for us as a dead city, and in this lugubrious dream full of grandeur, in this mass of vague ruins washed by a stream *which once broke against the echoing bridges* but which now had been *restored to the bent and murmuring rushes,* he still perceived three monuments of a more substantial, more indestructible nature which suffice to tell our history.[37] Imagine, if you will, the French language as a dead language. In the schools of new nations, the language of a once great people, the French people, is being taught. In what authors do you suppose the professors, the linguists of that time will derive their knowledge of the principles and beauties of the French language? Will it be, I ask, in the bedlams of sentiment, or what you call sentiment? But these productions, which are your favorites, will be, thanks to their inaccuracies, the least intelligible and the least translatable, for there is nothing more obscure than error and confusion. If, in that period less distant perhaps than modern pride may imagine, the poems of Théophile Gautier should be discovered by some scholar enamoured of beauty, I can imagine, I can understand, I can see his joy. And so that is the real French language, the language of great minds and of subtle minds! With what delight his eye will scan all these poems, so pure and so carefully embellished! How all the resources of our beautiful language, incompletely known, will be surmised and appreciated! And what glory for the intelligent translator who will want to wrestle with this great poet, whose immortality is preserved among debris more heedful than the memory of his contemporaries! In his lifetime he had suffered from the ingratitude of his own people; he had waited a long time, but finally he is rewarded! Discerning commentators establish the literary bond which connects us with the sixteenth century. New light is thrown upon the history of succeeding generations. Victor Hugo is taught and interpreted in the universities; but every literary man knows that the study of his resplendent poetry should be completed by the study of the poetry of Gautier. Some even perceive that, whereas the majestic poet was swept away by enthusiasms often unfavorable to his art, the precious poet, more faithful, more concentrated, never departed from it. Others notice that he has even added new vigor to French poetry, that he has enlarged its repertory and increased its vocabulary, without ever violating the strictest rules of the language which he was commanded by birth to speak.

Fortunate man! How worthy of envy! He loved only the Beautiful, he sought only the Beautiful, and when a grotesque or ugly object encountered his glance he was able to extract from it a mysterious and symbolic beauty! Endowed with a unique faculty as powerful as fate, he expressed tirelessly and without effort, all the attitudes, all the aspects, all the colors that nature adopts, as well as the intimate meaning contained in all the objects that are offered to the contemplation of the human eye.

His glory is both twofold and single. For him, idea and expression are not two contradictory things which can be reconciled only by a great effort or by cowardly concessions. Perhaps he alone has the right to say without pomposity: *There are no inexpressible ideas!* If, in order to wrest from the future the justice which is due Théophile Gautier, I have imagined a France that has vanished, it is because I know that the human mind can better conceive the idea of justice when it consents to leave the present. In much the same way, the traveler can better understand the topography of the surrounding country by climbing to a higher elevation. I do not wish to cry like the cruel prophets: These times are close at hand! I do not invoke any disasters, even to bring glory to my friends. In an effort to prove my contention, I have merely invented a fable for minds that are weak or blind. For among the living who are most discerning, who does not understand that someday Théophile Gautier will be cited as one cites La Bruyère, Buffon, Chateaubriand, that is to say, as one of the surest and rarest masters of language and style?

❦ HÉGÉSIPPE MOREAU

PREFACE

Baudelaire's essay on Hégésippe Moreau, a classic example of literary demolition (*éreintement*), was so devastating an attack that it proved unacceptable both to Eugène Crépet and to Catulle Mendès, editor of *La Revue Fantaisiste*. Even when it finally appeared in 1868 in the posthumous edition of Baudelaire's writings, it still aroused bitter comment although Moreau had been dead for thirty years.

Baudelaire's criticism of Moreau is in marked contrast to the poetic criticism of his essay on Marceline Desbordes-Valmore. In the *Salon of 1846* he had maintained that the best criticism is that which is amusing and poetic. Had his criticism of Moreau, amusing as it is, been less savage, the two essays might well be considered as illustrations of his dual ideal.

As a poet and a man, Moreau represented everything that Baudelaire most despised. He was the very antithesis of the aesthetic and spiritual ideal that Baudelaire incorporated in his conception of the dandy. His vulgarity, his lack of originality, his undisciplined life and art, his failure to recognize the aristocratic beauty of suffering, and, last but not least, his acceptance of the democratic ideal were in direct contradiction to the views that the critic had upheld in his analysis of dandyism. It is significant that Baudelaire was always infuriated by "simpletons preaching democracy."

Hégésippe Moreau (1810–1838), a minor Romantic poet whose life was marked by poverty and dissipation, is chiefly remembered for a collection of poems, *Le Myosotis* (1838) and for a volume of short stories, *Contes à ma Sœur*. Much of his poetry was anticlerical in spirit. Baudelaire's judgment of Moreau has been confirmed by posterity.

⋟⋞⋟⋞⋟⋞

The same reason that makes one life unhappy makes another happy. Gérard de Nerval drew from his vagabondage, which for so long was his great joy, a melancholy for which suicide finally seemed the only possible outcome, the only possible remedy. Edgar Poe, a great genius, slept in the gutter, overcome by drunkenness. Prolonged outcries, relentless execrations followed these two in death. Everyone wished to dispense with pity and repeated the hasty judgment of egoism: why pity those who deserve to suffer? Besides, our century likes to consider anyone who is unfortunate as impertinent. But if this unfortunate creature joins intelligence to poverty; if, like Gérard, he is endowed with a brilliant, active, luminous mind, quick

344

to learn; if, like Poe, he is a great genius, profound as heaven and as hell, ah then, the impertinence of misfortune becomes intolerable! Would it not seem that genius is a reproach and an insult to the masses! But if the unfortunate individual has neither genius nor knowledge, if there is nothing superior, nothing impertinent about him, nothing that prevents the rabble from putting itself on his level and consequently from treating him as an equal, it then becomes evident that misfortune and even vice can become a boundless source of glory.

Gérard wrote many books, travel books or short stories, all marked by good taste. Poe produced at least seventy-two short stories—one as long as a novel—exquisite poems in a style astonishingly original and perfectly correct, at least eight hundred pages of miscellaneous criticism, and lastly a book of lofty philosophy. In short, both Poe and Gérard were, in spite of their faults, excellent men of letters in the broadest and most delicate meaning of the word, bowing humbly to the inevitable law, working, it is true, when they chose and as they pleased, in accordance with a more or less mysterious method, but active, industrious, making use of their dreams or their meditations; in short, pursuing their profession with zest.

Hégésippe Moreau who, like them, was an Arabic nomad in a civilized world, is almost the antithesis of a man of letters. His literary baggage is not heavy, but the very lightness of this baggage has allowed him to reach fame more quickly. A few songs, a few poems, half classical, half romantic in taste, do not appall sluggish memories. In short, everything turned out well for him; never was spiritual fortune more favored. His poverty has been counted as work, the disorder of his life as misunderstood genius. He wandered about, and he sang when he felt like singing. We are familiar with those theories that justify indolence which, based exclusively on metaphors, allow the poet to think of himself as a bird, chattering, flighty, irresponsible, elusive, and flitting from branch to branch. Hégésippe Moreau was a spoiled child who didn't deserve to be one. But this marvelous good fortune should be explained, and before speaking of the engaging talents that led us to believe for a time that he would become a real poet, I am anxious to expose the fragile but enormous scaffolding of his excessively great popularity.

In this scaffolding every good-for-nothing and every vagabond is a post. In this conspiracy, every ne'er-do-well without talent is naturally an accessory. If it were a question of a truly great man, his genius would serve to lessen pity for his misfortunes, while many a mediocre man can aspire, without being too absurd, to rise as high as Hégésippe Moreau; and, if he is unfortunate, he naturally finds himself eager to prove through the example of the latter that all unfortunate people are poets. Was I mistaken in saying that the scaffolding is enormous? It is set up right in the midst of mediocrity; it is built with the vanity of misfortune: inexhaustible materials!

I said the vanity of misfortune. There was a time when it was fashionable for poets to complain, not about mysterious, vague sorrows that are hard to define, a sort of congenital poetic malady, but about very specific honest-to-goodness suffering; for example, poverty. People said proudly: I am hungry, I am cold! It was considered honorable to put this filth in verse. No modesty warned the poetaster that, lie for lie, it would be better for him to present himself to the public as a man wallowing in Asiatic wealth and living in a world of luxury and beauty. Hégésippe fell into that great antipoetic vice. He talked a great deal about himself and he wept a great deal over himself. More than once he aped the portentous posturing of the Antonys and the Didiers, but he added what he considered an additional charm—the angry and peevish gaze of the democrat.[38] Spoiled by nature, to be sure, but doing very little to perfect his gifts, he threw himself headlong into the multitude of those who cry unceasingly: "O hardhearted nature!" and who reproach society for having *robbed them of what is theirs.* He made of himself a certain ideal character, damned but innocent, doomed from birth to undeserved sufferings.

Un ogre, avant flairé la chair qui vient de naître,
M'emporta, *vagissant,* dans *sa robe de prêtre,*
Et je grandis, *captif,* parmi ces écoliers,
Noirs frelons que Montrouge essaime par milliers.

That *ogre* (an ecclesiastic) in *his priest's garb,* his ill-smelling and repulsive priest's garb, must really have been monstrous to have carried off thus the *wailing* little Hégésippe. Cruel kidnapper! The word *ogre* implies a definite taste for raw flesh; why else would he have *sniffed his flesh?* And yet we see by the following line that young Hégésippe was not eaten, since, on the contrary, he grew up (a *captive,* to be sure) like five hundred other fellow-students whom the ogre also didn't eat, and to whom he taught Latin, which allowed the martyr Hégésippe to write his native tongue a little less badly than all those who have not had the misfortune of being taught by *an ogre.* You have doubtless recognized the tragic *priest's garb,* the old cast-off monk's garment stolen from the cloakroom of Claude Frollo and of Lamennais.[39] There we have the romantic touch as Hégésippe Moreau felt it; then we have the democratic note: *Black hornets!* Do you really grasp the full profundity of that word? Hornet is the antithesis of bee, a more interesting insect because, like young Hégésippe, a poor little bee imprisoned among the hornets, it is industrious and useful from birth. You see that he is no more fastidious about democratic sentiments than he is about romantic expressions, and that he understands the matter about as well as the Masons who call priests lazy and good-for-nothing.

Those four wretched lines sum up very clearly the moral note in the poetry of Hégésippe Moreau. A Romantic convention artificially imposed upon a dramatic convention without being fused with it. There is nothing in him but conventions that have been joined and harnessed together. All this does not make a homogeneous unit, that is to say a unified whole, but rather something like a bus load of people. Victor Hugo, Alfred de Musset, Barbier, and Barthélemy one after another supply him with something.[40] He borrows from Boileau his symmetrical form, dry, hard, but brilliant. He brings back to us the antiquated circumlocution of Delille, which, like a useless, affected old lady, parades most incongruously in the midst of the lewd, coarse images of the school of 1830.[41] Occasionally, he livens up and is carried away in the classical manner, as is customary at Le Caveau, or else he cuts up the lyric sentiments into couplets in the manner of Béranger and of Désaugiers; he succeeds almost as well as they with the ode made up of separate parts.[42] See, for example, "Les Deux Amours." A man yields to banal love, while his memory is still full of an ideal love. It is not the sentiment, the theme, that I am criticizing; although very commonplace, it is profound and poetic in nature. But it is treated in an antihuman manner. The two loves alternate, like the shepherds in Virgil, with a tiresome mathematical symmetry. That is Moreau's great misfortune. Whatever the subject or genre, he is someone's pupil. His only originality lies in adding vulgarity to a borrowed form, if anything so universal as vulgarity can be called original. Although always a schoolboy, he remains a pedant, and even in the sentiments which least lend themselves to pedantry he brings certain habits from the Sorbonne and the Latin Quarter. His is not the voluptuous pleasure of the Epicurean; it is rather the monastic, steamy sensuality of the loutish pedant, the sensuality of the prison and of the dormitory. His amorous jesting has the coarseness of a schoolboy on vacation. *The commonplaces of lewd morality,* odds and ends of the last century which he warms up again and spouts with the gross silliness of a child or a street urchin.

A child! That is certainly the right word, and it is from this word and all its implications that I shall derive everything that I have to say in his praise. Some will doubtless find, even supposing that they are in agreement with me, that I have carried my disapproval too far and that I have exaggerated its expression. After all, that may well be true; but even if it were true, I shouldn't see much harm in it and I wouldn't consider myself very guilty. Action, reaction, praise, cruelty become alternately necessary. Equilibrium must be re-established. That is the law, and it is a good law. We must not forget that we are dealing here with a man whom people have wanted to make prince of poets in the country which has given birth to Ronsard, Victor Hugo, and Théophile Gautier, and that recently there has been a great hue and cry about raising a monument to him by public subscription, as if it were a question of one of those prodigious men whose neglected tomb is a blot on the history of a people. Are we dealing with one of those wills at grips with adversity, such as Soulié and Balzac, with a man entrusted with great duties, accepting them humbly and struggling unceasingly with the growing monster of exhaustion? [43] Moreau did not like suffering; he did not recognize its beneficence and he did not suspect its aristocratic beauty! Besides, he has not experienced that kind of hell! To ask so much pity and so much love from us, the person himself must be tender and compassionate. Has he known the tortures of an unappeased heart, the stifling pain of a soul that loves and is misunderstood? No. He belonged to that class of travelers who are satisfied at little cost, and who are content with bread, wine, cheese, and *the first woman who comes along.*

But he was *a child,* always impudent, often gracious, sometimes charming. He has the flexibility and the unexpectedness of childhood. In literary youth, as in physical youth, there is a certain freshness which makes us excuse many imperfections. Here we find what is worse than imperfection, but also we are sometimes charmed by what is better than youthful freshness. In spite of this mass of imitations from which, child and schoolboy as he always was, he could not escape, we sometimes find the accent of irrepressible truth, the sudden, natural accent which cannot be confused with any other accent. He truly possesses charm, a gift freely granted; he, so stupidly impious, he, the silly parrot of the simpletons preaching democracy, he should have given thanks a thousand times for this charm to which he owes everything—both his fame and the excuse for all his literary faults.

When, in this mass of borrowings, in this litter of vague and unintentional plagiarisms, in this explosion of bureaucratic and academic wit, we discover one of those unexpected miracles which we mentioned a moment ago, we feel something which resembles immense regret. It is certain that the writer who in one of his good moments hit upon "La Voulzie" and the song of "La Ferme et la Fermière" could have rightly aspired to a better fate. Since Moreau has sometimes succeeded—without study, without effort, in spite of bad company, without any interest in recalling happy hours at will—in being so frankly, so simply, so gracefully original, how much more original he would have been and how much more frequently, if he had accepted the rule, the law of work, if he had perfected, schooled and stimulated his own talent! Everything leads us to believe that he would have become a remarkable man of letters. But it is true he would not be the idol of the indolent and the god of the cabarets. That is doubtless a *glory* for which nothing could compensate, not even real glory.

❧ GUSTAVE LE VAVASSEUR

PREFACE

Baudelaire's essay on Le Vavasseur can hardly be called literary criticism. It is rather a nostalgic recollection of the young Norman poet who years before had been one of his closest friends. What the critic says about Le Vavasseur's poetry is favorable enough but so brief that one senses his difficulty in writing about something for which he felt little or no real enthusiasm.

There is little question, however, about the warmth and sincerity of his feeling for the amiable young athlete whom he had known at the Pension Bailly and to whom he had entrusted his manuscripts when he was sent on a voyage by his mother and stepfather in 1841.

Louis-Gustave Le Vavasseur (1819–1896) was a minor Norman poet who came to Paris as a young man to pursue his studies. While living at the Pension Bailly, he founded the *Ecole Normande*, composed of himself, Baudelaire, Prarond, Dozon, and a few others. In collaboration with his friends Prarond and Dozon, he published a volume of verse which met with indifferent success. It is believed that Baudelaire had been asked to share in the venture but that, dissatisfied with the collaborative project, he withdrew at the last moment. In 1929 Jules Mouquet made a study of the collection of poems and concluded on very doubtful evidence that most of Prarond's poems had been written by Baudelaire and that those of Le Vavasseur showed obvious proof of his influence.[44]

After finishing his studies, Le Vavasseur returned to his home at Vire in Normandy where he became a respected and distinguished citizen. He held the office of mayor for thirty-six years, contributed to various literary papers, published five collections of poetry, and wrote a biography of Corneille.[45]

It is many years since I have seen Gustave Le Vavasseur; but I always think back with pleasure to the days when I was his constant companion. I remember that, more than once, on entering his room in the morning I found him, almost naked, balancing precariously on a scaffolding of chairs. He was trying to emulate the tricks which we had seen performed the night before by professional acrobats. The poet admitted to me that he felt envious of all feats of strength and skill, and that he had sometimes had the satisfaction of proving to himself that he was not incapable of *doing the same thing*. But don't think for a moment that, after this admission, the poet appeared ridiculous to me or that I thought less of him; instead, I would have been disposed to praise him for being so frank and so true to his own nature. Moreover, I remembered that many men, whose natures were as rare and noble as his, had felt equally envious of bullfighters, actors, and all those who excite enthusiasm in the circus or the theater by making a glorious public display of their persons.

Gustave Le Vavasseur has always been extremely fond of feats of strength. A difficulty has for him all the enticements of a nymph. He is delighted by obstacles; he is elated by witticisms and puns; there is no music more pleasing to him than that of triple, quadruple, or multiple rhyme. He is *ingenuously complex*. I have never seen a man who was so ostentatiously and so frankly Norman. Thus Pierre Corneille, Brébeuf, Cyrano, inspire more respect and affection in him than in anyone else who might be less fond of the subtle and tortured phrase and of the witticism that epitomizes and explodes like a pyrotechnical display.[46] If one can imagine, joined to this frankly bizarre taste, an extraordinary distinction of heart and mind and learning as solid as it is extensive, one will perhaps be able to get an idea of this poet who has left us and who, long since settled down in his own province, is doubtless bringing to his new and serious duties the same ardent and meticulous zeal that he formerly spent in elaborating his brilliant verses, so metallic in their sonorousness and shimmering light. *Vire et les Virois* is a little masterpiece and the most perfect sample of precious wit, reminiscent of the complicated tricks of fencing, yet not lacking, as some might suppose, in reverie and rhythmic melody. For, it should be repeated, Le Vavasseur is a man of vast intelligence and—let us not forget this—one of the most discriminating and practiced conversationalists that we have known in an age and in a country where conversation may be compared to the lost arts. Animated as it is, his conversation is nonetheless solid, meaty, provocative, and the suppleness of his mind of which he can be as proud as of that of his body, allows him to understand everything, to evaluate everything, to feel everything, even that which, at first sight, appears to be most alien to his nature.

⚜ THE RIDICULOUS MARTYRS
BY LÉON CLADEL

PREFACE

Baudelaire's review of Léon Cladel's *The Ridiculous Martyrs* was first published in the *Revue Fantaisiste* in 1861 and shortly afterwards as a preface to the novel itself in 1862.

From the testimony of Poulet-Malassis and of Cladel himself there is ample evidence that Baudelaire's collaboration was not restricted to the preface alone.[47] The unevenness of the novel with its marked discrepancies of style seems to indicate that it had undergone corrections and revisions by the poet and critic.

Given the mediocrity of the novel, Baudelaire's praise seems rather exaggerated. It can be explained in part by the fact that the critic himself had shared in its creation and even more by the appeal that its subject must have had for him. In the hero of *The Ridiculous Martyrs* Baudelaire obviously recognized much of himself and of his life. Like Alpinien, he was "as prompt to indulge his vices as to curse them"; like him also, he was "a self-confessor who absolves himself and glories in the penance that he inflicts on himself." To read Baudelaire's

Journaux Intimes or his correspondence is to recognize the accuracy of the portrait.

Tied in with the discussion of the novel are a few typical Baudelairean ideas, some of which had found expression in earlier essays. The critic's dissatisfaction with most of the young writers of his day is based on their concern with Realistic art and their failure to realize that it is the "visionary [who] creates reality."

On the subject of morality in art Baudelaire leaves no room for misunderstanding. He takes Cladel to task at one point for failing to remain sufficiently "cold and indifferent" and reminds him that formal moralizing is inimical both to true art and to true morality. In general, however, he is satisfied with the implicit morality of the novel and concludes approvingly that it "springs from the book as naturally as heat from certain chemical mixtures."

Léon Cladel (1835–1892) was a minor novelist who wrote realistic novels describing life in the district formerly known as Le Quercy.

According to Poulet-Malassis Baudelaire's interest in Cladel was short-lived, though he is also known to have corrected the manuscript of *Amours Eternelles* which Cladel had dedicated to him. The collaboration left an enduring impression on the novelist who wrote an interesting account of it in a memoir called "Chez Feu mon Maître." [48]

One of my friends, who is also my publisher, asked me to read this book, assuring me that I would enjoy it.[49] I consented only with the greatest reluctance, for I had been told that the author was a young man, and the young men of today, with their brand-new faults, inspire in me a distrust that is sufficiently justified by those which have distinguished them at all times.

When I am in contact with Youth, I feel the same uneasy sensation as when I meet a forgotten schoolmate, now a speculator on the Stock Exchange, who isn't prevented by the twenty or thirty intervening years from addressing me in familiar fashion and slapping me on the back. In short, I feel that I am in bad company.

However, the friend in question had guessed right; something had pleased him which was to excite me; it was certainly not the first time that I have been mistaken, but I do believe it was the first time that I felt so much pleasure in being mistaken.

In the Parisian gentry there are four distinct categories of young people. The one—rich, stupid, lazy, worshipping no other gods but lechery and gluttony, those muses of disreputable old men—does not concern us in any way. Another—stupid, caring only about money, the third god of old men—is destined to make a fortune and does not interest us any more. Let us go on. There is a third category of young people, who *aspire to make people happy* and who have studied theology and politics in *Le Siècle*.[50] It is usually composed of insignificant lawyers who, like so many others, will succeed in putting on a false front before an audience, in aping Robespierre, and in *declaiming serious* things like him, though doubtless in a style less pure than his, for grammar will soon be as forgotten as reason, and at the rate at which we are progressing toward darkness, there is reason to believe that by the year 1900 we will be plunged into absolute blackness.

The reign of Louis-Philippe, towards its end, was already producing numerous specimens of dull-witted youths who were Epicureans or speculators. The third category, made up of a gang of politicians, sprang from the hope of seeing the *miracles* of February [1848] renewed.

As for the fourth category, I don't know how it originated, although I saw it come into existence. By itself, doubtless, spontaneously, like the infinitesimal microorganisms in a decanter of contaminated water, the great French decanter. It consists of literary youths, *realistic* youths who, emerging from childhood, devote themselves to *realistic* art (we must have new words for new things!). What distinctly characterizes them is a decided, inborn hatred of museums and libraries. Yet they have their classics, Henri Murger and Alfred de Musset in particular.[51] They do not know with what bitter mockery Murger spoke of *Bohemianism;* and as for the *other,* it is not his noble attitudes that they strive to imitate but his fits of self-conceit, his bragging about his indolence, the moments when, strutting like a traveling salesman, chewing a cigar, he would slip away from a dinner at the embassy to go to a casino or to a lively salon. From his complete confidence in genius and inspiration they derive the right not to submit to any mental gymnastics. They don't know that genius (if indeed the indefinable germ of a great man may be called that) must risk breaking its bones a thousand times in private, like a clown learning his trade, before dancing in public; that inspiration, in a word, is only the reward for daily work. They are bad mannered, have stupid love affairs, are as conceited as they are lazy, and pattern their lives on certain novels, just as kept women twenty years ago tried to look like the pictures of Gavarni, who has perhaps never set foot inside a cheap dance hall. Thus the man of intelligence moulds the people and the visionary creates reality. I have known some poor wretches whose heads were turned by Ferragus XXIII and who seriously planned to form a secret coalition in order to share, like a rabble dividing up a conquered empire, all the functions and the wealth of modern society.[52]

It is this pitiable small coterie that M. Léon Cladel wished to portray—with what malicious energy the reader will see. The title, with its antithetical construction, had piqued my curiosity, and little by little as I became absorbed in the manners that were depicted, I appreciated its true significance. I saw passing before my eyes the *martyrs* of stupidity, of conceit, of debauchery, of indolence precariously built on hope, of absurd love affairs, of egoistic wisdom, etc.—all *ridiculous,* but real *martyrs,* since they suffer for the sake of their vices and sacrifice themselves to them with an extraordinary good faith. Then I understood why it had been predicted that the work would fascinate me; I was discovering one of those satiric books, one of those books of *dry humor* whose comic character is all the more intelligible since it is always accompanied by the pomposity which is inseparable from the passions.

All this evil society with its vicious habits, its reckless manners, its incurable illusions, has already been painted by the animated brush of Murger; but the same subject, put in competition, can produce several pictures that are equally remarkable for different reasons. Murger jests in describing things that are often sad. M. Cladel, who lacks neither humor nor pathos, relates with *artistic* solemnity facts that are deplorably comic. Murger slurs over and quickly shrinks away from scenes which would disturb his sensitive spirit, were he to contemplate them too long. M. Cladel is intensely insistent; he does not want to omit a single detail or forget a confidence; he opens the wound to show it better, closes it again, pinches its livid lips and makes a pale, yellow blood spurt out. He handles sin as a keen observer, turns it this way and that, examines the circumstances closely, and displays in the analysis of evil the conscientious fervor of a casuist. Alpinien, the chief *martyr*, does not spare himself; as prompt to indulge his vices as to curse them, he offers in his constant oscillation the instructive spectacle of incurable disease veiled beneath periodic repentance. He is a self-confessor who absolves himself and glories in the penance that he inflicts on himself until he gains, by further stupidity, the honor and the right to condemn himself again. I hope that a few people of our century will be able to recognize themselves in him with pleasure.

The disparity between the tone and the subject, a disparity which is perceptible only to the judicious and disinterested observer, is a comic device whose power is immediately apparent; indeed I am surprised that it is not used more often by painters of manners and by satirists, especially in matters concerning Love, a veritable storehouse of humor that is seldom exploited. Great as one may be, and insignificant as he may be in relation

357

to the infinite, pathos and grandiloquence are permissible and necessary. Humanity is like a colony of those insects of the Hypanis river about which such pretty fables have been written, and the ants themselves can adopt for their political affairs the elevated style of Corneille, proportioned to their size.[53] As for insects in the mating season, I do not consider petty those figures of speech which they use to moan out their passions; every attic hears every evening tragic tirades which will never be useful to the Comédie-Française. M. Cladel's psychological insight is very great; that is his strong point. His art, detailed and blunt, turbulent and fevered, will one day be confined, without any doubt, in a stricter and more dispassionate form which will throw a more intense light on his moral qualities and expose them even more clearly. There are passages where, as a result of this exuberance, one can no longer discern the qualities from the faults. That would be excellent if the fusion were complete; but unfortunately, at the same time that he delights in the exercise of his clear intelligence, his sensibility, furious at having been dammed up, explodes suddenly and indiscreetly. Thus, in one of the best passages in the book he shows us a good man, an honorable and intelligent officer, old before his time, who weakened by anxieties and the dangerous remedy of drink, is exposed to the taunts of his barroom companions. The reader is aware of the former moral grandeur of Pipabs, and this same reader will himself suffer at seeing the martyrdom of this once brave man, smirking, capering, groveling, declaiming, jesting, in order to obtain from his young tormentors . . . what? the charity of a last glass of absinthe. Suddenly the author's indignation is expressed in stentorian tones by one of his characters who quickly puts those jeering daubers in their place. The speech is very eloquent and very stirring; unfortunately, the personal note of the author, his natural revulsion is not sufficiently veiled. The author is still visible under his mask. The highest art would have consisted in remaining cold and indifferent and in leaving all the merit of indignation to the reader. The effect of horror would have been increased. That formal morality benefits therein is indisputable; but art loses thereby, and with true art, true morality: implicit morality never loses anything.

The characters of M. Cladel do not shrink from any confession; they display themselves with a nakedness that is instructive. The women—one, whose animal sweetness, whose emptiness perhaps, gives her a false sphinxlike appearance in the eyes of her bewitched lover; another, an affected modiste, who has lashed her imagination with all the nettles of George Sand—curtsy to each other as in high society and call each other *madame!* with gushy politeness.

Two lovers spend their evening at the *Variétés* and attend *La Vie de Bohême;* returning to their hovel, they quarrel in the style of the play; better still, each of them, forgetting his own personality, or rather confusing it with the character he likes best, lets himself be addressed by the name of the character in question; and neither one nor the other perceives the travesty. Here we have Murger (poor departed soul!) transformed into a spokesman, into a dictionary of the *Bohemian* language, into the *Parfait Secrétaire des Amants* in the year of our Lord 1861. I don't believe that in view of such an incident anyone can dispute M. Cladel's power of sinister caricature. Still another example: Alpinien, the first and foremost *martyr* of this cohort of *ridiculous martyrs* (one must always come back to the title), in order to escape the intolerable misery that results from his immorality, his indolence, and his vagabond reverie, takes it into his head one day to undertake the strangest pilgrimage ever mentioned among the foolish religions invented by idle and impotent recluses. Since love, that is to say dissoluteness, debauchery elevated to the level of a counterreligion, has not brought him the hoped for rewards, Alpinien chases after glory and, wandering in cemeteries, he implores the images of great men who are dead; he kisses their busts, begging them to tell him their secret, the great secret: "What can I do to become as great as you?" If they had been capable of giving good advice, the statues could have answered: "Stay at home, meditate, and scribble on a lot of paper!" But this simple method is beyond the comprehension of an hysterical dreamer. Superstition seems more natural to him. In fact, this story so sadly gay, makes one think of the new calendar of the saints of the *Positivist* School.

Superstition! I said. It plays a great role in the solitary and inner tragedy of poor Alpinien, and it is not without a pleasurable and painful compassion that one sees his tired mind—where the most childish superstition, obscurely symbolizing universal truth as in the brain of nations, is fused with the purest religious sentiments—return to the salutary impressions of childhood, toward the Virgin Mary, toward the fortifying song of the bells, toward the comforting dusk of the Church, toward the family, toward his mother—the mother, always ready to receive with an open heart *failures*, prodigals, and aspiring bunglers! It may be hoped that from that moment on Alpinien is half saved; he needs only to become a man of action, a man of duty day in and day out.

Many people believe that satire is made with tears—sparkling and crystallized tears. In that case, blessed be the tears that furnish the occasion for such delightful and rare laughter, whose very brilliance demonstrates the author's perfect health!

As for the morality of the book, it springs out of it as naturally as heat from certain chemical mixtures. It is permissible to make slaves drunk in order to cure gentlemen of drunkenness.

And as for its success, which is unpredictable, I shall simply say that I desire it, since it might spur the author to new success, but that this success, so easy, moreover, to confuse with a momentary vogue, would not diminish in the slightest all the good that the book leads me to believe will come from the soul and the talent that have conspired to produce it.

❧ SELECTED BIBLIOGRAPHY

Accaputo, Nino. *L'Estetica di Baudelaire e le sue Fonti Germaniche.* Turin, 1961.

Asselineau, Charles. *Charles Baudelaire, sa Vie et son Œuvre.* Paris, Lemerre, 1869. Reprinted in *Baudelaire et Asselineau,* Textes recueillis et commentés par Jacques Crépet et Claude Pichois. Paris, Nizet, 1953.

Austin, Lloyd James. *L'Univers Poétique de Baudelaire.* Paris, Mercure de France, 1956.

Bandy, W. T., et Claude Pichois. *Baudelaire devant ses Contemporains.* Monaco, Editions du Rocher, 1957.

————. *The Influence and Reputation of Edgar Allan Poe in Europe.* Baltimore, Edgar Allan Poe Society, 1962.

————. *Corpus Baudelairiana* (forthcoming). This will be an exhaustive bibliography of works by and about Baudelaire.

Baudelaire, Charles. *Œuvres Complètes de Charles Baudelaire,* ed. Jacques Crépet (in collaboration with Claude Pichois for the three final volumes). 19 vols. Paris, Conard-Lambert, 1922–53. *Les Fleurs du Mal* (1 vol.). *L'Art Romantique* (1 vol.). *Curiosités Esthétiques* (1 vol.). *Petits Poèmes en Prose* (1 vol.). *Les Paradis Artificiels* (1 vol.). *Œuvres Posthumes* (3 vols.). *Histoires Extraordinaires* (1 vol.). *Nouvelles Histoires Extraordinaires* (1 vol.). *Aventures D'Arthur Gordon Pym* (1 vol.). *Eureka* (1 vol.). *Histoires Grotesques et Sérieuses* (1 vol.). *Correspondance Générale* (6 vols.).

————. *Œuvres Complètes de Baudelaire,* ed. S. de Sacy (in collaboration with Claude Pichois). 2 vols. Paris, Club du Meilleur Livre, 1955.

————. *Œuvres Complètes,* ed. Gérard Le Dantec (revised by Claude Pichois). Pléiade Edition. Paris, Gallimard, 1961.

————. *Les Fleurs du Mal,* ed. Antoine Adam. Classiques Garnier. Paris, 1959.

————. *Les Fleurs du Mal,* eds. Jacques Crépet et Georges

Blin. Paris, Corti, 1942. Reprinted with addenda in 1950.

————. *Curiosités Esthétiques, L'Art Romantique et Autres Œuvres Critiques*, ed. Henri Lemaitre. Classiques Garnier. Paris, 1962.

————. *The Mirror of Art*, trans. and ed. Jonathan Mayne (a selection of Baudelaire's essays on art). London, Phaidon; and New York, Doubleday, 1955.

————. *Selected Critical Studies of Baudelaire*, ed. D. Parmée (only the introduction is in English). Cambridge University Press, 1949.

————. *Charles Baudelaire, Critique Littéraire et Musicale*, ed. Claude Pichois. Paris, Colin, 1961.

Billy, André. *Sainte-Beuve, sa Vie et son Temps*. 2 vols. Paris, Flammarion, 1952.

Blin, Georges. *Baudelaire*. Paris, Gallimard, 1939.

————. *Le Sadisme de Baudelaire*. Paris, Corti, 1948.

Butor, Michel. *Histoire Extraordinaire, Essai sur un Rêve de Baudelaire*. Paris, Gallimard, 1961.

Carter, A. E. *Baudelaire et La Critique Française, 1868–1917*. Columbia, University of South Carolina Press, 1963.

Catalogue de L'Exposition Organisée pour le Centenaire des Fleurs du Mal. Paris, Bibliothèque Nationale, 1957.

Crépet, Eugène. *Baudelaire. Etude Biographique*. Revue et complétée par Jacques Crépet. Paris, Messein, 1906. Several reprintings.

Crépet, Jacques. *Propos sur Baudelaire*, ed. Claude Pichois. Paris, Mercure de France, 1957.

Fairlie, Alison. *Baudelaire: Les Fleurs du Mal*. London, Arnold, 1960.

Ferran, André. *L'Esthétique de Baudelaire*. Paris, Hachette, 1933.

Gilman, Margaret. *Baudelaire the Critic*. New York, Columbia University Press, 1943.

————. *The Idea of Poetry in France*. Cambridge, Harvard University Press, 1958.

Hubert, J. D. *L'Esthétique des Fleurs du Mal*. Geneva, Cailler, 1953.

Huyghe, René, et alii. *Baudelaire*. Paris, Hachette, 1961.

Hyslop, Lois Boe and Francis E. *Baudelaire on Poe.* State College, Pa., Bald Eagle Press, 1952.
————. *Baudelaire: A Self-Portrait.* London and New York, Oxford University Press, 1957.
Jones, Mansell. *Baudelaire.* New Haven, Yale University Press, 1952; and Cambridge, Bowes and Bowes, 1952.
Laforgue, Dr. René. *The Defeat of Baudelaire.* London, Hogarth Press, 1932.
Massin, Abbé Jean. *Baudelaire entre Dieu et Satan.* Paris, Juillard, 1946.
Mossop, D. J. *Baudelaire's Tragic Hero.* London, Oxford University Press, 1961.
Mouquet, Jules, et W. T. Bandy. *Baudelaire en 1848.* Paris, Emile-Paul, 1946.
Peyre, Henri. *Connaissance de Baudelaire.* Paris, Corti, 1951.
————. *Baudelaire, A Collection of Critical Essays,* ed. Henri Peyre, Englewood Cliffs, N. J., Prentice-Hall, 1962.
Pichois, Claude, et François Ruchon. *Iconographie de Charles Baudelaire.* Geneva, Cailler, 1960.
Pommier, Jean. *La Mystique de Baudelaire.* Paris, Les Belles Lettres, 1932.
————. *Dans les Chemins de Baudelaire.* Paris, Corti, 1945.
Porché, François. *Baudelaire: Histoire d'une Âme.* Paris, Flammarion, 1945.
Prévost, Jean. *Baudelaire. Essai sur l'Inspiration et la Création Poétiques.* Paris, Mercure de France, 1953.
Proust, Marcel. *On Art and Literature,* trans. Sylvia Townsend Warner. New York, Meridian, 1958.
Quennell, Peter. *Baudelaire and the Symbolists* (new edition). London, Chatto and Windus, 1955.
Raymond, Marcel. *From Baudelaire to Surrealism.* New York, Wittenborn, 1950.
Rhodes, S. A. *The Cult of Beauty in Charles Baudelaire.* 2 vols. New York, Institute of French Studies, Columbia University, 1929.
Ruff, Marcel. *L'Esprit du Mal et l'Esthétique Baudelairienne.* Paris, Colin, 1955.

————. *Baudelaire, l'Homme et l'Œuvre*. Paris, Hatier-Boivin, 1955.

Sartre, Jean Paul. *Baudelaire*, trans. Martin Turnell. London, Horizon, 1949; and New York, New Directions, 1950.

Starkie, Enid. *Baudelaire*. London, Faber and Faber, 1957; and New York, New Directions, 1958.

Tabarant, Adolphe. *La Vie Artistique au Temps de Baudelaire* (new edition). Paris, Mercure de France, 1963.

Turnell, Martin. *Baudelaire. A Study of His Poetry*. London, Hamilton, 1953; and New York, New Directions, 1954.

Vivier, Robert. *L'Originalité de Baudelaire* (new edition). Brussels, Académie Royale, 1953.

Vouga, Daniel. *Baudelaire et Joseph de Maistre*. Paris, Corti, 1957.

⚘ LIST OF ABBREVIATIONS

For the sake of simplicity, the following abbreviations will be used for reference to the Crépet-Pichois edition of Baudelaire.

AGP   *Aventures D'Arthur Gordon Pym*

AR   *L'Art Romantique*

CE   *Curiosités Esthétiques*

CG   *Correspondance Générale* (6 vols.)

E   *Eureka*

FM   *Les Fleurs du Mal*

HE   *Histoires Extraordinaires*

HGS   *Histoires Grotesques et Sérieuses*

NHE   *Nouvelles Histoires Extraordinaires*

OP   *Œuvres Posthumes* (3 vols.; vol. 2 contains the *Journaux Intimes.*)

PA   *Les Paradis Artificiels*

PPP   *Petits Poèmes en Prose*

≪ NOTES
ᐠ TO THE INTRODUCTION

1. AR, p. 219.
2. CG, V, 21.
3. CG, V, 281.
4. See Randolph Hughes, "Baudelaire et Balzac," *Mercure de France* (November, 1934), pp. 476–518.
5. AR, pp. 168–169.
6. Henri Peyre, *Connaissance de Baudelaire* (Paris, 1951), p. 27.
7. AR, p. 153.
8. CG, IV, 52, note 1.
9. AR, p. 22.
10. Jacques Crépet, *Propos sur Baudelaire*, ed. Claude Pichois (Paris, 1957), p. 46.
11. Baudelaire's relation to Stendhal is also discussed by Jean Pommier in *Dans les Chemins de Baudelaire* (Paris, 1945), and by Henri Lemaitre in *Curiosités Esthétiques, l'Art Romantique* (Paris, 1962).
12. CG, III, 38.
   For Baudelaire and Musset, see Jean Pommier, "Baudelaire et Musset," *Mélanges d'histoire littéraire et de bibliographie offerts à Jean Bonnerot* (Paris, 1954), pp. 355–364.
13. CG, V, 75.
   For Baudelaire and Dumas *père*, see Jean Dagens and Claude Pichois, "Baudelaire, Alexandre Dumas et le Haschisch," *Mercure de France* (October 1957), pp. 357–364.
14. CG, II, 66.
15. CG, II, 358.
16. In a letter to Ancelle (February 6, 1866), just a few days before he wrote the letter listing the writers who did not belong to the "modern rabble," Baudelaire indicated that he was planning to publish an article entitled "Sainte-Beuve or Joseph Delorme judged by the author of *Les Fleurs du Mal*." CG, V, 250.
17. Peyre, *Connaissance de Baudelaire*, p. 145.
18. AR, p. 199.
19. AR, p. 238
20. CE, p. 287.
21. CE, p. 223.
22. AR, p. 209.
23. AR, p. 198.
24. CE, p. 88.
25. CE, p. 197.
26. AR, p. 69.
27. NHE, p. XXI.
28. AR, p. 239; AR, p. 8.
29. *Chivers' Life of Poe*, ed. Richard Beale Davis (New York, 1952), p. 96.
30. AR, p. 66; CE, p. 199.
31. CE, pp. 77–78; CE, p. 197.

32. CE, p. 200.
33. FM, p. 369.
34. CE, p. 224.
35. AR, p. 172.
36. OP, II, 63–64.
37. W. T. Bandy, "New Light on Baudelaire and Poe," *Yale French Studies*, No. 10 (1953).
38. See Marcel Ruff, *Œuvres Complètes de Baudelaire* (Paris, Club du Meilleur Livre, 1955), II, 9.
39. For Baudelaire at the time of the Revolution of 1848, see Jules Mouquet et W. T. Bandy, *Baudelaire en 1848* (Paris, 1946).
40. AR, p. 9; AR, p. 399.
41. OP, I, 299.
42. CE, pp. 272–273.
43. AR, p. 96.
44. CG, I, 322–323.
45. PA, p. 69.
46. CG, III, 168.
47. CE, p. 310; CE, p. 275.
48. AR, p. 15; CE, p. 280.
49. PA, p. 161.
50. CE, p. 142.
51. HE, p. XXVII; PA, pp. 178–179.
52. "Le Parfum" in the sonnet sequence Un Fantôme (FM, p. 63).
53. Marcel Proust, *Le Temps Retrouvé* (Paris, Gallimard, 1949), p. 73. Elsewhere (in *Contre Sainte-Beuve*, which has been translated as *On Art and Literature*), Proust calls Baudelaire "the greatest poet of the nineteenth century" and criticizes Sainte-Beuve for failing to recognize the quality of imagination in *Les Fleurs du Mal*.
54. CE, p. 163.
55. PA, p. 161; AR, p. 60.
   Matisse expressed an analogous attitude when he wrote many years later: "I should like to recapture that freshness of vision which is characteristic of extreme youth, when all the world is new to it." (A. E. Gallatin, *Of Art*, New York, 1945, p. 16.)
56. CG, I, 368; NHE, p. XV.
57. AR, p. 206.
58. Lloyd James Austin, *L'Univers Poétique de Baudelaire* (Paris, 1956), p. 172 et passim.
59. Margaret Gilman, "From Imagination to Immediacy in French Poetry," *The Romanic Review* (February, 1948), pp. 30–49. See also her books, *Baudelaire the Critic* and *The Idea of Poetry in France*.
60. See note 37.
61. CE, p. 168.
62. For a discussion of Mrs. Crowe, see G. T. Clapton, "Baudelaire and Catherine Crowe," *Modern Language Review*, XXV (1930), 286–305.
   See also Margaret Gilman, *Baudelaire the Critic*, p. 241, note 11.
63. AR, p. 9.
64. Ibid.
65. CE, p. 88; CE, p. 262.
66. AR, p. 165.

67. CG, I, 404; CG, V, 36.
68. AR, p. 320.
69. FM, p. 374.
70. CG, III, 338.
71. NHE, pp. XX and XXI.
72. AR, p. 355.
73. AR, p. 119.
74. AR, pp. 184–185; AR, p. 297.
75. AR, p. 284.
76. Joseph de Maistre (1753–1821), author of *Les Soirées de Saint-Pétersbourg*, made a very powerful impression on Baudelaire's mind. In his *Journaux Intimes* he wrote: "De Maistre and Edgar Poe taught me how to think" (OP, II, 79). De Maistre combined political conservatism with theological doctrines about original sin that appealed to Baudelaire's sense of omnipresent evil forces in man and nature. For an extended discussion, see Daniel Vouga, *Baudelaire et Joseph de Maistre* (Paris, 1957).
77. NHE, p. XX.
78. AR, p. 401.
79. CG, IV, 198.
80. OP, I, 330.
81. PA, p. 240.

🎴 NOTES
TO THE TEXT

1. See commentary on Baudelaire's review of *Stories by Champfleury*.
2. CE, pp. 465–466.
3. In his notes on *Les Liaisons Dangereuses* Baudelaire writes, "A great man is never a meteorite" (OP, I, 331).
4. S.–G. Chevalier (1804–1866), who called himself Gavarni, was a notable lithographer and caricaturist of the period.
5. Although Baudelaire praised Haussoullier very highly in the *Salon of 1845* and defends his praise here, he never discussed his work again. Recently Jonathan Mayne discovered Haussoullier's picture in England and published it in his excellent illustrated edition of Baudelaire's art criticism, *The Mirror of Art*.
6. Raoul Rochette (1789–1854), an archaeologist of the day.
7. The passage from the German writer Ernst Hoffmann (1776–1822), whose fantastic stories Baudelaire admired, expresses very well his own sense of physical and spiritual analogies and correspondences. The theory of correspondences is one of the keys to Baudelaire's aesthetics.
8. Raphaël de Valentin is the hero of Balzac's *La Peau de Chagrin*.
9. Hero of a play of the same name (1831) by Dumas *père*.
10. The reference is to Lacenaire who was executed in the prison of La Grande Roquette where the Abbé Montès was a chaplain.
11. Fontanarès was the hero of Balzac's play *Les Ressources de Quinola* (1842), set in the 16th century; the others are heroes from Balzac's novels.
12. Some years later Baudelaire wrote extensive notes on *Les Liaisons Dangereuses* by Choderlos de Laclos, but they were never developed for publication. It may be noted that three of the authors mentioned are German. Nino Accaputo has stressed (probably too much) the influence of German idealism on Baudelaire in his recent book, *L'Estetica di Baudelaire e le sue Fonti Germaniche* (Turin, 1961).

    The work of the Reverend C. R. Maturin (1782–1824) also had an especial appeal for Baudelaire. Maturin is best known for *Melmoth the Wanderer* and *Bertram*.
13. Emile Deroy (1823–1846), an intimate friend of Baudelaire who painted the remarkable portrait of the poet that hangs in the Versailles Museum.
14. The French, English, and Russian navies defeated the Turkish fleet at Navarin in 1827.
15. See the prefatory note to Baudelaire's essay on Auguste Barbier, published in 1861.
16. It is generally agreed that this is an allusion to his stepfather, General Aupick.
17. Victor Cousin (1792–1867) was a brilliant lecturer at the Sorbonne and an eclectic philosopher who exercised great influence on French thought.
18. The Spanish play to which Baudelaire refers is Calderón's *El Mágico Prodigioso*.

19. A few years later Baudelaire wrote the poems entitled "L'Irréparable" (1855) and "L'Irrémediable" (1857).
20. René, the hero of a highly romantic tale by Chateaubriand (1768–1848) which introduced the *mal du siècle* into French literature. In a poem to Sainte-Beuve (1844) Baudelaire had written very differently about René (CG, I, 61–64).
Obermann, hero of a Romantic novel of the same name by Etienne Senancour (1770–1846).
Werther, the hero of a novel of the same name by Goethe which had an important influence on French literature in the early 19th century.
21. Pierre–Joseph Proudhon (1809–1865), author of *Avertissement aux Propriétaires*, was a socialist philosopher who made a strong impression on Baudelaire at the time of the Revolution of 1848. Baudelaire soon lost interest in his ideas and later in life wrote some rather sarcastic comments about him to his friends.
22. Emile Augier (1820–1889), popular playwright, author of *Gabrielle, Le Gendre de M. Poirier*, and *Le Fils de Giboyer*.
23. Louis Reybaud (1799–1879) author of the satirical novel *Jérôme Paturot à la Recherche d'une Position sociale* (1843) and its sequel *Jérôme Paturot à la Recherche de la Meilleure République* (1848).
Pierre Leroux (1797–1871), a socialistically minded idealist and author whose pantheistic views influenced some of the novels of George Sand
Eugène Viollet-le-Duc (1814–1879), architect and writer, is best known for his books on medieval architecture and his restorations of medieval buildings.
24. Hippolyte Castille, an obscure journalist who was one of Baudelaire's friends. He is reported to have said at one time: "That Baudelaire is a touchstone: he is invariably disliked by fools." See *Baudelaire devant ses Contemporains*, Bandy and Pichois (Monaco, 1957), p. 1.
25. Arnaud Berquin (1749?–1791), author of children's books that were still being read in the 19th century.
26. Emile Augier had won the Montyon Prize from the Academy for his verse play *Gabrielle* (1849), which Baudelaire ridicules at the beginning of his article.
27. *Reisebilder.*
28. Four years earlier, in 1848, Baudelaire had written: "No more tragedies, no more Roman history. Aren't we greater than Brutus?" (OP, I, 198). The same rejection of classicism is evident in the *Salon of 1846* in which he puts Balzac above Homer.
29. It has been suggested that the reference may be to Louis Ménard.
30. Cimabue (1240?–1302?), early Florentine painter.
31. The opposition to images expressed here seems inconsistent with everything else that Baudelaire ever wrote on the subject. In the *Salon of 1859* he wrote: "From my earliest youth, my eyes filled with paintings or engravings, could never be satisfied, and I think that worlds could come to an end, *impavidum ferient*, before I would become an iconoclast" (CE, pp. 279–280), and in his *Journaux Intimes* he noted: "Glorification of the cult of images (my great, my sole, my first passion)." (OP, II, 114).
Perhaps the "Moslem rage" against images was the result of a

momentary surfeit of visual experiences. As Baudelaire says in *Advice to Young Men of Letters*, "All true men of letters abhor literature at certain times. . . ."

Henri Lemaitre has argued that Baudelaire's objection is to an empty, formalistic kind of art resulting from "an immoderate love of form." See Henri Lemaitre, *Curiosités Esthétiques, L'Art Romantique*, Classiques Garnier (Paris, 1962), p. LIX.

32. Johann J. Winckelmann (1717–1768), German archaeologist and writer, the author of an influential history of ancient art.

33. This comment did not appear in Baudelaire's article in 1855 and seems to have been added after the publication of Pierre Leroux's poem, *La Grève de Samarez*, in 1863. CE, pp. 483–484.

34. Gustave Courbet (1819–1877), the Realist painter was on friendly terms with Baudelaire for several years, beginning in 1848 when he painted his first portrait of the poet. Within a few years temperamental and doctrinal differences brought their close association to an end.

35. Max Buchon, minor Realist poet and friend of Courbet, who translated the works of the German dramatist and poet, Friedrich Hebbel.

36. François Bonvin (1817–1887), minor Realistic painter admired by Baudelaire.

37. Antoine-Auguste Préault (1809–1879) was a sculptor who at one time formed part of the circle around Courbet. Although Baudelaire was not fond of sculpture, he enjoyed Préault's brilliant conversation.

38. This sentence is presumably an allusion to Courbet's second portrait of Baudelaire, which has a prominent place in Courbet's canvas, *The Painter's Studio*, and which seemed to ally him with the Realistic School.

39. Jacques de Vaucanson (1709–1782), a designer of automatons.

40. PA, p. 161.

41. OP, I, 268.

42. W. T. Bandy, "New Light on Baudelaire and Poe," *Yale French Studies*, No. 10 (1953).

43. OP, I, 263.

44. *The Centennial Celebration of Baudelaire's Les Fleurs du Mal* (Austin, University of Texas Press, 1958), p. 32.

45. CG, I, 380.

46. From Baudelaire's prose translation of *The Raven*. Baudelaire translated only three other poems of Poe: the sonnet "To my Mother," used as the dedication to *Histoires Extraordinaires*; and "The Haunted Palace" in *The Fall of the House of Usher*.

47. "On his throne of brass, mocking Destiny soaks their sponge in bitter gall, and Necessity twists them in its vise."

48. The Goncourt brothers in their *Journal* mention a convict thus tattooed. OP, I, 568.

49. The tercet is from Gautier's *Ténèbres*. The lines may refer to an ancient legend that an eagle dropped a tortoise on the head of Aeschylus.

50. The biographers and critics were P. Pendleton Cooke, James Russell Lowell—so it is thought—and Nathaniel P. Willis.

51. Rufus Griswold edited Poe's works (Redfield edition) after the poet's death.

George Graham, editor of *Graham's Magazine,* published in Philadelphia.

52. It is thought that the "philosopher of figures" was Emile de Girardin (1806–1881), publisher of the popular newspaper, *La Presse,* and of various journalistic books.

53. Poe was born in Boston in 1809.

54. It was Poe's brother Henry who went to Greece (HE, p. 408).

55. John P. Kennedy, popular novelist, author of *Horse Shoe Robinson.* At one time he was Secretary of the Navy.

56. Poe was really forty at the time of his death.

57. Juvenal, *Satire X,* verse 167.

58. Gérard de Nerval (1808–1855), poet and prose writer who is now being increasingly recognized as one of the great poets of the 19th century. He has been called a precursor of 20th century "hallucinatory" writing.

59. John Neal (1793–1876), novelist and critic of American literature and art.

60. Baudelaire wrote a long dedication to Mrs. Clemm when his translations began to appear serially in *Le Pays,* in 1854. A shorter dedication, followed by a translation of Poe's poem "To my Mother" was used when the first volume of translations, *Histoires Extraordinaires,* appeared in 1856.

It is sometimes believed that his admiration for Mrs. Clemm was increased by the failure of his own mother to fully appreciate his literary ambitions.

61. The phrenological interpretation of Poe is based on the theories of Johann Lavater (1741–1801). See G. T. Clapton, "Lavater, Gall et Baudelaire," *Revue de Littérature Comparée,* XIII, Avril–Juin (1933), 259–298.

Presumably Baudelaire had in mind Sartain's engraving in the Redfield edition. Poe himself once wrote: "Phrenology is no longer to be laughed at."

62. The phrase "a worm that would not die" comes from Poe's *Morella.*

63. Delacroix, to whom Baudelaire gave a copy of his translations, did not relish the comparison with Poe.

64. NHE, p. 378.

65. OP, II, 84.

66. HE, p. 438.

67. E, p. 233.

68. AR, p. 170.

69. E, p. 154.

70. Critic Armand de Pontmartin is supposed to have been one of the "unenigmatic sphinxes."

71. Cf. Baudelaire's poem. "Le Coucher de Soleil Romantique." FM, p. 247.

72. The critic Barbey d'Aurevilly (who was the first to speak of the "secret architecture" of *Les Fleurs du Mal*) had referred to Poe as a *jongleur.*

73. "Marginalia," CCXXIX.

74. *Le Diable Amoureux* was written by Jacques Cazotte (1719–1792).

75. "Marginalia," CCXLII.

76. Allamistakeo appears in Poe's story, "Some Words with a Mummy."
77. *Italiam fugientem,* from Virgil, *Aeneid,* Book V, lines 628–629.
78. "Marginalia," CCXXXVI.
79. Vitzilipoutzli, a misspelling of Widzipudzili, an Aztec god, the personification of war, mentioned by Musset in the manuscript version of the dedication of *La Coupe et les Lèvres.*

    Teutatès, the god of the Gauls to whom human sacrifices were made.
80. A garbled version of a passage in an article published in *Le Pays,* January 26, 1855.
81. This passage was taken from "The Poetic Principle" by Poe.
82. "Marginalia," CCXXXIX.
83. The next few pages are a translation and adaptation from "The Poetic Principle."
84. The discussion of *The Raven* is based on Poe's article, "The Philosophy of Composition." Baudelaire translated both "The Philosophy of Composition" and *The Raven* (in prose) and prefaced them with an interesting short note entitled "The Genesis of a Poem."
85. In early French poetry the term is used of lines in which the final rhyme is found again within the line. The name is derived from Léon de Saint-Victor who set the fashion of such verses.
86. Robert Kanters, "Je Considère le Poète comme le meilleur des Critiques," *Baudelaire* (Collection Génies et Réalités, Paris, 1961), pp. 198–199.
87. AR, p. 563.
88. Margaret Gilman, *Baudelaire the Critic* (New York, 1943), p. 99.

    See also, "Two Critics and an Author: *Madame Bovary* judged by Sainte-Beuve and by Baudelaire," *The French Review* (December, 1941), pp. 138–146.
89. Flaubert, *Selected Letters,* trans. and ed. Francis Steegmuller (New York, 1954), p. 138.
90. CG, IV, 129.
91. This is an allusion to Baudelaire's own unhappy experience with the French court that had condemned six of the poems of *Les Fleurs du Mal* and fined him 300 francs for having offended public morality.
92. The Marquis de Custine (1790–1857) was among the few who supported Baudelaire in 1857 at the time of his prosecution for *Les Fleurs du Mal.* The poet admired him as an embodiment of the dandy.
93. Charles Barbara (1822–1866), minor writer and friend of the poet.
94. Féval, Soulié, and Sue were popular novelists of the day. Of the three, Eugène Sue was the most popular and most admired for his melodramatic and often tendentious novels. He is best known as the author of *Les Mystères de Paris* (1842–1843) and *Le Juif Errant* (1844–1845).
95. Paul de Kock, another popular author whose comic and sentimental novels were widely read both in England and France.
96. Although more than one half of *La Tentation de Saint Antoine* had appeared in *L'Artiste,* it was not published in book form until 1874.
97. CG, II, 345.
98. Letter to his mother, CG, II, 66.

99. Jacques Crépet, *Propos sur Baudelaire*, ed. Claude Pichois (Paris, 1957), p. 19.
100. Georges Poulet, *Etudes sur le Temps Humain* (Paris, 1950), p. 305.
101. AR, p. 488.
102. *Méditations Poétiques* (1820) and *Harmonies Poétiques et Religieuses* (1830) by Lamartine.
103. Probably the volume entitled *Vers* (1843), written by Prarond, Le Vavasseur, and Dozon, three friends of Baudelaire who had invited him to contribute to the collection.
104. Hugo, *Les Voix Intérieures*, XVI, "Passé."
105. *Les Jeunes-France* (1833), a novel in which Gautier gaily satirized the group of flamboyant, young Romantics of whom he had been a leader for a short time.
106. The long quotation, taken from "New Notes on Edgar Poe" (1857), is a translation and paraphrase of passages from Poe's essay, "The Poetic Principle."
107. The page that follows is basically a repetition of ideas expressed in "The Respectable Drama and Novel."
108. Emile Augier.
109. The reference is to *L'Amour* (1858) by Jules Michelet, the eminent historian (1798–1874).
110. Lines from an unidentified poem.
111. M. Coquelet, a figure who appears in Gavarni's lithographs. M. Pipelet, a concierge in Eugène Sue's *Les Mystères de Paris*.
112. The familiar lines are from Poe's poem "To Helen."
113. The brief discussion of the English painters recurs in the *Salon of 1859*.
    For Kendall, see F. W. Leakey, "Baudelaire and Kendall," *Revue de Littérature Comparée*, Janvier-Mars (1956), 53–63.
114. Terence, *The Self-Tormentor*, I, 1, 25.
    Terence's word order is not exactly that of Baudelaire's version.
115. PA, p. 58.
116. Baudelaire's praise of Delacroix came at a time when the artist was still under heavy attack. One critic had written: "This is a painful spectacle. We are at the deathbed of a genius." By way of appreciation Delacroix wrote an exceptionally cordial note to Baudelaire, thanking him for treating his work as if it were that of a "great painter of the past," and adding, "you put something of yourself in everything you do." CE, p. 493.
117. PA, p. 53.
118. For Catherine Crowe, see G. T. Clapton, "Baudelaire and Catherine Crowe," *Modern Language Review*, XXV, No. 3 (1930), 286–305.
119. See Joseph C. Sloane, "Baudelaire, Chenavard, and 'Philosophic Art,'" *Journal of Aesthetics and Art Criticism*, XIII, No. 3 (March, 1955), 285–299; also Sloane's book, *Paul Chenavard* (Chapel Hill, University of North Carolina Press, 1962).
120. CE, p. 169.
121. The article to which Baudelaire refers had appeared in 1852. M. Fétis, the author of *Biographie Universelle des Musiciens*, was one of the leading critics of the day.
122. Paul Scudo (1806–1864), music critic of the *Revue des Deux Mondes*.

123. Passage taken from Liszt's *Lohengrin et Tannhäuser* (1851). Baudelaire was a friend and admirer of Liszt and dedicated his prose poem, "Le Thyrse," to him.
124. "Correspondances."
125. Cf. Baudelaire's strong belief in the dual nature of man: "There is in every man and at all times two simultaneous impulses, the one toward God, the other toward Satan." OP, II, 93.
126. The Princess de Metternich, wife of the Austrian ambassador, who apparently did not read the brochure that Baudelaire had sent to her. OP, II, 95.
127. Writers other than M. Franck Marie, among them Champfleury, also protested against the discourteous reception of the opera.
128. The play to which Baudelaire refers was *Les Funérailles de l'Honneur* by Auguste Vacquerie.
129. *Tannhäuser* was not performed in Paris again until 1895.
130. CG, III, 81.
131. CG, V, 39–40.
132. CE, p. 105.
133. See *Théophile Gautier* and *Salon of 1859*.
134. Charles Fourier (1772–1837), a theoretician of social reform, author of *Théorie de l'Unité Universelle*.
135. Emmanuel Swedenborg (1688–1772), whose ideas on correspondences were strongly influential on Baudelaire's thinking.
136. Ezekiel 3:1–3.
137. Juvenal, *Satire I*, verse 79.
138. Allusion to the poem, "Melpomène," in his volume *Iambes* in which Barbier attacks the immorality of Romantic drama.
139. Two popular poets of the period whose works were known for their sentimentality.
140. An allusion to an obscure writer, Mathieu Dairnvaell, who had collaborated with Baudelaire about twenty years earlier in writing *Mystères Galans*.
141. From *Médée*, Corneille's first tragedy.
142. Alexandre Erdan (1826–1878), an anticlerical journalist who campaigned for phonetic spelling.
143. Hippolyte Delaroche (1797–1856), fashionable, academic painter. Casimir Delavigne (1793–1843), popular dramatist and poet.
144. *Les Cariatides*, written in 1841, but not published until 1842.
145. Although Baudelaire once reproached Jules Janin for excluding sadness and horror as sources of literary inspiration, he himself returned to the theme of felicitous moments on several occasions (OP, II, 62). See also his praise of Delacroix for painting "the soul in its beautiful hours" (CE, p. 298). It will be remembered that he blames Moreau for not deliberately "recalling happy hours."
146. Sainte-Beuve; article on Senancour in *Portraits Contemporains*.
147. Cf. Baudelaire's poem "Elévation."
148. Cf. Baudelaire's prose poem "La Chambre Double."
149. Cf. Baudelaire's poem "La Vie Antérieure."
150. A fundamental principle of Baudelaire's own poetic art.
151. J. P. Florian (1755–1794), author of pastoral romances, fables, etc.

152. Baudelaire had done something analogous in his poem "L'Invitation au Voyage."
153. AR, p. 557.
154. For Scheffer (1795–1858), conventional Romantic painter, see Baudelaire's comments in Chapter XIII of the *Salon of 1846*.
    Peter Cornelius (1783–1867), German painter of mural pictures of historical subjects.
155. For Asselineau's comments, see Eugène Crépet, *Baudelaire* (Paris, 1906), p. 301.
    For Baudelaire's remarks to his mother, see his letter of August 10, 1862 (CG, IV, 100).
156. Probably the Abbé Jean-Baptiste Marduel, parish priest of Saint-Roch from 1749 to 1787, or the nephew who succeeded him.
157. In a letter to M. de Saint-Réal, Joseph de Maistre had written: "I don't know what a scoundrel's life is like; I have never been one; but a decent man's life is abominable" (AR, p. 562).
158. Later in the essay Baudelaire compares Guys to La Bruyère.
159. Baudelaire once wrote of the Marquis de Sade: "It is always necessary to come back to de Sade, that is to *natural man*, in order to explain evil" (OP, III, 12).
160. *De l'Amour*, Chap. XVII.
161. Here Baudelaire is simply restating the theories expressed in *Les Soirées de Saint-Pétersbourg* by Joseph de Maistre.
162. Baudelaire's statement that fashion is a sublime deformation of nature has a startling similarity to a remark made by Gauguin: "Nature may be violated and brought, by sublime deformation, to a permanent beauty" (A. E. Gallatin, *Of Art*, New York, 1945, p. 11).
    The painter, who was not afraid of arbitrary color, would have been delighted by Baudelaire's statement: "I should like to see fields colored red and trees painted blue. Nature has no imagination." This comment, reported by Jules Levallois, in *Mémoires d'un Critique* (AR, p. 464) is really based on a remark made by Pétrus Borel in *Champavert*, according to Enid Starkie. These views are clearly the basis of much modern theorizing about art.
163. Baudelaire was expressing the same idea in a negative way when he said: "Woman is *natural*, that is to say abominable" (OP, II, 87).

✠ NOTES
TO THE APPENDIX

1. Letter written in March, 1864 (CG, VI, 52).
2. Mme. de Scudéry (1607–1701), minor writer, best known as the author of *Le Grand Cyrus*.
3. OP, I, 492.
4. The title of a novel by Balzac.
5. According to a note of the Vicomte Spoelberch de Lovenjoul (*Un Dernier Chapitre de l'Histoire des Œuvres de M. de Balzac*, 1880), the rich businessman was the publisher Curmer.
6. The "small young man" was Edouard Ourliac, one of Baudelaire's earliest acquaintances in the literary world. Years later, in his essay on Pétrus Borel, Baudelaire called Ourliac a "small-town Voltaire."
7. The Rue de Navarin was the street on which Gautier lived.
8. The lover of tomcats was Gérard de Nerval. The reference to the Opéra-Comique is an allusion to Nerval's love for the actress, Jenny Colon.
9. In his early years Baudelaire did not think highly of Gautier as a journalist. Later, Baudelaire dedicated *Les Fleurs du Mal* to Gautier, calling him an "impeccable poet" and a "perfect magician."
10. Baudelaire's reference to an Indian necklace may have been prompted by his interest in the American painter Catlin. In the French text Baudelaire refers specifically to the Osage Indians. See also Robert Beetem, "George Catlin in France: his relationship to Delacroix and Baudelaire," *Art Quarterly*, XXIV, No. 2 (Summer, 1961), 129–145.
11. FM, pp. 362–363.
12. Edgar Quinet (1803–1875), liberal-minded historian who also wrote some philosophical poems, one of which was entitled *Prométhée*.
13. Papety and Scheffer were popular academic painters. See Chapter XIII of the *Salon of 1846*.
14. Paul Holbach (1723–1789), materialistic philosopher who was associated with the Encyclopedists.
15. Marc Désaugiers (1772–1827), popular poet and song writer associated with Le Caveau, a literary and social club.
16. Mme. de Warens (1700–1762), a kind woman of easy morals who was Rousseau's protectress from 1729 to about 1742.
17. According to Crépet, this paragraph is based on a statement in Emerson's *The Conduct of Life* (AR, p. 527).
    For Baudelaire's relation to Emerson, see Margaret Gilman, "Baudelaire and Emerson," *The Romanic Review*, July–September, 1935, pp. 211–244.
18. The writers in question were the popular novelists, Eugène Sue and Paul Féval.
19. Jules Janin (1804–1874), a successful drama critic and academician, heartily disliked by Baudelaire.
20. Editor of *Le Globe* (1806–1880).
21. The text of 1846 reads: "the frequently mediocre articles" (AR, p. 529).

378

22. *Kean, ou Désordre et Génie*, by Alexandre Dumas *père*, was produced in 1836. Sartre adapted this play for the drama of the same name that he wrote in 1954.
23. Unfortunately, Baudelaire's own mistress, Jeanne Duval, belonged in the first category.
24. The print maker of Champfleury's story was Rodolphe Bresdin (1822–1885) who adopted the name Chingachgook from James Fenimore Cooper's novel, *The Last of the Mohicans*. In garbled French it became Chien-Caillou. In 1861 Baudelaire wrote a letter to Gautier urging him to welcome Bresdin, who was returning to Paris after an absence of twelve years, and to study his work (CG, III, 273–274).

    Bresdin was one of Odilon Redon's teachers. According to Redon, Gautier's poem *La Comédie de la Mort* was inspired by one of Bresdin's lithographs, but it seems obvious that the reverse was true. The poem was written in 1838 and the print was done in 1854.

    For information on Bresdin, see the Catalogue of the Redon-Moreau-Bresdin Exhibition at the Museum of Modern Art (New York, 1962). An important exhibition of Bresdin's work was held at the Bibliothèque Nationale in 1963.
25. Henri Monnier (1799–1877), actor, writer and caricaturist. He created the comic figure, M. Prudhomme. Baudelaire wrote about his work in an article, "Quelques Caricaturistes Français," published in 1857.
26. *Le Compère Mathieu* was written by Henri de Laurens (1719–1797) in the libertine spirit of the 18th century.
27. OP, I, 230.
28. The book had the subtitle *Symphonie Fantastique*.
29. For Asselineau, see *Baudelaire et Asselineau*, eds. J. Crépet and C. Pichois (Paris, 1953).
30. CG, I, 372–377.
31. Jean-Paul Richter (1763–1825), German writer.
32. Ovid, *Tristia*, V, 10, 37.
33. "Thou art the Man," the title of a story by Poe.
34. To celebrate the centenary of her death, the Bibliothèque Nationale organized an important exhibition of her work in 1959.

    For further information see Eliane Jasenas, *Marceline Desbordes-Valmore devant la Critique* (Geneva, 1962).
35. Probably an allusion to his attachment to his own mother.
36. Jean-Paul Richter whose work *Titan* was adapted in French by Philarète Chasles in 1835.
37. "A l'Arc de Triomphe," from *Les Voix Intérieures*.
38. Antony, the first of a long line of infamous heroes in a drama of the same name by Dumas *père* (1831).

    Didier, hero of Hugo's play *Marion de Lorme* (composed in 1829 but not performed until 1831).
39. Claude Frollo, archdeacon in Hugo's novel *Notre Dame de Paris*.

    F. R. de Lamennais (1782–1854), religious writer of unorthodox views who finally broke away from the church.
40. Auguste Barthélemy (1796–1867), writer known for his satiric pen.
41. Jacques Delille (1778–1813), popular writer and translator of Virgil and Milton.
42. Pierre Béranger (1780–1857) and Marc Désaugiers (1772–1827),

popular poets and song writers associated with the literary and social club called Le Caveau.

43. Frédéric Soulié (1800–1847), a writer who struggled to make a living in business to compensate for his lack of recognition as a writer.

44. See Jules Mouquet, *Charles Baudelaire, Vers Retrouvés* (Paris, 1929).

45. Professor W. T. Bandy has just discovered an article on Baudelaire's *Salon of 1845* written by Le Vavasseur and published in an Abbeville newspaper. The article will soon be republished with scholarly notes (information furnished by Professor Bandy in a letter).

46. Brébeuf (1618–1681), a minor Norman poet, author of *Entretiens Solitaires*.

47. For a discussion of Baudelaire's role in the composition of the novel, see William Aggeler, "Baudelaire's Part in the Composition of Léon Cladel's *Les Martyrs Ridicules*," *Studies in Philology*, LVIII, No. 4 (October, 1961), 627–639.

48. See Eugène Crépet, *Baudelaire* (Paris, 1906), pp. 235–249.

   See also Judith Cladel, *Maître et Disciple—Charles Baudelaire et Léon Cladel* (Paris, 1951).

49. Auguste Poulet-Malassis (1828–1878).

50. *Le Siècle*, newspaper to which Baudelaire had a violent antipathy.

51. Henri Murger (1822–1861), author of *Scènes de la Vie de Bohême*.

52. Ferragus, leading character in Balzac's novel of the same name.

53. The Hypanis is a river in ancient Sarmatia. Cf. Aristotle, *History of Animals*.

 INDEX